1995

Decolonization
&
Independence
in Kenya

D1557368

Eastern African Studies

B.A. OGOT
& W.R. OCHIENG'

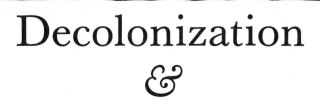

Decolonization
&
Independence
in Kenya

1940–93

James Currey
LONDON

$E \cdot A \cdot E \cdot P$
NAIROBI

Ohio University Press
ATHENS

James Currey Ltd
54b Thornhill Square
London N1 1BE

East African Educational Publishers
Kijabe Street, P.O. Box 45314
Nairobi, Kenya

Ohio University Press
Scott Quadrangle
Athens, Ohio 45701, USA

© B.A. Ogot & W.R. Ochieng' 1995
First published 1995

1 2 3 4 5 99 98 97 96 95

British Library Cataloguing in Publication Data
Decolonization and Independence in Kenya,
1940–93. — (Eastern African Studies)
  I. Ogot, Bethwell A. II. Ochieng',
William R. III. Series
967.62

ISBN 0-85255-706-X (James Currey Cloth)
ISBN 0-85255-705-1 (James Currey Paper)

Library of Congress Cataloging-in-Publication Data
Decolonization and independence in Kenya / edited by B.A. Ogot and
W.R. Ochieng'.
    p. cm. — (Eastern African Studies)
  Includes bibliographical references.
  ISBN 0-8214-1050-4. — ISBN 0-8214-1051-2 (pbk.)
  1. Kenya—Politics and government—1963-1978. 2. Kenya—
Politics and government—1978- 3. Kenya—Politics and
government—To 1963. 4. Decolonization—Kenya—History
20th century. 5. Kenya—Colonial influence. I. Ogot, B.A.
(Bethwell A.) II. Ochieng', William Robert.
III. Series: Eastern African Studies (London, England)
DT433.58.D4 1995   92-21440
967.62—dc20   CIP

Typeset in 10/11pt Baskerville
Colset Pte Ltd, Singapore
Printed in Great Britain
by Villiers Publications, London N3

Contents

v

Part Two

The Kenyatta Era
1963–78

Part Three

The First *Nyayo* Decade
1978–88

Contents

Part Four

Epilogue
1989–93

Nine

List of Contributors

Bethwell A. Ogot is the Director of the Institute of Research and Postgraduate Studies at Maseno University College, Kisumu. He was educated at Makerere University, St Andrews University and at the School of Oriental and African Studies, London University. Among his numerous publications are *A History of the Southern Luo* (EAPH) and, as editor, *Kenya Before 1900* (EAEP). He was a President of the UNESCO's International Committee for the Drafting of a General History of Africa; he edited Volume VI: *The Nineteenth Century until the 1880s*.

William R. Ochieng' is Principal and Professor of History at Maseno University College, Kisumu. He was educated, and then taught, at the University of Nairobi. He has taught in the United States at Stanford University and UCLA and, elsewhere in Kenya, at Kenyatta and Moi Universities. Among numerous publications, he is author of *A History of Kenya* (London) and *A History of the Kadimo Chiefdom of Yimbo* (Nairobi) and editor of *Themes in Kenyan History* (EAEP, James Currey and Ohio University Press) and, with Robert M. Maxon, of *An Economic History of Kenya* (Nairobi).

E.S. Atieno-Odhiambo is Professor of History at Rice University. He was educated at Makerere University and then at the University of Nairobi, where he went on to teach. He is the author of *The Paradox of Collaboration and other Stories* (Nairobi) and, with David William Cohen, of *Siaya: The Historical Anthropology of an African Landscape* (James Currey, EAEP and Ohio University Press) and *Burying S.M.: The Politics of Knowledge and the Sociology of Power* (Heinemann, New Hampshire, James Currey and EAEP).

List of Contributors

Robert M. Maxon is Professor of History at West Virginia University. He has also taught at Moi University. He was educated at Duke, Syracuse, Columbia and Makerere Universities. He is, among numerous publications, author of *John Ainsworth and the Making of Kenya* (Washington) and *East Africa: An Introductory History* (Nairobi).

Peter Odhiambo Ndege is Head of the History Department at Moi University. He was educated at Makerere, Kenyatta, Nairobi and West Virginia Universities. He is a contributor to *Themes in Kenyan History* and *An Economic History of Kenya* (Nairobi).

Wunyabari O. Maloba is Associate Professor of History and Coordinator of the African Studies Program at the University of Delaware. He was educated at Nairobi and Stanford Universities. He is the author of *Mau Mau and Kenya* (Indiana University Press) and of a number of articles on nationalism and decolonization.

Prologue

On Decolonization

W.R. OCHIENG' & E.S. ATIENO-ODHIAMBO

The undermining and final dissolution of the European colonial empires in Asia and Africa has been one of the most distinctive themes of the twentieth-century world. Like all major human events, the historians have discussed it in stages, their vision clearing and expanding as their emotions have dwindled.

Like their cousins in the other social science disciplines, historians can be inclined to wrap themselves in the isolating greatcoat of their 'country' and their 'period'. Thus, the withdrawal of the imperialists from their former colonies was, to start with, viewed in terms of the triumph of nationalism over imperialism. This view would later be given a fillip by the gallant heroics of the Front de Liberation Nationale (FLN), Movimento Popular de Libertaçao de Angola (MPLA), Front for the Liberation of Mozambique (Frelimo), Partido Africano da Independencia da Guiné e Cabo Verde (PAIGC), Zimbabwe African National Liberation Army (ZANLA) and other liberation armies which drove the Portuguese, French and British out of their colonies.

But time has a way of sobering humanity, including historians. Through prolonged contemplation and comparison of events, or comparison of the way in which different colonial societies coped with colonialism, different questions were asked and different approaches to the study of the collapse of empires were adopted. The questions that were originally asked in the study of decolonization included: What factors and forces were crucial in the decision of the Europeans to disband their empires? At what stage did the decolonization process begin? A lot of time and vitriol were spent in discussing and answering those questions, but it was later realized that the concept of decolonization transcended them, that other equally crucial but complementary questions needed to be asked and answered to make the discussion of decolonization complete. What, for example, did the nationalists wish to do after independence? Did they achieve their goal? If not, has decolonization been achieved? How did the colonial powers intend to relate to their former colonies after the transfer of power? Have they realized their vision? If yes, has decolonization been compromised?

Thus, decolonization as a theme is a much wider concept than the mere 'winning of independence' or 'transfer of power'. That explains the question: Why should decolonization be discussed beyond the era of independence? It entails the exploration of dreams, the analysis of struggles, compromises, pledges and achievements, and the rethinking of fundamentals. A large number of historians would consequently like to situate the beginning of this exploration during the Second World War, when the signs of the crack in the colonial edifice are clearly discernible. Others would like to start the exploration at the end of the First World War, arguing that, while the period of the Second World War and after was of clear relevance to certain later decolonizations, in the main its continuity lay backward to the age of classical European expansion, not forward to the era of imperial dissolution. In respect of Kenya we would like to situate the discussion of decolonization from the point when Kenyans (as *wanainchi*) abandoned their former neophyte politics of accommodation and began to agitate for *uhuru*, because the concept of decolonization is very closely tied up with notions of liberation. In Kenya the beginnings of territorial nationalism, including the roots of the Mau Mau liberation front, are clearly traceable to the period of the Second World War. Kenya's first territory-wide nationalist party, the Kenya African Union (KAU), was formed in 1944, while the Mau Mau struggle was the brainchild of the returned veterans of the Second World War. By the mid-1950s the key African nationalists, people like C.M.G. Arwings-Kodhek, Tom Mboya and Oginga Odinga, were very clear that they wanted *uhuru*. Crucial in the narrative on the 1955–63 period was the Nkrumah Revolution in Africa, a feat that first raised the possibility and then realized the actuality of African independence in the full glare of colonial world. Nkrumah showed the way, rhetorically and organizationally – first to C.M.G. Arwings-Kodhek, arguably the leader of the Kenya Africans in 1955, then to Tom Mboya in 1958, and to Oginga Odinga in the same year. In terms of moment it was the Nkrumah Revolution that most catalysed the decolonization of the African mind for independence, and this happened well before the Macmillan 'wind of change' speech in Cape Town in 1960; indeed, the latter was a realization after the fact. For, by 1959, it had dawned on the Kenyan historian B.A. Ogot that independence was coming. The when, however, was less certain; but only for a year, for the Lancaster House Conference of 1960 placed it as a negotiable agenda, and in three years *Wiyathi* – freedom – had come and Kenya became the land of the African, the *mundu muiru* as the Mama Uhurus referred to us.

Decolonization thus entailed the push and pull of events, episodes and ideas, with the forces and logic of African nationalism dictating the initiative. We want to believe that a contrary explanation which stresses voluntarism on the side of the occupying European forces simply attempts to camouflage the flow of history in order to suit the egos of the imperialists.

That Kenya gained independence through her nationalist initiatives is not in doubt. What is debatable is whether the long-term goals of the nationalists, which included complete Africanization of the country's politics, economy and culture, have been realized. It is this notion of decolonization that extends its definition beyond the date of *uhuru*. The thrust of most of the chapters at hand argues that the original dreams of the nationalists have not been achieved in the economic, cultural and political fields. While this is largely true, there is a need to situate this conclusion within the broader canvas of a world whose military, economic and cultural bases have been rapidly changing in the last three decades, culminating in the Soviet cataclysm. Who in today's world is culturally, economically and politically independent?

Meaning of the State

It is generally accepted that independent Kenya did not effect a major ideological, or structural, break with the colonial state and that all she did was to expand the former colonial administrative and economic infrastructures. This has often led to Kenya being labelled a 'neo-colonial' state in economic, political and cultural fields. Indeed, one of the few major books that have been published on independent Kenya was subtitled: 'The Political Economy of Neo-Colonialism'.[1] While the 'neo-colonial' appellation is generally regarded in Kenya as offensive, it is, nevertheless, important to recapitulate the salient features of the colonial state, for independent Kenya has borrowed substantially from it. This recapitulation is crucial for a clearer analysis of subsequent institutional continuities and changes in independent Kenya. But, first, let us define what is meant by the state.

There are as many definitions of the state as there are ideological perspectives.[2] For the purpose of this book, however, the state will be defined as an organ of society which arises out of the development in society of irreconcilable antagonisms, or struggle, among social classes with conflicting economic interests. When a society is divided into separate classes, the ruling class has to create a strong organization which helps to control the rest of the society.[3] As long as the oppressed classes are not yet ripe for their self-liberation, so long will they, in their vast majority, recognize the existing order of society as the only possible one. However, as they mature in self-awareness, they begin to agitate for their rights.

Thus, the state is the institution which the dominant social class creates to wield coercive power over other classes it seeks to rule, dominate and exploit. It is an institution conceived to look as if it stands above, or outside, class conflicts so that it may keep the conflicts within the bounds of law and order.

Under capitalism the ruling class wants the working people and peasants to believe that the state represents the interest of all classes in society. However, the object of the state is to enable the dominant class to establish, protect and enhance their economic, political and cultural interests and to suppress those of the ruled.[4] Indeed, as we shall shortly see in the course of this chapter when discussing colonial labour policies, state credit institutions and land policies, the state, particularly in Third World countries, plays a fundamental role in human, resource and capital mobilization on behalf of and in the interest of the bourgeoisie.

The state, therefore, has not existed from all eternity. There were societies, like those in precolonial Kenya, which managed without it, and which had no notion of the state or state power. However, 'at a definite stage of economic development, which necessarily involved the cleavage of society into classes, the state became a necessity because of this cleavage'.[5]

Terrestrially, the state has a definitive territory, or land, under its control. In the normal structure and composition of the state, the executive, the legislature and the judiciary form the most essential components of the secular state. The branches of the state are manned by many officials who manage them. These include policemen, judges, civil servants and soldiers. A state is never neutral. It is a machine that forces other classes to do what the ruling class wants. It is an organization for the protection of the possessing class against the non-possessing classes. It is, in short, an organ for the maintenance of one class over the others.[6]

The Inherited Colonial State

In the ten years between 1895 and 1905 the land that we today call Kenya was transformed from a footpath 600 miles long (between Mombasa and Kisumu) into a harshly politicized colonial state. Kenya's people, before the imposition of colonial rule, 'were like the American nation, made up of strangers, both adventurers and refugees'.[7] The transformation of Kenya from a polyglot of strangers into a coherent state was the work of force. The British, according to John Lonsdale, employed violence on a locally unprecedented scale, 'and with unprecedented singleness of mind', to usher Kenya into the twentieth century. The imposition of colonial rule in Kenya entailed the process of Westernization and capitalist penetration of African economies. Colonialism then effected the articulation of indigenous modes of production within the capitalist mode of production and the integration of African economies into the Western capitalist system of market relations.[8]

With very few exceptions the Europeans occupied the top of the colonial economic, political and social pyramid. Their salary scale was the highest in the colonial state. Although there were only 61,000 Europeans in 1960 – compared with 169,000 Asians and 7.8 million Africans – about 40 per cent of the total wage-bill of that year accrued to them. The Europeans also monopolized the best professions and dominated the industrial, banking, mining and commercial life of the country. In addition, they manned the top posts in the civil service and owned most of the large-scale farming production and the best and richest land in the Kenya Highlands. These covered approximately 7.5 million acres, or about 3.1 million hectares, and constituted 50 per cent of the arable land and 20 per cent of Kenya's highly productive areas. By 1960, 4,000 European farms accounted for 83 per cent of the total agricultural exports of the country.[9] European domination of the economy and society was effected through legislation and was buttressed by the armed forces, particularly in the period of militant African nationalism, between 1950 and 1963.

Below the Europeans were the Asians (Indians, Pakistanis, Goans) and Arabs. They owned a large part of small-scale agricultural and industrial production; handled the bulk of the retail and wholesale trade throughout the country; manned middle-level and clerical posts in the civil service; operated most of the transport and construction business; and provided skilled and semi-skilled labour.

At the bottom of the colonial social and economic pyramid were the vast numerical majority of the population, the Africans, the general majority of whom were peasants who lived by subsistence farming in Kenya's rural areas. But there were other social classes, and ethnic divisions, among the Africans. The roots of this division lay in pre-colonial history, but the colonizing bureaucracy exploited this fact for administrative reasons, which situation they also complicated by creating 'tribal' boundaries and 'reserves'.

Throughout the colonial period the colonial government, European settlers and other immigrant races needed labour and could not do without African workers. The European settlers, in particular, had exceptionally large farms – an average of over 2,400 acres per occupier in 1932. There was therefore only one solution, to make the Africans work for them. But this the Africans had neither reason nor inclination to do, 'unless the Europeans had been willing to pay in wages more than Africans could earn from farming on their own account. But such wages would have meant little or no profits for the Europeans.'[10]

To compel Africans to turn out to work for the Europeans and Asians, labour and economic legislation was enacted to facilitate labour recruitment and to deny Africans access to profitable cash-crop production and commercial credits. Some of the best African land, as we have already noted, was alienated for European use, thus limiting African agricultural production and access to fresh land. Hut and poll taxes were also imposed and the need to find yet more money forced young men to offer their services to the European settlers and Asian traders. Sir Percy Girouard, one of the first Governors of Kenya put this very clearly:

> We consider that taxation is the only possible method of compelling the native to leave his reserve for the purpose of seeking work. Only in this way can the cost of living be increased for the native . . . and it is on this that the supply of labour and the price of labour depends.[11]

Thus Africans became liable for all sorts of taxes levied on their huts, wives or even their mere existence. It was because of these factors that the African working class came into being. Gradually the African population in the 'reserves' rose until by the 1920s it became less and less necessary to use either law or force to turn them out for labour.

Thus, pressure on land, rural poverty and the need to find money with which to pay taxes were the most persuasive factors in the creation of 'voluntary' labour in Kenya. Young educated Africans were also attracted to towns to enjoy modern amenities and to acquire money with which to buy land and pay bride price. The era of 'free' labour had arrived in Kenya. It rose from the manipulative logic of capital and its pattern depended on the nature of penetration of capitalism in the various parts of the country. For example, those areas of Kenya, such as Central Province and Nyanza, which were penetrated earlier by capitalism and Western influences produced the earliest migrant labour.

However, the people who turned out to work for the government, Europeans and Asians cannot be called proletarians, in the strict meaning of the term, for they continued to own their small plots of land in their rural districts. In addition, the African working class was not a homogeneous group. In respect of security of employment and level of income, teachers, clerks, lawyers, interpreters, skilled workers, nurses and domestic servants enjoyed a privileged position compared with the semi-proletariat class of poorly paid, ill-fed and badly housed manual workers and farm-labourers. It was because of its income and the social prestige which it enjoyed that this class has been called a petty-bourgeois class. It is the class that threw up the earliest modern African nationalist agitators and leaders, who increasingly questioned the legality of colonialism and who eventually led Kenya to independence.

We have already spoken of the emergence of the African petty bourgeoisie and working class in the womb of colonialism; but it is also instructive to note the emergence and gradual evolution of the African capitalist class during the same period. Research findings of Gavin Kitching, Nicola Swainson and Michael Cowen indicate that this class had been forming since the 1920s and that the principal source of

accumulation for this bourgeoisie was trade, land and agriculture. Before
independence its development was impeded by the limits imposed on it
by settler capitalism, but by 1960 the economic and political weight of
the indigenous owners of capital was already decisive.[12] We are told, for
example, that between 1955 and 1964 their capital accumulation
increased from £5.2 million to £14.0 million per annum.

But, while the above motif represents the general picture of Kenya's
class composition and economic differentiation on the eve of independence, it should also be noted that in the period between 1960 and 1963 –
with independence in sight – the configuration of Kenya's class society
had begun to markedly transform, with political power gradually shifting
into the hands of the African petty bourgeoisie. This period was
characterized by a huge exodus of former European settlers and civil servants and Asians, who sold their property and left in fear of what *uhuru*
portended. It was also characterized by 'flight' of capital out of the country. 'Only a damn fool would not sell,' said Colonel Grogan, the doyen
of European settlers and their most outspoken mouthpiece.

The incoming African government responded to the inevitability of
uhuru and European and Asian exodus by promoting the African petty
bourgeoisie into important and key posts in the civil service, the military,
educational institutions and industries. This Africanization of key posts
in the civil service would be of crucial significance in the future economic
and social development of the postcolonial state. In her book *The Development of Corporate Capitalism in Kenya*,[13] Nicola Swainson tells us that this
petty-bourgeois class, in collaboration with its ruling counterparts in the
government, would use the power of the state through the mechanism
of licensing to acquire private capital to effect access into certain areas
of the economy, such as trade, land and good jobs.

Thus, independent Kenya inherited the colonial economic structures
and classes. During the short period of independence these structures
and classes would undergo rapid transformations – disintegration of
some, formation of others and new realignments.

Notes

1. C. Leys, *Underdevelopment in Kenya: The Political Economy of Neo-Colonialism* (London, Heinemann, 1975; James Currey 1988).
2. A.I. Salim, *State Formation in Eastern Africa* (Nairobi, Heinemann, 1984), pp. 1–5.
3. C. Mathema, *Wealth and Power: An Introduction to Political Economy* (Harare, Zimbabwe Publishing House, 1988), p. 16.
4. F. Engels, in K. Marx and F. Engels, *Selected Works*, Vol. 3 (Moscow, Foreign Languages Publishing House 1966), p. 327. Also see V.I. Lenin, *The State* (Peking, 1970), p. 14.
5. F. Engels, quoted in Neil J. Smelser (ed.), *Karl Marx on Society and Social Change* (Illinois, University of Chicago Press, 1973), p. 21.
6. Ibid., p. 20.

7. H.G. Mwakyembe, 'The Parliament and Electoral Process', in Issa G. Shivji (ed.), *The State and the Working People in Tanzania* (Dakar, Council for the Development of Social and Economic Research in Africa (CODESRIA), 1986), p. 32.
8. J. Lonsdale, 'The Conquest State: 1895–1904', in W.R. Ochieng' (ed.), *A Modern History of Kenya* (Nairobi, Evans Brothers, 1989), p. 7.
9. T. Zeleza, 'The Establishment of Colonial Rule: 1905–1920', in Ochieng', *Modern History*, pp. 35–36.
10. R.S. Odingo, *The Kenya Highlands: Land Use and Agricultural Development* (Nairobi, East African Publishing House, 1971), p. xix. Also see F. Furedi, *The Mau Mau War in Perspective* (London, James Currey, 1989), p. 9.
11. Leys, *Underdevelopment*, p. 29.
12. *East African Standard* (Nairobi, 8 February 1913), quoted in I.G. Shivji, *Class Struggles in Tanzania* (Dar es Salaam, Tanzania Publishing House, 1975), Vol. 1, p. 32.
13. N. Swainson, *The Development of Corporate Capitalism in Kenya* (London, James Currey, 1980).

Introduction

The Invention of Kenya

E.S. ATIENO-ODHIAMBO

Nations are in the making once again, this time in Eastern Europe and Southern Africa, and with momentous consequences for the historian of nationalism. A hundred years ago, writes David Bradling, the Cambridge historian of Latin America, nations used to grow – or, better still, evolve. 'Then the fashion changed and they were made, or simply emerged. Nowadays they are imagined or invented.'[1] Kenya's trajectory partly falls within this umbrella. Made into a colonial state *ex nihilo* through colonial conquest and imperial fiat at the end of the last century, it became a settler state in the inter-war years, only to be transformed by African struggles for civil liberties, human rights, democratic participation, workers' rights, peasant independence, spiritual space, elective representation and civic responsibility in the period between 1945 and 1963. These were struggles for freedom – *Uhuru*. Historians of the 1960s referred to the phenomenon as African nationalism, and often as mass nationalism. Yet what these struggles yielded immediately was more limited: the capture of the state power in 1963. The challenge ahead lay in making a nation out of the past: nation-building in other words. Historical consciousness was to play a vital role in this quest for national identity. And historians of Kenya have, in the past thirty years, had to grapple with this ambiguity as the central agenda. What role can, nay, must, historians play in shaping national identity? How does one make the writing of history into a creative principle that links the intellectual enterprise with the demands of everyday life? These demands of everyday life have in Kenya's postcolonial experience involved a concern with national unity, patriotic endeavour, economic development, social and spiritual space, the valorization of the cultural heritage and the definition of Kenya's place in the world. It is these demands – and they encompass the totality of the lived experiences of everyone in the family, at school, in the workplace, in the community and in the process of governance – that

1

have defined what is or should be the legitimate province, or the 'territory of the historian', in Emmanuel LeRoy Ladourie's words. Kenya, as a new nation, has demanded a new postcolonial history.

This history has had to be invented, assembled together, arranged around the metaphor of struggle. This metaphor entails seeing our history of the past fifty or so years as a moral enterprise: against the injustice that is colonialism; against poverty, ignorance and disease; against the drudgery of rural life; against the foreignization of the cultural ecology; against the intervention of alien ideas in the indigenous discourses on nation-building. It has also been a moral enterprise for the decolonization of consciousness. The historian in postcolonial Kenya has recognized that daily living is always the site of struggle: *The Struggle for the School*, in John Anderson's title, is apt as a forerunner to other struggles for land, for health, for housing, for water, for the environment. It is these struggles that have constituted rural and urban political discourses; the self-same struggles have also remained the core agenda for the developmental state, and for the many constituencies of the civil society that have continually urged the politics of vision as an attainable reality within our lifetimes.

This book takes the same credo for struggle as its motto: Jomo Kenyatta's pride in struggle, *Tulipigania Kama Simba*, is its perpetual refrain. The invention of an independent Kenya has involved the transformation of the political arena both globally and locally. These transformations are the subject of the first three chapters by Wunyabari Maloba, Atieno Odhiambo and Bethwell Allan Ogot. Jomo Kenyatta remains the pivotal agency in this postcolonial transformation – the goal of which was economic, social and political independence. The chapters by William Robert Ochieng' and Robert Maxon take up the challenge of evaluating the fifteen years of the *Pax Kenyatta*. The third section of the book is bold: it seeks to cover the very recent past, a period for which, strictly, it is not yet possible to write history according to the archival canon. Yet the writing of contemporary history is a task that cannot rightly be passed on to others. Part of the enterprise involves the imposition of an evaluative personal judgement on contemporary events. This can best be done if the project of historical writing is seen as involving the accumulation of the legacy of the past, and the passing of it to the next generation. The chapters on the Moi era therefore look backwards to the recent past, as well as forwards, as they must, to the future. Secondly, writing on the contemporary scene provides an opportunity to deploy the didactic role of history, which is to reconcile – Mwigwithania in Kenyatta's words – the many strands of struggles and interpretations, by falling back to a common, invented history, one of a common, continuing struggle. After thirty years of independence, history should teach Kenyans the value of tolerant patriotism. This book is presented in that spirit.

Note

1. David Bradling, review of *The Invention of Argentina* by Nicholas Shumway, in *New York Times Book Review* (13 October 1991), p. 11. For imagination of nations see Benedict Anderson, *Imagined Committees: Reflections on the Origin and Spread of Nationalism* (London, Verso Editions, 1983). For the invention of traditions see Eric Hobsbawm and Terence Ranger (eds), *The Invention of Tradition* (Cambridge, Cambridge University Press, 1983).

Part One

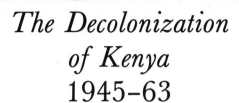

*The Decolonization
of Kenya
1945–63*

One

Decolonization:
A Theoretical Perspective

WUNYABARI O. MALOBA

The performance of African countries more than twenty-five years after the attainment of political independence has not been impressive. Hunger, political strife, severe limitation on civil liberties have all grown in intensity, leading many observers to conclude sadly that 'African independence has been an abysmal failure'.[1] This harsh assessment, it needs to be emphasized, has not been limited to external agencies and foreigners, many of whom can easily be accused of malice. Many local evaluations and appraisals of the economic, social and political performance of African countries have tended to provide evidence of stagnation and even regression in development.[2] Economic stagnation has been recorded despite 'vast amounts in aid between 1962 and 1978'.[3]

In the area of politics, there has been a proliferation of states under authoritarian rule or army rule, in which there has been loss of civil liberties, often the result of regimes seeking to maintain themselves in power by suppressing political rivals. This suppression, often brutal, has 'curtailed the openness of debate and public wooing for support, on which politics as an activity must inevitably thrive'.[4]

This chapter seeks to discuss the general idea of decolonization, especially as it relates to Africa. The aim is to show how the present conditions in Africa can be ideologically and institutionally linked to the colonial and imperial past. Without comprehending this tragic linkage, Africa's poverty and misery become the results of ill-fortune, a curse or some inexplicable haunting set of circumstances.

I

African nationalism in the 1960s had one overriding aim: to attain political independence. Kwame Nkrumah, correctly regarded as a premier Pan-Africanist, impressed this point on young nationalists by urging them to seek first the political kingdom and all else would be added unto them.[5] In his view, Ghana's independence had of course to be linked to the total liberation of Africa or else it would be meaningless. Nkrumah saw this political independence as a first crucial step in the drive towards continental unity, which alone would save Africa from political weakness and economic stagnation. Projecting this scheme with unyielding focus, and even obsession, Nkrumah probably scared many newly independent African states eager to defend their *uhuru* from 'Nkrumah's interference'. Clearly, by the time the Organization of African Unity (OAU) was formed in May 1963, African leaders were more eager to maintain their separate national seats of power than surrender to a continental government.[6] Yet more than sixteen years after Nkrumah's death it may be worth while to open debate on his programme and see whether it was a hollow formulation or a far-sighted formula for unity and development whose demise was unfortunate for the continent.

The drive for continental unity by Nkrumah and other Pan-Africanists set off from the premiss that in unity is strength, that, individually, African countries were weak and could not achieve economic independence or safeguard their national sovereignty. As producers of raw materials, African countries would not be able to influence international terms of trade in their favour nor would they industrialize. And, without industrialization, sustained economic development would be impossible to achieve, leading to unemployment, underemployment and eventually political unrest.[7]

Political independence was viewed, even by conservative nationalists, as the path to redress the economic and social neglect and injustices of the colonial era. Colonialism had not developed Africa nor was it constituted to do so. This can be stated even while acknowledging the variety of views on this issue.[8] Economically, colonialism had linked Africa tightly to the world capitalist system dominated by Europe and later the USA. African countries, it needs to be repeated, produced raw materials and imported selected manufactured goods – each largely determined by colonial capitalism. There were, to be sure, enterprising Africans during the colonial era. Some became cash-crop growers or traders, others were absorbed as workers or miners. In each case, however, Africans did not control the economic system in which they were absorbed nor did they determine their economic fortune. Compromises were made by colonial rulers, sometimes in the implementation of policy or even its formulation – but this should not be taken to mean that Africans controlled colonialism.

It would be folly to argue that Africans were passive participants in colonial capitalism. Certainly, tax rebellions or difficulties in labour recruitment or cash-crop cultivation might cause a modification for colonial policy, but this is far from controlling and determining the fate of colonialism, especially before the era of nationalism after the Second World War. 'The Europeans', Basil Davidson aptly reminds us, 'were still in command', and they 'used this command to impose an institutionalized relationship between Africans and Europeans – between Africans and the capitalist systems that Europeans were then developing – of a specific and colonial nature'.[9] This remained the case throughout the colonial period and completely nullified the so-called benefits that Africans derived from colonial rule. Walter Rodney argued convincingly that the sum total of benefits accruing from this colonial relationship 'was amazingly small' for Africa.[10] What had happened during colonialism was selective investment by European and other foreign capitalists in those enterprises that promised immediate profit with little risk. These enterprises had not been conceived as part of a coherent national economic plan for development but rather for their profitability to foreign investors.

Politically, colonialism was a dictatorship. It was imposed by violence and maintained by violence. Ruling with utter indifference to the opinions of the governed – the Africans – colonialism perfected a reign of terror by silencing its opponents through detentions, exile, even outright extermination. There is hardly an African country that does not have its list of martyrs of freedom – those nationals that were killed, imprisoned or detained for opposing specific or general colonial policies. Colonial administrators were appointed and not elected. They owed their allegiance to foreign centres of power, represented in the colonies by governors. They were not accountable to Africans for their actions nor did they pretend to be constrained in their actions by local opinions. Because they were part of a dictatorial system they relied on force of arms to implement their policies. It is generally argued that without local collaborators colonial administrators would not have managed to control all the territories. This is true. Yet it should be added that these collaborators were not masters but servants of an oppressive system.

This system was socially racist. The era of modern imperialism in the nineteenth century, which of course marked European expansion in Africa, was also the era of scientific racism. As part of the most vibrant branch of social Darwinism, racism and 'racist mythology [were] compatible with much mainstream Western science deep into the twentieth century'.[11] Western scientists and academics articulated the theory of a 'great chain of being' in which white people were 'at the top and the black people at the bottom of the human part of the chain, close to orangutans at the top of the non-human part'.[12] This racism given 'scientific' respectability was a distinct part of the culture of imperialism as Europeans advanced in Africa and was often used as a justification for this expansion.

Colonial administrators frequently came back to this theory of scientific racism to justify their policies. In Kenya, for example, Sir Charles Eliot refused to consider using indigenous Africans as the agents of commercial agricultural production after the railway had been constructed. In dismissing the possibility of using Africans as agents of commercial agricultural production, Eliot based his objections on moral, cultural and technological grounds. Although, according to Eliot, 'The African is greedy and covetous enough . . . he is too indolent in his ways, and too disconnected in his ideas, to make any attempt to better himself, or to undertake any labour which does not produce a speedy visible result.' He added that the African's mind 'is far nearer the animal world than is that of the European or Asiatic, and exhibits something of the animal's placidity and want of desire to rise beyond the stage he has reached'.[13]

More than thirty years after Eliot's tenure as governor, Sir Philip Mitchell was still reiterating the inferiority of the African. In his most famous colonial document, *The Agrarian Problem in Kenya*, Mitchell strove to offer the origin, development and solution of the agrarian problem. The document, however, reflected Mitchell's views on Africans and their problems. He was convinced that there had been no African precolonial development. Africans, according to him, had no

> wheeled transport and (apart from camels and donkeys of the pastoral nomads) no animal transport either; they had no roads or towns; no tools except small hoes, axes, wooden digging sticks and the like; no manufactures, and no industrial products except the simplest domestic handiwork, no commerce . . . no currency . . . they had never heard of working for wages.[14]

To such a people, therefore, it was expected that the white man should carry on his civilizing mission and introduce them to modernity and contact with human civilization. Africans, Mitchell reminded his audience, had no history, religion or culture of their own. 'They are a people who, however much natural ability and however admirable attributes they may possess, are without a history, culture or religion of their own and in that they are, as far as I know, unique in the modern world.'[15]

Racism, of course, entailed profound paternalism. The colonial administration knew the way and Africans had to follow. After all, as Mitchell insisted almost by way of final verdict, Africans were, in 1890, 'in a more primitive condition than anything of which there is any record in pre-Roman Britain'.[16] In the case of Kenya, colonial policies would, then, be based on the support of white settlers, who were supposed to civilize Africans and bring prosperity to the colony.

For the rest of Africa under British rule, Lord Lugard, whose book, *The Dual Mandate for British Tropical Africa*, was compulsory reading for any British colonial administrator, set the tone of racism and paternalism. He set out to identify 'African characteristics', especially of the Bantu, whom he found to be a 'happy, thriftless, excitable person, lacking in self-control, discipline and foresight' and who, although courageous and courteous, had 'his thoughts . . . concentrated on the events and feelings of the moment, and suffers little apprehension for the future or grief for the past'.[17] Lugard concluded that Africans were 'childlike races of the world'.[18]

Culturally, colonialism operated from the racist principle that barbarism pervaded Africa and therefore there was no culture to be salvaged. Missionaries in their evangelical duties championed this outlook, condemning centuries-old African religions and cultures, seeking to replace and in some cases succeeding in replacing them with Western European culture. As schooling and Christianity spread, so did Westernization. But this Westernization under colonialism was also a tool of control, achieved through the creation of new cultural loyalties and value systems and therefore subcultures within African countries. The French assimilation policy, even if only partially successful, sought to create French men and women out of Africans. Portugal, poor and repressive, also championed its own variety of assimilation, although by 1959

> after barely five centuries of 'civilizing mission' in Africa, less than 1 per cent of the African populations of Guinea-Bissau, Angola, and Mozambique could be classified as civilized by Portuguese standards; that is could read, write, and speak Portuguese, professed the Roman Catholic religion, had regular employment or business, and lived according to Portuguese standards.[19]

The Portuguese 'civilizing mission' was propagated in spite of the fact that by 1970 about '30% of the population of Portugal was officially classified as illiterate',[20] and therefore could not have qualified to be Portuguese!

Colonialism, therefore, not only despised African people but also denigrated their cultures and their abilities to effect change, to improve themselves. Under colonial rule, Fanon reminds us, 'The native is declared insensible to ethics; he represents not only the absence of values, but also the negation of values. He is, let us dare to admit it, the enemy of values, and in this sense he is the absolute evil.'[21] To fully appreciate the emotional charge that often accompanied the struggle for African independence, one has to know that this was also a struggle to regain African dignity and respect. How is this related to decolonization?

II

As a social, economic and political phenomenon and process, decolonization represents much more than the attainment of political independence – sometimes referred to as the transfer of power. In the transfer of power the national political élite assume the administrative responsibilities and duties previously discharged by the colonial authorities. They administer a sovereign nation. It makes little difference how they come to assume this position of political power. In those countries that had an armed struggle this stage is reached through the forcible ouster of previous foreign rulers, although this can be preceded by negotiations. This was true in Algeria, Angola, Mozambique and even Kenya. Where there has been no armed struggle, the transfer of power follows negotiations after the agitation for independence, e.g. in Tanzania, Uganda and Botswana. Most of the French colonies in West Africa achieved their political independence through this route.

Decolonization, on the other hand, implies an achievement of economic, social and political freedom from former colonial masters. In the context of this discussion, decolonization refers to the 'emancipation of Asia and Africa from European control, economic no less than political'.[22] Since it is supposed to signal an emancipation from alien control, decolonization cannot be adequately discussed and comprehended without acknowledging its emotional side, even its spiritual content rooted in the desire of those previously dominated seeking freedom and dignity. As it happens, the desire to be free includes cultural renewal and reassertion. Cultural nationalism tends to precede political nationalism. Political freedom given demonstration in the transfer of power must be seen as a major component of decolonization, but not the whole of it. Economic freedom, cultural reassertion, political empowerment of the local population, are all components of the phenomenon and process of decolonization. And so, while it is vital to deal with political independence, it is worth while to recall that the exercise of this independence can be considerably impaired by lack of economic independence and a neglect of cultural renewal and even social disintegration brought on by a clash over values – especially social values of different social classes.

One of the key aims of decolonization is economic freedom. Activists and ordinary citizens in supporting the struggle for independence expect an improvement in their living conditions. This desire to 'live better' explains political support for nationalists and nationalism. There is no African political party that did not promise better living conditions for its citizens during the struggle for *uhuru*. There was a general outcry against the economic exploitation of 'our resources by colonialists'. To achieve economic independence, the attainment of political independence was seen as a crucial step.

But colonialism was, as already stated, more than arbitrary racist rule. It was also an era of capitalist domination of Europe over Africa. Its economic mission was exploitation, and this was done without regard to Africa's development. The expansion of cash-crop production, mineral exploitation and even limited manufacturing did not enrich Africa but the Western capitalist countries. This entrenched in Africa the phenomenon of underdevelopment.[23] It is now becoming common and respectable in Western scholarship to denounce the underdevelopment theory by showing how generalized its deductions are and therefore how inadequate it is to explain the economic relationship between Africa and the West. Michael F. Lofchie, for example, has argued that 'the bimodal division of the world into core and peripheral societies is grossly over-simplified' and that this theory rests 'on an extremely doubtful inter-pretation of Western history: namely that the wealth of industrial nations has come about through their pillage of the agricultural surplus from peripheral regions'.[24] It may be worth while to note here that it is not the lack of evidence that is the problem. The problem is Western scholar-ship seeking to shift the blame and place it on Africans as being largely responsible for their misery and in the process, through a system of sophisticated formulation, exonerating the West from responsibility for creating and perpetuating Africa's plight. It is also worth pointing out that Lofchie suggested a capitalist alternative for Africa, arguing that 'capitalism has the capacity to stimulate African development and, over time, to improve the material conditions of its peoples'.[25]

But can the inherited economic institutions develop Africa and usher in economic independence? In this respect it may be instructive to recall the tragic experience of Latin America. After more than four hundred years since the Spanish *conquistadores* landed in the hemisphere, Latin America remains poor, underdeveloped and stagnant. 'Everything, from the discovery until our times,' Eduardo Galeano laments, 'has always been transmuted into European – or later United States – capital, and as such has accumulated in distant centers of power. Everything: the soil, its fruits and its mineral rich depths, the people and their capacity to work and to consume, natural resources and human resources.'[26] This tragic experience has led Galeano to the conclusion that 'Latin America is the region of open veins'. The exploitation of Latin America by the West has been facilitated by the presence of a distinct ruling class that works in close alliance with foreign companies, banks and other economic enterprises. This class has become, in Galeano's angry phrase, 'pimps of misery' and in the process mortgaged the sovereignty of their countries 'because "there is no other way"'.[27]

In Africa, the problem of economic independence has two major inter-related complex components. In the first instance, the inherited econo-mic institutions in many countries do not have the capacity to lead to sustained growth and development. They were established to exploit and not to develop these countries. They therefore offer 'no reliable founda-tion for a better future'.[28] The second problem concerns the leadership. Many of those that assumed political leadership on the attainment of *uhuru* also inherited this exploitative system. This included the salary structure, economic privileges, power and authority for a few. It has, for example, been noted that in former British colonies 'the corresponding patterns of remuneration characteristic of the public sector during the colonial rule remained largely intact'.[29] These high salaries, higher than those earned by Africans, were offered to attract European personnel to '"inhospitable" and distant parts of the world' and also to maintain a standard of living higher than that of 'the natives'. Can the same reasons be given for post-independent salary structures?

The salary structure further illustrates the degree to which most colonial economic institutions have persisted. In Kenya there are a number of studies that convincingly demonstrate this reality.[30] In most of Francophone Africa, France has maintained a tight economic hold on its former colonies. This is especially true in finance. 'The Bank of France guarantees convertibility of the CFA franc, the common currency, at a fixed rate with the French franc', and 'African banks keep two thirds of their foreign exchange holdings under French control'.[31] This is besides trade monopolies and management contracts which allow the French to continue to have a crucial voice in economic policy decisions.

There is, therefore, a crucial linkage between inherited institutions and political (and even economic) leadership. Economic decolonization cannot be realized if these institutions are left intact and especially if a few people in positions of power exploit them to enrich themselves and leave the rest of the population poor and stagnant. Opulent living by the élite abounds in Africa, Asia and Latin America, and yet this has never been seen as an indicator of economic emancipation. Often this extravagant life style is the result of wealth 'derived in large measure from patronage and manipulation of political authority'.[32] It has been observed, for example, that in Nigeria the oil boom in the 1970s was marked by remarkably 'lavish spending and corruption on a massive scale',[33] which 'failed to raise the general prosperity of the Nigerian people'.[34]

The political élite has in many countries either established joint ventures with foreign companies or entered the field as local competitors. On one level this can be seen as a step towards localization of the economy and therefore potentially positive. Close scrutiny reveals, however, that this strategy has yet to lead to economic independence. If the local bourgeoisie buy shares in local subsidiaries of transnational corporations (TNC), this does not make the corporation national in orientation, emphasis or outlook, nor does it cease to perform its exploitative role. Most of the shareholders in such enterprises tend to be powerful members of the ruling élite, who provide political protection for foreign economic ventures. It needs to be emphasized that the participation of the national bourgeoisie within an inherently exploitative system does not make the system any less injurious to national development and prosperity.

Since independence in Kenya, 'there are some indications that the national bourgeoisie has . . . been able to Kenyanise sections of international capital. A few Kenyan cartels have gained controlling interests in some subsidiaries of T.N.C.'[35] These cartels, however, have run into problems of 'expansion of internal markets' and inability to gain access to international markets guarded jealously by capitalist countries not eager to promote any meaningful industrialization in Africa. As a result, 'the possibility of Kenyan cartels having large holdings in transnational companies is limited',[36] nor can it be viewed as a viable foundation for sustained and integrated national economic development. There is, however, the possibility of Kenyan capital emerging on its own.

The failure of Africa to feed itself is the clearest sign of 'African agrarian malaise',[37] of poor agricultural performance, often the result of mistaken official policies. Famine has gripped many countries for a long time. The Sahel and now Ethiopia and Sudan, among others, continue to be plagued by food shortages, invariably resorting to foreign food aid to avert total annihilation of some groups of citizens. There are problems of climate, of 'rains not coming in time', but most experts will eagerly point out with alarming evidence that national agrarian policies in many African countries have favoured cash crops at the expense of food crops.[38] Transport infrastructure and technical investment have been directed towards reviving cash crops, which fetch foreign exchange, while on the whole assigning food crops secondary status. This leads to hunger, starvation, food shortages and then the need to import food, which tends to have disastrous consequences on local food production efforts.

Food shortages and the need for imports are not limited to those countries with a 'harsh climate' or those in which 'rains have not come in time'. Countries with vast agricultural potential do import food, and sometimes even get addicted to this practice. Nigeria became a net food importer at the height of the oil boom, when agriculture became neglected in spite of the country's vast potential for food production. It has also been noted that, even in drought conditions, some African countries have managed to increase their total harvest of cash crops.[39]

Production of cash crops and economic development are perennial vexing problems in Africa's complex relationship of economic dependence on the West. 'Terms of trade', by which is meant 'a relationship between import and export prices that is unfavourable'[40] to Africa, have often been seen as the key ingredient in Africa's poverty and lack of progress towards sustained development. It is presumed that, if Africa received better prices for its raw materials, then it would develop and even become independent of the West. On the whole, this is a problematic presumption. It is unlikely that 'primary procedures' can launch an independent existence within a system which thrives on 'institutionalized subjection' of these countries and which refrains from capital and technical redistribution that might lead to equity of opportunity and capacity among the participants. Better terms of trade might lead to a gradual elimination of starvation and shameful food shortages. What is problematic is whether this state of affairs, which can be called dignified stagnation, is the desired end of economic emancipation. In dignified stagnation there are no chronic food shortages, starvation – or identifiable national development. The point at issue is that even if this relationship of dependency were made to perform efficiently it would only serve to 'reinforce the system' of exploitation and 'not change it'. The characteristic feature of this relationship, which is exploitation, would not change.

Political decolonization has perhaps been the most evident and celebrated aspect of African independence in the last thirty years. African governments in charge of African states is surely a memorable event on the world stage. It arouses pride among the citizens and people of African descent in the African diaspora. African political independence is taken to be synonymous with African freedom. Even for those who may not be keen to grapple with the complexities of other aspects of decolonization, political independence has generally been seen as a major step in the rebirth of African dignity and pride. It is therefore vital to enquire as to why Africans sought this political independence.

The colonial state in Africa was, as already remarked, a ruthless dictatorship. It ruled without consultation. Even when 'parliaments' or consultative councils were established in different territories, 'these were dominated by an official majority which could be relied on to vote as solidly for any policy or programme introduced by the Governor',[41] and therefore did not constitute democratic rule. The demand for independence by Africans must be seen in the light of seeking democratic rule. Alien rule was hated, but above that there was the desire to participate in the government process, to influence decisions and policies, to have a local government in the hands of 'sons and daughters of the soil' who would be accountable to the citizens for their actions. Arbitrary rule, which was characteristic of colonial rule, was loathed because it was essentially an exercise of power without consultation or restraint. At the heart of colonial rule was the premiss that the state and the subjects did not have identical aims, and since the state 'knew better' it discharged the responsibility of forceful guidance while the subjects were to follow meekly and gratefully.

For political independence to continue to be a crucial aspect of the general phenomenon of decolonization, it must lead to a revision of these colonial relationships between the state and the citizens. Political empowerment of the citizens after independence is pivoted on massive participation in the political process. It should be remembered that the denial of participation in national politics was one of the emotional grievances that galvanized mass nationalism against colonial rule. To colonial masters Africans were children[42] and therefore could not participate in politics. Politics, decision-making and the ability to act with restraint were beyond the capacity of 'children'. Political independence, in reversing these attitudes, must dispel the myth that politics are

16

dangerous. Participation in national politics should not be seen as a dangerous thing.

There have emerged in Africa regimes that are authoritarian, one-party states or military juntas. Invariably each of these regimes has been noted for suppression of political dissidents, arbitrary rule and erosion of civil liberties. In Zaïre, for example, 'When Gen. Mobutu took over the government in November, 1965, he instituted a dictatorship'[43] that has been brutal. 'In 1966 he had four politicians hanged for plotting against him',[44] and he has remained in power due to Western aid. Amin's brutality in Uganda is well known and so is Banda's eccentric and dictatorial rule in Malawi.

A general tendency has arisen in Africa of limiting political pluralism and mass participation in politics. Even in those one-party states where 'competitive politics' have been allowed, this has been under tremendous scrutiny from the government and has generally produced no opponents to official policies or critics of the dominant political élite. Several reasons have been advanced to explain this practice. Multiplicity of political parties and other centres of opposition have been viewed as contributing to national instability. One-party states are also viewed as being uniquely suited to accelerating development since they can 'easily take decisive policy positions, which may be viewed as necessary for achieving development goals, particularly those that may meet with opposition either from the masses or from certain entrenched interests'.[45] Lastly, it has been vigorously argued that the multi-ethnic composition of African countries leads to 'tribalism', since 'different parties tend to represent different ethnic groups'.[46] This last reason comes dangerously close to the imperial position that colonialism and especially the colonial state stopped 'tribal warfare' in Africa and imposed peace. Whatever reason may be given to justify authoritarian rule, there can be little doubt that lack of political pluralism and mass political activism and participation tends to postpone the erection and growth of the political culture of tolerance. It also avoids the establishment of institutional guarantees for peaceful dissent and it unfortunately always equates dissent with sedition.

'Tribalism' and ethnic-based political parties are to a large degree indicative of the failure of national politics. It has become common in Africa for 'the political parties that captured the wave of nationalistic agitation' to lose 'their cohesion and sense of purpose'.[47] This loss of purpose, accompanied by suppression of political rivals and dissidents, can lead to what Mazrui calls 'retribalization' of politics.[48] When the national centre is viewed as unfair and especially when ethnic calculus is employed in the disposal of national assets and opportunities, those not included may opt for sectional identification as a sure source of strength and safety. Nigeria has provided the now classic example of 'retribalization' of politics that led to a brutal civil war. 'In Kenya, Luo ethnicity has probably significantly deepened since independence, partly in defensive reaction to some government policies.'[49] This became especially true in the period between 1966 and 1969 during the tumultuous lifespan of the Kenya People's Union (KPU), a self-styled socialist party led by Oginga Odinga that drew most of its support from Nyanza Province among the Luo.

During this period, the government used its monopoly over the economy, the legal system and paramilitary agencies to frustrate KPU's operations and especially its bid to enlarge its membership. The government 'became a major employer of salaried labour, the chief and sometimes the sole dispenser of development funds, trade licences, and other amenities, and influenced the circulation of information through its control of the communications media'.[50] This monopoly over economics and power enabled the government to halt a possible advance of KPU outside Nyanza Province. This became especially true in Central Province where the government, under Kenyatta, 'was determined to keep the Kikuyu from splitting along economic and party lines'.[51] The point at issue is that government sanctions made membership in an opposition party or forum too costly to bear.

'Retribalization' of politics, economic mismanagement, social chaos and sheer self-interest have led armies to intervene in national affairs in many countries in Africa. Army coups, mutinies or army-dominated governments mark a variety of political administration. On one level, it can be argued that armies intervene because politics have failed. Yet this conclusion is mistaken, for army coups are political occurrences and army rule is far from being non-political. What makes army coups an expensive mistake in Africa is that they interfere with and derail the general evolution of political institutions – especially the maturation of democratic institutions. They reinforce the legacy of authoritarian rule and government without restraint or direct accountability. They delay the development of political pluralism and they create the false impression that the problem at hand is basically one of efficiency and not of institutions. Besides, 'military regimes which have come to power in Africa are not necessarily more successful than the regimes they succeeded.'[52] In Nigeria, the army was not immune from the scandalous corruption that accompanied the oil boom, nor is Mobutu's paramilitary government an example of efficiency and justice.[53]

The cultural identity of Africans is perhaps one of the most controversial aspects of the phenomenon of decolonization. Political independence did not lead to cultural decolonization or necessarily to reafricanization. As it happens, the process of cultural identity of Africans continues to endure the effects of colonialism, foreign religious impact, educational values and the culture of the villages. In his praise of peasants as the only legitimate agents of revolution in Africa, Fanon singled out the villages as locations of true indigenous culture, inhabited by a people with 'a stony pride' who would support the revolution.[54] The distrust of the 'town people' by the peasants was based, according to Fanon, on their overt Westernization and their conversion to alien values.[55]

Why should culture be considered an important aspect of decolonization? The essential importance of culture is because it is integrally linked to the restoration of the dignity and identity of a people. It would be difficult to separate restoration of the dignity of Africans from respect for African culture. Dignity and, with it, cultural pride are especially important in the context of analysing a people whose past has been dominated by alien rule and culture. Alien rule and culture routinely disparaged African culture and it can therefore be said that colonialism was hostile to the growth of local culture.

Culture is, of course, linked to a people's history. 'Culture, whatever the ideological or idealist characteristics of its expression,' Cabral states, 'is thus an essential element of the history of a people.'[56] This history and culture, which together become a summary of a people's values, identity and aspirations, need political independence in order that they may find a favourable climate in which to grow and develop once more. Two crucial issues come out of this. In the first instance, culture is not static and, secondly, culture has a definite material base.

In the liberation of Guinea-Bissau, Cabral argued against the romanticization of African culture, which can include 'unselective praise; systematic exaltation of virtues without condemning defects; blind acceptance of the values of the culture without considering what is actually or potentially negative, reactionary or regressive'.[57] None the less, Cabral concluded that culture was crucial in national liberation struggles. Liberation had to involve what he called 'the confluence of the cultural levels of the social categories available for the struggle'. The 'cultural levels' had then to be transformed by the liberation movement 'into the national cultural force which serves as a basis for development of the armed struggle and is a condition for it'.[58] The liberation movement, while refraining from the negative aspects of African culture, was in fact a 'representative and defender of the culture of the people'. Political independence was therefore linked to cultural freedom and a reassertion of cultural identity. 'A people who free themselves from foreign domination will not be culturally free', Cabral insisted, 'unless, without underestimating the importance of positive contributions from the oppressor's culture and other cultures, they return to the upwards paths of their own culture.'[59]

Since the development of culture has a material base, it is folly to talk of cultural decolonization without economic decolonization. The economy and the values it generates and reinforces do affect the texture of any culture. In the context of Africa, this involves understanding the degree to which foreign economic exploitation and cultural dominance are linked to the cultural development of Africans. According to Amilcar

Cabral, 'national liberation exists when, and only when, the national productive forces have been completely freed from all kinds of foreign domination'.[60] What have been some of the observable realities?

Many countries in Africa have experienced what Mazrui has termed 'cultural dis-Africanisation',[61] the result of fast-paced but shallow Westernization. It would, however, be accurate to say that this 'cultural dis-Africanisation' had its roots firmly planted on the continent during the era of colonialism. Political independence has accelerated the pace of this phenomenon. How can it be that independent African countries have allowed this to happen? Much of it has to do with the desire to be like the West, to acquire 'Western standards' and values, in other words to be 'modern', which in many cases is taken to be synonymous with being Western in orientation and emphasis. The other explanation may lie in the absence of any concerted national effort at cultural renewal. There are also the inherited cultural institutions of government, law, education and scholarship which have continued to operate on Western models.

In former French colonies, France continues to exercise a central cultural role. In recent years this has revolved around the use of the French language, 'whether as mother tongue, or as an official language, or as a medium of instruction, or as a language preferred for international discourse'.[62] But this solidarity extends beyond language. It also becomes a vehicle for the dissemination of French cultural values – a 'French mode of thinking, a manner of approach, a set of assumptions, and a cultural heritage'.[63] Both moderate and radical leaders apparently subscribe to this 'interest in maintaining the integrity of the French language' and culture. One of these leaders is Léopold Sedar Senghor, until January 1980 President of Senegal. Known throughout the world as the popularizer of black values, the poet of Negritude, Senghor 'also believed deeply in France's genius and its civilising mission in Africa'.[64] While in power, he secured a privileged position for French economic interests in Senegal.

Although some countries, such as Zaïre, have had an 'authenticity' drive, this has been shallow and has not interfered with the country's economic and cultural dependency on the West.[65] Part of the problem has been an official neglect of indigenous cultural values in spite of rhetoric which extols their supremacy. The other problem is what may be called 'selective resurrection' of those aspects of local culture which reinforce the power and authority of the leaders – e.g. ruling like an African monarch, but without corresponding cultural institutional restraints on power.

Development, progress and the drive towards full decolonization have to harmonize with culture. African culture, it needs to be repeated, is not hostile to development or progress. Nor is it accurate to argue that the destruction of indigenous culture is an inevitable casualty of development. Examples abound in the world where economic progress has been crafted on culture – for example, in Japan. If culture is to lead to reaffirmation of identity and dignity, it must be closely woven in a country's institutions – in politics, economics and individual relations. It is only in this way that it can cease to be considered a relic of the past to be preserved as a tourist attraction.

'Dis-Africanisation' of Africa and its culture has international dimensions that should be considered. This is particularly relevant to Africa's relationship with the African diaspora. If African culture is destroyed, and if values associated with the continent are hard to find in existence, then Africa denies its descendants overseas a source of cultural inspiration.

Conclusion

This chapter has argued that decolonization is a phenomenon of multiple dimensions. Although it is convenient to look at political independence as the most visible and dramatic form of decolonization, it would be a mistake to equate it with decolonization. This is a process which encompasses economic independence, cultural renewal, identity, integrity and a drive towards an independent existence not unduly interfered with from overseas. Political independence provides the first and most crucial forum from which to pursue these interrelated goals as a bid is made for development and for political empowerment of the local population.

There is a point at which political leadership can in fact, through its policy decisions, subvert national efforts towards decolonization. In Nigeria, Chinua Achebe has in forthright terms stated that the leadership is the problem. 'The Nigerian problem is the unwillingness or inability of its leaders to rise to the responsibility, to the challenge of personal example which are the hallmarks of true leadership.'[66] Leadership does not merely govern and administer but also co-ordinates a national thought process towards an uplifting national vision of where the society should proceed after attaining political independence. This can be the case even if some of these goals were stated on party platforms before *uhuru*.

It has been repeatedly pointed out in this chapter that adherence to the colonial model of administration leads to authoritarian rule impatient with opposition or restraints on its power. Maintenance of inherited economic institutions tends to reinforce exploitation of the country by foreign (or even local) companies and does not provide a viable model for national economic development. These institutions reinforce neo-colonialism. But, as Amilcar Cabral observed, 'so long as imperialism is in existence, an independent African state must be a liberation movement in power, or it will not be independent'.[67] A successful liberation movement thrives on massive national political mobilization, on adopting a realistic revolutionary theory, but above all on having an ideology of liberation which aims to give its supporters peace, development, dignity and independence. It is willing to acknowledge mistakes and revise its strategy but never the goal of independence. Its leadership provides the example: ever vigilant, ever loyal to the ideals of the liberation movement and therefore the uplifting vision of the country. The vision of successful liberation movements in Africa and in the Third World has been egalitarian, non-discriminatory, non-repressive, non-racist and vehemently opposed to exploitation.

Notes

1. Michael Crowder, 'Whose Dream was it Anyway?', *African Affairs*, 86 (342) (January 1987), 10.
2. See, for example, Ali Mazrui, *The Africans* (Boston, Little, Brown & Co., 1986). See also Economic Commission for Africa reports and even appraisals by the OAU in the 1970s and 1980s. As an example, Edem Kodjo, former OAU Secretary-General, said, in 1978,

   Africa is dying. If things continue as they are only eight or nine of the present countries will survive the next few years. All other things being equal, absolute poverty, instead of declining, is likely to gain ground. It is clear that the economy of our continent is lying in ruins . . . Our ancient continent . . . is now on the brink of disaster.

   (Cited in Lloyd Timberlake, *Africa in Crisis* (Philadelphia, New Society Publishers, 1986), p. 8.)
3. G.M. Carter and Patrick O'Meara, 'Introduction', *African Independence: The First Twenty Five Years* (Bloomington, Indiana University Press, 1985), p. xii. Also see S.K.B. Asante, 'International Assistance and International Capitalism: Supportive or Counter Productive', in Carter and O'Meara, *African Independence*.
4. Ali Mazrui, 'Current Sociopolitical Trends', in Frederick S. Arkhurst (ed.), *Africa in the Seventies and Eighties* (New York, Praeger Publishers, 1970), p. 49.
5. P. Olisanwuche Esedebe, *Pan Africanism* (Washington, DC, Howard University Press, 1982), p. 199.
6. Ibid., p. 224. Esedebe concludes (p. 225) that the hatred of Nkrumah and his administration 'was allowed to overshadow a question of fundamental importance. The result was that the delegates rejected immediate political unity opting for consultation and functional co-operation.'
7. Ibid., p. 225.
8. For a more recent evaluation of these views see Adu Boahen, *African Perspective on Colonialism* (Baltimore, The Johns Hopkins University Press, 1989).
9. Basil Davidson, *Can Africa Survive?* (Boston, Little, Brown & Co., 1974), p. 17.
10. Walter Rodney, *How Europe Underdeveloped Africa* (Washington, DC, Howard University Press, 1982), p. 205.
11. Leonard Thompson, *The Political Mythology of Apartheid* (New Haven, Yale University Press, 1985), p. 13.
12. Ibid.
13. Sir Charles Eliot, *The East Africa Protectorate* (New York, Barnes & Noble, 1966), p. 92.
14. Sir Philip Mitchell, *The Agrarian Problem in Kenya* (Nairobi, Government Printer, 1947), p. 2.

15. Ibid., p. 3.
16. Ibid.
17. Lord Lugard, *The Dual Mandate for British Tropical Africa* (Hamden, Connecticut, Archon Books, 1965), p. 69.
18. Ibid., p. 72.
19. Richard Gibson, *African Liberation Movements* (London, Oxford University Press, 1972), p. 195.
20. Ibid.
21. Frantz Fanon, *The Wretched of the Earth* (New York, Grove Press, 1963), p. 41. Fanon continues and says that colonialism regards the native as 'the corrosive element, destroying all that comes near him; he is the deforming element, disfiguring all that has to do with beauty or morality; he is the depository of maleficent powers, the unconscious and irretrievable instrument of blind forces'.
22. Prosser Gifford and W.M. Roger Louis, 'Introduction', *Decolonization and African Independence* (New Haven, Yale University Press, 1988), p. x. They add that decolonization 'can also imply cultural and psychological freedom. It can include the liberation achieved by those who have found or rediscovered their true identity.'
23. See Rodney, *How Europe Underdeveloped Africa*. This theory of underdevelopment, of course, owes a lot to Paul Baran.

    Baran was the first to argue that the destiny of underdeveloped countries was distinctively different from that of the areas that had experienced capitalist development at an earlier date . . . Baran stigmatised monopoly capital as a cause of stagnation, in both the advanced and the underdeveloped countries . . . Baran differed from his predecessors essentially in regarding the development of capitalism in the underdeveloped countries as a different process from that which the advanced countries had gone through at an earlier period of history.

    (Anthony Brewer, *Marxist Theories of Imperialism* (London, Routledge & Kegan Paul, 1980), pp. 20 and 132.)
24. Michael F. Lofchie, 'African Agrarian Malaise', in Carter and O'Meara, *African Independence*, p. 172. For a detailed analysis of the controversies surrounding the underdevelopment theory, see Magnus Blomstrom and Bjorn Hettne, *Development Theory in Transition* (London, Zed Books, 1984).
25. Lofchie, 'African Agrarian Malaise', p. 185.
26. Eduardo Galeano, *Open Veins of Latin America* (New York, Monthly Review Press, 1973), p. 12.
27. Ibid., p. 13. Galeano further observes that Latin America's ruling classes 'have no interest whatsoever in determining whether patriotism might not prove more profitable than treason, and whether begging is really the only formula for international politics'.
28. Davidson, *Can Africa Survive?*, p. 4.
29. Paul Bennel, 'The Colonial Legacy of Salary Structures in Anglophone Africa', *Journal of Modern African Studies*, 20 (1) (1982), 127.
30. See, for example, Nicola Swainson, *The Development of Corporate Capitalism in Kenya, 1918–1977* (Berkeley, University of California Press, 1980); Gavin Kitching, *Class and Economic Change in Kenya* (New Haven, Yale University Press, 1980). Colin Leys' work, *Underdevelopment in Kenya* (London, Heinemann, 1975), is still useful, although the author has subsequently revised his views considerably on the validity of the underdevelopment theory.
31. Mort Rosenblum, *Mission to Civilize: The French Way* (New York, Doubleday, 1988), p. 222.
32. Carter and O'Meara, 'Introduction', p. xiii.
33. Crowder, 'Whose Dream?', p. 8.
34. Ali Mazrui and Michael Tidy, *Nationalism and New States in Africa* (Nairobi/London, Heinemann Books, 1984), p. 272.

35. Larry Ray and Kate Currie, 'State and Class in Kenya: Notes on the Cohesion of the Ruling Class', *Journal of Modern African Studies*, 22 (4) (December 1984), 588.
36. Ibid.
37. Lofchie, 'African Agrarian Malaise', p. 185.
38. See Timberlake, *Africa in Crisis*, p. 74.
39. Ibid., p. 19. Timberlake points out that in 1983–84, when there was a drought in the Sahel, 'five Sahelian countries – Burkina Faso, Mali, Niger, Senegal and Chad – harvested a record 154 million tonnes of cotton fibre (up from 22.7 million tonnes in 1961–62)'. During this period the Sahel imported food on a record scale. Timberlake's conclusion: 'The fact that cotton can be grown but grain cannot has more to do with government and aid agency policies than with rainfall.'
40. Davidson, *Can Africa Survive?*, p. 26.
41. Crowder, 'Whose Dream?', p. 15.
42. Mitchell, while governor of Kenya, postulated that 'the people whom it is customary to describe in this country as educated Africans' had the same amount of education as twelve-year-old white children. See B.A. Ogot, 'Kenya Under the British, 1895–1963', in B.A. Ogot (ed.), *Zamani* (Nairobi, East African Publishing House, 1968), p. 283.
43. Mazrui and Tidy, *Nationalism*, p. 274.
44. Ibid.
45. Ruth Berrins Collier, 'Political Change and Authoritarian Rule', in Phyllis M. Martin and Patrick O'Meara (eds), *Africa* (Bloomington, Indiana University Press, 1977), p. 297.
46. Ibid.
47. Mazrui, 'Current Sociopolitical Trends', p. 49.
48. Ibid.
49. Ibid., p. 50
50. Susanne D. Mueller, 'Government and Opposition in Kenya, 1966–9', *Journal of Modern African Studies*, 22 (3) (September 1984), 407.
51. Ibid., p. 412.
52. Collier, 'Political Change', p. 308.
53. Wyatt MacGaffey, 'The Policy of National Integration in Zaire', *Journal of Modern African Studies*, 20 (1) (March 1982), 88.
54. Fanon, *Wretched of the Earth*, p. 61. It is worth while pointing out here Fanon's famous dictum that 'in the colonial countries the peasants alone are revolutionary, for they have nothing to lose and everything to gain'. Also see p. 126.
55. Ibid., p. 112.
56. Amilcar Cabral, *Unity and Struggle* (New York, Monthly Review Press, 1979), p. 142.
57. Ibid., p. 150.
58. Ibid., p. 151.
59. Ibid., p. 143.
60. Ibid.
61. Mazrui, *The Africans*, p. 11.
62. Keith Panter-Brick, 'Independence: French Style', in Gifford and Louis, *Decolonization*, p. 103.
63. Ibid.
64. Boubacar Barry, 'Neo-Colonialism and Dependence in Senegal, 1960–1980', in Gifford and Louis, *Decolonization*, p. 294.
65. Wyatt MacGaffey, 'Policy of National Integration', p. 104.
66. Chinua Achebe, *The Trouble with Nigeria* (London, Heinemann Books, 1983), p. 1.
67. Cabral, *Unity*, p. 116.

Two

The Formative Years 1945–55

E.S. ATIENO-ODHIAMBO

Kikuyu future, European future, Asian future – All human future.
(Ehrenfels, 1960: 45)

Introduction: Colonial and Postcolonial Discourses

As an event there was no 'decolonization' in Kenya in the period between 1945 and 1955. Rather, this age was the first time since the Devonshire Declaration 1923 that the colonial discourse in Kenya once again assumed its multiplex dimensions: 'imperial' within the Colonial Office, 'the second colonial occupation' within the White Highlands, 'opposition' among the African populace in the reserves, in the *bomas* (often called towns) and in the settler farms, and 'sitting on the fence' amongst Asian *dukawallahs* (or petty shop-keepers) from Vanga to Lodwar. African memory recalls this period as 'the Age of 210' (Paper 210 on East African Federation), the period when both the settlers and the colonial state nearly forced them into an East African Federation designed by the settlers; when the empire first reached the villages on ex-Second World War Land-rovers with OHMS (On His Majesty's Service) number plates and DARA (Development and Reconstruction Authority) inscriptions – the latter a signal for forced or compulsory labour that led to the women's revolt against the same in Muranga in 1947, provided a name, Okuta, for an age-group and a religion, Dini Ya Maria Ragot, among the Luos and led to the emergence of rural populism and the rise of men like Oginga Odinga and J.T. Ole Tameno as defenders of their peoples against forced land consolidation and loss of grazing rights in the forests respectively. The Age of 210 was also the age of fear: fear that the settlers intended to collar more of Bukusu land and Pokot rights to graze in the highlands, giving vibrance to the Dini Ya Msambwa (DYM) and to Dini ap Mbojet among the Kipigis. It was also a seasons of fear of final loss of access to and security in the White Highlands by the many Luo squatters in Kisumu/Londiani district, Gikuyu in Nakuru and Naivasha districts, Nandi and Elkumi in TransNzoia and Uasin Gishu districts. The Age of 210 was also the age of pronounced urban poverty and hunger in the settler farms and in the *bomas*. In a capsule, it was an age of *matatizo*, which restlessness served as an agency to action: to strikes, to demonstrations, to a struggle for religious autonomy, to Mau Mau, to the second colonial conquest of Kenya by the empire in the 1953–54 period. At its terminal date, all the actors had been forced to rethink the history of the colonial past of the previous fifty years, and were all caught busily reworking the interstices of the colonial order to accommodate the hard past and the dim future. The period of 1953–55 witnessed these reworkings: of the role of the British army in colonial governance; of the British in the wider arena called their East African Dependencies; of the constitutional order within the Colony and Protectorate of Kenya; of the nature of a possible African politics, and its attempted encapsulation in two recognizably British models, the trade union and the political party.

Some thirty to forty years hence, in the 1980s and early 1990s, in the era of postcolonial discourse, armchair academics might seek to impose both a baptismal name – Decolonization – and a historical order – Process – to all this *mgogoro* (tumult). Three sobering considerations must be reintroduced into this project. First, African history has been through this type of semantic quest before. In dealing with the period of the first European conquest and colonization of Africa at the beginning of the twentieth century, some Africanists of the 1960s introduced 'resistance' as an entry into the heroic discourses about 'protonationalism', 'nationalism' and 'African initiatives'. At the end of the day, all this does not take us much further than where Julius Caesar left us two millennia before: he came, he saw, he conquered, in spite of the resistances of all the barbarians of Gaul and England. Secondly, the oral histories of the 1945–55 period, whether collected from an Indian *dukawallah* at Asembo Bay, a Pokomo chairman of the Young Buu Association, a Boer settler in the Wanjohi Valley, a market-woman in Saraturnin, Baringo, or a leading collaborator like Senior Chief Amoth Owira – all would fail to recognize their involvement in a process with an end called decolonization at our time. Thirdly, and this is crucial, decolonization, even when used by Western academics (Louis and Gifford, 1988), still remains an Aesopic term, which sanitizes struggle, eliminates contradictions and smuggles a plan – God's or empire's, it does not matter – into Kenya's history. The hidden agenda behind its ascetic tone is, however, clearly semantic, the 'granting' of independence by Britain to Kenya in 1963.

This chapter argues against this 'granting' assumption by taking as its credo Kenyatta's oft-cited and reverberating battle-cry:

Tulipigania Kama Simba!
  We fought like lions!
Tulinyakua Uhuru Yetu Kamili!
  We grabbed our true independence.

The Political Economy

The history of this period begins, and ends, with what the historian David Anderson has called 'the tyranny of property', the question of who was to own land in Kenya in these years, and of the relation of people to land. It was the encapsulation of the experiences of the past forty years of colonialism; in 1945 the basic question was whether the nature of property – 'White Man's Country' – and the control of land as a resource – entrenched through the 1939 White Highlands Order in Council – were going to be the same, and, if not, in what manner and by what means they were going to be altered. In the White Highlands the settlers sought to increase their numbers through closer settlement and their acreage through expanded production.

Then there was developmental colonialism as state policy, which involved the further privileging of the settler sector of the economy (McWilliam, 1963). In addition to closer settlement involving the settling of young white soldiers on land, there was the provision of training for them through the setting up of Egerton College for their exclusive use. More significantly, the process of the mechanization of settler agriculture, begun during the Second World War years, became more intensified. This was the cutting edge: mechanization meant expansion in the capitalist forms of production and the liquidation of manual and ox-drawn labour from the highlands. It also meant expanded production on the land. Modern technology rendered squatter hoe cultivation obsolete for the settlers, and made squatter occupation of agricultural space into an anachronism. Capital and technology drove the squatters from the surface of the land: thereafter the squatters became a surplus population, and the logic of history took on its inexorable course. The pseudo-feudal patronage relations between settler and squatter were terminated, and a reserve army of a landless discontented populace was spurned into the cauldron of Kenya's looming conflict.

Wyn Harris, the Acting Labour Commissioner in 1946, considered that there were as many as 250,000 African squatters living in forests and on settler lands (Youe, 1987: 210). Half of these were Agikuyu. In the ensuing years it was this population that had to be whittled down – and was – by a combination of state coercion and settler rejection. This was particularly vexing because both settler and squatter agriculture had enjoyed substantial prosperity during the Second World War-induced economic boom. From 1947 squatters were being subjected to oppressive labour contracts and to a reduction of their economic opportunities. The idea was to destroy the economic basis for squatter existence as a peasantry; to transform them from peasants into a rural proletariat, working for white farmers who for the first time were to develop their employer-labour relations along strictly capitalist wage-labour lines. To achieve these goals new contracts were drawn up during and after the war. The squatters were now required to work 270 days of the year rather than the previous 240 days. In addition they were required to limit their stock to 15. Squatter resistance ensued: at least 3,000 refused to sign the new contracts in the Rift Valley.

Meanwhile, squatters living in government forests pitted themselves against the Forest Department and against capitalist concessionaires. In the case of the Lembus Forest, the Tugen pastoralists have sustained their claim that they had a right to the pastures therein from the 1920s. The Forest Department had from 1938 intended to restrict the numbers of animals and the cultivation rights that the Tugen enjoyed, as well as insisting on removing the squatters at will. In response, the squatters mounted a campaign, after the war, desiring to be annexed to Baringo District (Anderson, 1987: 262–5). The Tugen campaigned hard for this in the period 1948–51, culminating in their petition to the Secretary of State. Kenya African Union (KAU) politicians and political leaders, such as J.L. Ole Tameno, came to the forest to speak with the squatters (Moi was absent!) in 1952. Tameno not only wrote to the Chief Native Commissioner, but also tabled a motion in the Legislative Council on 5 November 1952 defending the Lembus squatters. By March 1956 the Tugen had won the argument, and in 1959 the forest became part of Baringo.

The squatters of the Uasin Gishu plateau, who were mainly pastoralists, also faced the assault in the years after 1946. Repatriation of their stock to the reserve was the strategy adopted by them. In 1950, about 53,000 head of cattle were voided out of the district into the surrounding reserve (Youe, 1988: fn. 59). In the subsequent years the whites-only District Councils were given full authority to pass anti-squatting legislation and pursued this aim vigorously, as the lands of the north-west Rift became increasingly mechanized and settler agriculture became intensely capitalized.

In all areas, then, the state, but more particularly the settlers, found themselves face to face with their erstwhile guests, the squatters, who also regarded these lands as home and as property. The eviction of squatters did not mean 'termination of contract' to the latter. Rather they experienced being homeless and propertyless in the lands of their birth. Their struggles against this abyss from 1946 onwards must be seen as a struggle about existence, about *mugunda*, land as household and property, and about being. Being a landless human was a contradiction that was both epistemologically and existentially unacceptable to a 'rational' African in the 1940s.

The bitter struggles against the second colonial occupation (Lonsdale and Low, 1976) – the decision by the British imperial government to settle more white people in the highlands, to protect this enclave through financial and agro-economic privilege; and by the colonial settlers to mechanize production in the highlands, thereby throwing out hundreds of thousands of squatter families – make sense only in these notions. about property and the context of personhood and agency.

Similarly, in the African reserves, the issues of access, decried in all colonial reports as 'unnecessary fragmentations', and of control over herds – known as overstocking – in the light of a deteriorating biosystem raised not only questions of control but also of authority. Chiefs found themselves pitted against their wards as the former sought to extend their landholdings. The landless *ahoi* and guest residents, *jodak*, found their lot worsening, as founder lineages sought to control more of patrimonial property. Iltiamus pastoralists found themselves locked in struggle against the Tugen for access to the Lembus Forest pastures, while the Nandi stepped up cattle liberation against all the *lemek* non-Kalenjin settler, Luo and Luhya in the Nyando and Kipkarren valleys. There were, in addition, gender struggles, exemplified for example in Muranga women's resistance to forced labour, Nandi women's struggles over the control over the household economy (Oboler, 1985), and struggle of the women of Majengo and Shauri Moyo in Nairobi about ownership of private property (White, 1990).

As in the settled areas, developmental colonialism exacerbated the tensions in the African reserves, where the colonial state sought to arrest the consequences of deterioration of land that had been so eloquently attested to by all witnesses to the Kenya Land Commission a decade before (Coray, 1978). The new programmes, but particularly the agency of the African Land Development Board, made new demands: soil erosion was to be arrested through bench terracing. This led to a demand for compulsory unpaid labour from both men and women, for part of the week. These demands were unpopular country-wide. They generated protests and resistance from Kaya Duruma to Sio Port. But they also generated fear of further loss of land among the Kipsigis and the Agiryama to name but two. The attendant developmental agenda, namely the reafforestation of such hills as Maragoli and Kiboswa, Kisumu, only deepened these suspicions: the white man wanted the programme to succeed so as later to gain access to these hills. The Avalogooli protested and the Luo earned the sobriquet of 'obstinate' from Elspeth Huxley (Huxley, 1960). The bottom line is that colonial developmentalism detonated agrarian struggles (Bates, 1989).

These agrarian struggles took an acute form in the immediate post-war years, as the returned Second World War soldiers, *Keya*, sought to invest their wartime savings in shops, tea-rooms, water-mills, transport lorries and passenger buses (*Chakra* or *Oyiwe*) and found themselves placed in direct competition against the inter-war chiefly and *karani* (clerical) elements in rural society, but more directly against the Asian traders whose primary line of accumulation had been as collectors of produce: such men as *Ogonji* (Govindji Karsandas Karia) had built their rural wealth by being the grain produce and cotton buyers at Ndere, Luanda and Nambale in the inter-war years. It was this same niche that rural entrepreneurs like Oginga Odinga sought to fill. Under the motto of *Kinda e teko, Riwruok e teko* (In struggle lies strength, Unity is strength), Odinga mobilized the traders, teachers, chiefs, plus 'ladies and gentlemen' into the premier African enterprise of western Kenya during this period: the Luo Thrift and Trading Corporation (Odhiambo, 1976). Like the vegetable project in Karatina, enterprises like this one sought to establish an alternative vision of the future, a future where African accumulators would become independent gentry. This spirit ran against the ethos of the colonial society, which still placed the primacy of the pace and locomotion of history on the white settler, and which really still saw the African as a *pagasi* – unskilled labourer. Hence the sense of grievance against blocked opportunities among the Africans, which pitted them against their administratively dominated local Native Councils, which made the plethora of by-laws for, or rather against, genuine African free enterprise. The rural entrepreneur was, at the same time, an available local notable and communicator: politicians like Jomo Kenyatta sought them out in their itinerant quest for contact and legitimacy in the reserves. The tea-kiosk in rural Kenya became the rendezvous for private meetings, political and economic, between the political entrepreneurs and the local big men, *andu awe*. From them the politicians accessed the market-women as well. The tea-kiosk was to loom large at the Kapenguria trial of Kenyatta and his other five colleagues, as evidence was adduced relating to what Kenyatta had said at Thomsons Falls or at 01 Kalou. Rural enterprise, frustrated at every turn, sought political avenues of expression.

Two political avenues were open to the local notables. One was to link up to the existing KAU, and there is sufficient evidence that the tours of the KAU leaders of 1951–52 alarmed the state precisely because there was a waiting audience for the leaders virtually across the country. Hence their cancellations (PRO: CO 822/435). But an equally political decision could be made by elements from these same strata: to 'collaborate' by accepting official positions in the colonial system as functionaries. B.A. Ogot has argued that the history of collaboration is equally compelling in Kenya's narratives of nationalism (Ogot, 1972). The present author has likewise made a point worth reiterating still: really there were no permanent collaborators or resisters in the colonial enterprise (Odhiambo, 1974). The whole situation smacks of a paradox, as Bob Maxon has illustrated in the career of John Kebaso, who was a radical of the Odinga type in the mid-1940s, collaborated in the next decade, but still emerged as a pillar of Gusii 'nationalism' – Gusii in Kenya African National Union (KANU) – in the 1960s (Maxon, 1989). At any rate, the logic of history did not delineate such neat camps. On his being nominated to the Legislative Council for his presumed pliability, Moi was sent for by two such polarities: Achieng' Oneko was sent by Odinga to bring him to Kisumu to radicalize him before he proceeded to Nairobi. Clearly there existed porous fences, through which one could seep in the quest for political space and a relevant political arena: Kikuyu Central Association (KCA) today, KAU tomorrow and Mau Mau on the third day.

Related to this idea of property was the idea of progress, a very important component of African political thought at this time. Its African origins lay in the *Jamoko/Muthamaki/Mundu Mue/Omwami/Mundu Munene/ Omogambi* tradition, the African idea of life and success that encouraged individual accumulation of property in land, cattle and women. The settlers and the African colonial chiefs, court interpreters and livestock traders, as well as Indian shopkeepers, had been the exemplars of this ideal in the previous forty years. The returned soldiers very quickly put this idea of progress into action, buying the ex-Kenya African Rifles (KAR) lorries and buses, building shops in the village markets. At the same time, some African *asomi*, such as W.W.W. Awori and Tom Mbotela, derived the idea of progress from the books they read, and brought into the current discourses such ideas as the 'Universal Rights of Man'. All the educated people associated elective representation as part of this corpus of progress, and such founders of the Kenya African Study Union (KASU) as Samuel Onyango Josiah and Barrack Okeno embraced the idea of constitution-writing as a step in the direction of progress (Spencer, 1985). Next, this idea of progress was associated with speaking on behalf of the many. The contributions of the nominated Members of the Legislative Council are replete with these concerns. Eliud Wambu Mathu and Beneah Apolo Ohanga over and over again reiterated the need to grant Africans education and grandualist constitutional representation. Mathu was known then for his slogan: 'Half a loaf is better than none' (Roelker, 1976: 88–106). Ohanga espoused the values of Christianity and civilization (Nyabera, 1976). The columns of the Legislative Council Hansard of the period have Daniel arap Moi pleading for dips, water-holes and access to highland pastures for the northern Kalenjin peoples. At the level of praxis, perhaps the most penetrating of them was Oginga Odinga's Luo Thrift and Trading Corporation, which sought to create an economic kingdom as well as a national identity for the Luo rural and urban communities. Odinga also represented the idea of progress at another level: cultural unity, in his founding of the Luo Union during these years (Odinga, 1967). Yet the most poignant pointers to the idea of progress were the many clan associations that emerged in Mombasa, Nakuru, Nairobi, Kampala and Dar es Salaam in these years. They were all concerned with the creation of a moral community that emphasized thrift, accumulation and co-operation, and also took care of the new arrival in town, the unemployed, the dead, but also repatriated prostitutes to the Nyeri, Nandi, Samia or Bunyala Navakholo reserves (Tamarkin, 1973).

Nyokonyoko: The Texture of Everyday Life

The common colonial discourse about the Africans in this period was that they were 'sullen', and an exploration is necessary because it explains why ordinary people, undertaking day-to-day chores, would sustain an interest in anticolonial sentiments. The answer lies in the fact that every-day life was a constant annoyance. The 'colour bar' – the exclusion of Africans from goods and services enjoyed by Europeans – was a signify-ing marker of this period. Europeans, Asians and Arabs alike had a stake in *kala-ba*, and dished it out on Africans with impunity. With *kala-ba* came annoyances, experienced most acutely by 'houseboys', who were *shenzi* in English and *suthru* in Hindi: dogs in daily parlance. But also humiliations – of an African boy being stripped naked at Hardinge Street bus-stop by an English woman on suspicion of being a pickpocket, in spite of his St Peter Clavers' School uniform and despite the fact that his father was the police inspector in charge of Spring Valley (Juma Okola, pers. comm.). And spite . . ., as when Jamndas Dewji of Luanda spat into Mathayo Ogundo's eyes . . . just for the heck of it. Also: Low wages. Inadequate unsanitary housing in urban areas. Police raids for the *kipande*. Dreary manual dock labour. The capricious and arbitrary cattle quarantine laws and by-laws. Endless pasturing work from three in the morning to four in the afternoon for the settler herdsmen at Hoey's Bridge. Inadequate schooling. Compulsory bench terracing. Limited licences for African traders, and discriminatory infrastructural support. Dissatisfied, unemployed returned soldiers. *Ayahs* prohibited from enter-taining on *memsahib*'s compound and dismissed on the spot when caught. The humiliations of colonial medicine, with males suspected of venereal disease parading so as to be seen on Bahati road, Nairobi. *Pumbavu* as a compliment and *chura, afriti, kafiri, mshenzi* as descriptions of African being by the Busaidi Arab aristocracy in Mombasa. *Toa Kofia* (Take your hat off). The frustrations of being an independent *dobi* in Kaloleni. 'Fogoff' ('Fuck off'). *Peksen*, that frequent raid into the household any time, and *toa risiti*, account for your personal acquisitions because you are all potential thieves anyway, circulating goods through *blek*, the second economy. The numerous court fines paid really to court officials, or its alternative, *jela rumenda* or *jela ndogo*. The latitude of insults practised by everyone against the African: *bladi-Swaini, Kaffir, sokwe mutu, kuma nina, fakni, nugu waheed*. All these seared on the individual and collective memory. The determination of whites that blacks were opaque, as captured in an English woman's question to Tom Mboya in 1951: 'Is there *anybody* here?' (Mboya, 1963). The frustrations of semi-professionals in the workplace, with the constant reminder that they could neither think nor act right because of their colour (Gicaru, 1958). The daily received knowledge that all Africans were liars. The regard of all African women in towns as potential prostitutes; and the treatment of their economic activities as adjuncts to prostitution. The running harassment of food vendors and the informal sector as illegal hawkers (Onstad, 1990). The *tikiti ya kodi*, tax receipts that were to be permanently on your body. The arbitrariness of dispersal – *seksen* – or arrest by the police and *askari kanga: utamaliza hapo mbele* – it will be settled at the police depot. *Kanyaga*, the ubiquitous trespass laws in towns and on settler farms. The banishment of African laughter from European neighbourhoods because Europeans were eating, or *mamsap analala*. Men like Enos Opondo Aginga had to learn how not to laugh in the Government House kitchen. The *kiboko* for corporal punishment, meted out in generous dosages by *Kaburu* boys – *Bwana Mḏogo* – to African elders, and the requisite *sarut* as a thank you afterwards. Promises broken! The lot of cosmopolitan Africans who saw their future in terms of blocked opportunity: they were to be African Assistant Administrative Officers for ever, Achieng' Oneko lamented at Ruringu Stadium on that 25 July 1952 meeting. Even graduate Joel Mechack Ojal could not be served tea at the Kisumu Hotel, and Doctors Kinya, Likimani, Onyango and Mwathi could not operate outside Racecourse Road. All the pent-up frustrations that social historians study as preconditions to a revolutionary situation, and which explain the dilemma in Ngugi wa Thiong'o's *A Grain of Wheat* (1965): How could Ngotho the cook kill Mr Holand's son when the same cook carried the boy on his back only yesterday? He did. He had lived through enough of *ubaguzi wa rangi, kala-ba*. And this is why, as Tom Mboya wrote later, the one word *uhuru* – freedom – galvanized all these pent-up energies into mass political struggles (Mboya, 1963).

Jomo Kenyatta

The question was, what was to be done? The KAU suggested one way: organize politically. The Kenya settlers another: preserve white rule. The colonial state suggested yet a third: give the Africans a vent – this did not imply a way – in the African District Councils. Elijah Masinde preached the need for a spiritual kingdom. Men like Asa Osanya defended the dignity of individual humanity: when a settler slapped him, he hit back, causing a tumult one Nakuru afternoon in 1948. Some individuals subverted the imperial rhetoric by naming their African *shenzi* dogs Churchill (T.R. Odhiambo, pers. comm., April 1991). Others sought gradual accommodation into the structures of colonialism – as chiefs, nominated locational, district and Legislative Councillors. Some became revivalists, and perplexed the African world by millenarian behaviour that included hugging mothers-in-law and, it was rumoured, flouting other more private canons. As they sang in Luanda Doho in 1949, the world had gone 'Adventist'.

Yaye Yaye	Alas, Alas
Piny ti olokore	The world has become
Adwentist!	Adventist
Yaye Yaye	Alas! Alas!
Piny ti olokore	The world has become
Adwentist!	Adventist!

(B.A. Ogot: Dodo)

Enter Jomo Kenyatta, the 'quintessential African', as C.R.L. James referred to him. Kenyatta was, of course, the man with the message: the dismantling of colonialism. His return in 1946 inspired the younger wo/men away from engaging in what were essentially settler/employer politics confined to Kenya. Rather, he showed the direction: settler colonialism could only be dismantled from London. He thus weaned the age-group of Oginga Odinga from the politics of local focus – i.e. arguing with the District Commissioner in the Local Native Councils – and into the concern with independence (Oginga Odinga: pers. comm., 18 May 1982). This was the centrality of Kenyatta. That he tried to work with the chiefs, or got disillusioned (Abrahams, 1956), or failed to run KAU (Spencer, 1985; Throup, 1987), or was ousted from control of Nairobi KAU in 1951 (Kaggia, 1975) are all beside the point. He was the man who, in his own words, held the lion by the tail; who declared that the tree of freedom must be watered with blood. The Mau Mau proper, that is, people who were still young enough to fight militarily, looked up to him and did not abandon his message in the forest. They sang of him as their Messiah. Kenyatta of course was guilty of 'managing Mau Mau', the Mau Mau of the minds that he had liberated by his presence and oratory, from Elburgon, where the likes of Wasonga Sijeyo caught on to the message in 1948, to that spectacle of a meeting at Ruringu stadium, Nyeri, on 25 July 1952.

Anake wa 40: Towards Mau Mau

The linkage between KCA, KAU and Mau Mau lies in the triple membership of the youth in all three. Tamarkin identifies them in his discussion of the social basis of Mau Mau in Nakuru. 'The Mau Mau leaders in Nakuru were mostly young Kikuyu in their twenties, uneducated and uninfluenced by European missionaries. Most of them were petty traders struggling to make a living, having recently come to town from the farming hinterland where they had lived as squatters on European farms' (Tamarkin, 1978: 248). These young men acted as messengers, guards and look-outs during oathing ceremonies. 'It is on such potentially para-military duties of the young group that attention must be focused when attempting to trace the origins of the future guerilla movement' (Tamarkin, 1976: 123). From 1948 these guards took a special oath different from the old KCA oath in two forms: the goat replaced the Bible in the *Muma wa Thenge*, and the youth committed themselves to steal arms and to kill as a matter of duty. In 1950 the youth in Nakuru made a formal breach with the KCA and formed their own committee. A. Ngunjiri became their chairman, and this militant committee subsequently evolved into a District Committee. Ngunjiri, however, maintained contact with the KCA committee, which sanctioned the new *muma*. But by mid-1951 the youth had imposed forced oathing for the achievement of unity on all Gikuyu, and both the KCA and KAU branch leaders cowered into abstention, or oblivion. By late 1951 the militants baptized themselves as *Kiama Kia Bara*, the fighting group. In their growing militancy, they replaced Ngunjiri with Wachira Rugi as their chairman. He presided over a committee of illiterate ex-squatters in their twenties who had become petty traders. This was a volatile group, with no stake in the town or in the system as a whole. 'They had nothing to lose except their petty-trade which barely gave them a living' (Tamarkin, 1976: 29).

Nairobi was an 'outcast' city in these years: a city of the African poor; the wages of the employed were low, even by the standards of the time. David Throup (1987) has identified the unemployed and unmanageable crowd living marginally, on the edge of criminality according to the state, striving to make a living on their wits, as 'men in the middle' (Kabiro, 1973), housing themselves in the Kamkunji slums below Majengo and at Kariobangi. The African locations were a republic all of their own at night. In any case the Ugenya Inspector Juma Ja Kondiek and his few *askari* at Shauri Moyo police station could not control an unlit location. And so the oathing and the arming went on, and the linkages with the Gikuyu countryside were forged as young men carried arms, as taxi-drivers shuttled the leadership of the KAU and the trade unions, and as Mau Mau 'justice' installed itself in the town: Bildad Kaggia confesses to have strangled a 'traitor' in a taxi in 1951 (Kaggia, 1975). Thus the urban poor were an important political class in the Nairobi of the postwar years and in the making of Mau Mau. Comprising the unemployed, hawkers, *chupa na ndebe* collectors, pickpockets, thieves, prostitutes and beer-sellers, this stratum was an available mass for political activism.

They turned up at the KAU rallies, listened to Chege Kibachia's African Workers Federation agitation and joined Dominic Gatu's *Anake wa 40*. They created 'outcast Nairobi', the ungovernable republic that was the African locations; robbing, spivving, fighting back any police raids (Furedi, 1973: 282) but also oathing in preparation for Mau Mau. The movement ran a protection racket, through which it got funds from Asian and African businessmen.

Ironically, when the KAU leadership was arrested in late 1952, it left the leaders of the Muhimu, their movement, as the only political organization in Nairobi. Eliud Mutonyi and his committee thus intensified their collection of ammunition, medical supplies and the recruitment and deployment of the fighters (Mutonyi, n.d.). This urban leadership had a parallel and comparable construct in the settler farms, where an organic leadership had developed among the subalterns on the farms. Furedi in one of his earlier articles argued that the Gikuyu squatter society was undifferentiated along class lines, by asserting that the colonial administration failed to 'form a core of loyalist Kikuyu to fight on their behalf', in contrast to the reserves where 'a group of missionary Kikuyu literati, landowners and businessmen closely tied to the colonial system, constituted the basis for a class of collaborators' (Furedi, 1974: 498). His analysis suggests that, although there had emerged a substratum of a sub-élite of headmen, milk clerks, drivers, house servants, artisans, traders and teachers within the farms, this sub-élite was not alienated from the ordinary run of the squatters. Rather, they lived on the farms, together with their families, and became the organic intellectuals of the Mau Mau movement:

> This group of traders, artisans and farm teachers played a pivotal role in the movement on the grassroots. It was from their ranks that arose the leadership of the Mau Mau in the Highlands . . . [But], living on the farms, they were an integral part of the squatter community. In a sense they were the most successful and enterprising element of that community – and not unnaturally were seen as the 'natural' leaders of the squatter political movement. (Furedi, 1974: 500)

Furedi cites Gitau Gathuri of Dundori as one such man, as well as the *nyapara* Kinyanjui wa Mutegi. It was these respected people who were first oathed, and who then took charge of the oathing on the farms. Those who would be loyal to the settlers were intimidated out of their positions in the 1950–51 period. Thus the artisanal class played a crucial role, turning the movement from being merely a rural peasant protest into 'a considerable force with a clear anti-colonial dimension. They thus had a central role in the spreading of the movement and the formulation of the radical perspective' (Furedi, 1974: 503).

Kanogo has taken Furedi to task over this interpretation, arguing against the latter's emphasis on Mau Mau leadership as having arisen out of the subaltern elements in the settler farms. Kanogo argues that the *nyaparas* and artisans, being close to the *mzungu*, were always regarded with suspicion by the ordinary squatters. Her fieldwork data showed that it was the elders rather than *nyaparas* who were the first to be oathed on any farm. They constituted a select few, chosen, 'not because they held positions of importance within or without the settler set-up, but because of their political insight, respectability and "the wisdom of God"' (Kanogo, 1977: 24). Be that as it may, it is possible to agree that, given the constraints that had been imposed on squatter property accumulation since the 1930s, there is no dialectical contradiction between being old and being a *nyapara*. Plus, the labouring poor were old by the age of thirty: it was backbreaking labour: *Kamiti n'Omuliro*, Kamiti is hell, they said of the sisal plantations outside Nairobi. What is pertinent is that these *gathee* (young elders), *karanis* and *nyaparas* were the cosmopolitan element, with '*habari*', news from the Elburgon markets and from Nairobi and Makuyu. They were the men who linked the squatters to both the reserves and the towns. In a word, they were mobile, carried ideas and routinized the discourses on anticolonialism.

But they were not always men. Both Tabitha Kanogo (1987) and Cora Ann Presley have highlighted African women in Mau Mau, reminding the reader of the role that the latter played as organizers or as disseminators of nationalist ideas in the period between 1947 and 1956. Their role was crucial and was recognized as such by British Officials, who regarded them as 'the eyes and ears of Mau Mau'. As fighters, the women fought as members of the forest 'gangs'; they were active participants in the rural network of information and supplies; they were victims of screening, detention, villagization and the slowed-down release through the 'pipelines'. In sum, they were a crucial component of the struggle (Presley, 1986). This involvement was recognized by the colonial state, which began detaining women activists under the Emergency Orders in 1952. Women political leaders in Kiambu like Wambui Wagarama, Nduta wa Kore, Rebecca Njeri Kairi, Priscilla Wambaki and Mary Wanjiko were among the first 'subversives' to be detained. This did not deter activism, however, as those left behind were actively involved in administering oathing ceremonies and supplying materials – food, medicine and guns – to the forest fighters. Such a leader was Wanjiru Nyamarutu of Njoro (Kanogo, 1977: 248-9). In the course of the war 'nearly eight thousand women' were detained at Kiambu. Presley's informants recalled the horrors of detention: physical assault, forced labour, material deprivation. Her conclusion is an important one, namely that the history of Mau Mau as a rural movement would be incomplete without the integration of women's activism into its historiography.

Mau Maus of the Mind

Students of this period have had to contend with 'the myths of Mau Mau' – those 'meanings' or 'explanations' that have been given to the movement by its various interpreters since the late 1940s. These meanings in turn have spewed forth labels – structural semantics – which have been deployed in many discussions on Mau Mau. Their variety – resort to barbarism, return to the jungle, failure to cope with modernity and civilization, anti-Christian, anti-European, African savagery; nationalist, tribalist or independence movement; class action by the peasants and lumpenproletariat – is all a reflection of the positions of the interpreters of the movement. They may well have nothing to do with the historical movement called Mau Mau. The historian, however, is obliged to assess what all this intellectual activity has been for over the last forty years. *It has been about the production of knowledge, the production of history, and the use of that knowledge, that history, by the various contending segments of society.* As is now evident this production is a constant and continuous exercise (Cooper, 1988). In this vein, it is not peculiar to Kenya. The French Revolution is still a very keenly debated event in the history of the world; Chou en Lai once remarked that it is too early to discuss the true meaning of it! Historians world-wide still debate the origins of the First World War. Within Kenya, Mau Mau will continue to command this pre-eminence, for its real significance lies in the fact that it was a conjuncture, a meeting-point for all the forces of history, economic, social and ideological, that had shaped Kenyan societies in the first half-century. The 'Myths' become useful only in this regard: they help the student of history to raise basic questions regarding cause, meaning, explanation and the uses and abuses of history. They also enable the practising historian to take personal responsibility for the past and future, as was most evident in the recent exchanges between Kenyans Ali Mazrui, Atieno Odhiambo, Bethwell Allan Ogot, Ngugi wa Thiong'o and Godfrey Muriuki on the BBC programme, 'Tampering with the Past' (BBC, 14 April 1991).

The flip side to this coin is that the production of knowledge about Mau Mau has never been the exclusive monopoly of the Kenyans. As a media event, Mau Mau received substantial journalistic coverage in the *New York Times* in the USA, the *New Statesmen and Nation* in Great Britain, the *Johannesburg Star* in South Africa and the *Times* of India (Odhiambo, 1981b). As an experience of black people, it commanded the early attention of African American intellectuals, such as Martin Kilson (Kilson, 1955) and Bill Cayton, the editor of the black newspaper, the *Courier*. As a cultural event, it attracted the attention of the urban youth of Harlem, who took to 'Mau Mau-ling' and to calling themselves 'Jomo X Kenyatta', as well as the rural poor in Jamaica, who devised a Mau Mau dance step and expressed an interest in the *panga* as a weapon of liberation. The South African government banned the purchase of the *panga* by Africans. This production line has continued: Robert Ruark's *Something of Value* has, after all, been read by more people world-wide than its home-grown counterparts, Ngugi wa Thiong'o's early novels, *Weep Not Child* and *A Grain of Wheat*. And Ruark's academic reincarnation by Robert Edgerton in *Mau Mau: An African Crucible* (1989) will continue this trend, in spite of the plea from mainstream historians for a return to sanity (Maxon, 1991). The challenge actually lies outside the trope of academic versus popular narratives. Rather, it lies in the question: why does the non-African non-nationalist enjoy the Ruark genre? Why was a purported historical novel of Kenya, Barbara Wood's *Green City in the Sun* (1988), visibly advertised in London's Baker Street underground station wall mural, and not Likimani's *Passbook Number F47927* (1985), its feminist predecessor in the market? The answer: there are not one but many forms of 'knowledge' about Mau Mau (Lonsdale, 1990).

The Other Mau Maus

The historian John Lonsdale has emphasized the need to address the question of Gikuyu political thought at this time (Lonsdale, 1987), for on it hinge questions of Gikuyu nationalism, Mau Mau as nationalism, the linkages between Gikuyu and Kenyan nationalism and the subsequent 'Mau Mau debate' of the 1980s (Lonsdale, 1991; Odhiambo, 1992). This chapter will not revisit this terrain. Rather, what needs reiteration, particularly for the 1990s, is the *material basis of the many nationalisms extant among the Gikuyu at this time*. For those who believed in Western 'progress' and the culture of possessive individualism, Mau Mau was an embarrassment because it harked back to the moral community of the nineteenth century, when a Mogikoyo was bounded by his indissoluble membership to a household, *nyumba*, a lineage (*mbari*), age-group (*riika*), and access to communal property, *gethaka*. *Nyumba na riika itiuumaguo* – one cannot contract out of one's *nyumba* or *riika* (Muriuki, 1974). The cultural nationalism of Mau Mau underscored the values of unity, brotherhood (this is the substantive meaning of the oat) and struggle and conversely warned against betrayal. This cultural nationalism, however, posed no contradiction to the wider Kenyan nationalism, whose common line was anticolonialism, except for its local oathing paraphernalia. The political nationalism of Mau Mau, *Wiyathi*, freedom, was equally elastic, for the Mau Mau *Nyimbo* (songs) testify eloquently enough to their simultaneous commitment to the House of Mumbi, to the Gods of Kerenyaga, to liberating the land and to a future Kenya ruled by Kenyatta (Kinyatti, 1980).

The discussion of Gikuyu political thought brings to the fore the necessity of 'the other Mau Maus' taking place in Kenya at this time. A poignant beginning is at Hola Massacre, 1959. One of the eleven martyrs was a Turkana. A pithy statement was recorded by David Anderson from an Iltiamus informant: 'Trespassing in the settler farms and government forests was our war: it was our Mau Mau' (David Anderson, pers. comm., June 1989). The Banyala of Mulukhoba (Port Victoria) were, in 1953, fully mobilized by people like Mukudi, took the *nakhabuko* oath of unity and empathized with the wider struggle in the highlands (Ogula, 1974). The Mau Mau raiders of Athi River prison in 1953 included a contingent of Luo combatants (Kabiro, 1973), and the intelligence reports from Kampala and North Mara cited a movement of Luo Mau Mau guerillas, known as Onegos, who sought to link the Mau Mau war and the agitation of the Baganda for the return of their Kabaka from exile in England. It was the Onegos who threatened to sabotage the ceremonial royal opening of the Owen Falls Dam at Jinja in 1954 (PRO: CO 822/780; WAR/C/749). The Meru participation in Mau Mau has been recorded, as was the Embu. The Dini ya Msambwa was the Mau Mau of the Ababukusu (Wipper, 1977) as well as of the Pokot. Led by an elusive female spiritual medium, Chepusia, the Pokot played hide-and-seek on both sides of the Kenya/Uganda border against British levies until 1956. Was Kenyatta's 1967 claim that 'we all fought for *uhuru*' true in this regard at least?

The Nemesis of Mau Mau: Loyalism

The theme of loyalism has a long pedigree in Kenya's political history, beginning from the very first Kikuyu Association and maturing in the inter-war years (Clough, 1990). Kenyanist historians and literary commentators have often associated loyalism with the chiefs. W.R. Ochieng' has seen in them no stooges or self-seekers but an integral part of the African's struggle for progress and dignity (Ochieng', 1972: 46–70), while the thrust of Clough's work lies in recognizing the southern Kiambu loyalists as competitors in the political arena against a rival fraction of the Kiambu élite that sought power. Tamarkin sees the Mau Mau loyalists 'as having entered in the political struggle to defend legitimate group interests, to promote their political ideals and even to fight for what they regarded as the interests of their fellow Africans' (Tamarkin, 1978: 248). Ogot, on his part, reminded his readers of the ambiguous terrain out of which loyalism has operated in Kenya: 'Ideology and principles seem to have played, and continue to play, a more subsidiary role in Kenyan politics than loyalism' (Ogot, 1972: 147).

Both Ogot and Tamarkin agree that the Mau Mau young men were opposed by the elders in the countryside (Ogot, 1972) and in Nakuru (Tamarkin, 1978: 248). In the latter township, as in Nairobi (Spencer,

1985), the urban sub-élite that comprised the leadership of the KAU and the KCA pitted themselves against the militancy and the violence of the young men. In both cities, the elders lost the control of both organizations to the militants by 1951. It appears that for two years the Mau Mau had a field day in both cities.

The loyalists regained their initiative after the Declaration of Emergency, as part of the state campaign against the Mau Mau. Loyal Africans were organized by the administration from early 1953, and for the following three years the Home Guard formed the backbone of loyalism – bullying, screening, depriving, exploiting the women (Ngugi, 1965). Initiative lay in their hands; they became the Kikuyu leaders: J.F.G. Kanyua in Nakuru, Chiefs Waruhiu, Josiah Njonjo and Nderi, above all Chief Githu. Kanyua denounced Mau Mau in mid-1953 as 'an evil and unhealthy organization' which was 'destructive to the well-being of my people' (Tamarkin, 1978: 250). This brand of loyalism looked beyond the Mau Mau, to a multiracial Kenya where the key word would be 'happiness', a re-echoing of the theme of progress propounded earlier in this chapter. The Agikuyu needed reconditioning, and Christianity and moral regeneration. Loyalists espoused Christianity fervently, and formed the Torchbearers Association as the vanguard for this regeneration. Such worthies as Parmenas Keritu, David Wanguhu, David Waruhiu and Reuben Karari came to endorse the idea 'that Black and White need each other in the task of building a prosperous and peaceful Kenya'. The Torchbearers were the counterparts to the Capricorn African Society, the European front for multiracialism in this regard (Kanogo, 1974). They were also strongly fortified by revivalism; many were 'saved', sang *Tukutenderza Yesu* heartily, and saw Mau Mau as an evil force against Christ. They died, some of them, for their faith, and their hagiographers have elevated them to 'martyrs'. Their position in society is more explanatory: they were the rural and urban Gikuyu élite: businessmen, *karani*, chiefs, councillors. They were leaders, with a legitimate pedigree deriving from the Kikuyu Association of the early 1920s.

Out of loyalism emerged the Home Guard, a force of over 100,000 Agikuyu who fought and defeated the Mau Mau at the level of the households and the ridges. Theirs was the real victory, for they divided the spoils – land – of the Mau Mau among themselves. In this sense, the KAR and the British '*ma Joni*' were their mercenaries who were merely paid a salary. The debate about whether Mau Mau was a civil war among the Agikuyu is legitimate only to this extent: the Home Guard made it so, in the progress of the struggle. The Mau Mau attacked the Home Guard because the latter had set up their posts in the villages, were on the lookout for the Mau Mau and frustrated recruitment and supplies (Thurston, 1987: 60).

Narrative

The colonial settlers declared war on the Africans through eight emergency bills passed in the Legislative Council on 25 July 1952. This declaration by the white tribe thus preceded the state by close to three months. On 20 October, the state followed suit and declared its own war against its subjects. The settlers and the state thus allied, they took their war to the Gikuyu villages and to Nairobi and Nakuru and the settled areas. Gikuyu youth were flushed out, and the men among them – '*meni*' – went to the forests. There they ran into an army in the making: the organizers of the Land Freedom Army had not expected the settlers and the state to strike so soon, and so did not have a standing army by 20 October 1952. But they improvised in the struggle in every way, from chains of command, lines of supply, ammunition, oathing, prophecy, political education and bravado. They had the Bible for a text, a youthful memory of Gikuyu mythology, and an orator in Dedan Kimathi wa Ciuri. Within three months they were ready to strike out of their '*Mbuchi*' – forest posts – back into the villages. They took on the colonial police and army. Successfully enough for the empire to bring in Her Majesty's troops. The Mau Mau fought against the empire, the state, the settlers and the Home Guards for a period of two years. By 1955 they had been defeated militarily in the forests. They had also been defeated by the Home Guard in the villages. More specifically they were defeated by villagization, by the detention camps, by the desertion of the *thareda*, those who surrendered, by the double-dealing of the *Komerera*, by the detention camps and by the rehabilitation pipelines. Some people won the war: the Home Guard and their followers: about 10% of the Agikuyu population. They not only won the war against the Mau Mau; they had won allies in Britain – the army and the Colonial Office – in the course of the war. In this feat they did a political somersault over the settlers, who were the other losers in the war. The settlers lost the colonial state and lost the White Man's Country. The future of everybody stood starkly at stake because of the Mau Mau. In this sense the rhetoric of Mau Mau – land and freedom – became the turning-point around which future Kenyas were to be built. Isaac Deutscher has repeatedly drawn attention to the ironies of history: surely this must be one of them, that Mau Mau rhetoric won the war even as the protagonists who caused it all, the settlers and Mau Mau, were about to be shunted off to the foot-notes of history. The second irony is also a paradox; Mau Mau played a constructive role, albeit unwittingly, in that the military defeat of the Mau Mau militants cleared the political arena and enabled the loyalists to re-emerge as nationalist politicians in the postcolonial society and made moderate competition a legitimate and effective vehicle for *utetezi* – the agitation for African independence.

Conclusion: Towards an Alternative Future

In 1946 the Labour Government in Britain initiated those changes that were to transform African cultivators into peasants and European farmers into capitalists, through the injection of over £3 million into Kenya's agriculture. This funding enabled some Africans to enter into the petty commodity production of tea and coffee in Gusii and Meru. By 1952 there were 10,069 Africans licensed to grow coffee. These numbers were to swell as a result of the Swynnerton Plan, a move aimed at 'capturing' more of the cultivators and transforming them into peasants. With funding to the tune of £7.95 million, Swynnerton recognized the challenge of agrarian unrest, but turned it on itself by planning and dividing Africans along class lines: the landed yeomanry on the one hand and the landless would-be labourer/proletariat on the other. The Swynnerton Plan was significant in that it pulled the rug from under the Mau Mau's feet: it gave land to the Home Guard, the collaborators, those who stayed at home, the wo/men in the middle, and for the first time destroyed the *muhoi* option for the landless Agikuyu. It amounted to a mental revolution for those at the bottom: henceforth they had no kin, no ancestral land, no marginal marshlands in the reserves to go to. Swynnerton said this to nearly one-third of the Agikuyu population. A new Gikuyu society was born – propertied and propertylessness – and left to face an uncertain future, with different inputs into the politics of independence in the 1956-63 period, and into the Gikuyu reconquest of the Rift Valley under Kenyatta's leadership afterwards.

The propertied Agikuyu fell back on the politics of moderation, progress and representation. They were at their most eloquent in the representations they made to the East Africa Royal Commission in the 1953-55 period. In this they were not alone: the appendix to the report lists virtually anyone who was anyone among the Africans of Kenya as having given evidence. The report led the imperial government to an appreciation of the deepening colonial crisis in East Africa, and strengthened the case for a developmental strategy. Again, this would have a bearing on the World Bank approach to Kenya's future, as evidenced in the bank's involvement in 'land reform' in the 1960s (Leo, 1984: 69-118). Swynnerton thus captured the peasantry for the World Bank and the capitalist world system.

The colonial state, for the umpteenth time, also faced up to the question of an alternative future (Gordon, 1986). First, 'Mau Mau revealed to the British government that Kenya's metaphorical handful of Whites – comprising throughout the colonial period a mere one per cent of the total population – was unable to control burgeoning mass nationalism' (Youe, 1987: 209). The imperial army had intervened to suppress Mau Mau, but both General Erskine and General Lathbury, the successive British commanders, were clear that the ultimate solution to Mau Mau had to be political. In this they were at one with the colonial state, whose improvisations – call them constitutional changes – mirrored an attempt to perpetuate the state's stewardship. Token constitutional changes included first the inclusion of settler leaders in the War Council, then the inclusion of an African, B.A. Ohanga, in the Executive Council, and finally the begrudging admission that there ought to be a new colonial constitution. In 1955 this constitutionalist future was very much in the balance. Not only Michael Blundell but C.M.G. Argwings Kodhek, the *de facto* Kenya African leader in that year, agonized about the future model. So did the urban workers of Nairobi and Mombasa. In the former city, meticulous paperwork by Tom Mboya and W.W.W. Awori saw the formalization of negotiation as a weapon in the salary and welfare struggles of the workers (Singh, 1980); in the latter the strike weapon illuminated alternative possibilities of mass mobilization (Cooper, 1987). Confrontations between capital and labour were, of course, political and once again raised the question of an African future.

And let us not forget *The Hollow Men*, T.S. Eliot's reminder that all life, political life particularly, 'ends/Not with a bang but a whimper'. The settlers tried to salvage their hegemony through whimpering manœuvres. The recalcitrant ones among them, such as Ferdinand Cavendish-Bentinct, stuck to their agenda of no concessions over white power and privilege. Others, such as Michael Blundell, espoused multiracialism from 1954 onwards (Gordon, 1977). The Capricorn Africa Society and the United Kenya Club became their fall-back. Not to be outdone, the Anglican Church in 1955 also conceded that Festo Olang' would be the first African Assistant Bishop of Mombasa.

How does the historian tie up all these different communities of thought, action and discourse into a narrative on Kenya's nationalism? Foucault argues somewhere that when people engage in a discourse it creates boundaries, but that the boundaries do not define exclusive categories. So be it with the Kenyan discourse. Howsoever one looks at it, from the hilltops of Kasigau to the salt-pans of the Gabbra plains, Kenya between 1945 and 1955 was a land of commotion – *matata*.

Bibliography

Abrahams, Peter. 1956. *A Wreath for Udomo* (1st American edn). New York, Knopf.
Abuor, C. Ojwando. n.d. (before 1971). *White Highlands No More: A Modern Political History of Kenya*, Vol. 1. Nairobi, Pan African Researchers.
Anderson, David. 1987. 'Managing the Forest: The Conservation History of Lembus, Kenya, 1904–63', in David Anderson and R. Grove (eds), *Conservation in Africa*. Cambridge, Cambridge University Press, pp. 249–268.
Bates, Robert H. 1989. *Beyond the Miracle of the Market: The Political Economy of Agrarian Development in Kenya*. Cambridge, Cambridge University Press.

Berman, Bruce. 1990. *Control and Crisis in Colonial Kenya: The Dialectic of Domination.* London, James Currey.

Berman, B.J. and J.M. Lonsdale. 1990. 'Louis Leakey's Mau Mau: A Study in the Politics of Knowledge'. 31st Annual Meeting of the African Studies Association, Baltimore, 1–4 November.

Clayton, Anthony. 1984. *Counterinsurgency in Kenya.* Yuma, Manhattan, KS, Sunflower University Press.

Cleary, A.S. 1990. 'The Myth of Mau Mau in its International Context', *African Affairs,* 89 (355), 227–245.

Clough, Marshall S. 1990. *Fighting Two Sides: Kenyan Chiefs and Politicians, 1918–1940.* Niwot, CO, University Press of Colorado.

Cooper, Fred. 1987. *By the African Waterfront: Urban Disorder and the Transformation of Work in Colonial Mombasa.* New Haven, Yale University Press.

Cooper, Fred. 1988. 'Mau Mau and the Discourses of Decolonization', *Journal of African History,* 29, 313–320.

Coray, Michael S. 1978. 'The Kenya Land Commission and the Kikuyu of Kiambu', *Agricultural History,* 52 (1), 179–195.

Darwin, John. 1984. 'British Decolonization Since 1945: A Pattern or a Puzzle?', in R.F. Holland and G. Rizvi (eds), *Perspectives on Imperialism and Decolonization.* London, Frank Cass, pp. 187–209.

Edgerton, Robert B. 1989. *Mau Mau: An African Crucible.* New York, The Free Press.

Ehrenfels, U.R. 1960. 'Mau Mau and Why', *The Light Continent.* Bombay, Asia Publishing House, pp. 23–45.

Furedi, Frank. 1973. 'The African Crowd in Nairobi: Popular Movements and Elite Politics', *Journal of African History,* 14 (2), 275–290.

Furedi, Frank. 1974. 'The Social Composition of the Mau-Mau Movement in the White Highlands', *Journal of Peasant Studies,* 1 (4), 486–505.

Furedi, Frank. 1989. *The Mau Mau War in Perspective.* London, James Currey.

Gadsden, Fay. 1980. 'The African Press in Kenya, 1945–1952', *Journal of African History,* 21, 515–535.

Gicaru, Muga. 1958. *Land of Sunshine: Scenes of Life in Kenya Before Mau Mau.* London, Lawrence and Wishart.

Gordon, David F. 1986. *Decolonization and the State in Kenya.* Boulder, Westview Press.

Gordon, F.G. 1977. 'Mau Mau and Decolonization: Kenya and the Defeat of Multi-racialism in East and Central Africa', *Kenya Historical Review,* 5 (2), 329–348.

Great Britain. 1955. *East Africa Royal Commission 1953–1955 Report,* Cd. 9475. London, HMSO.

Huxley, Elspeth. 1973 (*c.* 1960). *A New Earth.* Westport, CT, Greenwood Press.

Kabiro, N. 1973. *Man in the Middle.* Richmond, BC, Canada, LSM Press.

Kaggia, Bildad. 1975. *Roots of Freedom, 1921–1963: The Autobiography of Bildad Kaggia.* Nairobi, East African Publishing House.

Kanogo, T.M.J. 1974. 'Politics of Collaboration and Domination? Case Study of the Capricorn Africa Society', *Kenya Historical Review* 2 (2), 127–142.

Kanogo, Tabitha M.J. 1977. 'Rift Valley Squatters and Mau Mau', *Kenya Historical Review,* 5 (2), 243–252.

Kanogo, T.M.J. 1987. *Squatters and the Roots of Mau Mau, 1905–63.* London, James Currey.

Kennedy, Dane. 1989. 'The Political Mythology of Mau Mau'. American Historical Association, San Francisco, 26–31 December.

Kilson, Martin L. 1955. 'Land and the Kikuyu: A Study of the Relationship between Land and Kikuyu Political Movements', *Journal of Negro History,* 40 (2), 103–153.

Kinyatti, Maina Wa. 1980. *Thunder From the Mountains: Mau Mau Patriotic Songs.* London, Zed Press.

Kitching, Gavin. 1980. *Class and Economic Change in Kenya: The Making of an African Petite Bourgeoisie.* New Haven, CT, Yale University Press.

Leo, Christopher. 1984. *Land and Class in Kenya*. Toronto, University of Toronto Press.

Likimani, Muthoni. 1985. *Passport Number F47927: Women and Mau Mau in Kenya* (with an introductory essay by Jean O'Barr). London, Macmillan.

Lonsdale, J.M. 1986. 'Explanations of the Mau Mau Revolt', in Tom Lodge (ed.), *Resistance and Ideology in Settler Societies*. Johannesburg, Ravan, pp. 168-178.

Lonsdale, J.M. 1987. 'La Pensée politique Kikiyu et les idéologies du mouvement Mau-Mau', *Cahiers d'Etudes Africaines*, 27 (3-4), 107-108, 329-357.

Lonsdale, J.M. 1990. 'Mau Mau's of the Mind: Making Mau Mau and Remaking Kenya'. African Studies History Seminar Paper, University of Witwatersrand, 22 March.

Lonsdale, J.M. 1991. 'The Moral Economy of Mau Mau. Wealth, Poverty and Civic Virtue in Kikuyu Political Thought', in J.M. Lonsdale and B.J. Berman (eds), *Unhappy Valley, Vol. II, Violence and Ethnicity*. London, James Currey, pp. 315-504.

Lonsdale, J.M. and D.A. Low. 1976. 'Towards the New Order, 1945-63', in D.A. Low and Alison Smith (eds), *History of East Africa*, Vol. 3. Oxford, Clarendon Press, pp. 1-65.

Louis, Roger and Prosser Gifford (eds). 1988. *Decolonization in Africa*. New Haven, Yale University Press.

McWilliam, Michael. 1963. 'Economic Policy and the Kenya Settlers, 1945-48', in K. Robinson and F. Madden (eds), *Essays in Imperial Government Presented to Margery Perham*. Oxford, Blackwell, pp. 171-192.

Maughan-Brown, David. 1985. *Land, Freedom and Fiction: History and Ideology in Kenya*. London, Heinemann.

Maxon, Robert. 1989. *Conflict and Accommodation in Western Kenya: The Gusii and the British, 1907-1963*. Fairleigh, NJ, Dickinson University Press.

Maxon, Robert. 1991. 'Mau Mau Books are Welcome, But . . .', *Weekly Review*, 15 March, 31-32.

Mboya, T.J. 1963. *Freedom and After*. London, Deutsch.

Muriuki, Godfrey. 1974. *A History of the Kikuyu to 1904*. Nairobi, Oxford University Press.

Mutonyi, Eliud. n.d. 'Mau Mau Chairman'. Mss., John Lonsdale collection.

Ngugi wa Thiongo. 1965. *A Grain of Wheat*. London, Heinemann.

Nyabera, Helen. 1976. 'Biography of B.A. Ohanga'. BA Dissertation, Dept of History, University of Nairobi.

Oboler, Regina S. 1985. *Women, Power, and Economic Change: The Nandi of Kenya*. Stanford, CA, Stanford University Press.

Ochieng', W.R. 1972. 'Colonial African Chiefs - Were They Primarily Self-seeking Scoundrels?', in B.A. Ogot (ed.), *Politics and Nationalism in Colonial Kenya*. Nairobi, EAPH, pp. 46-70.

Odhiambo, E.S. Atieno. 1974. *The Paradox of Collaboration and Other Essays*. Nairobi, East African Literature Bureau.

Odhiambo, E.S. Atieno. 1976. '"Seek Ye First the Economic Kingdom": A History of the Luo Thrift and Trading Corporation (LUTATCO) 1945-56', in Ogot, B.A. (ed.), *Hadith 6: Economic and Social Change in East Africa*. Nairobi, EALB, pp. 165-185.

Odhiambo, E.S. Atieno. 1977. 'Rebutting "Theory" with Correct Theory', *Kenya Historical Review*, 5 (2), 385-388.

Odhiambo, E.S. Atieno. 1981a. 'Who Were the Mau Mau?' Historical Association of Kenya Annual Conference Paper.

Odhiambo, E.S. Atieno. 1981b. 'The International Press and Mau Mau'. Historical Association of Kenya Annual Conference Paper.

Odhiambo, E.S. Atieno. 1991. 'Kenyatta and Mau Mau', *Transition: An International Review*, 53, pp. 147-152.

Odhiambo, E.S. Atieno. 1992. 'The Production of History in Kenya: The Mau Mau Debate', *Canadian Journal of African Studies*, 25 (2), pp. 300-307.

Odinga, Oginga. 1967. *Not Yet Uhuru*. London, Heinemann.

Ogot, B.A. 1972. 'Revolt of the Elders', in B.A. Ogot (ed.), *Politics and Nationalism in Kenya*. Nairobi, EAPH, pp. 134–148.

Ogot, Bethwell A. and Tiyambe Zeleza. 1988. 'Kenya: The Road to Independence and After', in Prosser Gifford and Wm. Roger Louis (eds), *Decolonization and African Independence*. New Haven, Yale University Press, pp. 401–426.

Ogula, Paul A. 1974. 'A Biography of Chief Mukudi of Bunyala', *Kenya Historical Review*, 2 (2), pp. 175–186.

Onstad, Eric. 1990. 'History of the Nairobi Hawkers, 1902–1970'. MA Thesis, Dept of History, University of Nairobi.

Presley, Cora Ann. 1986. 'Kikuyu Women in the "Mau Mau" Rebellion', in Gary Y. Okihiro (ed.), *In Resistance, Studies of African, Caribbean and Afro-American History*. Amherst, University of Amherst Press, pp. 53–70.

Prunier, Garard. 1987. 'Mythes et histoire: les interprétations du Mouvement Mau Mau de 1952 à 1986', *Revue Française d'Outre-mer*, 74 (277), 401–429.

Public Record Office (PRO), London. Series CO 822, WAR/C/749. East African Origin War Office Correspondence.

Roelker, Jack R. 1976. *Mathu of Kenya*. Stanford, Hoover Institution Press.

Singh, Markan. 1980. *Kenya's Trade Unions 1952–1956*, edited by B.A. Ogot. Nairobi, Uzima Press.

Spencer, John. 1985. *KAU, The Kenya African Union*. London, PKI.

Stichter, Sharon B. 1975. 'Workers, Trade Unions and the Mau Mau Rebellion', *Canadian Journal of African Studies*, 9, 259–275.

Tamarkin, M. 1973. 'Social and Political Change in a Twentieth Century African Community in Kenya'. Unpublished PhD Thesis, London University.

Tamarkin, M. 1976. 'Mau Mau in Nakuru', *Journal of African History*, 17 (1), 24–32.

Tamarkin, M. 1978. 'The Loyalists in Nakuru During the Mau Mau Revolt and Its Aftermath, 1953–1963', *Asian and African Studies*, 12 (2), 247–261.

Throup, D.W. 1985. 'The Origins of Mau Mau', *African Affairs*, 84 (336), 399–435.

Throup, David W. 1987. *Economic and Social Origins of Mau Mau*. London, James Currey.

Thurston, Anne. 1987. *Smallholder Agriculture in Colonial Kenya: The Official Mind and the Swynnerton Plan*, Cambridge African Monographs 8. Cambridge, Cambridge University Press.

Walton, John. 1984. 'The Mau Mau Revolt', *Reluctant Rebels, Comparative Studies of Revolution and Underdevelopment*. New York Columbia University Press, pp. 104–139.

White, Louise S. 1990. *The Comforts of Home: Prostitution in Colonial Nairobi*. Chicago, University of Chicago Press.

Wipper, Audrey. 1975. 'The Maendeleo ya Wanawake Movement in the Colonial Period: The Canadian Connection, Mau Mau, Embroidery and Agriculture', *Rural Africana*, 29, 195–214.

Wipper, Audrey. 1977. *Rural Rebels: A Study of Two Protest Movements in Kenya*. Nairobi, New York, Oxford University Press.

Wood, Barbara. 1988. *Green City in the Sun*. New York, Random House.

Youe, C. 1987. '"A Delicate Balance": Resident Labour on Settler Farms in Kenya, Until Mau Mau', *Canadian Journal of History/Annales Canadiennes d'Histoire*, 22, 209–228.

Youe, C. 1988. 'Settler Capital and the Assault on the Squatter Peasantry in Kenya's Uasin Gishu District, 1942–1963', *African Affairs*, 88, 393–418.

Three

The
Decisive Years
1956–63
B.A. OGOT

Reform Response to Mau Mau

The struggle against Mau Mau had exacted a political price from the British imperialists. Their military occupation of Kenya could not last indefinitely, but neither could they return the country to the status quo ante. Reform became imperative. The colonial regime now saw the need to broaden the basis of collaboration at the national level to include Africans within the political and economic structures of the colonial society. The main objectives of these colonial reforms were to create a base upon which a collaborative African leadership could emerge and to undermine the support of Mau Mau freedom fighters.

1954 was a watershed year in Kenya's tortuous road to independence. Not only was it the year of the draconian 'Operation Anvil' in Nairobi, which put thousands of Africans in detention camps, but it also saw the birth of the Swynnerton Plan, the Carpenter Committee Report, the Lidbury Report and the Lyttelton Constitution, all of which in their various ways embodied new state policies, which reflected, and further shaped, the underlying structural changes in Kenya's political economy.

Roger Swynnerton was an official in the Department of Agriculture. His plan provided the funding and the rationale for the land consolidation programme and enclosure movement which, from the turn of the 1950s, had come to be regarded as an essential prerequisite for an agricultural revolution in African areas. The main objective of the Swynnerton Plan was to create family holdings which would be large enough to keep the family self-sufficient in food and also enable them to practise alternate husbandry and thus develop a cash income. It was envisioned that 600,000 African families would have farming units of approximately ten acres a family, which would raise their average productivity in cash sales from £10 to £100 a year after providing for their own needs. The land reforms were accompanied by the removal of the remaining restrictions against African production of lucrative cash crops, such as coffee, tea, pyrethrum, hybrid maize and dairy products.

In drawing up his plan, Swynnerton assumed twenty years would be needed to implement it. Coffee was to expand by 5,000 new acres per year, reaching 71,000 acres in 1968; tea was to reach 70,000 acres by 1968; pyrethrum, 48,300 acres.[1] The Agricultural Department annual reports show that there was rapid growth in small-farm (African) marketed output. It rose from US$8.6 million in 1953 to US$25 million in 1961. It was also during this period that major regional differences between Central and Nyanza Provinces, which hitherto had been at par in marketed agricultural output, took place. Land reform was spreading rapidly in Central Province at a time when Luo political leadership was successfully mobilizing against its implementation in Nyanza Province.

There was also the danger that the increased prosperity of Kikuyu farmers and the fact that most of the funds secured for African agriculture was going to be spent in Kikuyu areas could be interpreted by other groups as a reward for rebellion. Sir Evelyn Baring, the Governor, saw this danger clearly, and he made sure that land consolidation was introduced in at least two other areas, namely, the Nandi and Kericho districts.[2]

The Carpenter Committee Report proposed minimum wages for African families in urban areas.[3] The conditions imposed by the State of Emergency and the desire of the imperial government to create a middle class among the African population enabled the government to adopt these reforms of the wage structure. The Kenya Labour Department encouraged the formation of employers' organizations to help facilitate the growth of collective bargaining. The Department also assisted in the maintenance and development of trade unions, which saw the emergence of Tom Mboya as the articulate spokesman of the workers. A new look in labour–management relations was developing, which was to lead to tripartite agreements involving the Federation of Kenya Employers (FKE), the Kenya Federation of Labour (KFL) and the government.

Finally, the Lidbury Commission on the Civil Service accepted the principle of equal pay for equal work. Government employees of all races were to receive equal salaries and conditions of service. As a further extension of the principle of equal pay, the Commission recommended that women should receive the same basic pay as men. This recommendation was an important move in the deracialization of Kenya society. The Commission also recommended that the government should work towards the eventual policy of recruiting its officers from local sources. In the mean time, however, the inducement principle was to continue to be applied to overseas recruits.[4]

The Report of the East African Royal Commission issued in 1955 gave an added fillip to the momentum of reform. It was highly critical of government policies towards African agriculture, and it called for the deracialization of the Kenya highlands. Furthermore, it called for increased numbers of Africans in administrative and management positions. Looking to the future, the Report recommended 'the integration of the African rural population into the world economy'.[5]

But these reforms, which were intended to increase the opportunities for Africans in the colonial society and to integrate them more effectively into the changing pattern of the economy, could not contain African politics. Nor could African politicians be 'pocketed', because the land and other economic reforms that had been introduced, while benefiting indigenous capitalist interests, fell far short of popular demands.

For example, the land consolidation programme had repressive political objectives. In the words of the Special Commissioner for Central Province, 'Thus land consolidation was to complete the work of the Emergency: to stabilize a conservative middle class, based on the loyalists; and, as confiscated land was to be thrown into the common land pool during consolidation, it was also to confirm the landlessness of the rebels.'[6]

The Forfeiture of Lands Act was passed in December 1953. It provided for the confiscation of land individually owned by so-called 'terrorists'. It is estimated that, by 1956, 3,510 people had already forfeited their land under this Act.[7] Moreover, the 'villagization' policy (based on the model of the fortified villages of the Malayan Emergency) that accompanied land consolidation was explicitly designed to break links between Mau Mau fighters and their supporters, buttress the position of the loyalists and seal the landlessness of the former. Between May 1954 and August 1956, about 1,077,500 Kikuyu and Embu people had been herded into 854 villages.[8]

Political Party Formation and Ideology

The indigenous, Asian and international capital marginalized settler capital in the 1950s. By the mid-1950s the value of goods manufactured in the country exceeded the total value of settler agricultural production.[9]

As the economic fortunes of the settlers declined, the traditional centres of power in the colonial state apparatus were undermined. Growing African nationalism forced open the gates of African representations to the central structures of the colonial state, which ushered in more fierce struggles over who would ultimately control the state and the policies it would pursue. Thus the rather cavalier attitude of some 'radical' historians towards constitutional struggles is unwarranted. The association of struggle exclusively with armed struggle has led some historians in Kenya to treat the period up to 1955, when Mau Mau was active, as the peak of African nationalism, and the subsequent years as marking nothing more than a humiliating retreat into 'betrayal' and eventual 'neo-colonialism'.[10]

It would perhaps be more correct to describe the post-1955 period as marking the gradual abandonment of the Mau Mau alternative. Mau Mau – a liberation movement, unlike Frelimo or the Zimbabwe African National Union (ZANU) – never transformed itself into a political party, thus leaving room for district and later national political organizations, such as the Kenya African National Union (KANU) and Kenya African Democratic Union (KADU), which were never liberation movements, to emerge.

It might be a salutary reminder, both to those who dismiss Mau Mau's contribution to Kenya's decolonization and others who see the suppression of the movement as marking the end of the nationalist struggle, to note that Kenya's tortuous constitutional road to independence started in earnest with the introduction of the Lyttelton Constitution in 1954, at the height of the British anti-Mau Mau crusade. The Lyttelton Constitution introduced a new central government structure based on a ministerial system which included African and Asian Ministers and conceding the principle of multiracial representative parity between Europeans and non-Europeans. Under the new ministerial system the division of agriculture into separate and independent departments was ended when the two were appointed under the Ministry of Agriculture. A separate Ministry of Finance was also created to plan and co-ordinate overall national economic development.[11] This system broke up the hitherto powerful centralized Secretariat, undermined the powers of the Provincial Administrative Officers, and opened up the state to professional politicians, including vocal African nationalists. The colonial regime had hoped that 'middle-class' Africans would become part of a shared community of interests integrated into the colonial order. But the Africans had different perspectives. The new African 'middle classes', in both the urban and the rural areas, saw competition with the immigrant groups, Europeans and Asians, and ultimately with the colonial regime itself, as the way to ensure their continued upward mobility. Indeed, it was these African politicians who derailed each constitutional plan, beginning with the Lyttelton Constitution itself, which had been intended to last until 1960.

Political accommodation to the so-called colonial reforms by Africans, including the majority of their leaders, had thus become impossible. The realities were mass arrests and population removals, brutal torture in detention camps, the intensive and sometimes forced labour recruitment campaigns conducted in Nyanza and Southern Provinces in order to replace the repatriated and detained Kikuyu, Embu and Meru workers, continued coercive enforcement of soil conservation programmes, and generalized fear and terror that was life in the Kenya of the 1950s. The stakes were now simply too high. No wonder when attempts were made in 1955 to relax the ban but limit African political associations to districts they failed to contain the expressions of nationalist aspirations and goals in these geographically contrived organizations. The first one to be formed in Nairobi, in December 1955, was the Kenya African National Congress under the leadership of C.M.G. Argwings-Kodhek, the 'Mau Mau lawyer'. Kodhek's action was in defiance of the general colonial ban of colony-wide political parties. It was refused registration until it modified its name and focus.

The Congress was then registered in April 1956 as the Nairobi District African Congress, with Argwings-Kodhek as president, M. Chege as vice-president and C. Kiprotich as general secretary. The Congress's cry of 'Africa for the Africans' was seen as a serious threat to the Europeans and Asians in Kenya. When the 1957 African elections were announced, a split took place within the Congress, which led to the formation of the Nairobi People's Convention Party (NPCP), with Tom Mboya as its president and C. Kiprotich as secretary-general. It soon emerged as the best-organized and -disciplined mass party in Kenya, with Mboya attempting to turn it into a country-wide nationalist party. Other district associations that emerged at this time were the Mombasa African Democratic Union, the African District Association (Central Nyanza), the Abagusii Association of South Nyanza District, the South Nyanza District African Political Association, the Taita African Democratic Union, the Nakuru African Progressive Party (1955), the Nakuru District Congress (1958), the Abaluhya People's Association and the Nyanza North African Congress.

But this was not the first time that the colonial government was attempting to restrict African political activities to the district level. From 1924, when the Local Native Councils were established, to 1944, when the Kenya African Union (KAU) was formed, the colonial government encouraged the Africans to air their political demands through these local institutions.

KAU, which represented the first national political party to be established in Kenya, was proscribed on 8 June 1953 because, it was alleged, it had been used as a cover for Mau Mau. It had lasted barely nine years and was poorly organized, especially at the grass-roots level. Moreover, the party had failed to establish itself over the whole country. This meant that most Kenyans lacked any experience in party organization and national consciousness was underdeveloped. Between June 1953 and June 1955, political parties were prohibited; and from June 1955 to 1960, they were allowed, but at district level and outside Central Province. This was because, according to the then Colonial Secretary, Alan Lennox-Boyd, KAU had been the source of pre-Emergency militancy and violence and therefore no country-wide party like KAU was ever to be allowed again in Kenya.[12]

One major consequence of the formation of these district organizations was that the pace of political development among the various districts continued to be uneven and parochialism rooted in ethnic loyalties was encouraged at the expense of African unity. The other effect of the period of district-based political associations was the emergence of the local powerful figures who would in future resist attempts at political centralization by colony-wide political organizations such as KANU.

It should, however, be noted that when the district political organizations were allowed in 1955, they continued to be prohibited in Central Province. A nominated Advisory Council for the province was later established to allow the loyalists to discuss government policy. An articulate section of the Kenya population was thus denied participation in politics. So, when other districts were developing district organizations and establishing patron–client relationships, Central Province was forcibly cut off from open political organizing at a crucial time before independence.

But, despite these political and legal constraints, an African political élite was emerging that skilfully used its position to undermine European political influence and gain dominance that allowed it to move Kenya towards independence with great rapidity. More often than not, the petty-bourgeois African politicians, not the colonial governor or his overlords in London, held the initiative and dictated the pace of events. The imperial-inspired reforms, including the Lyttelton Constitution, did not initially represent any explicit programme of decolonization. They were essentially piecemeal, *ad hoc* responses to intensifying political struggles within the country. When the back of Mau Mau had been broken after 1955, the colonial officials lulled themselves into the conviction that it would take another generation before Kenya could be considered for self-government. Such was the quality of imperial prescience that, as late as January 1959, the Colonial Secretary, Lennox-Boyd, and the East African Colonial Governors' meeting in the ornate chambers of Chequers agreed that Kenya would not achieve her independence until after 1975, following Tanganyika and Uganda.[13] The Colonial Secretary and the Governors agreed that the three main British interests involved in Kenya were the military bases, essential for British global strategy, the need to ensure that the country remained economically linked with the West and the need to protect the interest of the immigrant communities.[14] On his return from that conference, Governor Evelyn Baring toured the settler areas in May 1959, assuring the European farmers that Kenya would not be independent for another fifteen years and during that period Kenya would be a 'fortress colony' containing a British army base. But a dramatic change in the policy of the British Government seems to have taken place after the general election in October 1959. Baring received a gloomy letter from Sir Fredrick Crawford, Governor of Uganda saying:

> It looks to me as though we have 'had' Africa, and nothing remains but the dreary prospect of toning down the more outrageous claims of African

nationalists. Perhaps the solution is to declare a time-table for here and Tanganyika, say 1970; do all we can to make them ready between now and then; and then leave the place to the denizens and to the human misery that will result for most of them.[15]

In January 1960, Iain Macleod, the new Colonial Secretary, accepted the principle of independence under African majority rule in Kenya within three years. On 3 February 1960, Prime Minister Harold Macmillan, who was on a tour of Africa, told the South African Parliament that 'The wind of change is blowing through this continent and whether we like it or not this growth of political consciousness is a political fact and our national policies must take account of it.' Why did Macmillan suddenly decide to change his views about British policy in Africa? What happened to the grand imperial timetable drawn up at Chequers? History intervened.

In 1957, Africans were allowed to elect eight representatives to the Legislative Council, on a 'qualified franchise' that gave up to three votes to 'persons of income, education or active government service, while denying most Africans any franchise whatever'.[16] Mr (later Sir) Walter Coutts, a senior civil servant who was the Commissioner appointed to investigate methods of selecting African members of the Legislative Council, admitted that the majority of Africans who gave evidence before him were in favour of universal adult franchise. He, however, decided to recommend a qualitative franchise. In Nairobi, for example, there were only 2,384 registered voters, although the city had an African population of over 100,000. Of these, 655 had one vote, 1,066 had two votes and 663 had three votes, making a total of 4,776 votes.[17] In Nakuru district, it was reckoned that there were 95,000 Africans with homes in the area, but only 676 qualified as voters.[18] The highest registration in a Rift Valley district was in Nandi, which had 1,684 voters. Kajiado had 442 registered voters, Baringo 1,968 and Samburu 182. In the whole of Ukambani, there were 17,888 registered voters and in the Coast Province 7,912. In Central Province, severe disabilities were placed on the Kikuyu and the allied Embu and Meru peoples, because of the part they had played in Mau Mau. Only those who were able to prove that they actively supported the government as 'loyalists' in the fight against Mau Mau were allowed to register as voters. Of the 35,644 voters in the province, 21,145 were Meru. Small wonder, therefore, that the total number of registered African voters for the 1957 elections was only 126,508.[19]

To contest the eight seats with a total electorate of 126,508 were 37 candidates. In the Rift Valley, there were three candidates. One was J.M. Ole Tameno, who was a former member of the Legislative Council for the Rift Valley from 1952 to 1955, when he resigned. A Makerere-trained veterinarian, he believed that Africans were not yet ready for independence. J.K. Ole Tipis was another Maasai candidate, with 'mashambani' influence and a Capricornist. Trained at the Veterinary Training College, Ngong', he served in the Second World War. In his view, the Africans were not yet ready for self-rule. Daniel T. arap Moi, a former teacher who had joined the Legislative Council in October 1955, following the resignation of Ole Tameno, subscribed to the United Front policy issued by the then sitting African members.

In Nyanza South constituency, there were six candidates. There were J.J. Bonga, a former teacher and warrant officer in the army, from Karachuonyo, and F.K. arap Chumah, who was the incumbent and who entered the Legislative Council in 1955. He hailed from Kericho. The third candidate was J.K. Kebaso, who bluntly stated in his election manifesto that the Africans of Kenya were not yet ready for self-government. He was one of the founders of the KAU and was the first president of the Union's Nairobi branch. In 1945 he formed the Kisii Union and was the editor of its local district newspaper, *Sauti ya Bomani*. The remaining three candidates put forward various demands in their manifestos: L.G. Oguda, a former teacher, demanded undiluted democracy and the formation of national political parties; G. Orinda Okun promised to campaign for a Kenyan university, if elected; and Taita arap Towett, a social worker from Kericho, opposed multiracial schools because 'they will kill the African way of life'. He also believed in internationalism because economic isolation is suicidal.

Nyanza North constituency also had six candidates. J.D. Otiende was a former school teacher and newspaper editor and a former secretary-general of the KAU. He was the author of a book, *The Abaluhya People of North Nyanza*, and was at that time president of the Abaluhya People's Association. Then there was W.W.W. Awori, the then member for the constituency and a former vice-president and treasurer of the KAU. He was elected vice-president of KAU in 1947, when Jomo Kenyatta was elected president. In the same year, he started *Radio Posta*, the first African daily newspaper in Kenya. He was nominated to the Legislative Council in 1952. Surprisingly, he argued in his election manifesto that self-rule for Kenya should be deferred until the Africans were in a position to influence public affairs. The third candidate was C.N.W. Siganga, a graduate of the University of Wales, who had worked as a teacher and community development officer. Between 1952 and 1955, he was president of the Abaluhya People's Association. Then there was W.B. Akatsa, a graduate of Makerere and Hull University and a teacher and supervisor of schools. In 1957, he was president of the North Nyanza Progressive Party. The fifth candidate was Masinde Muliro, a graduate of Cape Town University, who had returned to Kenya in 1955 to teach at the Alliance Girls High School. He wanted an independent Kenya where all races and creeds would be protected. Finally, there was J.G.W. Kadima, a graduate of St Mary's School, Yala, and a businessman.

In Ukambani constituency, the contest was fought amongst three teachers. J. Nzau Muimi from Kitui was a Makerere graduate and a former teacher and supervisor of schools. He was the sitting member for Ukambani and believed that the Africans were not yet ready to govern themselves without the help of other races. The other two candidates were D.N. Mumo, a Makerere graduate and a teacher, who also served on the Machakos African District Council. He believed that Africa was fundamentally for Africans. M.J. Makilya, also a teacher and supervisor of schools, had studied local government administration in Britain.

In Nairobi, two of the candidates, Tom Mboya and C.M.G. Argwings-Kodhek, had already acquired a creditable record during the Emergency. Following the arrest of the KAU leaders, Tom Mboya had emerged as an articulate trade unionist and a nationalist. He outlined his election manifesto in the booklet *The Kenya Question – An African Answer*, which he wrote while in Britain in 1956. His election war-cry was 'to hell with European domination'. Argwings-Kodhek was a graduate of Makerere and the University of Wales, a former teacher and the first African lawyer in Kenya. He was nicknamed 'Mau Mau lawyer' by the white settlers, who hated his guts. His campaign slogan was 'Africa for the Africans'. The third candidate was the then sitting member, Muchohi Gikonyo, whose record in the Legislative Council was that of a moderate loyalist. He had gained political experience as a nominated member of the then Nairobi Municipal Council. He was reputed to be a fabulously rich wine merchant. His election motto was 'Rome was not built in a day'. The last candidate was J.M. Kasyoka, a Nairobi City Councillor, who was a loyalist and a Capricornist.

In Central Province, the main battle was between Bernard Mate, who was comparatively unknown, and Eliud Wambu Mathu, the then sitting member. Mate had recently returned from South Africa, where he took his university studies, and was posted to the Alliance Girls High School, Kikuyu, to teach. He had solid Meru support. Eliud W. Mathu was an experienced politician. He was the first African to be appointed to the Kenya Legislative Council, and throughout the Emergency he remained a member of the Legislative Council. A graduate of Fort Hare College in South Africa and Oxford University, he was a former teacher. The third candidate was David Waruhiu, a farmer and businessman, and a loyalist who hoped to gain sympathy votes resulting from his father's assassination.

The five candidates who presented themselves for election in Central Nyanza were H.D. Odaba, A.O. Odinga, B.A. Ohanga, G.N. Onyulo and E.P. Oranga. Odaba, who came from Samia, was a former teacher and school supervisor. In June 1953, he was appointed Assistant District Officer in the Rift Valley Province and in the same year he formed the Londiani African Civil Service Association and the Kikuyu Home Guard in the Londiani forest. He was elected acting president of the Nakuru

African Progressive Party in 1955. The second candidate, Oginga Odinga, was a Makerere graduate and a former teacher, who was president of Luo Union (East Africa) and founder of the Luo Thrift and Trading Corporation. He rejected, as selfish, oppressive, discriminative and undemocratic, any system resting power in the hands of a few immigrant aristocrats. He provided the stiffest opposition to B.A. Ohanga, who was the sitting member. A former teacher from Gem, Ohanga was the second African member to be nominated in 1947 and the first African to be appointed minister under the Lyttelton Constitution in 1954. He believed in gradualism and multiracialism. The fourth candidate, G.N. Onyulo, was a graduate of Maseno School. He was a clerical interpreter in the Judicial Department, a member of the Kisumu African Advisory Council, the Kisumu Municipal Board and the Central Nyanza African District Council. He was formerly secretary of the Kenya African Civil Service Association at Nakuru and Kisumu. He argued that Kenya must develop as an African state. The last candidate, E.P. Oranga, was a graduate of Makerere, where he obtained a diploma in agriculture, afterwards becoming an assistant agricultural officer. Since 1947, he had been a member of the Central Nyanza African District Council. Though a gradualist, he was nevertheless opposed to the Asian monopoly of trade in Kenya.

In the Coast constituency, six candidates vied for the seat. The sitting member, Jimmy Jeremiah, who had been appointed Parliamentary Secretary, had sat silent in the Legislative Council. The second candidate, Francis Joseph Khamisi, was a graduate of Kabaa High School, editor of *Baraza*, a pioneer Swahili newspaper from 1939 to 1945, and the general-secretary of the KAU (1944–47). During the campaign he allied himself with the Capricorn Society. Ronald Gideon Ngala, the third candidate, was a graduate of Makerere and Redland College, Bristol, a former teacher and supervisor of schools and a member of the Mombasa Municipal Board, who stated that true democracy must be the goal. The remaining two candidates were C.M. Mwashumbe, an intellectual lawyer, and D.M. Mwakio.

From the profiles of the candidates, it is evident that practically all of them were drawn from the middle class, with the overwhelming majority of them being teachers. The average level of education was high, with almost all of them having at least secondary school education, and a sizeable proportion having college and university education. Most of the candidates had either studied or worked in places outside their home regions.

On the other hand, the political horizon of the majority of the candidates was rather low. The then African sitting members issued their conservative United Front policy advocating gradualism or *pole pole* strategy. They said that the Colonial Office had to have ultimate control; loyalty to Kenya and the British Crown was a prerequisite; communal rolls were to be continued and Africans were to strive for a majority on the unofficial side of the Legislative Council. Such a platform was obviously too tepid, given the revolutionary situation in Kenya at that time.

Then there was a second group of *pole pole* candidates who subscribed to the Capricorn Contract, comprising J.D. Otiende, Francis Khamisi, Justus ole Tipis, J.M. Kasyoka and David Waruhiu. The Capricorn Contract stood for the establishment of true stability and confidence in the country; abolition of racial discrimination; gradual progress towards self-government; and the establishment of a common citizenship for all Kenyans.

In the election, the multiracialists and the Capricornists were faced with African nationalism. The outcome of the 1957 African election was therefore likely to be the acid test of the multiracial course which was set in motion in Kenya with the introduction of the Lyttelton Constitution.

Moreover, the objective of the Coutts Report was to ensure that the first African elected members of the Legislative Council would reflect the opinions of the 'middle-class' elements to whom multiracialism was directed. To the surprise of the colonial officials, the majority of the seats were won by supporters of African nationalism and opponents of multiracialism.

Daniel T. arap Moi, Bernard Mate and James Nzau won the Rift Valley, Central and Ukambani seats respectively.

Six of the eight previously nominated African members were removed by the voters: Eliud W. Mathu, B.A. Ohanga, W.W.W. Awori, J. Jeremiah, F.K. Chumah and M. Gikonyo. The two survivors were Daniel T. arap Moi and James Nzau.

The biggest election surprise was the defeat of Mathu by the comparatively unknown Mate. Perhaps the explanation lies in Mathu's behaviour and attitude during the Emergency. It is on record that Mathu supported Emergency legislation, acted as a liaison between loyalists and the colonial administration; and he 'condemned the revolt for its violence and experienced some guilt for being of the same ethnic background as its leaders'.[23] He opposed any compromise with any Mau Mau leaders, such as General China, who, he advocated, should be shot on sight. He stated: 'We must go into the forest whole hog and get these fellows shot dead, bring bodies and then burn them in Nairobi.'[24] These were the considered views of the most senior African legislator about those who were sacrificing their lives for the freedom of Kenya. Is it any wonder, therefore, that Mathu was rejected by the Africans in the 1957 elections?

As a result of these elections, a new generation of African politicians came to centre stage: Tom Mboya, Oginga Odinga, Masinde Muliro, R.G. Ngala and Daniel T. arap Moi, among others. They immediately grouped together under the African Elected Members Organization (AEMO), rejected the Lyttelton Constitution and refused to accept any

Table 3.1 Election Results, 1957: Number of Votes

Nairobi:	T.J. Mboya	–	2,138
	C.M.G. Argwings-Kodhek	–	1,746
	M. Gikonyo	–	238
	J. Kasyoka	–	133

The 4,255 votes cast represented an 89 per cent poll.[20]

Central Nyanza:	A.O. Odinga	–	9,316
	B.A. Ohanga	–	3,360
	H.D. Odaba	–	872
	G.N. Onyulo	–	642
	E.P. Oranga	–	402
South Nyanza:	L.G. Oguda	–	13,882
	J.K. Kebaso	–	8,200
	T. arap Towett	–	6,308
	J.J. Bonga	–	3,235
	G. Orinda Okun	–	1,299
	F. Kiprotich Chumah	–	721

The 33,645 poll in the South Nyanza constituency was the equivalent of 75 per cent of the total and the 14,592 votes in Central Nyanza amounted to a 74 per cent poll.[21]

Coast:	R.G. Ngala	–	3,406
	D.M. Mwako	–	2,539
	F.J. Khamisi	–	2,267
	C.M. Mwashumbe	–	712
	J. Jeremiah	–	488
North Nyanza:	M. Muliro	–	6,728
	W.W.W. Awori	–	6,071
	C.N.W. Siganga	–	4,438
	J.D. Otiende	–	1,753
	W.B. Akatsa	–	1,646
	J.G.W. Kadima	–	1,344

The poll was 78.5 per cent of the registered voters.[22]

ministerial post until Africans were granted fifteen more seats to give them a majority over the European and Asian elected members. Convinced that power now lay in London, not in Nairobi, they sent a delegation to London to press for a new constitution.[25] Within months of their election, the Lyttelton Constitution was dead.

In October 1957 the Lennox-Boyd Constitution was conceded, extending the multiracial formulation by raising African representation in the Legislative Council to fourteen, thereby giving Africans parity with the Europeans. In addition, African ministerial portfolios were increased to two. No more communal seats were to be created in the future and it was thought this constitution would last at least ten years. As a move towards common-roll elections in the future, the Legislative Council was to sit as an electoral college to choose twelve Specially Elected Members, four each for Africans, Asians and Europeans.

Within a month of its publication, AEMO had rejected the new constitution, which was, however, supported by the Europeans and Asians. The African elected members also decided to boycott the elections for the Specially Elected seats. The political temper was becoming more militant. In June 1958, Odinga earned himself the epithet of a 'radical' by mentioning, for the first time in the Legislative Council, that dreaded and most revered of names, Jomo Kenyatta, referring to him as a respected leader. In September, Mboya's NPCP called for 20 October, the date on which Kenyatta and other nationalists were arrested, to be observed annually as a day of fasting. The Africans demanded a new constitutional conference. By January 1959, all the elected African and Asian members, together with one European member, had walked out of the Legislative Council, formed the Constituency Elected Members Organization (CEMO) and dispatched a delegation to London. Calls to have the Emergency lifted and veteran political leaders released became more strident. Then, on 3 March 1959, the Hola Massacre took place, further inflaming the nationalists, and tarnishing Britain's image both at home and abroad.[26] Ian Macleod, Britain's new Colonial Secretary, later admitted that 'Hola helped to convince me that swift change was needed in Kenya'.[27]

Clearly, the African nationalists held the initiative. The imperial government was groping from one policy to another while the settlers were in disarray.

But, in spite of these political gains, the problem of an organizational focus for African nationalism in Kenya was already apparent by the middle of 1958. The disparity between districts was already evident during the 1957 African elections. The African members of the Legislative Council themselves were not elected under the umbrella of a national party which could enforce discipline. The March 1958 African elections held under the Lennox-Boyd Constitution brought in six more African members of the Legislative Council, further intensifying personality and leadership conflicts. In May 1958, African leaders attempted to form a Convention of African Associations to foster unity amongst district associations and to develop a common policy with the African elected members. But the colonial ban on colony-wide African political parties had not been lifted and therefore the proposed convention was refused registration. African political unity had therefore to continue to depend on the maintenance of cohesion and agreement amongst the African elected members. But this was becoming increasingly difficult. The formation of the Kenya National Party (KNP), supported by eight of the fourteen elected members and led by Muliro, Ngala, Moi and Towett, in July 1959 marked the first split in the ranks of African nationalists. The formation of the Kenya Independence Movement (KIM), led by Odinga, Mboya and Kiano, in August 1959 completed the polarization of African nationalism. This polarization was to be reflected in the two national political parties that were formed in the following year after the Lancaster House Constitutional Conference.

Meanwhile, the pressure of the nationalists compelled the imperial government to lift the State of Emergency in 1960. In mid-January of the same year, the first Lancaster House Constitutional Conference was convened. There was therefore a need for the African elected members to present a united front. They agreed to submerge their differences and appointed Ngala as their leader and Mboya as secretary. For the first time, the British Government conceded the principle of African majority rule in Kenya. A new Legislative Council of sixty-five members was announced by Macleod. Thirty-three of these members were to be elected from open seats, the first in Kenya's history. Twenty seats were to be reserved for minority groups, ten for Europeans, eight for Asians and two for Arabs. There were to be twelve National Members, four each for Africans, Asians and Europeans, to be elected by the Legislative Council. There were to be four African Ministers, three European Ministers and one Asian Minister. But the form and content of Kenyan independence was far from decided. The Governor was still to choose the Ministers, responsible government was not discussed and there was no provision made in the new constitution for a Chief Minister. But the European conservatives felt betrayed by the colonial government. One of their leaders, Briggs, called the new constitution 'a victory for Mau Mau'. Indeed, in these terminal stages of colonial rule, Kenya was gripped by severe crisis, whose overall effect was to accelerate independence and deepen the restructuring of Kenya's political economy from one dominated by white settlers to one dominated by a combination of indigenous and international capital.

The Politics of Independence Negotiations

In trying to explain these last few years of colonial rule in Kenya, a number of writers, using models derived from pluralism to systems analysis, have argued that decolonization was essentially a bargaining process between Africans and the two racial minorities, Europeans and Asians, with the British Colonial Secretary playing the role of umpire. Rothchild concludes that direct bargaining between 'the spokesmen of the three major races', which reached a peak at the turn of the 1960s, ended in 'a trade-off [taking] place between legal and constitutional concessions on the one hand and the acceptance, with certain limitations of African power, on the other'.[28] Like the pluralistic model on which his whole analysis rests, with its cultural determinism, Rothchild tends to absolutize racial and ethnic collectivities, ignoring the horizontal ties of class. More importantly, the way 'bargaining' is used connotes equality of the actors and a procedural smoothness to independence. The period between 1960 and 1963 was far from that. Writing a few years later, Wasserman tried to improve the 'bargaining' thesis by underscoring the fact that, by the end of the 1950s, the settler bloc was fractured into divergent conservative and liberal camps, each with increasingly distinct social bases, priorities and tactics. The conservatives were led first by Group-Commander Llewelyn Briggs and later by Sir Ferdinand Cavendish-Bentick. They represented the interests of small farmers and the more recently arrived settlers and centred on the Convention of Associations (before regrouping under the Kenya Coalition in 1960). The conservatives, who feared any moves towards deracialization, wanted to preserve the status quo by trying to rekindle the *laager* mentality in Kenya Europeans. The European liberals, led by Sir Michael Blundell, supported the move towards multiracialism, which was supposed to offer a possible alternative to an early all-African government. The liberals had their political base among the business and professional communities and the older, larger and more wealthy farmers. They organized themselves in a new political party, the New Kenya Group, which was the first Kenya political party to be open to members of all races. The group sought to build up, and align with, a moderate African middle class.[29]

According to Wasserman, the actual form of decolonization depended on the outcome of the interaction between the rise of the nationalist power and the adaptive response of the colonial regime. He therefore contends that the major goal of colonial administration in Kenya from 1960 onward was to thwart the development of African political organizations which might challenge the inherited political economy. Accordingly, decolonization was a dual process of bargaining and socialization, with independence as the ultimate end. 'From this perspective the decolonization process was not so much the *upward* development of an indigenous African political movement, as the *downward* manipulation of the movement into a system.'[30]

Wasserman's 'consensual decolonization', in which the liberals succeeded in locking Kenya into a neo-colonial system, finds echoes in much
of the dependency literature on Kenya.[31] However, the settlers,
whether liberal or conservative, should not be confused with the agents
of multinational firms, whose members in Kenya were increasing and
whose links with African producers and merchants were growing. The
liberals certainly did not have the power to build up an African middle
class (which at any rate had been long in formation in spite of the settlers), with which they could 'align'. Indeed, the liberal agenda – first,
to create a multiracial state as an alternative to all-African government,
then, to destroy Kenyatta politically by forming a government without
him and, finally, to divide African politicians and force a *majimbo* (decentralized) constitution with minority safeguards – all failed miserably.
Where then was the liberal success that Blundell and his associates have
been credited with? The bargaining thesis assumes there was merely a
functionist game of system maintenance. History is turned into a parody
of voluntarism and continuity.

The dream of turning Kenya into a 'White Man's Country' was given
burial at Lancaster House. The settlers felt betrayed. Briggs died in
London soon after the Constitutional Conference, a lonely and depressed
person. Thousands of settlers fled from Kenya in fear of their lives, property and pride, as the 'native' cries of '*uhuru na Kenyatta*' (freedom and
Kenyatta) became deafeningly close to realization. Others ran down
their farms as they waited to be bailed out by the British Government.
The Blundells hoped in vain that the transitional period would last for
at least ten years, giving them enough time to manipulate African
'moderates' in order to institutionalize settler representation and participation. But history did not permit such 'bargains' to be made. In fact,
Blundell himself became so disillusioned with politics that he soon turned
his whole attention to making money![32]

The Economics of Decolonization

The economic crisis following the first Lancaster House Constitutional
Conference was of such proportions that capital flight reached £1 million
a month, the Nairobi Stock Exchange fell sharply, the building industry
virtually collapsed and unemployment shot up dramatically.[33] The
economy was contracting precisely at the time that tens of thousands of
detainees were being released and restrictions against Kikuyu, Embu
and Meru workers had been dropped. That old festering wound of the
Kenyan polity, land, threatened to open once again, while the labour
system witnessed a return of the convulsions of the post-war years.

After the Emergency was lifted, many of the returning detainees and forest fighters either found that their lands had been forfeited and redistributed, or their previous landlessness had been irrevocably confirmed through the land consolidation programmes, which had been fully taken advantage of by pre-Emergency landowners and loyalists. Incidents of rioting, illegal squatting and land seizures were reported from the Central Province. There was also apparently a revival of oathing, an ominous development, which a decade earlier had served as a prelude to the outbreak of Mau Mau.[34]

In response to this impending explosion, the 'yeoman' and 'peasant' schemes only introduced in 1961 as a means of bailing out the settlers and buying off the expanding African agrarian bourgeoisie, were quickly abandoned in favour of a more comprehensive land settlement programme that would include at least some of the landless.[35] Thus were born the controversial land settlement programmes that would collectively be known as the Million Acre Scheme, after the 1.2 million acres which were allocated to 35,000 families in the 1960s. The Scheme was funded by the British Government, the Colonial Development Fund and the World Bank to the tune of £7.5 million. The involvement of international capital was seen in imperial as well as settler circles as the best guarantee against possible ravages of nationalist expropriation; it would take a daring government indeed to offend the World Bank.[36] The nationalists, with the exception of the radical fringe opposed to the principle of compensation itself, came to see in land settlement a way of killing two birds with one stone: defusing rural unrest and promoting the interests of the African landed class. Other squatter settlement schemes were to be launched after independence. But over half of the settler lands were transferred almost intact by sale to wealthy Africans organized in partnerships or limited liability companies.[37] Thus a new land policy based on class, instead of race, was being established in Kenya.

The agrarian crisis was accompanied by a labour crisis. There was a resurgence of worker militancy despite the rising unemployment and the growing collaboration between the KFL and the FKE. The government, through the Labour Department, also came to see in collective bargaining a way of enticing trade unions into moderation. Thus was begun a long courtship of convenience between organized labour and industrial capital, with the state acting as a matchmaker. But the workers refused to consummate the tripartite marriage.

The threats to the labour control system that the labour unrest of 1960–63 provided, as well as the current agrarian crisis, were symptoms of, and themselves accelerated, the transition from the colonial to a postcolonial state and society. Ever since the Emergency and the direct intervention of the imperial state, the colonial state had become an area of fierce conflict, the result of which had been the rise of African representation and a corresponding diminution of the settler hold over state institutions. By 1960 imperial state intervention itself had become such that, during the 1960–63 interregnum, officials of the colonial state, from the field officers in the Provincial Administration to the Governor himself at the centre, had become functionaries. They were no longer active participants in the formulation of key policies, which were now being directly negotiated at Lancaster House between the Colonial Secretary and the African nationalists. The nationalists had come a long way. But the demise of the settlers, followed as it was by the adoption of the principle of majority rule by the imperial state and the subsequent exclusion of the colonial administrators in the great constitutional wrangles, had the effect of concentrating the struggle for power among the various factions of the nationalist movement. In other words, in the tempests of the transition to independence the centrifugal social forces held within the nationalist torrent threatened to burst open.

It is not a coincidence that the two main nationalist parties were formed following the first Lancaster House Constitutional Conference. In a sense, the formation of KANU and KADU was a crystallization of the apparent cleavages in the ranks of the African members of the Legislative Council which had led to the break up of CEMO in 1959 into the KNP, led by Ngala, Muliro and Moi, the future leaders of KADU, and the KIM, under the uneasy leadership of Mboya and Odinga, a schism that would linger on in KANU. Often these cleavages have been explained in terms of personality clashes or ideological tendencies, whereby KADU is labelled 'moderate' and KANU 'radical'.[38]

On 14 May 1960, at the second Kiambu meeting (the first was held on 27 March), KANU was founded, with James Gichuru as president (pending the release of Kenyatta), Tom Mobya as secretary-general, Odinga as vice-president, Ngala, elected *in absentia*, as treasurer and Moi, also elected *in absentia*, as assistant treasurer. But there were those African leaders who feared the dangers of a one-party state dominated by a few ethnic groups. Masinde Muliro had formed the Kenya African People's Party; the Kalenjin Political Alliance was formed in March–April to represent 900,000 Kalenjin-speaking peoples. Led by Moi, the Alliance stated its prior claim to control over land in the western highlands of Kenya. Then there was the Maasai United Front, which was concerned about the future of the Maasai land areas. In Mombasa, the Coast African People's Union, headed by Ngala, was formed to protect the interests of coastal Africans. On 25 June 1960, a conference was held at Ngong' outside Nairobi, attended by the leaders of these four newly formed parties and the Somali National Association. They were merged to form KADU, with Ngala as president, Muliro as vice-president and Moi as chairman.

While personality clashes and jostling for influence cannot be discounted altogether for an era noted for its turbulence and the presence of powerful figures with strong independent bases for support, they need not be overstated either. Indeed, the fiercest protagonists, Mboya and

Odinga, both Luo, were also members of KANU. The ideological labels, on the other hand, are precisely that, labels which mystify as much as they explain the sources and trajectory of the conflict. The broad programmatic similarities between KADU and KANU tend to be overlooked, so that the ease with which KADU dissolved itself into KANU in 1964 is then regarded as something sudden.[39] There were, of course, many contacts between the two parties, almost from the time of their formation. In 1961, the two parties agreed to an independence timetable as well as general economic policies.[40] Both parties held Kenyatta in high regard and demanded his early release. Indeed, both parties still hoped that Kenyatta when freed would be able to bring the two factions together to form one mass nationalist organization. However, these hopes received a temporary set-back. Following his release from detention in August 1961, Kenyatta decided to accept the presidency of KANU on 28 October 1961. But Kenyatta did not found KANU, nor did he dominate it or identify with it the way Nyerere controlled the Tanganyika African National Union or Nkrumah the Convention People's Party. He appeared to operate above party politics, relying more on his role as the founding father of the Kenya nation, a fact which was to make it easy for the parties to come together in 1964. All these points show that the differences between the two parties were more apparent than real. Indeed, as is discussed below, the two parties had gone a long way towards achieving national unity by the end of 1963. This is not to say that the parties did not see themselves or portray their conflict sometimes in precisely these terms, or that indeed the ideological differences were not real; rather, it is to suggest that ideological explanations alone are inadequate.

At the root of political factionalism during this period lay the conjuncture of approaching independence in a society suffering from acute uneven development. Uneven development in Kenya, as in other colonial formations, had historically corresponded to, and been intersected by, regional, ethnic and class factors.[41] In spite of the Emergency – in fact, because of it – the Central Province, populated mostly by Kikuyu, had continued its relatively fast level of development. This ensured that the Kikuyu petty bourgeoisie, numerically the largest in the country, would be central to any postcolonial dispensation. But during the Emergency political leadership of the nationalist movement had passed on to a petty-bourgeois leadership that was predominantly Luo, the second largest nationality in Kenya, inhabiting a region that had also been significantly penetrated by colonial capitalism, albeit in different forms. By the time the Emergency was lifted and Kikuyu leaders allowed to re-enter politics, the Mboyas, the Odingas and the Argwings-Kodheks were sufficiently entrenched not to fear for their positions and influence, although the overall scope of leadership conflict was broadened, thus making it more intense and open.

The same could not be said of the Rift Valley and Coastal regions and peoples where colonial capitalism was less developed and their petty-bourgeois classes were much smaller and more vulnerable at the national level. The Kalenjin peoples of the Rift Valley region, unlike the Luo, lived in close geographic proximity to the so-called European highlands bordering their areas. The Kalenjin feared the possibility not only that the Kikuyu would override these claims, but that they might also 'colonize' their areas, especially now that there were tens of thousands of landless Kikuyu agitating for land.[42] The official anti-Kikuyu propaganda of the Emergency and the exploitation of the rural unrest amongst the unemployed Kikuyu ex-squatters in the Rift Valley by radical political leaders, such as the young Mark Mwithaga in Nakuru and G.G. Kariuki in Laikipia, only served to inflate these fears. Meanwhile, the Coastal peoples had developed fears of economic domination by the 'up-country peoples', who already formed the bulk of the labour force. Concurrently, the conflict between the Coastal Africans, particularly squatters, and Arab-Swahili landholders had come into the open. Faced with this challenge, as well as the ominous development up-country, and buoyed by temporary economic and cultural revival, the Arabs began agitating for *Mwambao* or autonomy for the coastal strip. They formed their own political party, the Mwambao United Front, which demanded political union with Zanzibar. 'If for any reason', they stated in their memorandum to the second Lancaster House Constitutional Conference in March 1962, 'the Sultan of Zanzibar abdicated his sovereignty over Mwambao, it would necessarily follow that Mwambao would become an Independent Self-Governing State.' They went on to state quite categorically that they did not accept 'the right of any ruler or protecting power to come to any arrangement to hand over a free people to the control, rule or protection of an alien power without the consent of the permanent inhabitants of the territory concerned'.[43] This demand by the Mwambao United Front met with unqualified opposition from Coastal African political groups.[44] In other words, Coastal Africans both were opposed to the historic dominance of the Arabs and would not countenance the possibility of new domination by up-country peoples.

Underlying the broader regional cleavages, there were local social, economic and political divisions which provided a basis for local factional and leadership rivalries and future inter-ethnic and inter-regional political realignments. For instance, in September 1962, the Sabaot people from the Mount Elgon area formed the West Kalenjin Congress, with Daniel C.M. Moss as its president. The party was opposed to the recommendation of the Regional Boundary Commission to include Sabaot country in the Western Region, instead of in the Rift Valley Region with the rest of the Kalenjin. They also claimed Trans Nzoia East as Kalenjin land. In the 1963 elections, another ethnically based party, the African

People's Party (APP) was born. This was a political vehicle for Paul
Ngei, who broke away and formed his own party because he felt he
had not been accorded the appropriate national power and status by
the KANU leaders. In fact, both KANU and KADU were basically
loose coalitions representing diverse social forces with weak central
party machinery, so that almost from the beginning they were given to
internal political fissures and realignments. For example, in Nakuru
alone, KANU accommodated three social groups, represented by
former officials of the Nakuru District Congress, such as J.F. Kanyana
and S.K. Mwandia, who were ex-KAU chairmen who had turned
loyalist during the Emergency and were now operating within the
moderate wing of KANU; there were the ex-detainees and ex-freedom
fighters; and then there were the new leaders, such as Mark Mwithaga.
In Muranga, the nationalist movement encompassed the landed groups
and the colonial civil servants, the former detainees represented by
Bildad Kaggia and the 'ambiguous politics of new men' like Julius
Kiano and Kariuki Njiri.[45] Even in a district like Central Nyanza,
where the class distinctions were not yet fully developed, there were
two antagonistic KANU factions, led by Oginga Odinga and F. Odede,
coexisting within the same party. At the national level, the period
between 1961 and 1963 witnessed very fierce intra-party disputes within
KANU. The nationalist 'hardliners', represented by B. Kaggia, Paul
Ngei and Oginga Odinga, were engaged in an ideological battle with
the moderates, represented by Tom Mboya, James Gichuru and Julius
Kiano. The fact that these parties were formed in the midst of the
transition to independence meant that there was not enough time to
consolidate the party structure and therefore institutionalize the inter-
party conflict. Hence, the relative ease with which KADU dissolved into
KANU in November 1964. The merger of KANU and KADU was
a factor of critical importance in determining the stability of postcolonial
Kenya and its ability to survive periodic bouts of political strain. A
continuation of the multiparty system at that time would have exacerbated ethnic divisions and animosity and led to a multiplicity of political
groups, some representing ethnic or religious communities. Such fragmentation would have sapped national unity and undermined economic
development.

By then, of course, Kenya had attained her independence under
KANU. KADU's attempt to form a government with the help of European and Asian members in 1961, following the refusal of KANU to form
a government despite its electoral victory in the February 1961 general
elections, until Kenyatta was released, was a failure. KANU's popularity
soared. So did the party's militancy. Governor Rennison accepted
the inevitable and released Kenyatta on 14 August 1961. Two more
Constitutional Conferences were held in 1962 and 1963 to pave the way
for independence.

The Making of a Constitution and the Emergence of a National Consensus

As we have already noted above, political negotiations leading to independence are often discussed in terms of an unholy alliance between the African élite and the white liberals striking a neo-colonialist bargain with the metropolitan power. This is an over-simplification and a distortion of the facts. The truth of the matter is that a much tougher negotiation was carried out among the African leaders themselves, especially between KANU and KADU, which produced a national consensus upon which the Kenya constitution was based. This was the work of the African leaders themselves, for which they should be credited. The period between 1961 and 1963 is crucial for the making of the Kenya constitution.

By October 1961, it was evident that all hopes for a united Kenya under Jomo Kenyatta's leadership had been shattered by the fear of domination that gripped the non-Kikuyu–Luo nationalities at this time. Intimidation of and violence against political opponents were becoming widespread and public wrangling and open splits among leaders in the same party were rampant. A spirit of tolerance and understanding was necessary if political independence which guarantees freedom and equal rights for all was to be achieved. This was the biggest task facing Kenyans between 1961 and 1963. How they tackled it is an important aspect of the history of Kenya which we cannot afford to gloss over.

There were three Lancaster House Constitutional Conferences – 1960, 1962 and 1963 – but the most important one for constitution-making was the 1962 one, which lasted from 14 February to the first week of April. It hammered out the independence constitution under the chairmanship of the then Colonial Secretary, Reginald Maudling.

Soon after his appointment as Colonial Secretary, Maudling paid a visit to Kenya, in late November 1961. At the end of the visit, he issued a statement in Nairobi which was later to provide a valuable background to the Lancaster House Conference in 1962. In that statement, Maudling made it clear that the future of Kenya rested largely in the hands of Kenyan leaders and only in a subsidiary way in the hands of the British Government. But the great danger he saw in the country was fear: 'fear of discrimination, fear of intimidation, fear of exploitation'.[46] Regarding discussions about the constitution, he expressed the hope that these would concentrate on the facts rather than on an exchange of slogans. 'What we must determine', he wrote,

> is the nature and composition of the Central Government, the nature, composition and powers of other governing authorities, the protection of individual rights, including land titles and property rights, and the means whereby the stability of the Constitution may be secured, and law and order, which is absolutely fundamental to the happiness of Kenya, firmly preserved.[47]

This was broadly the agenda. It took Kenya leaders about seven weeks of hard negotiations in a cold English winter to hammer out the independence constitution. It took so long to produce precisely because the different parties sought to produce a foolproof constitution that would allay the fears of everybody and protect the rights of each citizen. The fact that they ended up with a constitution which has reasonably withstood the test of time – with a few amendments – is in itself a tribute to the foresight, tolerance and common sense of the Kenya constitution-makers.

The KADU parliamentary group, represented by Ronald Ngala, D.T. arap Moi and M.J. Seroney, among others, and advised by Sir Michael Blundell, Reggie Alexander and W.I. Havelock, initially presented a one-page statement on what they felt should constitute the main features of a federal constitution for Kenya.[48] They argued that, because of regional and group differences and imbalances, there was a genuine danger of discrimination and conflict between the different regions and groups. 'Domination by a political party, or personality, group or tribe, must be prevented in order to protect the political rights and fundamental freedoms of the individual and to insure the independence of the judiciary.' To achieve these aims, it was necessary to decentralize state power. They therefore proposed the creation of six regional authorities with legislative and administrative powers. They also proposed the establishment of a bicameral system, with the federal parliament consisting of a lower house elected on a national basis and an upper house elected by the regional assemblies voting as electoral colleges, both houses having substantially equal powers. The regions were to have equal representation in the upper house. Finally, the KADU document recommended that there should be no judicial decentralization. In other words, the judiciary was to remain a branch of the central government.

In response to questions and criticisms from the other parties attending the conference, Ronald Ngala, the leader of the KADU delegation, elaborated on some of the points they had raised in their brief memorandum. He emphasized, for example, that their main objective was that 'there should be a decentralization of power. Such decentralization must be to authorities which can implement and execute their responsibilities without depending on Central Government aid, either financially or in any other way.'[49] In other words, the regional authorities had to have independent legislative and financial powers.

In contrast to the brief document submitted by KADU, the KANU delegation tabled at the conference a detailed nineteen-page document divided into eight parts, which was tantamount to a draft constitution for an independent Kenya.[50] The delegation included Jomo Kenyatta, Oginga Odinga, Tom Mboya, Bruce MacKenzie and Fritz d'Souza, among others. Their document covered the nature and structure of the constitution, a Bill of Rights, local government authorities, land usage, the East African Federation and Amendments to the constitution. This lucid and readable document raised many fundamental principles and constitutional issues which are still relevant today. The constitution of independent Kenya was to a large extent an elaboration of this KANU document in conjunction with KADU's principle of democratic regionalism.

KANU stated as its aim the establishment of a civic society 'in which there is political freedom, human dignity and economic opportunity for all without discrimination. Such a society must rid every citizen of fear for his person, his property, or his basic and fundamental human rights.' The KANU delegation, however, observed that not all aspects of life in a country, in its administration or governance, and human or economic relations, can be the subject of constitutional provisions. 'For example,' they wrote, 'to give greater confidence to the lesser-developed areas, it will be necessary to put into effect a dynamic and urgent economic, agricultural and educational programme.'

At the Lancaster House Conference of 1960, it had been agreed that Kenya's independence constitution should be based on the Westminster model. This meant majority rule, with the majority party, for the time being, running the government, and the acceptance of an opposition party or parties, who, on their part, accept parliamentary rules and methods as the means of advancing their policies and in pursuance of their political activities. While endorsing this earlier decision, KANU now qualified it by saying that they did not insist 'on the establishment of a mere copy of the Constitution as practised in Westminster'. They fully realized 'that the future shall be based on ensuring a stable Constitution, suited to our circumstances and based on enshrined democratic principles and fundamental rights'.

Regarding the structure, it is interesting to note that KANU recommended a president and a prime minister selected by the majority party or appointed by the president. It also recommended that, under the circumstances obtaining at the time, a unicameral legislature was more appropriate and practical. They quoted, with approval, from Professor Mackenzie's paper circulated to the first Lancaster House Conference in 1960, which stated that

> A Second Chamber may be useful in many ways, but its basic powers are usually to play some part in ordinary legislation, and to take a more important part in Constitutional change. It may be that Kenya does not need a Second Chamber, an institution which adds something to the expense of Government and to delays in legislation.[51]

Detailed proposals were offered by KANU regarding fundamental rights. The party attached great importance to this section and stated categorically that 'The state shall not make any law which takes away or abridges the rights conferred by this part; any law in contravention of this clause shall be to the extent of such contravention void.' The section covered the right to equality, the right to freedom, safeguards as to arrest and detention, protection of life and personal freedom, freedom of religion, rights against exploitation, cultural and educational rights, the right to property, the right to a fair trial and the right to constitutional remedies.

Since KANU believed that the fundamental basis of the new constitution must be the observance of the rule of law, it strongly recommended, for this purpose, the presence and continuation of a properly established, fair and impartial judiciary, free from executive interference. Such an independent judiciary, they stated, could only be secured by adequate constitutional provisions. Following precedents in other Commonwealth countries, KANU proposed several provisions on the judiciary to be incorporated in the new constitution. These provisions covered the qualifications for judges, the establishment of a judicial service commission, the appointment of puisne judges and of the Chief Justice and, lastly, the removal of judges. On this last provision dealing with the removal of judges, it is ironic to note that it was KANU that originally formulated the clause that the independent Kenya was to find obnoxious. The KANU delegation had recommended that

> The Constitution should provide that no judge may be removed from office except for inability to perform the functions of his office for reasons of infirmity of body or mind or other cause or for his misbehaviour. The Head of State should not be permitted to remove any judge even on the grounds mentioned until the question of the judge's removal has been investigated and recommended by an independent tribunal comprising not less than three judges, or former judges, of a Supreme Court in some Commonwealth Country.

This recommendation was incorporated into the Kenya Constitution and it is therefore incorrect to argue, as many commentators have since done, that this provision represented one of the neo-colonial sections of the Kenya Constitution imposed on reluctant Kenya leaders by a departing colonial power.

The Kenya Coalition, led by L.R.W. Welwood and C.W. Salter, explained that they themselves had not submitted a constitutional paper as such because they were convinced that 'the suggestions which will form the basis of the Constitution must spring initially from the main African Parties'.[52] They therefore restricted themselves to offering comments on the KANU and KADU constitutional proposals.

They rejected KANU's argument that true national unity can only be achieved through a unitary form of government. They did, however, welcome the general tenor of KANU's Bill of Rights and the provisions to secure an independent judiciary; but they did not consider that the mere existence of a Bill of Rights or an independent judiciary provides adequate safeguards against possible abuse of power. They also suggested that there should be provision for minority representation in the legislature, at least during the transitional period. Regarding KADU proposals, the Coalition warned that

> the existence of strong local or regional authorities does not in itself guarantee the rights of the individual. A local authority can be quite as arbitrary as a Central government. It is therefore necessary to ensure that not only do local authorities act as a check on the Centre but that the Centre can act, if necessary, as a check on local authorities.[53]

For about seven weeks and in the cool and imposing Lancaster House, the African leaders had contributed substantially to the drafting of the Kenya Constitution in a sober and critical fashion. It was a big contrast to the rhetoric, slogans and name-calling exercises which characterized political rallies in market-places, stadiums or the Desai Memorial and Makadara Halls in Nairobi. The leaders had discovered how much they had in common; they got to know each other better, and this helped in reducing the suspicions and mistrust which had hitherto impeded political dialogue. And, by the time they left London, the delegates had agreed on the pattern for a future government which was to ensure a country free from fear, with people making their contributions to the rebuilding of confidence and stability. Thus was achieved a national consensus embracing general policy goals and institutional structures.

Following the Lancaster House Conference, a coalition government involving both KANU and KADU was formed. And, by July 1962, Kenya was already developing a sense of national purpose as signified by the decision of Ngala and Kenyatta to hold the first 'Kenya We Want' Convention in August 1962.[54] At the Convention, various committees were formed to examine in detail different topics, such as natural resources, land consolidation, education, economic development, the training of women, the establishment of parastatals, tourism, etc.

In April 1963, the Kenya Constitution, a 248-page document, was published. Several issues which had been left unresolved from the 1962 Conference, such as the powers of the regions, the distribution of revenue, the central government's ability or otherwise to dictate to the regions and the percentage needed in the senate and lower house in order to amend the constitution, were to be dealt with at the final Constitutional Conference, which was to be held in London in September 1963, to settle the final form of the Kenya Constitution.

KADU was particularly concerned about two major checks on finance and on the police that had become glaring from the published constitution. To a large extent, the regions were to finance themselves. They were also to be responsible for running all local and regional services.

To meet these commitments, each region was to derive revenue from customs and excise duties and consumption taxes on petrol and diesel fuels, the latter being distributed between the authorities according to the amount of fuel used by each region. Regional authorities had the right to receive a large share of all revenue received by the central government from customs and excise duties on items other than petrol and diesel fuels, and it was agreed that this money would be distributed between the regions in accordance with the size of their populations. Each regional authority was also to receive a special grant from central government to run its regional contingent of the police.

In addition, each region had to control the vitally important network of local government authorities within the region. In addition to receiving grants-in-aid from the regional authorities, these local authorities were to raise money by means of a new single graduated personal tax applicable throughout all regions. This tax replaced the then existing poll rates levied by local authorities and the personal tax previously levied by the central government.

From a regional viewpoint, these arrangements had several shortcomings. Firstly, the right to fuel duty and vehicle tax appeared to be the only firm right they had, the others being left largely to the discretion of the central government. As Tom Mboya rather sarcastically summed it all up, 'Regional Authorities will have a status inferior to that enjoyed by the Nairobi City Council at present.'[55] In the case of fuel tax, Mboya pointed out that, if the principal mode of transport in a region happened to be the camel, it was their hard luck. Added to this was the fact that the agreement to distribute revenue from other sources proportionate to population gave a big advantage to thickly populated regions, such as Central, Nyanza and Western. Moreover, the regions could not borrow money from abroad directly, although the Nairobi City Council already enjoyed that privilege. Above all, under the constitution only the central government was empowered to impose taxation other than taxes specifically provided for.

The other major regional weakness concerned security. According to the constitution, the police force was an overall one for Kenya, under the control of the Inspector-General (Police Commissioner), but there were to be 'regional contingents'. Also, the General Service Unit could be sent to any region for forty-eight hours without the prior consent of the regional authority, and during that period they were to be under the direct control of the central government. Added to this, Section 97(2) of the constitution read: 'The executive authority for the Region shall be exercised so as (a) not to impede or prejudice the exercise of the executive authority of the Government of Kenya; and (b) to ensure compliance with any law made by the Central Legislature applying to that Region.'

Given these major shortcomings, it was evident that the '*majimbo*' arrangements were almost stillborn. There were too many hidden checks which, in effect, made the regions powerless.

As a prelude to independence, the so-called Kenyatta Elections – consisting of national, regional and local elections – were held in the second half of May 1963. The campaigns, however, were marred by widespread thuggery, bribery and intimidation. These activities were not confined to a few individuals of one party. The rot gripped both the major political parties, especially in areas where one party appeared dominant. In Bungoma, for example, where KADU, led by Masinde Muliro, appeared strong, acts of thuggery and terrorism were committed against KANU, led in the district by Elija Masinde, a former detainee and leader of *Dini ya Msambwa*. In Nyanza, on the other hand, a predominantly KANU area, much intimidation and thuggery took place between rival elements within KANU.

As generally expected, KANU swept the board in the independence elections. Kenyatta became the Prime Minister on *Madaraka* Day. KANU leaders embarked on a conciliatory policy, aimed at wooing KADU towards a merger. This was particularly evident in Kenyatta's speeches. Making his first official up-country tour since the elections, the Prime Minister, while addressing over 10,000 people in the Nakuru Stadium, introduced the new theme by saying:

> I would like to point out that the Government which is now in power is the Government of the whole of Kenya. It is not just for those who elected us. We shall care equally for those people who gave us their votes and those who did not. Those who do not agree with us have proper ways of making their views known. The opposition is formally recognized in our national Constitution, and can play a constructive role in nation-building . . . I believe firmly that if this country of ours is to prosper we must create a sense of national family-hood, *ujamaa*. We must bring all the communities of Kenya to build a united nation. In this task we shall make use of those attitudes of self-help, good-neighbourliness and communal assistance, which are such an important feature of our traditional societies.
>
> We shall build upon this spirit, adapting it and expanding it to deal with the task of creating a nation. We must forget all our differences of the past and work together to build the new Kenya of the future. Where there has been racial hatred it must be ended. Where there has been tribal animosity it will be finished. We must not dwell upon the bitterness of the past. I have known my share of suffering but I am not anxious to remember it now. Rather let us look to the future, to the good, new Kenya, not to the bad old days. If we can create this sense of national direction and identity we shall have gone a long way towards solving our economic problems.[56]

The final Constitutional Conference was to be held in London from 25 September under the chairmanship of the Colonial Secretary, Mr Duncan Sandys. There were fears from KADU leaders that KANU intended to abolish '*majimboism*' in London. There was apprehension in the air. But one major development took place prior to this conference which greatly facilitated it and, more importantly, moved Kenya still further towards consolidating the national consensus which had been hammered out in 1962.

KANU held a meeting at Machakos during which Ngei told the Akamba to forget the clenched-fist sign of the APP and switch to the raised finger of KANU. Kenya, he said, needed only one Prime Minister to lead it to independence. He then announced the dissolution of the APP.[57]

By November 1963, there were signs that Kenya's opposition party, KADU, was beginning to disintegrate. Two of its staunchest supporters, 'whistle-blow' William Murgor and John Seroney, announced that they were crossing the floor to sit with the government. Their defection must have come as a bigger blow to KADU's president, Ronald Ngala, than even the complete walk-out from the opposition by Paul Ngei's APP.

There was a Shakespearian touch to the brief notice issued by Messrs Murgor and Seroney. 'There comes a time', it began, 'in the careers of politicians, when they have to make an agonising reappraisal of their position.' The time had now come, they added. After considerable thought, said the two Kalenjin, they had come to the conclusion that they would be serving the best interests of their constituents by working within the government ranks in the National Assembly. A great task of nation-building lay ahead of Kenyans and they wished in the national spirit of *harambee* to 'associate their electorates with this noble task'. In conclusion, they announced: 'We renounce the Opposition whip and accept instead the Government whip in the National Assembly. We shall henceforth be guided in our politics by the policies of the Prime Minister, Jomo Kenyatta, and our Government.'[58]

What gave this announcement great significance was that it was precisely these two who a few weeks earlier had enthusiastically supported KADU's threat to the British Government that, if the party did not get satisfaction from the London constitutional talks, it would set up a republic within Kenya constituted by all the non-KANU areas. What had changed? Did they feel that the sands were running out for KADU and any form of opposition in Kenya?

As if that were not enough, another 'old faithful', Taita arap Towett, the poet and linguist, surrendered his post as KADU's political adviser and resigned from the party to sit as an independent in the National Assembly. These changes gave KANU ninety-three members in the Lower House against KADU's twenty-eight.

A few days before independence, Kenya's opposition party took another hard knock when its Chief Whip, Eric Khasakhala, joined in the drift to the government benches. He announced his decision at a meeting in Emukhaya in Western Region, and in the presence of the Minister for Home Affairs, Oginga Odinga, who told the enthusiastic crowd that one of the first fruits of Khasakhala's switch would be a journey to China at the head of a delegation of Bunyore people.[59]

All these developments, which occurred a few weeks before independence day, are relevant in discussing the ease with which KADU was, in the following year, to dissolve itself to join KANU. Practically all the signs were already pointing in that direction.

On the night of 12 December, the Union Jack was finally hauled down as Kenya's black, red, green and white flag was hoisted, ending sixty-odd years of colonial rule.

Notes

1. Colony and Protectorate of Kenya, *A Plan to Intensify the Development of African Agriculture* (Nairobi, Government Printer, 1954).
2. Charles Douglas-Home, *Evelyn Baring* (London, William Collins, 1978), p. 262.
3. Colony and Protectorate of Kenya, *Report of the Committee on African Wages* (Nairobi, Government Printer, 1954).
4. Colony and Protectorate of Kenya, *Report of the Commission on the Civil Services of the East African Territories and East African High Commission 1953–1954* (Nairobi, Government Printer, 1954).
5. Great Britain, Parliamentary Papers, 'East Africa Royal Commission Report, 1953–1955', Cmnd 9475 of 1955, p. 181.
6. Quoted in M.P.K. Sorrenson, *Land Reform in the Kikuyu Country* (Nairobi, Oxford University Press, 1967), p. 117.
7. Geoff Lamb, *Peasant Politics* (Lewes, Sussex, Julian Friedman, 1974), p. 11.
8. Ibid.
9. Kenya Government, *Economic Survey* (Nairobi, Government Printer, 1968), pp. 5, 105ff.
10. See, for instance, Maina wa Kinyatti, 'Mau Mau: The Peak of African Nationalism in Kenya', *Kenya Historical Review*, 5(2) (1977) pp. 285–311.
11. George Bennet, *Kenya: A Political History* (London, Oxford University Press, 1963).
12. J.N. Crowley, 'Colonial Policy and Nationalism in Kenya', PhD Thesis, University of Washington, 1967, p. 98.
13. Michael Blundell, *So Rough a Wind* (London, Weidenfeld & Nicholson, 1964), pp. 261–262; Douglas-Home, *Evelyn Baring*, pp. 284–285.
14. Douglas-Home, *Evelyn Baring*, p. 283.
15. Ibid., p. 285.
16. Colony and Protectorate of Kenya, *Report of the Commissioner Appointed to Investigate Methods of Selection of African Members of Legislative Council* (Nairobi, Government Printer, 1956).
17. *Kenya Weekly News*, Nairobi, 15 March 1957.
18. *East African Standard*, Nairobi, 12 March 1957.
19. *Kenya Weekly News*, Nairobi, 1 March 1957.
20. *East African Standard*, 12 March 1957.
21. Ibid., 13 March 1957.
22. Ibid., 12 March 1957.
23. Jack R. Roelker, *Mathu of Kenya: A Political Study*. Hoover Colonial Studies, edited by Peter Duigan and L. Gann (Stanford, CA, Stanford University Press, 1976), p. 121.
24. Ibid., pp. 126–127.

25. See Tom Mboya, *Freedom and After* (London, André Deutsch, 1963) and Oginga Odinga, *Not Yet Uhuru* (London, Heinemann, 1971).
26. For official accounts, see *Record of Proceedings and Evidence in the Inquiry into the Deaths of Eleven Mau Mau Detainees at Hola Camp in Kenya*, Cmd. 795 of 1959; *Documents Relating to Deaths of Eleven Mau Mau Detainees at Hola Camp in Kenya*, Cmd. 816 of 1959. London, British Government printers.
27. *Spectator*, London, 20 March 1964.
28. D. Rothchild, *Racial Bargaining in Independent Kenya* (London, Oxford University Press, 1973), p. 8.
29. Gary Wasserman, *Politics of Decolonization* (Cambridge, Cambridge University Press, 1976), pp. 16, 166.
30. Ibid., p. 15.
31. See, for example, C. Leys, *Underdevelopment in Kenya: The Political Economy of Neo-Colonialism* (London, Heinemann, 1974, James Currey 1988).
32. The settler exodus is reported in detail by Rothchild, *Racial Bargaining*; see also Blundell, *So Rough a Wind*.
33. Leys, *Underdevelopment*.
34. G. Lamb, *Peasant Politics* (Lewes, Sussex, Julian Friedman, 1974); J.T. Kamuchuluh, 'Meru Participation in Mau Mau', *Kenya Historical Review*, 3(2) (1975) pp. 193–216; and A. Njonjo, 'The Africanization of the "White Highlands": A Study in Agrarian Class Struggles in Kenya, 1950–1974', unpublished PhD thesis, Princeton University, 1977.
35. See C. Leo, 'Who Benefited from the Million-acre Scheme? Toward a Class Analysis of Kenya's Transition to Independence', *Canadian Journal of African Studies*, 15(2) (1981) pp. 201–223.
36. Ibid. pp. 201–223; see also H. Ruthenberg, *African Agricultural Production: Development Policy in Kenya, 1952–1965* (New York, Springer-Verlag, 1966); J.W. Harbeson, *Nation-Building in Kenya: The Role of Land Reform* (Evanston, IL, Northeastern University Press, 1973); R.S. Odingo, 'Land Settlement in the Kenya Highlands' in J.A. Sheffield (ed.), *Education, Employment and Rural Development* (Nairobi, East African Publishing House, 1967).
37. Leys, *Underdevelopment*, pp. 73–114; C. Leo, 'The Failure of the "Progressive Farmers" in Kenya's Million Acre Settlement Scheme', *Journal of Modern African Studies*, 16(4) (1978) pp. 619–638; and C. Leo, 'Who Benefited?'.
38. See, for instance, Leys, *Underdevelopment*, pp. 212–214, as well as the writings of the protagonists themselves, particularly Mboya, *Freedom and After*, and Odinga, *Not Yet Uhuru*.
39. C. Gertzel, *The Politics of Independent Kenya* (London, Heinemann, 1970), is correctly wary of using these labels, but still does not satisfactorily explain the dissolution of KADU into KANU in 1964.
40. See KANU–KADU Accord (Nairobi, 1961).
41. See Edward Soja, *The Geography of Modernization in Kenya* (Syracuse, Syracuse University Press, 1968). This is a study of differential resource distribution and the consequences of a colonial impact on resource growth and distribution in a developing country.
42. Gertzel, *Politics of Independent Kenya*, pp. 9–10.
43. Memorandum No. 16, Kenya Constitutional Conference 1962, Personal Archives.
44. K.M. Mambo, 'Political Activity among the Miji Kenda', Seminar Paper, Kenyatta University, 1983; A.I. Salim, *Swahili-Speaking Peoples of Kenya's Coast, 1895–1965* (Nairobi, East African Publishing House, 1973), Chapter 6; K.K. Janmohammed, 'Ethnicity in an Urban Setting: A Case Study of Mombasa', in B.A. Ogot (ed.), *History and Social Change in East Africa* (Nairobi, East African Publishing House, 1976).
45. Lamb, *Peasant Politics*, p. 16.
46. Personal Archives, Document K.C.C. (62) 15.

47. Ibid.
48. Personal Archives, Document K.C.C. (62) 4.
49. Personal Archives, Document K.C.C. (62) 11.
50. Personal Archives, Document K.C.C. (62) 3.
51. Personal Archives, Document K.C.C. (60) 5, paragraphs 44, 45 and 51.
52. Personal Archives, Document K.C.C. (62) 10.
53. Personal Archives, Document K.C.C. (S.G.) (62) 2.
54. *Reporter*, Nairobi, 21 July 1962.
55. *Reporter*, Nairobi, 27 July 1963, p. 11.
56. *Reporter*, Nairobi, 29 June 1963, p. 10.
57. *Reporter*, Nairobi, 21 September 1963.
58. *Reporter*, Nairobi, 23 November 1963, pp. 9–10.
59. *Reporter*, Nairobi, 7 December 1963.

Part Two

*The
Kenyatta Era
1963–78*

Four

Structural & Political Changes

WILLIAM R. OCHIENG'

Independent Kenya's Development Strategies

Kenya's colonial economy had been moulded into a distinctive pattern by the long years of colonial rule. It displayed characteristics typical of an underdeveloped economy at the periphery: the preponderance of foreign capital, the dominance of agriculture, the limited development of industry and heavy reliance on export of primary products and imports of capital and manufactured consumer goods.[1] This under-developed state of the economy meant that independent Kenya would have to formulate policies that would not only arrest Kenya's mounting urban and rural poverty and decay, but would also put the economy into the hands of the indigenous people. To meet these changes Kenyans would have to work hard to improve on existing infrastructural facilities, such as communications, hospitals, power supplies and educational and financial institutions.

Independent Kenya's leaders would also have to address themselves to the reversal of the export-orientated nature of Kenya's economy. Most of what was produced in Kenya during the colonial period was exported 'but most of the proceeds never returned for the development of the economy. Rather they were used for the development of Britain, the colonial power.'[2] The task of the *uhuru* government was therefore to formulate policies which would ensure that the citizens of Kenya had the greatest share of the subsequent development.[3]

The main principles and strategies of Kenya's development after independence were laid down in the Sessional Paper No. 10 of 1965 entitled 'African Socialism and Its Application to Planning in Kenya'. In this document the Kenya African National Union (KANU) government outlined its political and economic philosophies. The government rejected both Western capitalism and Eastern communism. Tom Mboya, who was then the Minister of Economic Planning and Development, contended that African socialism would guarantee every citizen, whether rich or poor, full and equal political rights. 'Under colonialism,' the Sessional Paper said, 'the people of Kenya had no voice in government; the nation's resources were organized and developed mainly for the benefit of non-Africans; and the nation's human resources remain largely uneducated, untrained, inexperienced and unbenefited by the growth of the economy.'[4] With independence Kenya intended 'to mobilize its resources to attain a rapid rate of economic growth for the benefit of its people'.[5] The main features of African socialism, according to the KANU government, were:

1 Political democracy.
2 Mutual social and political responsibility.
3 Various forms of property ownership so that nobody would have too much power.
4 The control of wealth so that it is used in the interest of society.
5 Freedom from want, disease and exploitation.
6 Progressive taxation to narrow the gap between the rich and the poor.

In particular, the KANU government stressed the wisdom of operating a mixed economy in which strategic and essential resources and services, such as railways and harbours, principal roads, airways, broadcasting and post and telecommunication, would be a government responsibility. 'We shall work towards a situation in which the roles of private enterprise and government are complementary to each other . . . without damaging the existing fabric of the economy.'[6]

On p. 17 of the Sessional Paper No. 10 of 1965 we also read as follows: 'We shall welcome both government and private investment in Kenya. We shall also encourage investors to participate jointly in projects with our own government.' So foreign capital was welcome but, to curtail their political influence in internal economic matters, foreign investors were expected to accept 'the spirit of mutual responsibility' by 'making shares in their companies available to Africans who wished to buy them, by employing Africans at managerial levels as soon as qualified people can be found; and by providing training facilities for Africans'. Nationalization, the document asserted, 'will be used only where the national security is threatened, or production resources are seriously and clearly being misused'. Otherwise, instead of spending the nation's limited resources on buying existing assets and businesses, such money could be more profitably spent on providing essential services.

It is important to conclude this section of the chapter by noting that in his preface to the Sessional Paper No. 10 of 1965 the President, *Mzee* Jomo Kenyatta, also underlined the fact that the economic approach of his government would be 'dominated' by the desire to ensure Africanization of the economy and public service. 'Our task remains to try to achieve these two goals without doing harm to the economy itself and within the declared aims of our society.'

As it turned out, Kenya's economic policies have been heavily geared towards a mixed economy rather than to socialism. Besides, right from independence, Kenya's leadership opted for a clear strategy of economic growth, based on a determination to keep existing ties with the major Western industrial nations, especially Britain, in order to gain foreign aid and investment, build overseas markets for her products and expand tourism. In addition, the KANU government concentrated on growth, rather than redistribution. Thus, nationalization and state ownership have not been practised to any significant extent since independence. Instead, Kenya has relied heavily on private ownership and market forces.[7] As a result, foreign investors and multinational corporations have found their way into the Kenyan economy in a big way and their influence has increased over the years.[8] Indeed, between 1964 and 1970, large-scale foreign investment in commerce and industry almost doubled in Kenya. For four years between 1967 and 1970, the average annual rate of inflow of foreign capital was £41.3 million, a total of £41.3 million.

Africanization of the Economy

The achievement of independence in 1963 had implications which extended beyond political change, to include economic and social changes as well. Besides bringing vital political decisions under the control of the indigenous bourgeoisie, independence also enabled some leaders to make important economic decisions which have enhanced the economic standing of the local bourgeoisie.

'Africanization', in particular, was one of the most emotive political slogans in the tumult before independence and Kenyatta's promise to the people. As we have already seen, before independence large-scale agriculture, industry and commerce were dominated by non-Kenyans. Europeans controlled agriculture and industry while commerce and trade were dominated by Asians. Thus, after independence one of the most urgent and pressing problems was to break the foreigners' dominance of the Kenyan economy and transfer it to Kenyans. Again, as we noted earlier, this objective was tackled through the mechanism of legislation and licensing.

The first legislation to this effect was the Trade Licensing Act of 1967, which excluded non-citizens from trading in rural and non-urban areas and specified a list of goods which were to be restricted to citizen traders only. These included most basic consumer goods, such as maize, rice and sugar, and the list was to be extended later on in the 1970s to include most commodities, such as textiles, soap and cement.[9] The Kenya

National Trading Corporation (KNTC), which had been formed in 1965 to handle domestic import–export trade, was also used extensively in the period after 1967 'as an instrument by the emergent bourgeoisie to penetrate the wholesale and retail sectors, which had formerly been the exclusive preserve of non-citizens'.[10] In 1975, the Trade Licensing Act was amended to the effect that all goods manufactured by foreign firms in Kenya must be distributed through the KNTC-appointed citizen agents. The firms to be excepted from these provisions were those producing semi-finished products for sale to other industries and those goods of a highly technical nature.[11] Again, as Swainson puts it, 'This cut out a substantial proportion of the wholesale trading profits to foreign corporations and brought a wide range of commodities under the control of African merchant capital.'[12]

Another important feature of the transfer of capital and economy into the hands of Africans has been the large-scale extension of credit through state credit institutions, such as the Agricultural Finance Corporation (AFC), the KNTC, the National Housing Corporation (NHC) and the Industrial and Commercial Development Corporation (ICDC). Established in 1963 and reconstructed in 1969, the AFC has been concerned primarily with providing credit for buying or rehabilitating large farms, although it sometimes extends credit to smallholdings as well. It also administers the Guaranteed Minimum Return programme for wheat and maize. By 1972 the corporation's credit to some 2,500 large-scale farmers and ranches had amounted to £12 million, plus some £2.5 million to 14,500 small-scale farmers.[13]

The ICDC, which has been in operation since 1964, is in charge of the Commercial Loans Revolving Fund, through which it helps progressive citizen traders, especially those who acquire business from non-citizens through the government's Kenyanization of trade programme. ICDC was conceived as the main vehicle for government participation in industry. Africanization was to be partly through the support of small businesses which were unable to obtain commercial bank credits and partly through the acquisition of equity in large farms for subsequent transfer to individual Africans.

Between 1964 and 1972 more than 2,542 citizen traders received financial assistance worth £3.5 million through this ICDC scheme, and between 1974 and 1975 total loans given out to 1,087 citizen traders and industrialists amounted to £2.7 million. By 1977 the assets employed by ICDC totalled nearly £31 million, of which 45 per cent was in loans and advances, 27 per cent in equity and 24 per cent in subsidiary companies.

The other corporations and agencies which the state has used for resource and capital mobilization and the transfer of capital to Kenyan citizens include the various co-operative societies, the Kenya Industrial Estates (KIE) – formerly a subsidiary of the ICDC, the Development

Finance Company of Kenya (DFCK), the KNTC, the NHC, the Kenya Tea Development Authority (KTDA) and the Industrial Development Bank (IDB), to mention only a few. The Kenyan citizen businessmen whom government measures sought to establish within the capitalist mode of production were, on the whole, small retail traders, bar-owners, small transporters, builders, *jua-kali* manufacturers, hoteliers and the like. Their members expanded as Asian and European competition was progressively excluded and credit was chanelled towards them on favourable terms. There is evidence that the proportion of establishments in retail and wholesale trade owned wholly or mainly by Kenyans increased from 48 per cent in 1966 to 80 per cent in 1971, and in retail trade alone from 55 to 89 per cent. While the above figures refer to Kenyan citizens in general, it is fair to bet that they point to the progress of Africanization.

Land Transfers and Agricultural Policies

Kenya is primarily an agricultural country; as such agriculture was regarded right from independence as the crucial springboard of Kenya's economic, industrial and social growth. Indeed, the majority of Kenya's industrial establishments are primarily concerned with the processing of food and other agricultural products. But Kenya's agricultural problems were acute at independence. As we have already noted, during the colonial period the cash-crop agricultural sector was completely dominated by European settlers, while African holdings were expected to grow food for the domestic market. As the land issue had been at the root of most of Kenya's political troubles, it was necessary to find a solution to it in the interest of stability and growth.

Perhaps the most important single set of decisions underscoring the future of African agriculture in Kenya came in the 1950s regarding African land tenure and registration. These decisions were contained in the recommendations of the East African Royal Commission of 1953–1955, which deprecated the system of African communal land ownership and argued for individual title-deeds, and also in the Swynnerton Plan ('A Plan to Intensify the Development of African Agriculture in Kenya') of 1954, which argued that the reform of African land tenure was a prerequisite of agricultural development. Consolidation, enclosure and registration of title, it was argued, would make credit obtainable for improvements and enable progressive farmers to acquire more land. Thus, the Land Registration (Special Areas) Ordinance of 1959 and the Registered Land Act of 1963 were enacted to achieve individualization of tenure among the African people.

The above land laws and the deracialization of the White Highlands in 1959 enabled the colonial government, under Governor Malcolm

MacDonald, and the postcolonial state, under Jomo Kenyatta, to effect
a near-revolution in land redistribution and in Kenya's agricultural
transformation in the period after 1960. For example, by the end of the
1950s, the Swynnerton programme, initiated in 1955, had been completed in the Kikuyu districts and it had been followed by the provision
of extension services and credit and, most important of all, by the
removal altogether of the ban on African-grown coffee and tea. The
results were spectacular. The value of recorded output from smallholdings rose from £5.2 million in 1955 to £14.0 million in 1964, coffee
accounting for 55 per cent of the increase.[14]

Elsewhere, in the country, the Kenya government pursued a vigorous
policy of food production and food surplus for export. The 1960s, in particular, were characterized by the large proportion of public expenditure
on the agricultural sector, particularly on land transfers and adjudica-
tion, research, veterinary services, training, livestock marketing, crop
development, machinery and soil conservation services. By 1970 the
government was strongly represented in the rural areas through its
agricultural extension services, which employed about 6,000 people.
This figure had jumped to 10,000 people by 1989.

We noted earlier that land was the most sensitive item in the
nationalist agenda. After independence the KANU government tackled
the land issue and landlessness by a massive resettlement of African
farmers on the previously European-owned farms. Funds were raised
from the World Bank (International Bank for Reconstruction and
Development (IBRD)) and the Colonial Development Corporation for
the purchase of farms and their settlement of a 'low density' to provide
annual monetary incomes, in addition to subsistence and loan charges,
of £100 and more. But a large number of farms were also transferred to
Kenyan citizens as intact units, usually with financial assistance from
public funds. Wealthy, indigenous Kenyans, including well-known per-
sonalities in public life, also bought farms directly from the departing
Europeans, usually with loans from the Land Bank.

By 1970 more than two-thirds of the old European mixed farms had
been given to 50,000 African families. The remaining third, roughly 1
million acres, which were still in European hands, as Colin Leys has
observed, would mostly be purchased over the next decade.[15] A further
4 million acres of ranch land and plantations of coffee, tea and sisal
seemed likely to remain for a long time in foreign hands because of their
very high capital value.

All these agrarian changes and policies did a lot to transfer capital
into the hands of indigenous farmers. We learn from Gavin Kitching
in his book *Class and Economic Change in Kenya* (Yale University Press,
1980) that in the period 1958–68 the gross farm revenue of African
smallholders in Kenya grew from a little under £8 million to over £34
million, an increase of 420 per cent in a decade. The largest single

item in this growth was coffee production, 'which was worth little over £1 million in 1958, and nearly £8.5 million nine years later'.

Stratification: Wealth and Poverty

One of the major objectives of the Kenyatta government after independence was to remove inequalities inherited from the colonial period. We read as follows in the Sessional Paper No. 10 of 1965: 'The state has an obligation to ensure equal opportunities to all its citizens, eliminate exploitation and discrimination, and provide needed social services such as education, medical care and social security.'

Some of the inequalities came into being as a result of the uneven penetration of capitalism and Western influence in the country right from the onset of colonialism. In this respect, it is noteworthy that a communications infrastructure was built in districts such as Kiambu, Nyeri, Meru, Siaya, Taita, Kakamega, Bungoma, Kisii and Machakos. It was also in these districts that the colonial government concentrated their agricultural innovations and experimentation. Kenyan towns, such as Nairobi, Mombasa, Kisumu and Nakuru, would also be centres of capital, industrial and commercial concentration. The vast areas of the Rift Valley, Coast Province and north-eastern Kenya were to lag behind in the development of labour, education and agriculture. It follows that at independence some parts of Kenya were highly economically developed and modern while the others were still using the indigenous modes of production.

To what extent has the postcolonial state guaranteed the promise of egalitarianism to her citizens? Has the spectacular growth of Kenya's economy since independence and the mechanisms of the transfer of wealth to the Africans, as discussed above, removed to any appreciable extent the inherited inequalities?

Definitions of poverty and justifications of personal wealth are usually controversial issues. Yet, if we observe a society in time, or through time, we may clearly observe forms of socio-economic inequality and we may categorize or measure with reference to any number of criteria. Among these would be land ownership, education or monetary incomes. But the moment certain individuals in society are seen to enjoy a higher standard of living than their compatriots an explanation is usually sought for.

A report compiled by the International Labour Organization (ILO) in 1972 was among the first to draw the attention of Kenyans to the problems of inequality and poverty during the Kenyatta era. The report pointed out:

> The development of the Kenyan economy has been accompanied by a growing imbalance within the country. The tendency of Nairobi and other urban areas

to grow at the expense of the rural, the richer regions in relation to the poorer, has led to growing imbalances between regions and different groups of the population.[16]

While acknowledging the excellent progress which Kenya had achieved since independence, a World Bank report of 1975 also identified unemployment, poverty and income distribution as the disappointing aspects of Kenya's development story: 'In many respects,' it said, 'the performance of the Kenyan economy has been quite remarkable in comparison to most other countries faced with similar problems. Only with respect to the growth of employment and its impact on the poverty of the lowest income groups has Kenya's performance been rather disappointing.'

It was clear from both the ILO and the World Bank reports that the much advertised Africanization of jobs in the public sector and the transfer of farms and businesses to a few petty bourgeoisie and peasants in the first decade of independence had only amounted to the replacement of a few Europeans, but this did not fundamentally alter the structure of the former colonial economy. Kenya's economy is still externally orientated, making it highly open and vulnerable to external factors. The country's external trade has also been characterized by large balance of trade deficits as imports continue to exceed exports. Thus, Kenya's economy does not generate adequate surpluses for reinvestment in, and expansion of, the economy. Despite the government's efforts to improve agriculture – the mainstay of the country's economy – declining international commodity prices and general deteriorating terms of trade have progressively pauperized the peasants, whose numbers have also been steadily increasing. Kenya's industries are also still dominated by multinational corporations and other foreign investors, who export their surpluses out of the country. In addition, the government's industrialization and investment policies tend to strengthen the dominance of multinational corporations. As a result, a pattern of dependence has emerged, with the multinationals providing capital and a technology which is not always appropriate to Kenya. 'The result of this', according to Professor J.K. Maitha, 'is establishment of high cost and capital intensive industries which tend to strengthen existing income inequalities by limiting labour absorption and producing inappropriate products.'[17]

If Kenya's economic performance has been both distorted and inhibited by its structural relationship to international capital, poverty within a large segment of Kenyan society has also been aggravated by secondary factors – including landlessness, adverse climate and soil conditions in some parts of the country, lack of adequate or relevant education, low wages, high cost of consumer goods and unemployment. For most Kenyan peasants, persistent poverty is also a result of lack of meaningful involvement in the monetary economy, as most of them still practise subsistence farming. Writing on inequality in Kenya, Hazlewood has noted: 'The greatest regional inequalities are the work of nature. One need look no further than the 307 mm of rainfall in North Eastern Province and the 1084 mm in Central Province to find a major cause of the inequalities between the two.'[18] Kenya continues to remain a land of a few rich people and millions of poor folk.

Conclusion

A number of conclusions arise from our discussion of the postcolonial state in Kenya and her economic inheritance. Foremost, the postcolonial state in Kenya has largely inherited the former colonial economic infrastructure and policies. Kenya's economy is also still dominated by multinational corporations and foreign capital. While the former ruling and farming European bourgeoisie departed at independence, their positions were largely inherited by an indigenous bourgeoisie, who are ruling in collaboration with international finance. Although it is demonstrable that the interests of the indigenous (or local) bourgeoisie and those of foreign capital are not harmonious, no fundamental structural changes have been made in the inherited colonial economy.[19]

Politics of the Kenyatta Era

Every country that has moved from colonialism to independence has sought to transform its inherited colonial institutions to serve the culture, needs and aspirations of the newly independent society. In Kenya, the desire for this transformation was often identified with the call for nation-building. Nation-building required that men of vision and men of public affairs be at the helm to define immediate and finite ends and to devise the means to those ends.[20] At the same time, it was also clear to Kenyan leaders that nation-building was critically dependent upon the development of sympathetic political and economic institutions, for, in the immediate preceding years, the people of Kenya had hoped that the attainment of independence would mark for them a transition from the realm of necessity to that of building a democratic socialist state strongly committed to pan-African ideals and world peace. 'The Colonial period had produced Kenya,' wrote George Bennet, 'it was up to its people to look beyond.'[21]

Thus, it was not surprising that on Independence Day Jomo Kenyatta appeared before the Kenya nation and announced that his government would build a democratic African socialist state. The idea was that the benefits of economic and social development would be distributed equitably, that differential treatment based on tribe, race, belief or class would be abandoned and that every national, whether black, white or brown, would be given an equal opportunity to improve his lot. Tom Mboya wrote:

> Our system of African Socialism will guarantee every citizen full and equal political rights. Wealth must not be permitted to confer special political concessions on anyone. The disproportionate political influence that has frequently been granted, openly or otherwise, to economic power groups in capitalist societies must not be permitted to gain a foothold in Kenya. Similarly, the fundamental force of religion, which has been denied in Communist countries, will be a definite feature of our society in which traditional religion provided a strict moral code. But political rights will not be contingent on religious beliefs.[22]

Brave words, but the radicals were not fooled by them. They had observed Kenyatta's performance very closely from the day he became Prime Minister on 1 June 1963, and what they had seen was not pleasing to them. They had also carefully listened to, and analysed, Kenyatta's Independence Day address, and had noted that, while Premier Milton Obote's speech at the same venue had dwelt on Kenya's bloody struggle for *uhuru*, Kenyatta's own speech inexplicably made no mention of 'the people who laid down their lives for the struggle'.[23] According to the radicals, Kenyatta had already forgotten the freedom fighters of the forests and detention camps, who were in danger of being overlooked 'because it suited the ambitions of the self-seeking politicians to divert our people from the real freedom aims of our people'.[24]

The young KANU government was faced with many problems. Politically, the KANU leaders faced serious ethnic and ideological divisions. There was the Somali question for those inhabitants of northern Kenya who had shown by their effective and total boycott of independence elections their desire not to stay in Kenya. There were also two political parties (the Kenya African Democratic Union (KADU) and the African People's Party (APP)) in opposition, which had to be contained.

Economically, the great task facing the KANU government was stimulation of development to meet the needs of the people. There was the ever-explosive issue of land shortage. There was the scarcity of capital, resources and skilled manpower. Immediate measures had also to be taken to expand the economy through industrialization, improved methods of farming and intensive training of local manpower. What is more, the economy was heavily in the hands of expatriates, who owned large companies, banks, hotels, extensive farms, shops and businesses. The government was faced with the need to correct this imbalance in favour of the Africans, without at the same time causing undue hardship to the expatriates, who were still a major source of capital and skilled manpower.

'Everything will come when we have political power' is how Kenyatta had expressed his practical approach to Oginga Odinga when the Kikuyu radicals were seeking allies with the Luo in the 1950s. Unlike his neighbour, Julius Nyerere in Tanzania, Kenyatta articulated no particular social philosophy. But there was to be no revolution after he took over power, as some of the old pan-Africanists had hoped and many of the colonialists feared. In the early years of independence he showed little interest in pan-African or international issues that would necessitate globe-trotting diplomacy. It also became very clear, soon after independence, that he was an African capitalist who would guide Kenya in that direction and rely on a trusted civil service to be the backbone of his regime.

Kenyatta and his associates preserved what they most needed from the colonial state, and particularly the law-and-order aspect. Institutions such as the provincial administration, police and army were taken over intact. Kenyatta even retained the services of European officers such as Ian Henderson, the police inspector who had prepared a case against him at Kapenguria, and Whitehouse, the District Commissioner who had been his gaoler at Lokitaung.[25] A British settler, Bruce Mackenzie, held the strategic Ministry of Agriculture, while another settler, Humphrey Slade, remained the Speaker of the National Assembly, and when an army unit threatened mutiny within a month of Kenya's independence Kenyatta's government did not hesitate to ask the British troops to put it down.[26] Kenyatta's call to forgive and forget became the keynote of his government. Youth-wingers and radical nationalists who spoke of revenge or change were roundly rebuked. In resisting calls by the radicals, Kenyatta was strongly supported by his colleagues in the conservative camp. Mboya said:

> there is no point in change for its own sake. Only if some special institution has utility within our special circumstances is it justified. Look at the political institutions. In most cases we have started off with those bequeathed to us by the former colonial powers. This is the system we have been used to working within. We may introduce certain superficial innovations but the principles and so much of the machinery remain the same. It is difficult to break away entirely, to steer a new course, to create institutions which are African, yet which are appropriate for modern society.[27]

White men and women who only a few months before had thought of Kenyatta and his team with revulsion now took Kenyan citizenship. 'Everything will be alright so long as the old man is there,' they said to each other.[28] We touch on the attitude of Kenyatta at this stage because, although he himself was a personification of conservative social forces and tendencies in the country, in the period after independence he would dominate the social scene, and a lot of the politics in the country would revolve round his political style. A pragmatic capitalist, Kenyatta would rule Kenya by manipulating factions, working through a relatively strong civil service and utilizing his ethnic base for the fulfilment of his ambitions. We would further like to argue that there were two transfers of power in Kenya: one from the British to Kenya's nationalists in 1963 and the second from the nationalists to Kenyatta in the period after he had eliminated Mboya and Odinga as political factors in Kenya. We talk of the second transfer of power because right from 1964 Kenya's nationalists in Parliament, for whatever reasons, would concede considerable political power to the President in a quick succession of constitutional amendments.[29] (The thirteen amendments which Parliament made on the Kenyan constitution during Kenyatta's rule are appended at the end of this chapter.) In the first three years of independence alone, seven substantial amendments had been made to the constitution and the eighth amendment was being discussed.[30] All these amendments were aimed at strengthening the hands of the executive, and there were complaints that these amendments were rushed through Parliament 'before the public had had time to consider the matters involved' and that 'they were designed to benefit the government in power'.[31] For example, the October 1964 Republican Amendment gave the President enormous executive powers, which enabled him to provide the so-called 'strong and wise government that Kenya's leaders believed to be essential at this stage of the country's growth'.[32] An Act rushed through Parliament in 1966, known as the Preventive Detention Act, would also dilute the Bill of Rights as entrenched in the constitution and enable the President to detain individuals without recourse to the courts 'in the interest of public security'. This authoritarian presidency, 'though initially a stabilizing factor for bourgeois rule, increasingly became a snare to this rule, and finally stood as a wall between the bourgeoisie and the popular masses, almost foredooming any hopes of the former taking the initiative of organizing the latter on their own political terrain'.[33]

The first two years of independence were years of political readjustment. The opposition Members of Parliament (both KADU and the APP) were lured to join KANU in the government. They immediately strengthened the conservative wing of KANU, but the ideological difference between the radicals and conservatives in KANU continued. The radicals accused the KANU government of betraying the pledges which they had made to the masses before independence.

Land policy, in particular, became a major bone of contention, and no one tried more conscientiously than Bildad Kaggia to put the government on the road to a land policy that would be good for the expansion of the Kenyan economy, the interests of the landless and the confidence of the poor people who had elected the *uhuru* government. On 5 September 1963, Kaggia wrote a letter to Bruce Mackenzie, the Minister of Agriculture, and told him:

Everyone in this country is well aware of the landhunger that has existed among Africans as a result of the robbery of their land by the British colonial imperialists. The logical method to solve the problem posed by this robbery would have been to nationalise all big estates owned by the Europeans and make them either state farms, so as to alleviate unemployment, or hand them to co-operatives formed by landless Africans.[34]

Apart from advocating free land distribution to the landless, Kaggia also called for free education and free medical facilities for the people, but nobody senior in Kenyatta's government listened to him. In fact, by championing the interests of the poor, Kaggia did not know that he was making many enemies among Kenyatta's close associates. Indeed, on 22 May 1964, the Prime Minister, *Mzee* Jomo Kenyatta, wrote to Kaggia and, among other things, told him: 'I am seriously concerned at your repeated attacks on the Ministry of Lands and Settlement, and with your interference with land consolidation in Fort Hall [Murang'a].'[35] This was a veiled warning to Kaggia, and a request to him to resign from the government if he did not like its policies. In June 1964, Kaggia resigned his parliamentary secretaryship in the Ministry of Education with the following comment: 'As a representative of the people I found it very difficult to forget the people who elected me on the basis of definite pledges, or forget the freedom fighters who gave all they had, including their land, for the independence we are enjoying.'[36]

Kenyatta and his close associates were not impressed. On many occasions, Kenyatta had made it abundantly clear that 'those Africans who think that when we have achieved our freedom they can walk into a shop and say this is my property, or go onto a farm and say this is my farm are very much mistaken, because this is not our aim'.[37] On 4 May 1965, Tom Mboya told an attentive Parliament: 'there is no society or country where social services are completely free. So far as the nation as a whole is concerned, every service must be fully paid for.'[38]

But the disagreement between the radicals and Kenyatta's government continued, and went beyond land, medical and educational issues. As we have observed already, the radicals were also calling for rapid Africanization of the civil service and the economy and the publication of a blueprint for economic and social development. Additionally, the radicals were pressing the government to honour party pledges on the necessity of an East African federation. More importantly, the radicals and conservatives differed on their attitude towards the state, the working-class movement and foreign policy. Was the state to be used by the nationalists now in power to create a capitalist class and various classes of property among the Africans or was the state itself to be the capitalist, preventing the accumulation of capital in private hands but encouraging it in the public sphere? Of course, the pro-West, conservative group preferred a free-market economy, 'in which the state superintended *laissez-faire* capital accumulation', while the radicals pushed for the public ownership of the means of production.

To placate the radicals, however, Kenyatta instructed Tom Mboya, his Minister of Planning and Economic Development, to formulate the famous Sessional Paper No. 10 of 1965. The publication of the Sessional Paper, in May 1965, sparked off fresh controversies and acrimony that eventually led to the breakaway of the radicals from KANU. The blueprint clearly had no intention of altering the inherited colonial economic and social structures, and particularly their law-and-order aspect. Kaggia argued: 'I do not mind calling our socialism African Socialism, Kenyan Socialism, Kikuyu Socialism, or even Luo Socialism, but I believe that whatever prefixes we use it must be socialism and not capitalism.'[39] Zephania Anyieni, a Member of Parliament, criticized the use of the term 'African Socialism'. If Kenyans were shy of calling their socialism scientific, then 'let us call it Kenyan Socialism'.[40] Kenyan academicians also dismissed the document as a 'fraud'. The document, according to Dharam Ghai, 'commits the government against a revolutionary break with the past in its attempt to transform society. The general policy, rather, is to build upon and modify the inherited economic and social systems.'[41] Ghai denied Mboya's contention that there were no economic classes in Kenya. He said, 'already in Kenya there is the nucleus of a new class among Africans, based on differences in wealth and education'.[42] According to Barak Obama, 'African Socialism', as contained in the document, remained 'undefined'. He added, 'it would have been more clear and logical to define African Socialism and then state its independence from scientific socialism. After all, how can one talk of the independence of something people do not know?'[43]

But Mboya disagreed with government critics who were calling for scientific socialism. He called them 'prisoners of foreign propaganda'. He said,

> it was our concern to define a system and to identify policies that will meet our needs, solve our problems and further our ambitions . . . Each country has its history, its culture, its own inheritance of economic institutions and resources, and its own problems. To impose on a people a rigid system [Marxism] that takes no account of their needs, desires, aspirations and customs is to court disaster and failure.[44]

Turning to the academicians, Mboya accused them of living in ignorance in their ivory tower. He pleaded with them to spare some time to think 'about our political and social philosophies'. This they should not do 'from the ivory tower with the aim of gaining some sort of self-satisfaction'.[45]

As the socialists in KANU increased their attacks on government economic and foreign policies, the conservative wing of KANU, led by

Kenyatta and Mboya, closed ranks. On platforms, shifting the weight of his elephantine frame from one foot to the other, waving his fly-whisk lazily, Kenyatta would say, 'it is a sad mistake to think that you can get more food, more hospitals or schools by simply crying communism'. His bleary, slow-moving eyes would sweep back and forth over the audience. His target was the people he suspected of building a following for themselves by preaching that all things the people wanted would be theirs if only they held out for communism.

> There is no room for those who wait for things to be given for nothing. There is no place for leaders who hoped to build a nation on slogans. For over forty years, I fought and sacrificed my active life so that this country could get rid of the yoke of colonialism and imperialism. Many sons and daughters of our land suffered and shed blood, so that our children might be free. You can therefore understand my personal feelings about the future. How can I tolerate anything that could jeopardise the promise to our children? Let me declare once more that, as Head of your Government, I shall combat with all my strength anyone that may be tempted to try to undermine our independence. This pledge holds true whether such forces operate inside Kenya or from without.[46]

Nearly every writer on the subject of socio-economic development following the transfer of power at independence notes that, whatever changes are required from the inherited system, the problem of increasing development capabilities is not only technical, but profoundly political as well. It is political because independence and consequent shifts of political power must respond to at least three new priorities effectively missing under colonial rule. First, in their enthusiasm for a new policy they expect and urgently demand of government new and expanded services. Secondly, they want these new services now, or at least as soon as possible. For government to make no effort to meet their demands is to risk political discontent. The need for a capacity to respond to various sources of popular demands is, then, the third priority.

Kenyatta and his allies never understood this or, if they did, they felt strong enough to stand their ground against the tide of popular frustration. Kenyatta's government had only inherited the colonial economic structure, but it never bothered to behave in a populist manner. Writing in 1967, after he had interviewed Kenyatta, Lawrence Fellows, the then *New York Times* correspondent in Nairobi, had the following interesting observation to make: 'In Nairobi, tall hotels and modern office buildings have sprouted from an underbrush of close-packed Indian shops and tin-roofed shacks, and African policemen direct the choking traffic with cool efficiency, but Kenyatta is holding back the tide of envious Africans wanting jobs that white men still hold.' Four years after *uhuru*, there were still 1,700 Britons in the civil service alone, some of them holding very important and strategic jobs. 'What is perhaps far more significant', wrote Fellows, 'is that Western businesses operate in Kenya without fear of nationalisation – in sharp contrast to nearby Tanzania.'

Talking to businessmen earlier in September 1964 at the City Hall in Nairobi, Kenyatta had made himself very clear; 'My Government realize that Africans must be integrated in the commercial and industrial life of the nation ... But we are determined that the development of African businesses and industries should be carried out without damaging the existing fabric of the economy.' An even more disturbing trend emerged from the figures of land transfers since independence. Of the total land transfers in the first year of independence, more than half of the farms had been acquired by the Europeans. Individual purchasers bought 1,185,299 acres of land, of which 70 per cent was acquired by Europeans. And, when the Mau Mau freedom fighters refused the ridiculous plots which Kenyatta's government was offering to them as 'settlement schemes', they were quietly rounded up by the police.[47]

It was not until his split with his first vice-president, Oginga Odinga, and the formation of the socialist Kenya People's Union (KPU) in March 1966, that Kenyatta began to hear clearly what the opposition to his regime was all about. He never reconsidered the stand of his government; if anything, his attitude hardened. He saw in his opponents paid agents of communism whose mission it was to dethrone him, and the socialist KPU platform simply confirmed his fear. Addressing a Kenyatta Day rally at Kamkunji, in Nairobi, on 20 October 1967, Kenyatta had the following to say:

> Brothers, there are those who ask, 'What is the Government doing?' And there are those who say, 'The Government has done nothing as yet.' But I am telling you, even if we have done nothing, I think every citizen should be proud of being free. Each man is free, and is no longer anybody's slave. For a man to say he is free, and that he is governing himself is a very important thing ... We all fought for *uhuru*, and it is only the cowards who used to hide under the beds while others were struggling who go about asking what the KANU government has done ... You all know KPU ... Ask them where (and how) they fought for *uhuru* ... What have the KPU ever done for anybody? As from today KPU are to be regarded as snakes in the grass. Let them try and re-examine their minds and return to KANU. If they do not do so, KPU should beware! The fighting for our *uhuru* is on. Whoever has ears to hear, let him heed this.[48]

As we said earlier, in March 1966 the radicals, led by Oginga Odinga, Bildad Kaggia, Achieng' Oneko, Joseph Nthula, Zephania Anyieni, Tom Okello Odongo and Oduya Oprong, broke away from KANU and formed the KPU, which was supported by urban workers, trade unions and students and advocated socialist policies. In his resignation statement, Oginga Odinga claimed that the country was being run by an 'invisible government'. This 'government':

represents first, international forces purely concerned with ideological colonization of the country and has no genuine concern for the development of the people. Secondly, it also represents the commercial interests, largely foreign, whose primary concern is big profits for the shareholders. Here, too, the interest of the people of Kenya is only secondary to the profits and understandably not their concern.[49]

Odinga proceeded to summarize the reasons for his resignation from KANU and government in the following words:

> It is fairly clear that there is pressure and desire that I should leave the Government. The authority concerned has, however, shown reluctance to say so openly to the public. If I thought that there was the slightest chance of putting things right from within the Government then this desire to remove me from office would worry me as indeed it has not done for the last one year. However, *wananchi*, my honest opinion is that the present Government has reached a point of no return. It can only do for the people the little that the underground master allows it to do. Its guiding star has become personal gain. I therefore find it impossible to be part of it, and my decision is that from now on I should be free to join *wananchi* in demanding that their voice be heard.[50]

On 17 April 1966, thirteen veteran trade unionists resigned from KANU to join the KPU. Among these were J.D. Akumu, O.O. Maka-Anyengo, V.G. Wachira, George Inguka and F.E. Omido. On 19 April 1966, five days after Odinga's resignation from the government, eighteen Members of Parliament and nine Senators announced that they had joined the KPU. In his resignation statement, Achieng' Oneko, a close aide to Kenyatta and fellow inmate in detention, stated that he had come to disagree with Kenyatta's 'policies as the head of KANU and the Government on foreign affairs, land, agriculture, the federation of East Africa, foreign loans and the failure of the Government to implement policies made public in the KANU manifesto of the 1963 General Elections'.[51]

The KPU's constitution defined its objective as the fight for the economic independence of the people of Kenya. Its manifesto said:

> The KPU will pursue truly socialist policies to benefit the *wananchi*. It will share out the nation's wealth equitably among the people and extend national control over the means of production and break the foreigners' grip on the economy . . . The KPU is committed to enlargement of the public sector of the economy, believing that, in so doing, the KPU government will be in a position to bring about more rapid economic development and a more equitable distribution of the fruits of the people's labour. This means that the KPU government will have to acquire control of the means by which this can best be brought about. Thus, those industries, like the public utilities, whose existence are vital for national economic independence should be nationalised.[52]

In their trade of words with KANU in the next three years, the KPU insisted that KANU's 'African Socialism' was simply a cloak for the practice of tribalism and capitalism. Oginga Odinga said in the KPU manifesto,

> These politicians want to build a capitalist system in the image of Western capitalism but are too embarrassed or dishonest to call it that. Their interpretation of independence and African Socialism is that they should move into jobs and privileges previously held by the settlers. If Kenya started *uhuru* without an African elite class she is now rapidly acquiring one. Ministers and top civil servants compete with one another to buy more farms, acquire more directorships and own bigger cars and grander houses.

The KPU claimed that under the KANU government the peasant for the most part remained as he always was and that the workers could no longer believe that the government was working on their behalf. For their efforts Kenyatta banned their party and threw the KPU leaders into detention in 1969. In the same year, Tom Mboya was gunned down in broad daylight in a Nairobi street, paving the way for smooth and personal rule for Kenyatta.

The Politics of the Kenyatta Succession

As the struggle between the radicals and conservatives raged, all was not well in the camp of the conservatives. One concern that had troubled the conservatives was who would succeed Kenyatta. It is not very clear how old Jomo Kenyatta was when he became Kenya's first president. My guess is that he was already 74 years old, and not in very good health. With the expulsion of the radicals from the ruling party, the issue of Kenyatta's succession became even more pressing for the various factions in KANU, particularly as between the President's Kiambu advisers and the supporters of the Secretary-General – Thomas Joseph Mboya.

Since his entry into national politics in 1952, as acting Kenya African Union (KAU) treasurer, Tom Mboya had always inspired both admiration and revulsion. By 1960, when he became the first secretary-general of KANU, Mboya was already the most articulate and visible of Kenya's politicians. He represented the new Africans – cosmopolitan, urbane, articulate and self-assured. He used to appear, it seemed, every other month on British television: cool, very confident and speaking his piece in measured yet emphatic tone, acting his interrogators and adversaries off the screen.

Mboya was an important point of contact between Kenya and the developed countries of the West. David Goldsworthy sums him up as a leader of intellectual brilliance, vast practical competence, fine judgement, great drive, courage and dedication.[53] Unlike most of his opponents and rivals, who only had vague ideas about what to do with independence, Mboya, by 1960, already had a very clear conception of the shape of the independent Kenya that he wished to see.[54] 'There were always two Mboyas in tandem,' Goldsworthy has observed, 'the militant nationalist and the orthodox developmentalist.' He became the leading theoretician of Kenyan nationalism. He was the ideologue of the development strategy in the critical years of transition from the colonial to the postcolonial order. Although he toyed for a while with socialist ideas, during the period of his study at Ruskin College, he eventually rejected scientific socialism and chose a pro-Western capitalist path for Kenya. Because of all his successes, many powerful politicians regarded him with much fear and jealousy. He was accused of being an agent of the West and, with Oginga Odinga out of the party in 1966, Mboya's enemies in the party, particularly Mbiyu Koinange, Charles Njonjo and Njoroge Mungai, began to worry about him, for Mboya was now visibly the clear successor to Kenyatta in the ruling party. Kenyatta himself had begun to fear Mboya, and had expressed to the American ambassador, William Attwood, his concern over American financial support of Mboya. 'I want you to see to it that the flow of these funds is stopped,' Attwood reports Kenyatta to have told him.[55] Definitely, the old man and his henchmen were worried about the organizational acumen of the young Mboya and, knowing that they had depended on Mboya to get rid of Odinga, they were now not sure whether Mboya would not turn round and manœuvre them out of power.

As Kenyatta's health deteriorated, the men around him began to panic. On one occasion, Mboya was openly criticized by Charles Njonjo over his American ties and purported political ambitions.[56] Under the cover of constitutional reform, a committee was established in July 1967 to review the constitutional provision on the President's succession. The move was aimed at blocking Mboya's path to the presidency. At that time, the constitutional guarantee empowered the National Assembly to act as an electoral college following the President's death and to elect a new president. Mboya, who had massive support in the Assembly, seemed to have the upper hand and this was uncomfortable for his enemies. After several abortive moves, a Bill was eventually passed in Parliament in June 1968 which provided for the vice-president's ascension to the presidency for ninety days pending elections, but as acting president, whose minimum age must be 35.

Although, to undiscerning observers, the issue of succession was over, the anti-Mboya faction in KANU still felt very insecure. Rumours began to circulate that Mboya was intending to leave his Nairobi constituency to stand in Nyanza. Others said that he was making a secret deal with Oginga Odinga for a place in the KPU. Although Mboya denied these rumours, his enemies did not believe him. At the same time, Kaggia was drawing more and more of the disgruntled Kikuyu into an alliance with the Luo in the KPU. The Kikuyu reacted to the threat as they had often done in the past. From early 1969, Kenyatta and his advisers persuaded themselves that in the interest of tribal solidarity they should start oathing. Once again the ridges of Kikuyuland began to seethe with activity, as lorry-load after lorry-load made its way to Gatundu to 'have tea with the President', the euphemism for the oathing ceremonies.[57] There they swore that 'the flag of Kenya shall not leave the House of Mumbi', i.e. Kikuyuland. Often participants took the oath on a flag of Kenya spread out on the ground.[58] On 5 July 1969, Tom Mboya was shot dead outside a chemist's shop in Nairobi's busiest quarter. Although the assassin, a Kikuyu, was later charged and hanged, the Luo did not forgive Kenyatta, for they felt that the assassin was his agent. When three months later Kenyatta visited Kisumu to officially open the hospital built with Soviet aid, he was pelted with stones and in the ensuing confusion some forty-three people were shot dead in the demonstrating crowd by Kenyatta's bodyguards. The KPU was immediately banned and its leaders thrown into detention, as the KPU was blamed for the fracas.

With the murder of Mboya, the banning of the KPU and the detention of its leaders, Kenyatta and his Kiambu clique could now breathe a deep breath of relief. Kenyatta mused,

> In a life of close association with the soil of Kenya, I have found joy and humility in the seasonal rhythms both of plant and animal life, and in the crafts of careful husbandry. But I have seen drought and flood, hail and tempest. I have seen locusts come and crops destroyed by virus or fungus, and livestock stricken by rinderpest or tick-borne disease. One must learn to suffer and endure, to replant and rebuild, to move on again. And as with farming, so with politics, the practitioner must never lose faith.[59]

Kenyatta's major enemies and headaches were now eliminated, and this paved a smooth road for his personal rule. Increasingly relying on provincial administration, the police and the Kikuyu-dominated army, Kenya after 1969 became a one-man show. Trade unions were curbed and intimidated, the boss of the government-controlled workers' federation, the Central Organization of Trade Unions (COTU), was hand-picked by the President. Even the Cabinet had little significance in the affairs of state. It met infrequently and executive power lay elsewhere. 'The real institutions of the State were Kenyatta and his court, the Civil Service and the armed forces, and the machinery of "technical assistance" and aid.'[60] Kenyatta's court was based primarily at his country home of Gatundu. The inner court consisted of a small group of Kikuyu politicians from his home district of Kiambu – Mbiu Koinange, James Gichuru, Njoroge Mungai and Charles Njonjo. It was quite rare for Kenyatta to travel or to appear in the public without one or other of these four Kikuyu politicians.

Politics is like a flowing river. Sometimes the river meanders lazily upon a gentle plain, sometimes it hurtles furiously on the face of a cliff. And so it was with the political life of Jomo Kenyatta. The brief calm which he experienced after the death of Mboya and the detention of Odinga did not last for long. There were still many outstanding bills to settle. As a pan-Africanist and national patriarch, he would have preferred to live above factional rivalry and vendetta, but his ethnic and ideological commitments kept dragging him through the murky waters of politics. By 1970 he was about 80. He was growing feeble and senile and the close advisers were beginning to worry again about his successor. In 1967 they had fiddled with the constitution to bar Mboya from succession. Should Kenyatta die now, the Vice-President, Daniel arap Moi, would automatically succeed him for at least ninety days, and there was no telling what Moi would do with the presidency during those ninety days.

But there was also the persistent problem of the radicals. As it turned out, the banning of the KPU did not eliminate radicalism in Kenya. The radicals now launched their activity from KANU's back-benches in Parliament – led by the populist member, J.M. Kariuki – and from the university. Unlike the KPU Members of Parliament, who had claimed to be socialists, J.M. (as he was popularly known) always regarded himself as a man of the people. He stood for 'justice and the equality of man'. Both in Parliament and on public platforms, J.M. championed the people's right to free medical services, education and land. On economic and social justice, he said: 'A small but powerful group of greedy, self-seeking elite in the form of politicians, Civil Servants and businessmen, has steadily but surely monopolised the fruits of independence to the exclusion of the majority of the people. We do not want a Kenya of ten millionaires and ten million beggars.' On the theme of nation-building J.M. said: 'It takes more than a National Anthem, however stirring, a Coat of Arms, however distinctive, a National Flag, however appropriate, a National Flower, however beautiful, to make a Nation.' J.M. was staunchly supported by peasants, students and nationalists such as J.M. Seroney, Martin Shikuku and George Anyona. According to them, KANU had failed to meet the challenge given by the people when they rallied behind it. Its greatest failure was the inability to 'forge several tribes into one nation since independence'.[61] By early 1975, Kariuki knew that a few people around President Kenyatta were plotting to harm him. He observed:

> My concern about the owners of property has been misconstrued as rebellion against the Government, and I have been accused of being controversial in matters affecting my brothers and sisters who happen to be less endowed with the material wealth of the world. If that is what controversy means, I do not regret the accusation.[62]

Kariuki was found murdered on Ngong' Hills in March 1975, and in the period leading to 1977 a number of radical politicians and academics, including Flomena Chelagat, George Anyona, Martin Shikuku, Ngugi wa Thiong'o and J.M. Seroney, were imprisoned or detained on criminal charges. Commenting on J.M.'s death, the *Weekly Review* of 24 March 1975 had the following to say: 'Kariuki's death instills in the minds of the public the fear of dissidence, the fear to criticise, the fear to stand out and take an unconventional public stance. For Kariuki was a dissident, the most celebrated of all dissidents in Kenya since independence.'[63]

Jomo Kenyatta's rule had always been dogged by the twin problems of his succession and radical dissidence. In the past, his regime had tackled the problems by imprisoning or detaining defiant opponents and challengers. But Vice-President Daniel arap Moi was a very different sort of person. He was loyal, humble, decent and a popular appointee of Jomo Kenyatta. His detention, dismissal or assassination would severely alienate domestic and international opinion. How, then, do you exclude him from succeeding the ailing Kenyatta?

Kenyatta's close advisers decided to adopt an earlier tactic which they had used to exclude Mboya from succession. Early in 1970, rumours were rife that a group of Kiambu politicians were already making a bid to change the constitution to allow for the position of an executive prime minister instead of an executive president. According to the stories, Kenyatta had already agreed to remain a nominal head of state. Nothing was said of what would become of the position of the vice-president, but the man most spoken of as likely to be named premier was Dr Njoroge Mungai, at that time Minister of Internal Security and Defence. As these rumours became commonplace, and embarrassing, the government was forced to clear the air. On 1 May 1970, the Attorney-General, Charles Njonjo, issued a statement and categorically denied that the constitution was about to be amended. He said: 'This rumour must have been started by some politicians who want a constitution to suit their ambitions. But the present constitution stands as far as I know.'[64]

The Attorney-General's assurance notwithstanding, the rumours persisted until 1976, when those bidding to change the constitution came out in the open. They included Njoroge Mungai, Kihika Kimani, James Gichuru, Paul Ngei, Jackson Angaine and Njenga Karume. Most of these people were members of the Gikuyu, Embu and Meru Association (GEMA) – a purported 'welfare association', which was founded in 1971 to consolidate the economic, social and cultural fortunes of its members. Their first public meeting was held at Nakuru on 26 September 1976, at which they described the existing constitutional arrangement as 'all wrong'. They opposed the provision which allowed the vice-president to succeed the president automatically, in the event of the reigning president retiring or becoming physically or mentally incapacitated or in the case of his death. Paul Ngei said: 'During the three months that allow the Vice-President to become President a lot of things can happen. If you give me that period I can really teach you a lesson and I can assure you it would not be a pleasant one.'[65]

On 3 October 1976, at a fund-raising meeting held at Gitithia Presbytarian Church of East Africa (PCEA) near Limuru, the Change-the-Constitution group again exhorted Kenyans to amend the constitution, in order to make it impossible for anyone 'to lead them by the nose'. Kihika Kimani said: 'Automatic ascension by the Vice-President to the presidency might allow an unscrupulous person every opportunity during his 90-day tenure of office to eliminate his political rivals. He could pick on a select few who will support his candidacy for President.'

Again, most Kenyans were not amused by these orchestrated campaigns to exclude Moi from the presidency. They questioned who were behind the Change-the-Constitution group. On 4 October 1976, the outspoken Member of Parliament for Mombasa Central, Shariff Nassir, became the first leader to publicly condemn those who were bent on amending the constitution. He called them 'day-dreaming, greedy and jealous people'. Stanley Oloitiptip, another opponent of the Change-the-Constitution group, said,'We reject *in toto* the suggestion paraded by some that our constitution is undemocratic and the precipitate panic and urgency for the suggested constitutional amendment by power-hungry, self-seeking and unpatriotic few. We strongly feel that the suggestion itself is unethical, immoral and borders on criminality and is very unAfrican.' Oloitiptip proceeded to collect ninety-eight signatures of members of parliament who were opposed to the Change-the-Constitution group. Two of Kenya's daily newspapers, the *Standard* and the *Daily Nation*, also jumped into the affray, with diametrically opposed views. Again, as was the case in 1970, the government was forced to intervene in this acrimonious hullabaloo, which threatened to break into a civil war. On 6 October, after a Cabinet meeting in Nakuru, the Attorney-General issued the following warning:

> In view of the recent sudden wave of statements at public rallies about the alleged need for amendment of our constitution, I would like to bring to the attention of those few who are being used to advocate the amendment, that it is a criminal offence for any person to compass, imagine, devise or intend the death or deposition of the president. Furthermore it is also an offence to express, utter or declare such compassings, imaginations, devices or intentions by publishing them in print or writing. The mandatory sentence for any such offence by a citizen is death, and any person who aids in any such offence by being an accessory after the fact of it is liable to imprisonment for life. Anyone who raises such matters in public meetings or who publishes such matters, does so at his own peril.[66]

This Cabinet statement ended the question as to whether there was going to be any amendment to the constitutional provision dealing with presidential succession. It also brought to an end the public controversy which the issue had generated, but it raised quite a number of questions in the minds of political observers. For example, had the Change-the-Constitution group got clearance from Kenyatta before they took to the warpath? Or had Kenyatta suddenly realized that the controversy was fraught with dangerous divisive trends and therefore changed his mind?

Conclusion

Kenya's social and economic performance under President Jomo Kenyatta is discussed in the first part of this chapter and in Chapter Five. It is, however, fitting – by way of conclusion – to highlight the major political features of Kenyatta's regime. First, we wish to observe that in the period between 1963 and 1978 the ruling national bourgeoisie under Kenyatta effected major constitutional changes that helped them to consolidate political power and to impose their political and economic dominance on the state. In the final analysis, these constitutional changes aimed at strengthening Kenyatta's personal rule, and in the process the ruling party, KANU, was neglected – and by extension participation by the *wananchi* in the political process. Whereas Kenya had emerged into *uhuru* with a very lively multiparty system, a vociferous parliament and an independent press, by 1970 freedom of speech was virtually a thing of the past and government critics were in detention. Second, we also wish to observe that, due to the Western and capitalist orientation of Kenyatta and his regime, Kenya's colonial heritage – laws, parliament, civil service, police, army, economy, education and provincial administration – remained largely unchanged and unsympathetic to and remote from popular wishes. This problem was aggravated by Kenya's heavy reliance on Western capitalist countries for skilled manpower, development and technical grants and trade. The highly personal style of government which Kenyatta's unique position created could be justified as giving confidence and stability to the new state, 'but to some it began to look as though the old colonial power had simply transformed itself into one where Kenyatta was a new-style Governor and the Kikuyu had replaced the Europeans as the top dogs'. There was a constant problem of unemployment, many of those out of work being school-leavers and former members of the Mau Mau forces. 'Old KCA [Kikuyu Central Association] leaders looked enviously at the smart cars, and European secretaries enjoyed by younger men, the fruits, their elders felt, of their sacrifices.'[67] There is, therefore, a lot of truth in Oginga Odinga's view that Kenya under Jomo Kenyatta was 'not yet *uhuru*'.

Appendix: Constitutional Amendments Under Kenyatta

1. The First Amendment of October 1964 abolished the office of the Prime Minister, who now became a strong executive President who was also the head of government, state and ruling party.
2. The Second Amendment abolished the office of the Regional President and the powers of the regions. The former regions now became provinces headed by provincial commissioners who were appointed directly by the President.
3. The Third Amendment of 1965 lowered the voting majority required to change the constitution from the original 90 per cent in the Senate and 75 per cent in the Lower House, to 65 per cent in both Houses.
4. The Fourth Amendment of 1966 stipulated that a member who failed to attend eight consecutive sittings of the National Assembly without the valid permission of the Speaker, or who was serving a prison sentence exceeding six months, would lose his parliamentary seat. The President could, however, use his discretion to pardon any such offender.
5. The Fifth Amendment of April 1966 laid down that any Member of Parliament who resigned from the party which had supported him at his election, but which had not been subsequently dissolved, must also resign his (or her) seat and fight a by-election.
6. The Sixth Amendment of 1966 empowered the President to declare a state of emergency in the country for twenty-eight days at a time, through a simple parliamentary majority, in order to handle any emergency that might arise in the country. Such powers could, however, be vetoed by a normal parliamentary majority of 65 per cent.
7. The Seventh Amendment of December 1966 abolished the Upper House (or Senate) to enable the government to secure the one-chamber legislature which it believed was essential for a strong central government.
8. The Eighth Amendment back-dated the Fifth Amendment, although those who joined KADU were not requested to resign to fight a by-election.
9. The Ninth Amendment stipulated a number of rules concerning presidential succession and election. First, any presidential candidate must be at least 35 years old. Second, a presidential candidate must be supported by a registered political party and at least 1,000 registered voters. Third, should the office of the president fall vacant for any reason, his vice-president would assume presidential powers for a period of ninety days, during which elections must be held to elect a new president.
10. The Tenth Amendment stated that any registered political party

that wished to participate in parliamentary elections must adopt a presidential candidate.

11. The Eleventh Amendment of 1975 declared the Kiswahili language a parliamentary language. A member could now use either Kiswahili or English in parliamentary deliberations.

12. The Twelfth Amendment of 1975 empowered the president to pardon someone guilty of election offences.

13. The Thirteenth Amendment of 1977 established the Kenya Court of Appeal, following the collapse of the East African Community, which had hitherto run the East African Court of Appeal.

Notes

1. W.R. Ochieng' (ed), *A Modern History of Kenya* (London, Evans Brothers, 1989), p. 213.
2. B.A. Ogot (ed.), *Zamani: A Survey of East African History* (Nairobi, Longman, 1974), p. 371.
3. E.S. Atieno-Odhiambo and P. Wanyande, *History and Government of Kenya* (Nairobi, Longman, 1989) p. 116.
4. Ibid.
5. Republic of Kenya, 'Sessional Paper No. 10: African Socialism and Its Application to Planning in Kenya' (1965), p. 1.
6. Ibid.
7. See Ochieng', *A Modern History*, p. 158.
8. J. Heyer, J.K. Maitha and W.M. Senga, *Agricultural Development in Kenya: An Economic Assessment* (Nairobi, Kenya Literature Bureau, 1976), p. 37. See also J.B. Ojiambo, 'Communication of Agricultural Information Between Research Scientists Extension Personnel and Farmers in Kenya', PhD thesis submitted to the University of Pittsburgh, 1989, pp. 19–25.
9. Heyer *et al.*, *Agricultural Development*, p. 37.
10. N. Swainson, 'The Rise of a National Bourgeoisie in Kenya', *Review of African Political Economy*, 8, January 1977, p. 39.
11. Ibid., p. 41.
12. N. Swainson, *The Development of Corporate Capitalism in Kenya: 1918–1977* (London, Heinemann, 1980), James Currey 1988, p. 189.
13. Ibid.
14. A. Hazlewood, *The Economy of Kenya: The Kenyatta Era* (London, Oxford University Press, 1977), pp. 164–165.
15. Colin Leys, *Underdevelopment in Kenya: The Political Economy of Neo-Colonialism 1964–1971* (London, Heinemann, 1975), p. 53.
16. International Labour Organization, *Employment, Incomes and Equality: A Strategy for Increasing Productive Employment in Kenya* (Geneva, ILO Office, 1972), p. 2.
17. J.K. Maitha, quoted in Heyer *et al.*, *Agricultural Development*, pp. 64–65.
18. Hazlewood, *Economy of Kenya*, p. 175.
19. Ochieng', *A Modern History*, pp. 212–214.
20. W.R. Ochieng', *A History of Kenya* (London, Macmillan, 1985), p. 144.
21. G. Bennet, *Kenya: A Political History: The Colonial Period* (London, Oxford University Press, 1963), p. 161.
22. T. Mboya, quoted in Ochieng', *History of Kenya*, pp. 147–148.
23. O. Odinga, *Not Yet Uhuru* (London, Heinemann, 1967), p. 253.
24. Ibid., pp. 253–254.

25. J. Murray-Brown, *Kenyatta* (London, George Allen & Unwin, 1972), p. 312.
26. Ibid., pp. 312–313.
27. T. Mboya, *The Challenge of Nationhood* (London, André Deutsch, 1970), p. 5.
28. Murray-Brown, *Kenyatta*, p. 313.
29. Reasons given to justify the creation of strong presidencies in Africa vary. Ali Mazrui has argued that there was a tendency in African nationalism to hero-worship freedom fighters and national patriarchs. Africans were also alleged to prefer to look at their presidents as monarchs. See Ali Mazrui, 'The Monarchical Tendency in African Political Culture', *British Journal of Sociology*, 18 (3) (1967); see also A. Mazrui, *Violence and Thought* (New York, 1969), pp. 206–230.
30. C. Gerzel, 'Kenya's Constitutional Changes', *East Africa Journal*, December (1966), p. 19.
31. Ibid., p. 30.
32. Ibid., p. 20.
33. P. Anyang' Nyong'o, 'State and Society in Kenya', *African Affairs*, 88 (351) (April 1989), p. 232.
34. B. Kaggia, quoted in Odinga, *Not Yet Uhuru*, p. 266.
35. Ibid., p. 266.
36. Ibid., pp. 266–267.
37. J. Kenyatta, *Suffering Without Bitterness* (Nairobi, East African Publishing House, 1968), p. 161.
38. Mboya, *Challenge of Nationhood*, p. 80.
39. B. Kaggia, quoted in Ochieng', *History of Kenya*, p. 148.
40. Ibid.
41. D. Ghai, 'African Socialism for Kenyans', *East Africa Journal*, June (1965), p. 15.
42. Ibid., p. 18.
43. B.H. Obama, 'Problems Facing Our Socialism', *East Africa Journal*, July (1965).
44. Mboya, *Challenge of Nationhood*, pp. 73–104.
45. T. Mboya, 'Kenya Intellectuals and the KANU Government', *East Africa Journal*, March (1967), p. 13.
46. J. Kenyatta, 'Kenya's Mixed Economy', *East Africa Journal*, November (1964), p. 18.
47. Murray-Brown, *Kenyatta*, p. 313.
48. Kenyatta, *Suffering*, pp. 340–348.
49. *East Africa Standard*, 15 April 1966.
50. Ibid.
51. *East Africa Standard*, 26 April 1966.
52. *The Manifesto of the Kenya People's Union* (Nairobi, Kenya People's Union, 1966), pp. 3–5.
53. D. Goldsworthy, *Tom Mboya: The Man Kenya Wanted to Forget* (London, Heinemann Educational Books, 1982).
54. His ideas are contained in his book, *Freedom and After* (London, André Deutsch, 1963).
55. W. Attwood, *The Reds and the Blacks* (New York, Harper & Row, 1967), p. 247.
56. G. Ndirangu, 'Tom Mboya', *Society*, 8 (July/August 1989), p. 5.
57. Murray-Brown, *Kenyatta*, p. 317.
58. Ibid.
59. Kenyatta, *Suffering*, p. vi.
60. Leys, *Underdevelopment*, p. 246.
61. Ochieng', *History of Kenya*, p. 154.
62. Ibid.
63. Ibid.
64. J. Karimi and P. Ochieng', *The Kenyatta Succession* (Nairobi, Transafrica, 1980), p. 21.
65. Ibid.
66. *Weekly Review*, 18 October 1976, p. 13.
67. Murray-Brown, *Kenyatta*, p. 316.

Five

Social & Cultural Changes

ROBERT M. MAXON

The Kenyatta era witnessed several examples of significant social change. Racial segregation would largely come to an end, the government undertook a massive expansion of educational and health facilities, and Africanization, in both the public and private sectors, had an increasing impact on Kenya's social structure. While these might seem dramatic and even revolutionary breaks with the colonial past, the main thread that runs through Kenya's social history during this period is, as in the political and economic spheres, the strong continuity that linked the initial years of independence firmly to the era that preceded it.

Kenyan Society and *Uhuru*

On the eve of independence, Kenya can be characterized as a plural society. That is, the population was made up of people representing different racial groups and diverse cultures. In addition to the African majority, there were small, but well-entrenched, European, Asian and Arab communities. In numerical terms, these immigrant groups constituted a small proportion of the total population. Europeans, Asians and Arabs totalled 3 per cent of the Kenya population, 2 per cent in 1969 and 1 per cent in 1979. Despite their small numbers and declining political influences, the European and Asian communities, in particular, wielded immense economic muscle in the commercial and industrial spheres at the time of *uhuru*, and they held front-rank positions in most professions and in the colonial state.

To both academic observers and the general public, moreover, Kenya in 1963 had the appearance of a society stratified by race. Social status was still largely determined by skin colour and racial group identification. Europeans stood at the apex of this structure as a privileged caste.

110

Below the whites in the colonial social hierarchy came the Asians and the Arabs. The African majority occupied the bottom rung of the social ladder. As in most such caste societies, segregation by race was a part of the Kenyan social system. The result of legal mandates and colonial social practice, schools, hospitals, clubs and various restaurants and hotels reserved admittance to selected, racially determined clientele. Urban housing patterns also reflected a strong segregationist pattern.

The racially stratified social structure was particularly evident in the areas of occupation, income and education. Non-Africans were prominent in the professions, in managerial positions and in the upper echelons of the civil service. In contrast, Africans constituted an extremely small percentage of professional and managerial groups. In 1964, for example, Africans made up only 3 per cent of the legal profession and 5 per cent of physicians and surgeons.[1] Income inequalities followed a similar pattern. Europeans earned far higher incomes, on average, than did the Asians, and both groups enjoyed significantly higher per capita incomes than did Africans.[2]

Educational inequality formed an obvious and important indicator of the racial caste structure. Colonial education in Kenya was not only characterized by segregated schools. It was, as in other parts of the world where racial segregation was practised, inherently unequal. African children had fewer educational opportunities than those of Europeans and Asians. The colonial state spent much more per pupil on the latter students than on Africans. This meant that, on the whole, the educational facilities (buildings, laboratories, books) provided for European and Asian children were far superior to those available to Africans.

Europeans had been the 'ruling class', dominating the colonial administration, and their status as a privileged caste reflected this.[3] Europeans occupied virtually all the senior posts in the civil service, and they were similarly dominant in industry and the professions. Historically, settler farmers had played a considerable role in the colony's agricultural economy. The overwhelming proportion of the European population was British in origin.[4] Despite this uniformity of nationality, Kenya Europeans were divided by class. Leaving aside the traditional dichotomy between settlers and officials, it is still possible to identify several strata among Europeans: the civil servant cadre, an agricultural upper class, an urban merchant class, a professional class (lawyers, doctors, dentists), a foreman and skilled wage-earner group, a multinational corporate class and missionaries.[5] With the exception of the farmers and the missionaries, the European population was concentrated in Nairobi and other urban centres.

Kenya's·Asian community was also largely concentrated in urban areas. However, Asians were far more divided in terms of national origin, language, religion and economic class. So much was this the case that it is undoubtedly illusory to refer to Asians as a distinct caste at all.

Most Asians prior to independence looked inward towards their families and sub-communities rather than outward as members of a single, united Asian community.[6] The most significant divisions amongst Asians were those based on religion and caste. The main religious differences in 1963 were Hindu, Muslim, Sikh and Christian. Within these categories, however, there existed numerous divisions or sub-communities (for example, Sunni and Shia Muslim groups, Patidars and Jains among Hindus).[7] Although Asians predominated in retail and wholesale trade at the time of independence, they also held numerous mid-level positions in the civil service, occupied posts as technicians and a number held professional positions (doctor, lawyer, teacher). In terms of income, the Asian community ranged from relatively poor to very wealthy, but the majority had what would be considered a moderate income.[8]

The Arab community was numerically smaller than either the Europeans or Asians. The great majority lived in Mombasa and other coastal towns. Though primarily engaged in agriculture and commerce, Arabs were also divided along class lines.

The European and Asian population of Kenya would be more profoundly affected by the changes that followed *uhuru* than the Arab community. One of the most important results of the political and economic changes was the reduction in the size of the European and Asian communities. Table 5.1 illustrates this population loss. It was caused, more than anything else, by the emigration of sizeable numbers of Asians and Europeans. Such emigrants felt unable to remain in a Kenya ruled by the African majority and one in which Africanization policies seemed to promise a loss of employment and/or business opportunities and of economic status. Such feelings were particularly manifested in the way the immigrant communities responded to the issue of Kenya citizenship.

With the advent of independence, the non-African communities were presented with a choice as to whether or not to adopt Kenya citizenship. Following the achievement of internal self-government on 1 June 1963, government leaders made no attempt to disguise their rejection of dual citizenship. They, and the African population at large, demanded total identification of the non-Africans with the newly independent state. The independence constitution allowed non-Africans a two-year period after December 1963 within which they could register as citizens. Yet, during the initial year of independence, only 3,911 did so.[9] The number of applications increased in 1965, but it is clear from the 1969 and 1979 censuses that the vast majority of Europeans and a considerable portion of the Asian population at independence left Kenya over the next fifteen years. For the latter, the overwhelming majority who did not become Kenya citizens took British passports. Table 5.2 indicates the number of European and Asian citizens residing in Kenya in 1969 and 1979. In contrast, the great majority of Arabs remained as Kenya citizens.

The two largest groups of Europeans to depart during the Kenyatta

Table 5.1   Kenya's Arab, Asian and European Populations, 1962–79

	1962	1969	1979	% Decline
Arab	34,048	27,886	39,146	+ 14.9
Asian	176,613	139,037	78,600	55.5
European	55,759	40,593	39,901	28.4

Source: *Statistical Abstract 1981.*

Table 5.2   Asian and European Citizens, 1969 and 1979

	1969	% of total Asian/ European population	1979	%
Asian	60,994	44	32,554	41
European	3,889	10	4,445	11

Sources: *Population Census 1969* and *Population Census 1979.*

era were the settler farmers and civil servants. The independent state adopted policies, with considerable British assistance, to facilitate the departure of both. For the latter, Africanization of the civil service brought an end to the need for their services. This process proceeded fairly rapidly; by mid-1967, the administrative cadre of the civil service was 91 per cent Africanized.[10] The buying-out of European farmers moved somewhat more slowly. By January 1971 there were still about 450 mixed farmers in Kenya.[11] By the end of 1978, virtually all the non-citizen European mixed farmers had sold out; however, a substantial number of sisal and coffee estates in the country remained in the hands of European owners.

While a substantial number thus left Kenya between 1962 and 1979, other factors operated to mitigate the loss in numbers of whites. As Table 5.1 illustrates, Kenya's European population declined very little between 1969 and 1979, and the percentage decline experienced in the 1962–79 period was much lower than that of the Asian population. As a result of government initiatives to spur economic development and foreign investment and the emergence of Nairobi as an important regional centre, greater numbers of European technical assistance personnel, embassy and United Nations staff and employees of multinational firms took up residence, usually on short-term contracts, in the country than had done so before. Thus the European population of Kenya stabilized at about 40,000 for most of the Kenyatta era, but it was quite different in character from prior to *uhuru*. The European population of 1979 was much heterogeneous than before and would lack the unity of the colonial era.

The Asian exodus after independence was the result of many of the same feelings that motivated that of the Europeans. Of particular importance, nevertheless, was the uncertainty felt by many Asian businessmen on the issue of Africanization of commerce. The latter was a government priority at *uhuru*, and in the first years of independence there was increasing public pressure to speed up the process of assisting African entrepreneurs to break the virtual Asian monopoly on trade in both the urban and rural trading centres.[12] Initial government programmes sought to extend credit to African traders and assist them in other ways, such as preferential treatment in the distribution of basic commodities. In late 1967, however, the government began a much more systematic approach to Africanizing retail and wholesale trade. The passage of the Immigration Act of 1967 gave the government greater means to control the non-citizen's working and carrying on business in Kenya. The Trade Licensing Act of the same year required the relicensing of all traders and gave the government the power to exclude non-citizen traders from certain areas and goods when it came into effect at the end of 1968.[13]

The immediate impact of these measures and the likelihood of the British government instituting much more stringent restrictions on Asian entry into that country was to spur a considerable upsurge in Asian immigration to Britain in late 1967 and early 1968. The rush to Britain subsided after a brief flurry. The British passports would be accepted by Britain, but it was stipulated that the stream of immigration should be spread over several years. Thus, for the remainder of the period under review, Asian immigration continued at a steady pace. There still remained a larger portion of non-citizen Asians than citizens in 1978, however.

For Kenya's Arabs, *uhuru* produced a rather different reaction. Though long regarded as a separate community on the coast, the majority of Arabs opted for Kenya citizenship after 1963 and fully identified with the ideals and aspirations of the new nation. According to Professor A.I. Salim, the Zanzibar revolution of January 1964

> reinforced the need and the resolve to integrate. The pronouncements of Kenyatta and other politicians that coastal Arabs were Africans were reassurances marked by action. As one of the smaller corporate bodies in Kenya, they have a fairly creditable position in the national life and government – a position they never held in the colonial days, during the segregation of races into unequal compartments.[14]

Writing in 1973, Professor Salim observed that the prevailing mood amongst Kenya Arabs was 'one of optimism and enthusiasm for participation in nation-building'. They were not nearly as apprehensive or uncertain about the future as Asians or Europeans.[15] In contrast to the latter, the Arab population increased between 1962 and 1979.

Another change that affected the non-African and African communities alike was the scrapping of segregation at independence. No longer would schools, hospitals or residential areas be reserved exclusively for whites or Asians. Segregationist regulations relating to public facilities were also dropped, and the government pressured formerly exclusive clubs to revise their membership requirements to allow affiliation from all racial groups. Along with these measures, the government sought also a change in non-African attitudes towards the majority of the population. President Kenyatta, on many occasions, attacked the colonial idea of African inferiority and warned non-Africans against *ubwana* or the boss mentality.[16] Moreover, Kenyatta's government did not shrink from taking punitive measures, such as deportation of those disrespectful to Africans, to promote respect and fair treatment of the majority by non-Africans. There is no doubt that these actions produced what Donald Rothchild has termed an 'expanding humanism'. Overt manifestations of superiority or *ubwana* were greatly reduced as a result.[17]

The scrapping of segregation and attacks on *ubwana* did presage a more egalitarian social structure, but Kenya's new leaders were not prepared to take egalitarianism to revolutionary lengths. In independent Kenya, stratification by race would go, but in its place would emerge stratification by wealth. Such stratification existed in all Kenyan communities before independence; it was the natural outcome of colonial capitalism. As such, it forms an important example of social continuity with the pre-independence period. After *uhuru*, economic status, rather than racial, became the most significant factor in social stratification. Africans, to cite one example, could live in any part of Nairobi that they wished as long as they had sufficient funds to buy or rent housing there.

The government's acceptance and, indeed, encouragement of this mirrored its decision to embrace capitalism and capitalist development models in the economic sphere. Kenya's leaders clearly showed their acceptance of a social structure marked by divisions according to economic status and wealth in their educational policies. Schools reserved exclusively for Europeans and Asians were opened to all races in 1964, but the government continued to operate most of those it controlled as high-fee schools. These charged higher fees than the schools Africans attended. For example, the fees at the Nairobi School (then Prince of Wales) were £375 per year in 1964 and at Lenana School (then Duke of York) £330, while those at Alliance High School were £60.[18] This situation meant that only a few African families could afford to pay the fees.

Gradually the numbers of Africans who could afford to attend the high-fee schools increased; the government helped this along by providing bursaries to needy students and its 1967 edict that all formerly European schools must increase enrolment of African students. By 1978, the vast majority of the pupils in such institutions as Nairobi and Lenana schools were African. However, these pupils were, almost without exception, drawn from the emerging African upper middle class, particularly from what may be termed the bureaucratic bourgeoisie. For those families that could afford it, these schools provided better facilities and superior amenities (e.g. swimming-pools) than the bulk of the nation's educational institutions. They thus furnish a clear example of the government's acceptance of inequalities based on wealth in the social sphere.

Turning specifically to the largest of Kenya's population groups at *uhuru*, the Africans, several characteristics stand out. Africans made up 97 per cent of Kenya's population in 1963. Far more lived in the rural areas than in cities and towns. The 1962 census showed that only about 7 per cent of the country's population lived in urban areas. Most Africans thus made their living from agriculture. The process of peasantization, at work throughout the colonial period, had produced large numbers of peasant households. The majority of these households would hold title to their land as the independent state continued the colonial policy of land consolidation and registration of individual title-deeds. Peasant households produced food for their own subsistence, and increasing numbers had begun to raise cash crops and to produce milk for sale. The majority of such peasant households relied on family labour.

The process of peasantization had accelerated in the 1950s and was greatly speeded up after independence. Cultivation of cash crops, particularly tea, coffee, pyrethrum and sugar-cane, increased dramatically, as did the sale of such crops by peasant households as the independent government sought to spur economic development in the largely underdeveloped reserves that had been created by colonial rule. Dairy output, aided by the widespread adoption of grade cattle by peasants, rose dramatically also. Within a decade of independence, the marketed output of Kenya's small-farm or peasant sector had come to equal that of the large farms.

This had a profound impact on rural social structure during the Kenyatta era. It speeded up the process of differentiation by wealth that had been at work since before the First World War.[19] Although the rural areas inhabited by Africans would continue to be characterized by low per capita incomes, by the end of the 1970s, a distinctive rural class structure had clearly taken shape in those districts most involved in commodity production for the market.[20]

At the lowest rung of the rural class structure were those households that were landless in that they had no land or insufficient land on which to produce crops for the family's subsistence. Most could, with difficulty, educate children only up to primary-school level. Male members of the household, in particular, were, as a result, forced to seek wage employment in the rural or urban areas. Colonial policies had created landlessness, but, despite land reforms, peasant landlessness continued after independence, and in some areas the process accelerated after 1963 as peasant holdings became ever smaller and households were forced into straddling between wage employment and agriculture and to sell land to make ends meet.[21]

Above the landless households were those that may be classified as poor peasants. These had retained land sufficient to provide for subsistence and reproduction, but were only marginally involved in the production of cash crops. More often than not, some family members were employed for wages as a necessary means of supplementing family income. Levels of education attained by the children of these households were normally minimal.

One of the most significant and rapidly expanding strata after independence may be termed the middle peasantry. These households owned sufficient land to provide for both subsistence and cash crops. Taking advantage of the spread of the latter, they were able to obtain a regular income from the sale of coffee, tea, sugar-cane or milk, together with food crops; with this income, they carried out improvements to their farms. They increased consumption of consumer goods and provided for the education of children to high-school level and beyond.

The small, but highly influential, upper strata in the rural class structure consisted of what may be termed the rich peasants or rural petty bourgeoisie. This was the rural group that, on the whole, benefited most from the economic and political changes brought by *uhuru*.[22] These households were, at independence, involved in a process usually termed straddling; that is, they were often involved in commercial agriculture while at the same time engaged in commerce as traders or transport owners, and were employed as teachers or local civil servants. Many of those employed as chiefs fell into this category. They were thus able to use income derived from the latter sources to invest in an expansion of agricultural activities through buying additional land and fertilizers and other inputs.

Taking full advantage of the economic opportunities offered by *uhuru*, the rural petty bourgeoisie continued the process of straddling after independence, increasing agricultural production, venturing into more lucrative trading activities and obtaining better jobs in the public and private sector for themselves and their families. They were also able to see a large proportion of their children obtain high-school and post-secondary education. In addition, the rural petty bourgeoisie would play an active and important role in local and national politics after independence.

This brief summary of rural stratification after independence clearly suggests an ongoing social process of differentiation. By 1978, this was having a very crucial impact in many parts of rural Kenya. While a small number of peasant households were materially bettering their economic and social status, a large number, according to most students of rural Kenya at the time, were facing a bleak future because of growing landlessness and rural poverty.[23] As noted earlier, this was not a process begun at independence, but rather represents a continuity from the colonial period. It was the product of colonial land policies, the rural development strategy adopted during the last phase of colonial rule and intensively implemented during the Kenyatta era.

This picture of a stratified rural Kenya in the 1970s needs to be qualified to some degree, however. Research carried out by Michael Cowen in parts of Central Province in the 1970s suggests a more complex rural situation. Cowen found that production for international markets tended to produce an equalization of incomes among the middle peasantry in particular. Such a phenomenon, which, Cowen argued, was supported by international capital, mitigated against pauperization in the rural areas as, over time, the trend towards equalization would act as a counter to differentiation.[24]

Turning to the urban areas, the petty bourgeoisie there would also emerge as a growing force after independence. That stratum included both those who had occupied this position before *uhuru* and those who had previously been employed but who struck off to self-employment on their own afterwards. It included traders, of course, but many were transporters, launderers, hotel and bar owners and building contractors. Particularly significant were landlords, who after independence were able to expand their urban property ownership as a means, similar to other parts of Africa, of capital accumulation.[25]

The largest socio-economic category amongst the urban African population at the time of independence was that of the worker/proletarian. As a result of the process of proletarianization during the colonial era, a working class had come into being. By the time of *uhuru*, migrant labour was no longer the predominant form among Kenya workers. Since the mid-1950s, government policy, increasing industrialization and the growing involvement of foreign firms in the Kenyan economy had combined to bring about a stabilization of the work-force. By the 1960s, the great majority of workers in the core sections of the economy spent the whole of their working lives in wage employment.[26] Thus the trend towards a more stable, skilled and better-paid labour force, begun as a response to the changing political and economic climate in the decade prior to *uhuru*, continued to characterize formal-sector employment after independence.

Wage employment was concentrated in the urban areas, especially in Nairobi.[27] After 1963, employment increases in Nairobi almost doubled that of all the other major towns. Employment in the capital and in other towns and cities grew fastest in the first decade after independence (an annual rate of 3.8 per cent).[28] The public sector grew faster than the private in the 1960s and 1970s. In 1967, the public-sector wage employment made up 35.5 per cent of the total. By 1978, this rose to 42.8 per cent.[29] Public-sector employment was concentrated in service industries while employment in the private sector was concentrated in agriculture and manufacturing.

The urban working class was also overwhelmingly male at independence, and this changed little during the succeeding years. For those employed by industry in 1977, for example, 17 per cent were women.[30] By 1979, only 4.5 per cent of the total female work-force was engaged in formal wage labour. Several reasons for this can be identified:

> Women in Kenya, as elsewhere in Africa, were heavily involved in agricultural production in addition to their household roles, and they also suffered from the burden of unregulated fertility. At the same time their access to opportunity structures of education and training were more limited than those of men.[31]

The majority of males that dominated the urban work-force had ties in the rural areas. They held land there or could expect to inherit title to land from their fathers. For many, nevertheless, this land, where the worker's wife often lived, was insufficient to provide the kind of means of subsistence that wage labour could. This ownership of land in the rural areas, which provided the urban worker with a foothold there as well as in the city, has sometimes been described as a semi-proletarian condition. That is to say, the worker is not entirely dependent on wages. Studies carried out in the 1970s, however, indicated that urban modern-sector jobs were subsidizing the rural areas through provision of money for taxes, school fees and consumption, rather than vice versa.[32]

Those holding modern-sector jobs hardly constituted the bulk of the urban work-force after independence. A large portion of the latter was made up of what Richard Sandbrook has termed 'the labouring poor'. Not a single class, the labouring poor comprised 'a congeries of strata whose only common trait is a hard and precarious living outside capitalist production'.[33] Included in this grouping were 'petty producers' and artisans, such as tailors or shoemakers. The growth of the tourist industry in post-independence Kenya led to a significant growth in the number of such artisans involved in the making of artefacts for sale to tourists. The category of labouring poor also included apprentices to artisans, as well as street hawkers, kiosk holders and casual labourers.[34]

It is also important to note that in both the urban and the rural areas there existed a sizeable group of unemployed. These were individuals for whom the employment opportunities available after *uhuru* did not expand fast enough. While the reasons for the continued existence of a large number of unemployed was primarily the result of economic factors, the phenomenon had important social implications. Both the government and international organizations have sought means to reduce the level of unemployment.[35] Not all the unemployed came from the same background or had the same interests. In fact, the urban unemployed ranged from what might be termed a lumpenproletariat of petty thieves to the educated unemployed. The latter grouping, by the middle of the

1970s, included a sizeable number of secondary-school leavers who spent substantial periods, usually supported by kin, in the urban areas looking for suitable employment.

The other identifiable African social group at independence was also by far the smallest in number: the bourgeoisie. Most, in 1963, were concentrated in the professions, the civil service and commerce. Those bourgeoisie, overwhelmingly male, who worked as lawyers, doctors or teachers as well as those in the middle levels of the civil service were particularly distinguished by the amount of Western education they had obtained, the majority outside Kenya, which was relatively much greater than for the rest of the African population. In most cases, they were the first generation of Africans to obtain higher education. Sometimes referred to as an educated élite, this group was greatly dissatisfied, on the whole, with the second-class status they were forced to endure in the professions and civil service in comparison with Europeans and Asians having the same qualifications. The African commercial bourgeoisie, though small in numbers, was likewise strongly aggrieved at the obstacles, chiefly in the form of colonial regulations, lack of credit and Asian competition, that lay in the way of African traders expanding their economic activities into urban property ownership, wholesale trade, large-scale transport ownership and manufacturing. It is thus not surprising that the bourgeoisie gave strong support to the nationalist movement and indeed provided, along with the rural petty bourgeoisie, most of its leaders.

Not surprisingly, this class played a prominent role and greatly expanded its economic, political and social influence after independence had placed political power in their hands. Africanization programmes rapidly brought the African middle class into control of the civil service, and the expansion of higher education increased the numbers of the educated élite. *Uhuru* also brought great opportunities for economic enhancement to the bourgeoisie. With government assistance, it was possible, for example, to buy large farms and to obtain exclusive wholesale licences and extensive credit. African businessmen would, from the middle of the 1960s, receive preference in trade and transport licensing, including the opportunity to operate shops in the main business districts of the largest cities. This resulted in many petty bourgeoisie being able to significantly enhance their class position through the accumulation of greater resources. Thus the Kenyatta era witnessed a significant expansion of the African middle class.[36]

One facet of this process should particularly be noted. This was the emergence of a bureaucratic bourgeoisie. The expansion of the public service formed the backdrop for this process; as it went forward, many high-ranking civil servants became involved in business ventures, manufacturing and property ownership.[37] This blending of government and commerce was given formal backing by the 1971 Ndegwa

Commission report. By the end of the Kenyatta presidency, it was not uncommon to find high-ranking civil servants, as well as government ministers, owning commercial and industrial enterprises, serving on company boards of directors and owning urban and rural property. Without doubt, the bureaucratic bourgeoisie, running the government and playing an influential economic role, emerged as one of the most influential fractions of the African middle class during the first decade and a half after independence. In 1975, Leys viewed this group as having a 'clear consciousness of mission: the image of a bureaucratic *corps d'élite* controlling, and dramatically expanding the modern sector in partnership with western capital'.[38]

The use of the state apparatus to promote class interests is hardly unique in a capitalist system, and it was by no means a revolutionary departure in independent Kenya. During the colonial era, chiefs and other members of the petty bourgeoisie were able to use governmental institutions at the location and district level to promote their economic interests.[39] Thus the process by which a bureaucratic bourgeoisie emerged and used the state for economic enhancement provides yet another example of the continuity that linked the colonial and independence periods in Kenya's history.

While the foregoing has emphasized the class divisions that existed among the African population of Kenya after independence, these were not the only significant social distinctions dividing them. Ethnicity, or ethnic identity, also formed an important dividing line. The colonial period had formalized and hardened ethnic divisions as the colonial rulers established a system of administration based on a division of Kenya by 'tribes'. This and the colonial policy of divide and rule had created forms of ethnic identity and solidarity, popularly dubbed tribalism, largely unknown in precolonial times.[40] Such ethnic identity was based on differences in language. The processes of peasantization and proletarianization had not significantly weakened the adherence to ethnic identity amongst Kenya's African population by the early 1960s. Rather, the converse appears to have been the case. Linguistic divisions 'provided ready-dug lines of cleavage along which other conflicts would be politicized as it became more and more important to the ordinary people that levers of social action should be in "friendly hands"'.[41]

This situation was little altered after independence. Despite economic change, modernization and rapid urbanization, ethnic identity continued to be a very important factor in Kenya's social equation. The growth of social mobility and state power may well have made the average citizen more likely to seek security in ethnic-based social welfare organizations and to look more favourably on the leadership of those who spoke his/her language.[42]

Despite frequent attacks on tribalism by political leaders, ethnic identity and loyalty continued to manifest a strong influence in Kenya society during the Kenyatta era. Political support, sports organization (particularly football), employment patterns and *harambee* efforts all reflected the pervasive influence of ethnicity. While expanding educational opportunities and the use of Swahili and English as media of instruction had the potential for breaking down ethnic barriers, the inherited educational system guaranteed that the majority of students attended schools only with fellow ethnic-group members at the primary level. Moreover, many of the social issues publicly aired during the initial decade of independence took on a pronouncedly ethnic or tribal character, as some ethnic groups, usually the Kikuyu, were said to be holding the best jobs in the public sector, having more schools and having assumed a dominant role in business or the trade union movement.

Yet, while ethnicity continued as a powerful social force into the independence period, it was not nearly so divisive a force as in some other African nations in the same period (e.g. Uganda and Nigeria). Official government policy sought to provide for an equitable division of resources and opportunities among all ethnic groups in the nation. While, as this chapter will illustrate, this was not always very successfully accomplished, ethnic rivalry, and its potentially devastating social and political consequences, was kept under control in newly independent Kenya. Nothing illustrates this more clearly than the smooth and peaceful transition of power that followed the death of President Kenyatta in August 1978. Despite some foreign predictions of possible ethnic disunity upon the demise of Kenya's first president, Daniel T. arap Moi's assumption of the presidency suggests that, at least among the political and economic élite, potential division and rivalry would not be allowed to compromise Kenya's social stability.

Population Growth and Urbanization

Two very critical features of independent Kenya's social scene were the twin factors of rapid population growth and urbanization. The former, in particular, provided the most powerful force underlying social change and social policy after 1963. Neither population growth nor urbanization was a new social force. Both had gathered momentum in the final years of colonial rule, but, after independence, they speeded up dramatically.

Table 5.3 shows the growth of population during the period 1962 to 1979. The expansion of Kenya's population has been staggering, as the rate of increase per annum for the period was almost 4 per cent, the highest in the world.[43] The rapid population growth was the result of a continued high birth-rate and lower mortality rate after independence. According to government estimates, the total fertility rate (the number of children born by a mother at the end of her reproductive period)

Table 5.3 Kenya's Population

1962	1969	1978
8,636,263	10,942,705	15,327,061

Source: Republic of Kenya, *Statistical Abstract 1981.*

stood at 6.8 children per woman in 1962, and by 1979 it had risen to just under 8 births per woman.[44] At the same time, the mortality rate, particularly among infants, declined dramatically.[45]

The population explosion was in many respects the direct outcome of social initiatives undertaken by the independent government. The considerable expansion of health services played a very important role, particularly in the dramatic drop in infant mortality rates. As better and more extensive health facilities and greater awareness of health and hygiene measures were provided for Kenyans, these had the effect of fuelling population growth. Also, it is apparent, the expansion of education helped to push the population explosion. Government studies suggest, for example, that the dramatically increased numbers of women attending primary school helped increase fertility. Exposure to primary education made women more conscious of better hygiene and nutrition, which reduces infant mortality.[46]

As Kenya's population increased, it became younger. The 1969 census showed that 48.2 per cent of the population was under fifteen years of age, and by the end of 1979, 59.8 per cent of the population was under twenty.[47] It goes without saying that this fact had immense social significance. The high rate of population growth threw heavy burdens on the educational and health services during the Kenyatta era and in the years that followed it. Any society which has 60 per cent of its population dependent on a much smaller economically active segment will be faced with substantial social and economic challenges in providing jobs and social services for the proportion under twenty years of age.[48] Kenya's rapid population growth could not help but have a very powerful impact on government social and economic policies.

The rapid population growth, which put a severe strain on social services, led inevitably to a concern to check the rate of expansion. The Kenya government was one of the first independent African states to support family-planning efforts as a means to this end. In its 1965 exposition of African Socialism, the government promised 'immediate steps' towards family-planning education 'because the present high rate of population growth makes extensive and intensive provision of social services more expensive'.[49] In early 1966 the government declared that it would 'pursue vigorously policies designed to reduce the rate of population growth through voluntary means'. A programme aimed at that goal was undertaken, starting in 1967, in co-operation with the

Family Planning Association of Kenya.[50] The programme operated on a free service basis as a part of the health service, but this produced little of the anticipated results. The census figures for 1969 showed that the rate of population increase had actually risen. Continued government concern led to support for a five-year family-planning programme, inaugurated in 1974 with the support of the World Bank. It aimed at reducing the growth rate to 3 per cent per annum, but the initiative came nowhere near achieving that goal.[51]

Despite much research by Kenyan and expatriate experts, an effective means of reducing the rate of population increase had not been found by the end of 1978. While it could be argued that the government's efforts lacked firm commitment, a more fundamental reason for the failure of the efforts to limit births in Kenya was the inability of those involved in the undertaking to fully understand the economic and social forces that fostered the high rate of fertility and to design effective means for mitigating them. As population increases continued at a world-leading pace through the 1970s, it is not difficult to conclude that the most signal failure of policies aimed at fostering social change in the Kenyatta era was in the field of family planning.

Rapid urban growth paralleled the rise in Kenya's population. After *uhuru*, in fact, the rate of urban growth exceeded that of the total population. This produced a growth in the number of urban areas and in the populations resident there. The 1979 census showed an urban population of 2,315,696 or 15 per cent of the total population of the nation. The census recognized 91 urban centres as opposed to 34 in 1962.[52] Table 5.4 provides data on the growth of Kenya's six largest cities between 1962 and 1979.[53] The patterns of urbanization illustrated by Table 5.4 were the result of well-established historical factors. Colonial development had brought about all the urban centres, and the growth after independence largely continued the trends begun after the Second World War.

Table 5.4 Growth of Population in Major Urban Centres, 1962–79

Centre	1962	1969	1979	Annual Rate of Growth	
				1962–69	1969–79
Nairobi	266,794	509,286	834,500	9.7	6.3
Mombasa	179,575	247,073	341,500	4.7	3.8
Kisumu	23,526	32,431	150,400	4.7	36.4
Nakuru	38,181	47,151	92,600	3.1	9.6
Eldoret	19,605	18,196	50,200	− 0.5	17.8
Thika	13,952	18,387	41,300	4.0	12.5

Source: Obudho and Obudho, 'Post-Colonial Urbanization' (see note 53).

Urban growth continued and accelerated after independence as a result of a number of factors. First there was the loosening of colonial restrictions on the movement and residence of Africans in urban areas after *uhuru*. Cities also experienced a high rate of natural population growth, and in many cases urban boundaries were expanded to include surrounding areas of population. Finally, and the major cause of urban growth, these years were characterized by a high rate of rural-to-urban migration.

Understandably, the latter factor attracted most attention from policy-makers and scholars. Rural-to-urban migration was brought about by a variety of push and pull factors. Among the former may be included rural land scarcity and poverty and rural–urban income differentials. Rural areas were comparatively starved of investment when compared with the cities in the 1960s and 1970s. Without doubt, the uneven development that marked Kenya's regions and the fact of rural differentiation were the most significant of all push factors.[54] Among the pull factors are numbered the monopoly of modern-sector employment in the urban areas, the greater availability and accessibility of schools and hospitals, and the superior transportation networks of the cities. The urban areas offer attractions as centres for entertainment opportunities and cultural exhibitions. The perceived availability of economic opportunities was certainly the most important factor in rural-to-urban migration.[55] One of the paradoxes of the rural-to-urban migration that marked Kenya's first years of independence was that the migrants included both the poorest and the most educated and well-to-do in rural society.[56]

As suggested earlier, urban migrants maintained ties with the rural areas. Moreover, not all urban migrants found employment within a short period of time. They became part of the pool of urban unemployed. This excess population created many social problems.[57]

The growth of the urban population in Kenya after independence was thus partly the result of what may be termed urban bias. The urban areas had better social amenities, employment and commercial opportunities than the rural areas. Young people, in particular, were attracted by the better opportunities for education and advancement in the cities. Moreover, urban growth itself was the cause of further urban bias on the part of the government. After *uhuru*, the state spent larger sums per capita on housing, schools, health centres and roads in the urban areas. Virtually all new industrial development was centred in existing urban areas. The growth of the urban population, the economic significance of the urban areas and the potential political and social volatility of such large centres as Nairobi and Mombasa led to further examples of urban bias, typical in the developing world, in the form of government edicts to fix and control rents, provide housing allowances and hold prices of essential foods at low levels for the benefit of the urban population; often this was accomplished, as in the case of food prices, at the expense of the rural population.

Despite the existence of urban bias, rapid urbanization rates after *uhuru* resulted in problems such as shortages of essential services, over-crowding and the mushrooming of slum areas. Infrastructural develop-ment proceeded far more slowly than urban growth, and a gap soon emerged between supply and demand for water supply, sewerage, houses and health facilities. By the mid-1970s, the shortage of urban housing was particularly pressing.[58] As a result of such shortages, the urban poor were pressed into slums, or an increasing percentage took refuge in squatter settlements on the outskirts of the cities, where people lived in temporary metal, cardboard or plastic dwellings. Such 'spontaneous settlements' lacked such essential services as water, refuse collection and transport, and they were viewed, not without reason, as centres for vice and crime by the other urban dwellers.

Despite periodic pleas from political leaders, including President Kenyatta, for a reverse of rural-to-urban migration and periodic attempts of urban authorities to demolish the squatter settlements, rapid urban growth and the accompanying social problems represented an ongoing issue of concern. While government officials could console themselves that the phenomenon of urbanization was not unique to Kenya in the developing world, the problems associated with rapid urban growth would not be solved quickly. They would continue to challenge develop-ment and social planners.

Education

Another major focus of government policy and development planning after independence was education. Education lay at the heart of the independent government's attempts to foster social change and promote development. Upon the achievement of internal self-government on 1 June 1963, the then Prime Minister Jomo Kenyatta identified three enemies – ignorance, sickness and poverty – to be overcome by an independent Kenya.[59] The Prime Minister and his government were under no illusions, however, as to the magnitude of the task before them. The nation needed to dramatically increase school enrolments in order to attain its development goals.

Within one week of independence, therefore, the government appointed the Kenya Education Commission, under the chairmanship of Professor S.H. Ominde, to survey the country's existing educational resources and advise the government on future strategy. After eight months, the Ominde Commission, as it came to be known, produced part one of its report, dealing with broad questions of policy. This was published in December 1964 and was followed by a second report presented to the government in mid-1965. The Commission's recommendations had 'a profound influence on national thinking on education'.[60]

Among its most significant and far-reaching recommendations, the Ominde Commission endorsed free primary education as 'a valid objective of educational policy' but recognized that this would take time to achieve. Primary education, the Commission held, could only be made free after it was virtually universal. Thus universal primary education would be the initial goal. The Commission also stressed that the government's efforts in primary education should be 'directed towards areas in which the percentage enrolment falls seriously below the national average'.[61] Most importantly, moreover, the Commission concluded that, given the new nation's need for highly trained manpower, too great an emphasis should not be put on primary education. To facilitate rapid economic development, secondary and higher education would have to receive highest priority.[62] The Commission also endorsed integration, with a single curriculum but different fee structures, for Kenya's racially divided school system.

The thinking of the Commission was reflected in other government planning documents produced during the first years of independence. Both the 1964–70 Development Plan and the 1965 policy statement interpreting the government's conception of African Socialism gave support to the goal of universal primary education.[63] However, the latter policy document maintained that immediate provision of free and universal education 'would bankrupt the nation and mortgage economic growth for generations'.[64] In particular, it laid far greater stress on the expansion of secondary education, rather than primary, so as to relieve the shortage of domestic skilled manpower. Thus the direction of greatest government emphasis was on the expansion of places in forms one to six so as to provide that trained manpower.[65]

Table 5.5 illustrates the expansion of education during the Kenyatta era. This confirms the more rapid expansion of secondary education after independence. Between 1964 and 1966, the number of secondary schools rose by 80 per cent and the number of pupils enrolled by 76 per cent; in contrast, primary enrolment grew by only 3 per cent while schools increased by 11.6 per cent. For the entire 1964–79 period, the number of secondary schools increased almost eightfold while the number of primary schools did not quite double. The largest share of development expenditure on education went to the secondary level. Mirroring secondary trends, enrolment in higher education also dramatically expanded. While 536 Kenya students were registered in universities in East Africa in 1963–64, just over 7,000 were similarly enrolled in 1978–79. By the latter date, Kenya had established two universities, the University of Nairobi and Kenyatta University.

A very striking characteristic of the rapid expansion of secondary

Table 5.5   Schools and Student Population, 1964–79

Year	Primary		Secondary	
	Schools	Students	Schools	Students
1964	5,105	1,010,889	222	35,921
1966	5,699	1,043,416	400	63,193
1970	5,123	1,427,589	783	126,855
1975	8,161	2,881,155	1,160	226,835
1979	9,622	3,398,246	1,773	370,703

Source: *Statistical Abstracts* 1965–1980.

education was the part played in it by *harambee* secondary schools. These schools, begun by local communities as self-help efforts, accounted for one-third of all secondary schools by the end of 1965. By 1978, more than half of Kenya's secondary enrolment was in unaided schools.[66]

The dramatic expansion of educational opportunities in the Kenyatta era is, in many respects, a striking success story. Although the goal of free and universal education was not achieved, trained manpower was made available for the Africanization of the public service within a decade. The teaching profession itself had been substantially Africanized by 1978. By that date, over 85 per cent of the primary-aged children had enrolled in school. The latter owed much to government decisions in 1971 and 1973 that provided for the abolition of fees through standard five.[67] The considerable strides made in providing education to greater numbers of Kenyans after independence is summarized in Table 5.6. While the 1969 census indicated that some 74 per cent of the population had received no schooling, that group constituted only 52 per cent of the population a decade later.

Besides increasing numbers of schools and pupils, the fifteen years after independence were also significant for several influential changes in policy and practice. One of the first to be implemented was the change from the elementary and intermediate school structure (4 + 4) to a primary-school curriculum of seven years. This alteration, which involved the dropping of the standard four examination, had been implemented by the end of 1966.[68] Whereas at independence the financing of primary education had been the responsibility of county councils, from 1970 it was taken over by the central government so as to relieve the severe strain caused on local government finance. In the area of curriculum, the English-medium programme, first begun in African schools in 1961, spread widely in primary schools. The Ominde Commission recommended its adoption and, by the end of the 1970s, English formed the medium of instruction from standard one in virtually all Kenyan schools.[69]

Table 5.6 Educational Achievement, 1969 and 1979: Percentage Completing Educational Levels

Province		None or not stated	Std 1–4	Std 5–7	Form I–IV	Form V +	Total
Central	1969	64	18	15	3	–	1,675,647
	1979	42	25	23	9	1	2,345,833
Coast	1969	79	8	9	3	1	944,082
	1979	64	15	13	7	1	1,343,794
Eastern	1969	76	13	9	2	–	1,907,301
	1979	42	30	21	7	–	2,179,851
Nairobi	1969	44	16	24	13	3	509,286
	1979	32	15	25	23	5	827,275
Northeastern	1969	97	2	1	–	–	245,757
	1979	94	3	2	1	–	373,851
Nyanza	1969	75	12	11	2	–	2,122,045
	1979	48	27	18	7	–	2,643,956
Rift Valley	1969	79	11	8	2	–	2,210,289
	1979	58	21	15	5	1	3,240,402
Western	1969	69	17	12	2	–	1,328,298
	1979	49	27	17	7	1	1,832,663
National	1969	74	13	11	2	–	10,733,202
Total	1979	52	23	17	7	1	15,327,061

Sources: *Population Census 1969* and *Population Census 1979*.

In expanding educational facilities, the government attempted to provide, as the Ominde Commission had recommended, facilities for those districts and provinces that had been educationally 'behind' in terms of numbers of schools and pupils so that they might catch up. As Tables 5.6, 5.7 and 5.8 indicate, this did not occur. Those provinces with the smallest percentages of primary- and secondary-school students (Coast and Northeastern) remained in that position from 1966 to 1978, as did the province having the highest percentage of pupils enrolled (Central).

In addition, Table 5.9 illustrates that, while considerable progress was made in increasing female enrolment in schools, girls continued to lag behind boys in school attendance despite their greater numbers in the population as a whole. This continued to be pronounced at the secondary stage, and was even more so at the university level.

Despite the success achieved in rapidly increasing school enrolment at all levels, the government's efforts in the field of education during the first decade and a half after independence have not escaped criticism. In addition to the failure to successfully redress the inherited regional imbalance in schools and enrolment, other criticism has centred on the appropriateness of the curriculum for Kenya. The curriculum for primary and secondary education was localized to some extent, but the bulk

Table 5.7 Percentage Primary School Enrolment by Province, 1966–78

Province	1966	1972	1976	1978
Central	24	24	20	21
Coast	6	6	6	6
Eastern	20	20	19	20
Nairobi	5	4	3	3
Northeastern	< 1	–	–	–
Nyanza	18	16	19	17
Rift Valley	14	15	18	19
Western	13	14	15	14

Source: *Statistical Abstracts* 1970–1980.

Table 5.8 Percentage Secondary School Enrolment by Province, 1966–78

Province	1966	1972	1976	1978
Central	24	23	24	24
Coast	11	9	6	5
Eastern	9	15	16	18
Nairobi	24	16	10	9
Northeastern	< 1	–	–	–
Nyanza	10	14	17	17
Rift Valley	10	13	12	13
Western	12	10	15	14

Source: As for Table 5.7.

Table 5.9 Percentage Primary and Secondary Enrolment by Gender, 1966–78

Year	Primary		Secondary	
	Male	Female	Male	Female
1966	62	38	74	26
1972	57	43	69	31
1978	53	47	60	40

Sources: *Statistical Abstracts* 1967, 1973, 1981.

remained as it had been inherited from the colonial era. It was thus 'élitist' and inegalitarian in nature, as it was 'designed to meet the interests and needs of a very small proportion of those who enter the school system'.[70] The heavy emphasis on literary education and the preparation for white-collar jobs is certainly open to question, since by the end of the 1970s considerably less than 20 per cent of those finishing primary school were able to enter government secondary school. The curriculum did little to prepare those leaving after standard seven for jobs in agriculture and industry.[71] In the words of Court and Ghai, 'The main feature of the period has been linear expansion rather than structural reform of the inherited system.'[72]

The crucial problem of the appropriateness of the curriculum for the employability of the graduates of the school system increasingly drew attention from the government and public. By the end of the 1960s, the absorptive capacity of the labour market had drastically decreased, particularly for those with lower formal credentials. Professor D.N. Sifuna has summed up the results of this situation very succinctly:

> The consequence of this situation was the pressure for higher and higher levels of formal schooling. And yet the pool of graduates far exceeded the number of places at the succeeding stage. This meant vigorous selection and indeed an onerous and highly competitive system of examinations at different educational stages. Examination became the sole criterion of one's eligibility to climb the educational ladder. Hence, the main function of the primary school is to select entrants for the secondary school, and the latter has an identical function with regard to admission to university.[73]

The need for education to prepare youth more appropriately for the kind of jobs and lives they would encounter on leaving the schools system was quickly recognized by educational and political leaders alike. The 1972 ILO report emphasized the need for greater emphasis on basic education, and recommended a restructuring of the educational system so as to better provide vocational bias and prepare school-leavers for the type of employment likely to be available in a developing nation like Kenya.[74] A 1975 National Committee on Educational Objectives and Policies also called for a restructuring along the lines suggested by the ILO report. Yet, despite these recommendations, the educational system continued to place emphasis on high-level manpower development.

The major reason for this was that, although government and educational leaders were well aware of the weaknesses in the system, there was no great public pressure for change. In fact, just the opposite was the case. As Professor Sifuna has stressed, 'any attempt to change the prevailing conception of the purpose of education, namely continuous expansion of higher education, met with public resistance'.[75] All social classes saw education as the route to material advancement, enhancing the prospects for wage employment for children and, given the nature of extended kinship relations in independent Kenya, whole families invested resources in the education of their young people. Thus any proposals for thoroughgoing change were not well received by either the rich or the poor. Most significantly, those in positions of leadership in politics and the civil service had little enthusiasm for change away from the system that had helped to make them part of the élite.

Seen in a broader social context, therefore, the educational system merely reflected the dominant economic, political and social structure and social norms of the time. Since educational systems largely reproduce rather than alter the economic and social structures of the societies in which they exist,[76] the decision to follow the capitalist, less egalitarian, path to development that marked the post-independence years led inevitably to the continuation of a social structure based upon wealth, which was characterized by large gaps between the rich and the poor. The educational system, shaped to meet the needs of a colonial élite, was, not surprisingly, largely continued as a most effective way of perpetuating the interests of the postcolonial political and economic élite and expanding its numbers. Even the most cursory survey of the Kenyatta era suggests that the system was most successful in accomplishing this end.

Health

As with education, improving health care was viewed as a priority by the independent government. As noted earlier, this was made clear by Prime Minister Kenyatta in his *Madaraka* Day message in 1963. His government's first development plan, covering the period 1965–70, emphasized the need to improve health as an important prerequisite for development. Specifically, the government aimed to increase the number of doctors while at the same time replacing expatriate physicians with Kenyans (Kenya had 7.8 doctors per 100,000 population at independence). The first step would be to provide a medical school at the newly renamed Kenyatta National Hospital. There was also a need to increase the numbers of registered nurses (then 22.8 per 100,000) since at independence there were virtually no African registered nurses (RNs) (nor was there any training institution open to African RNs at that time). The plan hoped to expand health facilities at least as fast as population growth, and it aimed at correcting the imbalance in health care facilities in favour of the rural areas. In particular, the government pointed to the development of rural health centres. These were described as 'the linchpin of Kenya's health policy'. They would be centres 'in which curative medicine is co-ordinated with preventive and promotive medicine'.[77] The long-term goal was to provide one such centre for every 10,000 population and to co-ordinate them with the government's hospital system so as to improve rural health standards.

These aims were further refined in the government's statement describing African Socialism and its application to Kenya and the development plan for the 1966–70 period. The former document set the ambitious goal of providing medical and hospital service for all who needed it without charge.[78] As with universal free education, this was a target that was not obtainable at once, but it would remain a stated aim of government policy for the years ahead. So too did the government commit itself to providing each district in the country with the means to ensure that all people had a 'minimum provision' of essential health services.[79] One of the first steps towards this goal was the introduction of free medical services for out-patients and children in 1965.

The revised development plan for the 1966–70 period reaffirmed the government's goal of bringing health services 'increasingly within the reach of all people', providing for an increase in medical services that would keep pace with the rate of growth of the country's population and reducing the existing 'disparity in the standard of health services provided in various districts'.[80] In addition, the plan stressed the need to increase the number of hospital beds, and for the implementation of programmes aimed at eliminating preventable diseases. Health centres continued to form the 'linchpin' of the government's health programmes, but its long-term goal was now revised to be one health centre for every 20,000 inhabitants.[81]

Tables 5.10, 5.11 and 5.12 illustrate the outcome of the government's efforts to increase the number of health professionals and health facilities during the period under review. These show that very significant advances were made in both areas. The rise in the number of doctors and dentists was particularly significant in that in 1962 more than three-quarters of doctors were expatriates, while in 1978 the majority were Kenyans. Likewise, the bulk of RNs in 1962 were non-African, but, by 1978, that situation had been reversed. While the government played a substantial role in the provision of health centres and dispensaries, it was not alone in spurring the expansion of facilities and beds shown in Tables 5.11 and 5.12. Private hospitals continued to be established and maintained by church and mission groups, and many of the health centres and dispensaries begun in those years were the result of self-help efforts from local communities.

The expansion of health-care facilities during the Kenyatta era represents one of the most successful social welfare initiatives of the period. Despite the fact that it was not always able to provide facilities to keep pace with population growth, that it came nowhere near providing a health centre for every 20,000 of the population by 1978,[82] and that there were only 9.5 doctors per 100,000 population in the latter year, most Kenyans had access to substantially improved health-care facilities at the end of the Kenyatta presidency. By 1979, for example, there were 42.8 RNs per 100,000. As Table 5.13 shows, a slight improve-

Table 5.10   Basic Health Statistics, 1963–78

	1963	1966	1974	1978
Doctors and dentists	948	910	1,242	1,596
Registered nurses	2,308	3,182	4,876	6,388
Registered midwives	900	1,067	2,171	NA

Sources: *Statistical Abstracts* 1967, 1973, 1980.

Table 5.11 Total Hospital Beds
(Government and Non-government)

1962	10,617
1970	14,537
1973	18,186
1978	26,922

Sources: *Statistical Abstracts* 1963, 1973, 1980.

Table 5.12   Health Care Facilities by Province, 1966 and 1978

Province	1966			1978		
	Hosp.	Health Cen.	Dispen.	Hosp.	Health Cen.	Dispen.
Central	29	31	68	47	41	154
Coast	23	11	58	23	18	137
Eastern	24	23	76	27	29	191
Nairobi	22	–	46	26	2	112
Northeastern	3	1	3	3	6	18
Nyanza	19	28	41	32	37	112
Rift Valley	41	45	132	52	65	317
Western	16	21	8	16	35	47

Sources: *Statistical Abstracts* 1967 and 1980.

ment occurred in virtually all provinces in the ratio of hospital beds per 1,000 population between 1964 and 1978. While low by standards of the developed world and unevenly distributed, Kenya's ratio of hospital beds, physicians and nurses per 1,000 population compared very favourably with those of other sub-Saharan African nations. As already noted, moreover, improved health care helped to foster the population explosion of these years. Kenyans experienced a definite improvement in life expectancy. By the end of the 1970s, average life expectancy had risen from forty-four years to fifty-five, the highest outside South Africa in the sub-Saharan region.[83]

Table 5.13   Beds per 1,000 Population, 1964 and 1978

Province	1964	National rank	1978	National rank
Central	1.19	3	1.60	3
Coast	1.72	2	1.80	2
Eastern	0.89	5	1.40	5
Nairobi	4.53	1	4.73	1
North Eastern	0.40	8	0.83	8
Nyanza	0.59	7	1.37	6
Rift Valley	1.15	4	1.44	4
Western	0.74	6	1.27	7

Sources: *Development Plan 1966–70* and *Statistical Abstract 1979*.

On the other hand, the government had least success in achieving its goal of reducing disparities in health-care facilities among Kenya's provinces and districts. This was to be accomplished, in considerable measure, by increasing and upgrading facilities in those parts of Kenya that had been most poorly endowed with hospitals, beds, health centres and dispensaries in colonial times. As Tables 5.12 and 5.13 suggest, nothing of the sort happened during the period under review. Those provinces with the fewest facilities and beds in 1964 and 1966 were, despite increases in both areas, still in that position in 1978. In fact, the province that increased its share of the nation's hospitals by the greatest percentage between 1966 and 1979 was Central (from 6 per cent of the total to 21 per cent). It could hardly be argued that this was the least well endowed of Kenya's provinces. At the other end of the scale, both Coast and North Eastern provinces experienced a drop in the percentage of hospitals sited there during the same period.[84] Not surprisingly, the 1979 census indicated that Central had the highest life expectancy of all Kenya's provinces (58.1 years for males and 63.6 for females).[85] As with education, therefore, the government's aim of equalizing social welfare facilities among the nation's regions remained still to be achieved.

Social Welfare and Development

From independence, development planners recognized a potential clash between the goals of speeding economic development and dramatically expanding educational and health-care facilities and opportunities and making them available to the citizenry at no cost. With limited financial resources at its disposal, the government continuously faced the choice of utilizing those scarce resources to foster purely economic development

Table 5.14 Percentage of Total Expenditure on Education and Health

	1963/64	1968/69	1974/75	1978/79
Education	11	11	20	15
Health	4	6	7	5
Total Social Services	17	22	31	25

Sources: *Statistical Abstracts* 1968, 1973 and 1980.

or to give greater emphasis to social welfare. There was no doubting that a better-educated and healthier population would facilitate more rapid development, but choices had to be made, in working out annual budgets, as to where expenditure would be most profitably allocated.

A common criticism of Kenya policy during this period was that far too large a share of the national budget went to financing welfare services, particularly education. Table 5.14 shows the share of total expenditure given to education, health and other social services for selected years between 1963 and 1979.

More particularly, the system can be criticized for consuming an increasing share of resources without any corresponding contribution to economic productivity. By the mid-1970s, it was estimated that the resources devoted to funding education were equivalent to nearly 12 per cent of gross domestic product (GDP).[86] According to Tony Killick, the educational system

> and the structure of economic incentives which underlies it, is criticized for producing an output inappropriate to the economy's needs, thus contributing to unemployment and technological backwardness in the rural areas. It is, furthermore, associated with interpersonal and interregional inequalities, contrary to the government's stated goals.[87]

While education's claim on national resources was large, Table 5.14 does not suggest that educational expenditure had taken an overwhelming share. Certainly the pattern indicated by the table is not one of runaway spending on education. While education made up a greater proportion of recurrent expenditure (26.6 per cent in 1976–77), it is, as Arthur Hazlewood suggests, 'a matter of judgement whether it amounts to a disproportionate share of national resources'.[88] Public support for the levels of expenditure noted above remained strong. Nor is it clear that a reduction in educational spending levels and the resultant loss of school places would have a beneficial economic or social effect. While many saw formal education as a selection mechanism for further education and salaried jobs, the role of education in raising general awareness and ability among a substantial portion of the population would seem to be a prerequisite for any kind of effective development efforts.

The *Harambee* Movement

What may be termed the *harambee* movement had a very profound impact on social policy and the provision of educational and health facilities during the Kenyatta era. The concept of self-help that undergirded the *harambee* (literally meaning 'let's pull together') movement was not, of course, unknown among Kenyan communities. During the precolonial and colonial periods, neighbourhood groups and those related by kin often pooled resources to accomplish tasks that would benefit the group as a whole (clearing trees, building roads, constructing primary schools). This self-help ideal was given new impetus and meaning at the time of the achievement of self-government. It received particularly strong backing from *Mzee* Kenyatta himself, who, following the triumph of the Kenya African National Union (KANU) in the 1963 elections, made *harambee* an appeal not only for self-help but for national unity as well. *Mzee* Kenyatta first proposed *harambee* to Kenyans, as a word that would 'express the mood we want to create', in late May 1963. He used the word again in his *Madaraka* Day speech.[89]

In the first two years after independence, Kenyans responded positively to the call of *harambee*. In addition to the building of roads and the construction of dams and water pipelines, self-help efforts were directed to the construction of health centres, dispensaries and schools. More than 2,500 such facilities were built during that period.[90] This rapid proliferation of such facilities, often the vehicles for personal political ambitions, caused some concern to development planners; both the Ominde Commission and the 1966–70 development plan recognized the important contributions that self-help efforts could make to national development, but stressed that, in order to make the maximum contribution, they must be planned and directed.[91] Nevertheless, rapid construction of *harambee* schools and other projects continued with little central direction. Observers could easily conclude that 'the ideal Harambee project seems to be one which is likely to be taken over by Government and to attract overseas aid but unlikely to be independently initiated by the Government'.[92] In 1977, Kenya had 222 private and *harambee* secondary schools; six years later 600 out of 981 high schools were *harambee*.[93]

Clearly people all over Kenya answered the President's call. Local communities raised money, elected school committees and started schools. Until 1968, the government exercised little control over the starting of such secondary schools. Once management had been recognized, the school could hire teachers and enrol students, following the same secondary syllabus as government-aided schools. The Ministry of Education could do little to slow down this process until the 1968 Education Act gave it greater powers to control registration of *harambee* secondary schools. Even with increased powers, the Ministry was under great political pressure from local communities and their leaders to register the schools and to bring them within the state-supported system.

Yet many have questioned, with good reason, the educational value of *harambee* secondary schools. The majority of the teaching staff in such secondary schools were 'untrained'. In 1970, for example, only 32 per cent of the teachers in *harambee* schools met official government qualifications for high-school teaching as opposed to 81 per cent in Ministry of Education-aided schools. Examination results in *harambee* secondary schools were significantly lower than in aided schools. Some 71 per cent of those who sat the form four exam in 1970 either failed (37 per cent) or received only a school-leaving certificate. Only 9 per cent of the *harambee* candidates sitting for that year's examination obtained a division I or II pass (as opposed to 32 per cent for government-aided high schools).[94] This meant that the graduates of *harambee* secondary schools did less well in admission to Form V places and had marginal success in the job market. The use of untrained teachers was not the only cause of the poor results. Most *harambee* secondary schools had inadequate facilities. Books and equipment were normally at the bare minimum. Libraries were usually inadequate, and many had no laboratories. Thus the curriculum for most such schools was dominated by traditional, non-scientific subjects. Vocational courses, particularly agriculture, were largely ignored.[95]

Yet another problem with the *harambee* movement has been that it has done little to reduce regional inequality in development and the provision of social amenities. While many schools, water projects and health facilities were constructed, the greatest proportion were put up in those provinces and districts that were already the most developed and were, in fact, experiencing the most rapid economic advancement during these years. The provision of health centres and dispensaries provides an illuminating example.

Despite criticisms, the *harambee* movement was, and remains, a shining example of successful self-help efforts in independent Kenya. The nation's people showed themselves ready to make sacrifices and work together for social and economic improvement on a scale that few Third World countries could match. Little wonder that the word *harambee* became the national motto. The concept retains, almost three decades after independence, a very powerful appeal as a mobilizational force among all social classes in Kenya.

In Search of a National Culture

With the achievement of *uhuru* came the recognition that, as an independent nation, Kenya needed to develop a national culture as a means of promoting and enhancing national unity, pride and patriotism. Moreover, there was a need to assert the utility of African cultural traditions, which had been subjected to a multifaceted assault under colonialism. Denigrated by colonialists and missionaries alike as 'primitive', African customs, beliefs and ways of life had been thoroughly bruised by the colonial period. Kenya's founding fathers 'sought to revive and enhance the dignity and relevance of Kenya cultural heritage'.[96] Culture, according to post-independence official thinking, was 'a unique way of life peculiar to a people, encompassing social institutions, values, norms and ethics as well as attire and various forms of artistic and literary expression'. It would find expression 'through the nation's unique artifacts, diversity of song, art, dance, theatre, literature and other traditions'.[97]

It was recognized that, for a nation to develop and maintain its particular identity, certain cultural values should be developed and promoted. Particularly significant for a new nation like Kenya in this regard was the development of a national language. Other elements of a national culture that drew interest during the Kenyatta era were the creation and adoption of a national dress, the preservation of monuments and structures of cultural interest, the promotion of Kenyan culture through the mass media, and the promotion of a national culture through song, dance and literature. Despite public awareness and some government support for the need to develop these facets of national culture, the first decade and a half of independence were marked by the search for, and attempt to attain, rather than the emergence of, a true Kenyan national culture.

Nothing illustrates this more clearly than the only partially successful endeavours to make Swahili Kenya's national language. Such a course enjoyed support from the new nation's political leadership; almost all made their public speeches in Swahili. Independence saw the elevation of the national service of the newly christened Voice of Kenya (VOK) to pride of place in comparison with the English-language radio service in terms of hours of broadcasting. Public notices and signs were altered so that the Swahili version came first and English second.

However, Swahili only came to partially fulfil the characteristics of a national language. For sometime after *uhuru*, English remained the sole medium for parliamentary debates. When Swahili finally became accepted for use in the legislature, it came merely to be co-equal with the English language. Throughout the period, moreover, English remained the medium of instruction at all levels of education. As late as 1978, many schools did not teach Swahili at all in Standards 1–3. English, rather than Swahili, remained the language of official government communications and for commerce and banking. It could thus not be contended that Swahili became a true national language.[98]

Moreover, attempts by designers and commercial interests to push for the adoption of male and female attire that would exemplify Kenya's African heritage met with even less success. Although prior to independence, many prominent politicians had worn beaded caps and other forms of traditional attire, this practice ceased virtually from the attainment of *uhuru*. Almost without exception, the political leadership adopted Western-style dress.[99] This was also true for the population at large. While tourists might be offered what was marketed as national dress, such attire was little seen amongst the populace.

The new government gave considerably greater support, on the other hand, to the preservation of monuments and structures of national interest. This was done both in the sense of fostering the preservation of monuments and sites deemed positive to the development of Kenyan culture and in the sense of eliminating those that did not. As examples of the former, the government expanded the number of protected sites and official support for the national museum. A number of Stone Age sites were treated in this way. As examples of elimination, city authorities removed the statute of Lord Delamere from Nairobi's city centre and gave African names to most of the streets bearing names reflecting the colonial era. While both initiatives had a positive impact, the effort to preserve and create national monuments and structures was hardly thoroughgoing. Far more attention at the national museum was given, for example, to human origins and the Stone Age than to more recent cultural periods. Despite some public support, moreover, relatively little was done to erect monuments to those who fought for freedom during the colonial period.

A somewhat greater positive impact on national culture came about from the promotion of Kenyan authorship and publishing. The government provided a means to this end through the East African Literature Bureau (after 1977 the Kenya Literature Bureau), which, after independence, gave much greater support to African, as opposed to expatriate, writers. So too did private publishing concerns. As a result, the first decade of independence witnessed the publication of significant historical and literary works, which directly enhanced Kenya's cultural heritage as an African nation. Kenya's traditional history was 'rediscovered' and widely disseminated. Yet these were focused on the experience of individual ethnic groups rather than the nation as a whole. It was also true that, since the bulk of the publishing firms operating in Kenya were foreign-owned, their main interest was in making profits rather than the encouragement of literary and other works that might foster and enhance the emergence of a national culture.

Considerable steps were taken during the Kenyatta era in the direction of promoting a more positive image of Kenya culture through the mass media. This was especially the case with the government-owned radio and television services. At independence, the latter consisted almost exclusively of programmes imported from British and American television. In the years that followed, VOK television increased, on more than one occasion after strong criticism of the nature of 'foreign' programmes by *Mzee* Kenyatta, the number of programmes in Swahili and those that catered for African audiences and which emphasized African music and dance.[100] VOK radio likewise, in both its English and Swahili services, gave increasing time to programmes that fostered an African identity and projected African rather than Western values.[101] Newspapers also moved to include more items relating to African traditions and culture for their readers after independence, and they portrayed a much more positive image of both than in colonial times. However, as both the main newspaper groups were foreign-owned, their dedication to the promotion of a national culture remained suspect.

Without doubt, the most successful moves towards a national culture during the Kenyatta era came in the fields of music, dance and literature. Although music, dance and theatre had, in theory, been promoted before independence by the Kenya Cultural Centre in Nairobi, the latter had catered almost exclusively for the interests of Kenya's Asian and European populations. As Dr Ndeti has argued, the constituent membership excluded Africans so that 'there was no way in which the centre could project African culture'.[102] Even some years after independence the Kenya Cultural Centre and the adjacent National Theatre strongly catered for expatriate interests and included non-Africans in positions of influence and control. Nevertheless, African music and dance received a strong boost after independence. Literally hundreds of traditional music and dance groups came into being. This owed much to the personal initiative of President Kenyatta. He insisted on the inclusion of African music and dance in all national celebrations, and he was regularly entertained by groups of such performers from all over the nation.[103] The schools drama and music festivals increasingly came to reflect African culture through songs and plays in Swahili or ethnic languages. A Kenyan literature also emerged as a number of African writers produced works that centred on the African experience and attempted to broaden understanding of African culture.

While these took an African perspective and made Africans the main focus of the novels and plays, it would be difficult to argue that this served to foster a truly national culture. The two prominent themes that characterized the literary works published in the first years of independence, the clash of cultures (Western and African) and the response to colonial injustices (through adopting the setting of the Mau Mau rebellion), did little to promote pride in African culture as Western culture emerged the winner.[104] This 'anti-African creed' did little to promote a positive image of African culture; written in English, moreover, these works were directed to a small portion of the African population.[105] Some change in this situation began to be apparent at the end of the 1960s as publishers and the public gave more attention to oral literature, which was much closer to the real lives of the African majority. The free Travelling Theatre of the University of Nairobi took drama to the common people and the themes treated, normally in Swahili, were much closer to their experiences and interests. In 1968, the literature syllabus at the University of Nairobi was 'decolonized', and a new Department of Literature was created with an Afrocentric bias.[106]

Despite these achievements, no national culture emerged during the Kenyatta era. First of all, although many facets of African culture were fostered and given pride of place, thus redressing the colonial hostility and neglect that traditional customs, music and dance had experienced, these reflected not a single national culture but rather the varied cultural heritage of Kenya's several ethnic groups. Partly this reflected the difficulty of welding together different, and often disparate, cultural traditions of the more than three dozen ethnic groups.

More significant, nevertheless, were two other factors. The continued encroachment of Western culture, as reflected in forms of dress, music and language, especially among Kenya's educational and economic élite, served to inhibit the emergence of a national culture. The latter was an inevitable by-product of the adoption of a capitalist development strategy that encouraged Western investment and the acceptance of an élitist, Western-orientated, educational system. In the words of R.M. Osotsi, the Western-educated élite who took over Kenya at independence fell back on the Western-orientated culture they absorbed during their formative years.

> Boarding school, baptism, and total alienation from traditional education processes had raised nothing but contempt in this elite for their own culture. This elite was now considered ready to take all the cultural reins of the new and young society. Nothing more disastrous could have happened culturally.[107]

In addition, as the then director of the Institute of African Studies at the University of Nairobi stressed in a 1980 explanation of the absence of a national culture, Kenya had not 'seriously addressed itself to culture' and the political ideology Kenya had chosen was 'inimical to indigenous traditions'. Kenya's founding fathers, he argued, 'presided over the adoption of western materialism as the chief cultural value in life'. This was not tolerant of Kenya's indigenous cultures.[108] Ngugi wa Thiong'o has emphasized (e.g. *Homecoming*, London, Heinemann, 1972) a somewhat similar explanation for the 'frustration of national cultures' in Africa. The African bourgeoisie, in his view, have adopted the social and cultural ambitions and practices of the European élite of colonial days; thus the order of the day for them has been 'skin-lighteners, straightened hair, irrelevant drawing-room parties, conspicuous consumption'.[109]

Whatever the reason, Kenya, unlike a number of African states, had not established a ministry of culture by 1978. Viewed in strictly economic terms, this was perhaps not surprising. The founding fathers of the new nation gave greater priority to economic development and the expansion of educational and health facilities. Only in 1972 did the government decide to set up a national body to co-ordinate cultural activities. When constituted, the Kenya National Council of Arts and Culture was to enhance national pride and sponsor cultural activities. It was placed under the Ministry of Co-operatives and Social Services, however, and that unit, understandably, gave far greater attention to those aspects of its charge rather than to culture. The establishment of a ministry of culture would have to await the first Nyayo decade. (For a more detailed discussion of culture, see Chapter Eight.)

Conclusion

The less than complete success in creating a new national culture should not obscure the fact that the Kenyatta era was marked by some significant successes of social policy. Educational and health-care facilities were dramatically expanded. By 1978, Kenya had taken giant steps towards achieving universal primary education. Places in secondary schools and universities were greatly increased as the nation went a long way towards meeting its needs for highly trained manpower. Large inroads were made in reducing illiteracy rates as a result of the educational expansion. Improvements in health care were equally impressive. As a result, Kenya had, by 1978, attained a more lengthy life expectancy than most other states in sub-Saharan Africa. In both health and education, independent Kenya achieved more in a decade and a half than the colonial state had accomplished in the preceding six decades.

One of Kenya's most significant successes was the peaceful ending of racial segregation. Schools, public facilities and social clubs were rapidly integrated with a minimum of tension and disruption. President Kenyatta's call to all races to forget the past and heed the call of *harambee* to pull together played a positive role in the process. When compared with the desegregation process in other parts of the world (e.g. the United States), Kenya's experience stands as a truly noteworthy achievement of the first years of independence. Some of the less successful social initiatives, on the other hand, were the failure of family-planning programmes to bring about a decline in the rate of population increase and the lack of progress in bringing about an equalization in educational and health-care facilities in all provinces of the nation.

Yet, for all the social changes that marked the Kenyatta era, their most striking feature was their non-revolutionary nature, the continuity that linked them firmly to the preceding colonial era. Despite changes in the composition of the population after *uhuru*, Kenya remained a plural society. Though stratification by wealth and class replaced that of race after 1963, this was not a new departure. The process of peasantization and proletarianization during the colonial period had led to the emergence of differentiation within African societies and to regional differentiation as well. The processes continued to exercise a similar influence after independence. Urban and population growth, which had begun in the colonial period, continued and speeded up following *uhuru*. Even in the educational sphere, the great expansion in numbers of schools and pupils was accomplished by largely retaining the essentials of the inherited colonial system. Given the economic policies followed by the independent government, this continuity in the sphere of social policy came as no surprise.

Notes

1. Republic of Kenya, *High-Level Manpower Requirements and Resources in Kenya 1964–70* (Nairobi, Government Printer, 1965), p. 29.
2. Donald Rothchild, *Racial Bargaining in Independent Kenya* (London, Oxford University Press, 1973), pp. 54–56.
3. Ibid., pp. 51ff. Alison Smith, 'The Immigrant Communities (1): The Europeans', in D.A. Low and Alison Smith (eds), *History of East Africa*, Vol. 3 (London, Oxford University Press, 1976), p. 457.
4. Rothchild, *Racial Bargaining*, p. 33.
5. Ibid. Smith, 'Immigrant Communities', pp. 460–461.
6. Rothchild, *Racial Bargaining*, p. 37.
7. Ibid., pp. 41–47.
8. The majority of male Asian employees interviewed by Rothchild in 1966 earned between £360 and £719 per annum. Ibid., p. 50.
9. Ibid., p. 188.
10. Ibid., p. 248.
11. *Daily Nation*, 7 January 1971.
12. Rothchild, *Racial Bargaining*, pp. 244–248.
13. Ibid., pp. 262–269.
14. A.I. Salim, *The Swahili-Speaking Peoples of Kenya's Coast 1895–1965* (Nairobi, East African Publishing House, 1973), p. 245.
15. Ibid., p. 246.
16. Jomo Kenyatta, *Suffering Without Bitterness* (Nairobi, East African Publishing House, 1968), p. 166.
17. Rothchild, *Racial Bargaining*, pp. 181–182.
18. Republic of Kenya, *Education Commission Report Part II* (Nairobi, Government Printer, 1965), p. 19.
19. Gavin Kitching, *Class and Economic Change in Kenya* (New Haven, Yale University Press, 1980), pp. 144–145; Colin Leys, *Underdevelopment in Kenya: The Political Economy of Neo-Colonialism* (London, Heinemann, 1975), pp. 50–117.
20. Leys, *Underdevelopment*, pp. 171–174; John Carlsen, *Economic and Social Transformation in Rural Kenya* (Uppsala, Scandinavian Institute of African Studies, 1980), pp. 190–192; Christopher Leo, *Land and Class in Kenya* (Toronto, University of Toronto Press, 1984), pp. 187–94.
21. Carlsen, *Economic and Social*, pp. 191–192.
22. The best historical account of this group is provided by Kitching, *Class*. See also Leys, *Underdevelopment*, pp. 148–165.
23. Carlsen, *Economic and Social*, p. 192; Leo, *Land and Class*, pp. 187–190.
24. Michael Cowen, 'Commodity Production in Kenya's Central Province', in Judith Heyer, P. Roberts and G. Williams (eds), *Rural Development in Tropical Africa* (New York, St Martin's Press, 1981), pp. 138–139; Michael Cowen, 'The Agrarian Problem: Notes on the Nairobi Discussion', *Review of African Political Economy* 20 (January–April 1981), 62.

25. Richard Sandbrook, *The Politics of Basic Needs: Urban Aspects of Assaulting Poverty in Africa* (Toronto: Toronto University Press, 1982), pp. 147–151.
26. Sharon Stichter, *Migrant Labour in Kenya: Capitalism and the African Response 1895–1975* (London, Longman, 1982), pp. 133–139.
27. Republic of Kenya, *Employment and Earnings in the Modern Sector 1977* (Nairobi, Government Printer, 1979), pp. 5–6.
28. Tiyambe Zeleza, 'The Labour System in Independent Kenya', in W.R. Ochieng' and R.M. Maxon (eds), *An Economic History of Kenya* (Nairobi, East African Educational Publishers, 1992).
29. Republic of Kenya, *Statistical Abstract 1977* (Nairobi, Central Bureau of Statistics, 1977), p. 265, and *Statistical Abstract 1981* (Nairobi, Government Printer, 1981), p. 239.
30. Republic of Kenya, *Employment and Earnings*, p. 18.
31. Zeleza, 'The Labour System'.
32. Stichter, *Migrant Labour*, pp. 146–147; E. Johnson and W.E. Whitelaw, 'Urban-Rural Income Transfers in Kenya: An Estimated Remittances Function', *Economic Development and Cultural Change*, 22 (April 1974), 473–479.
33. Sandbrook, *Politics of Basic Needs*, p. 156.
34. Ibid., pp. 157–163.
35. ILO, *Employment, Incomes, and Equality* (Geneva, ILO, 1972).
36. Ibid., p. 96.
37. Leys, *Underdevelopment*, pp. 194–195, 250.
38. Ibid., p. 197.
39. Kitching, *Class*, pp. 197–198; Robert M. Maxon, 'A Kenyan Petite Bourgeoisie Enters Local Politics: The Kisii Union, 1944–49', *International Journal of African Historical Studies*, 19 (1986), 451–452.
40. Christopher Wrigley, 'Changes in East African Society', in Low and Smith (eds), *History*, p. 532; John Lonsdale, 'When did the Gusii (Or Any Other Group) Become a Tribe?', *Kenya Historical Review*, 5 (1977), 123–133.
41. Wrigley, 'Changes', p. 531.
42. Ibid., p. 532.
43. The average global rate of increase per annum at the end of the 1970s was 1.8%. Republic of Kenya, *Economic Survey 1979* (Nairobi, Government Printer), p. 23. See also R.A. Henin, 'The Characteristics and Development Implications of a Fast Growing Population', in Tony Killick (ed.), *Papers on the Kenyan Economy Performance, Problems and Policies* (Nairobi, Heinemann, 1981), pp. 193–207.
44. Republic of Kenya, *Economic Survey 1979*, p. 24. Republic of Kenya, *Compendium to Volume I 1979 Population Census* (Nairobi, Government Printer, 1981), p. 11.
45. From an estimated 119 per 1,000 in 1969 to 83 per 100 in 1977. Republic of Kenya, *Economic Survey 1979*, p. 27; Henin, 'Characteristics', pp. 196–200.
46. Republic of Kenya, *Economic Survey 1979*, pp. 25–26.
47. Republic of Kenya, *Economic Survey 1981* (Nairobi, Central Bureau of Statistics, 1981), p. 29. According to the 1979 census, 18.6 per cent of the population was under five years of age!
48. Ibid., pp. 34–35.
49. Republic of Kenya, *African Socialism and Its Application to Planning in Kenya* (Nairobi, Government Printer, 1965), p. 52.
50. Republic of Kenya, *Development Plan 1970–74* (Nairobi, Government Printer, 1969), p. 500. Republic of Kenya, *Development Plan 1989–93* (Nairobi, Government Printer, 1989), p. 209.
51. Republic of Kenya, *Economic Survey 1979*, p. 24.
52. Republic of Kenya, *Population Census 1979* (Nairobi, Government Printer, 1981). Urban centres are those with 2,000 or more inhabitants.
53. This section on urbanization is based heavily on R.A. Obudho and Rose A. Obudho,

'The Post-Colonial Urbanization Process in Kenya', in Ochieng' and Maxon (eds), *Economic History*, pp. 405–444.

54. Sandbrook, *Politics of Basic Needs*, pp. 44–46.
55. Henry Rempel, 'The Extent and Nature of Population Movement into Towns', in R.A. Obudho (ed.), *Urbanization and Development Planning in Kenya* (Nairobi, Kenya Literature Bureau, 1981), p. 86.
56. Ibid., pp. 58–63; Obudho and Obudho, 'Post-Colonial Urbanization'.
57. R.B. Ogendo, 'Industrial Role of the Main Towns', in Obudho (ed.), *Urbanization and Development Planning*, p. 48.
58. Republic of Kenya, *Development Plan 1974–78*, Part I (Nairobi, Government Printer, 1974), p. 469.
59. *Sunday Nation*, 2 June 1963.
60. Republic of Kenya, *Ministry of Education Triennial Survey 1964–66* (Nairobi, Government Printer, 1967), p. 2.
61. Republic of Kenya, *Education Commission Report Part II*, pp. v–vi.
62. Ibid., p. v.
63. Republic of Kenya, *Development Plan 1964–70* (Nairobi, Government Printer, 1964), p. 101, and *African Socialism*, p. 39.
64. Republic of Kenya, *African Socialism*, p. 30.
65. Daniel N. Sifuna, *Development of Education in Africa: The Kenya Experience* (Nairobi, Heinemann, 1990), pp. 162–164.
66. Not all of this was in *harambee* schools, as private, non-community, schools came to enrol a sizeable number of pupils as well. Ibid., p. 165; Republic of Kenya, *Development Plan 1979–1983*, Part I (Nairobi, Government Printer, 1978), p. 157.
67. Sifuna, *The Kenya Experience*, p. 172.
68. Republic of Kenya, *Triennial Survey*, p. 2.
69. Republic of Kenya, *Kenya Education Commission Report Part I* (Nairobi, Government Printer, 1964), p. 13; D.N. Sifuna, *Short Essays on Education in Kenya* (Nairobi, Government Printer, 1980), pp. 139–143.
70. Sifuna, *Short Essays*, p. 104.
71. Michael P. Todaro, 'Education and National Economic Development in Kenya', in Killick (ed.), *Papers*, p. 276; Lawrence Lockhart, 'The Economics of Nine Years Education for All', in Killick (ed.), *Papers*, p. 284.
72. David Court and Dharam Ghai (eds), *Education, Society and Development: New Perspectives from Kenya* (Nairobi, Oxford University Press, 1974), p. 10.
73. Sifuna, *The Kenya Experience*, p. 167.
74. Ibid., p. 169; ILO, *Employment, Incomes and Equality*, pp. 238–249.
75. Sifuna, *The Kenya Experience*, p. 175.
76. Todaro, 'Education and National', p. 277.
77. Republic of Kenya, *Development Plan 1964–70*, p. 107.
78. Republic of Kenya, *African Socialism*, p. 30.
79. Ibid., p. 47.
80. Republic of Kenya, *Development Plan 1966–70* (Nairobi, Government Printer, 1966), p. 314.
81. Ibid., pp. 315–320.
82. It was one for 72,000 in 1978. Republic of Kenya, *Development Plan 1979–83*, p. 128.
83. Republic of Kenya, *Development Plan 1989–93*, p. 20.
84. Only in the case of health centres did Northeastern experience some advance: from 1 per cent of the national total in 1966 to 3 per cent in 1979.
85. Republic of Kenya, *Compendium*, p. 17.
86. Tony Killick, 'Introduction to Part VI: The Economics of Education', in Killick (ed.), *Papers*, p. 265.
87. Ibid., p. 267.

88. Arthur Hazlewood, *The Economy of Kenya: The Kenyatta Era* (Oxford, Oxford University Press, 1979), p. 218.
89. J. Owino-Ombudo, *Harambee, Its Origin and Use* (Nairobi, Transaction Publishers 1972), p. 56; *Sunday Nation*, 2 June 1963.
90. Republic of Kenya, *Development Plan 1966–70*, p. 325.
91. Ibid.; Republic of Kenya, *Education Commission Report Part II*, pp. 21–26.
92. E.M. Godfrey and G.C.M. Mutiso, 'The Political Economy of Self-Help: Kenya's Harambee Institutes of Technology', in Court and Ghai (eds), *Education, Society*, p. 271.
93. Clara Josephine Elsa Abreu, 'Self Help in Education: The Contribution of African and Asian Voluntary Organizations, 1900–1973 and the Development of Education in Kenya', MED Thesis, University of Nairobi, 1974, p. 363.
94. Ibid., p. 372.
95. Sifuna, *Short Essays*, pp. 110–111.
96. Republic of Kenya, *Kenya Official Handbook* (Nairobi, Government Printer, 1983), p. 204.
97. Republic of Kenya, *Development Plan 1989–93*, p. 256.
98. Kivuto Ndeti, *Cultural Policy in Kenya* (Paris, UNESCO, 1975), p. 47.
99. The major figure to hold out against this practice was Kenya's first vice-president, Oginga Odinga.
100. This was not without some controversy as, until the end of the 1960s, the great majority of television licences were held by non-Africans.
101. Ndeti, *Cultural Policy*, p. 28.
102. Ibid., p. 42.
103. Republic of Kenya, *Kenya Official Handbook*, p. 205.
104. R.M. Osotsi, 'The Theatre in Independent Kenya', in William R. Ochieng' (ed.), *Themes in Kenyan History* (Nairobi, Heinemann, 1990), p. 213, and S.O. Amuka, 'Oral Literature and Fiction', in ibid., p. 248.
105. Amuka, 'Oral Literature', pp. 247–248. I am particularly grateful to Dr Amuka for further elucidation on these points.
106. Ibid., p. 247.
107. Osotsi, 'The Theatre', p. 211.
108. B.E. Kipkorir, 'Towards a Cultural Policy for Kenya: Some Views', Institute of African Studies, University of Nairobi paper 131, 29 January 1980, pp. 1 and 5.
109. David Cook and Michael Okenimkpe, *Ngugi wa Thiong'o: An Exploration of His Writings* (London, Heinemann, 1983), pp. 209–210.

Part Three

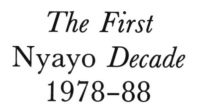

The First
Nyayo *Decade*
1978–88

Six

The Economics
of Structural Adjustment

ROBERT MAXON & PETER NDEGE

During the period 1978–88, the Kenya economy encountered severe difficulties and was presented with formidable challenges as it sought to sustain the impressive record of growth that marked the Kenyatta era. By the mid-point of the first *nyayo* decade, it had become apparent to the government and the private sector that the 1980s were a far cry from the 'golden age' that marked the period 1964–75. The Kenya economy was beset, during the first ten years of the Moi presidency, with economic problems of both external and internal origin. The government's response would be the economics of structural adjustment.

As to the former problems, the continued world economic crisis of the 1970s, the increase in crude oil prices in 1979 and the world recession that followed in its wake had a negative impact on the Kenya economy. Throughout the decade, moreover, Kenya's major exports were subject to considerable fluctuations in prices, and this helped to hold back sustained economic expansion. As examples of the latter, the droughts of 1979–80 and 1984, which brought food shortages in their wake and necessitated large imports of grain, provided severe setbacks for the economy as a whole. Gross national product (GNP) per capita fell from US$420 in 1980 to US$330 in 1987.[1] The gross domestic product (GDP) growth rate fell to 3.8 per cent during 1980–87 (as opposed to 6.9 per cent for 1965–80).[2] The government was forced, as a result of these and other factors, to take the unprecedented action of issuing several major sessional papers during the decade, through which it sought to lay down strategies for meeting these difficulties. Most involved the adoption of what came to be known as structural adjustment policies (SAP). One of the first, *Sessional Paper No. 4 of 1980 Economic Prospects and Policies* scaled down the development programme in light of the impact of the oil price rises; another, *Sessional Paper No. 4 of 1981 National Food Policy*, sought to establish policies that would attain self-sufficiency in food production following the food shortage of 1979–80; the *Sessional Paper No. 4 of 1982 on Development Prospects and Policies* outlined SAP to be adopted to deal with the continuing severe financial crisis, which had produced GDP growth rates even slower than the revised target of the 1980 sessional paper; a fourth, *Sessional Paper No. 1 of 1986 Economic Management for Renewed Growth*, represented a further attempt to reorientate priorities and policy, through SAP. It was hoped that these would enable the Kenya economy to better meet the challenges of the 1980s and the succeeding decade.

These initiatives achieved some measure of success. For example, self-sufficiency in maize, though interrupted by the 1984 drought, had been achieved by the end of the 1980s. On the other hand, a number of negative economic trends manifested themselves, and indeed worsened, during the same period. The nation's balance of payments remained firmly in the red, much of the 1980s witnessed double-digit annual infla-tion rates and the public debt rose dramatically, particularly as a result of foreign borrowing. The first *nyayo* decade was thus not an easy time for Kenya's economy. More than anything else, the experience of these years served to emphasize what is perhaps the most fundamental factor in twentieth-century Kenya's economic history, the dependent nature of the economy.

The Policy Framework

The theme of continuity that marked the presidency of Daniel arap Moi, clearly emphasized by his choice of *nyayo* (footsteps) as the watchword of his administration, was nowhere more apparent than with regard to economic policy. Moi's ascendancy to the presidency in August 1978 was marked by no significant change in the development strategy and economic planning that had emerged during the Kenyatta era. This was hardly surprising as those classes and economic interest groups that had been influential during the Kenyatta era maintained that posture under the new leadership.

The Kenya government remained committed to a capitalist-orientated, mixed economy and economic policies that aimed at creating and sus-taining a high rate of economic growth. Among the most significant of the latter were measures which guaranteed private property ownership and the encouragement of foreign investment through legislative provi-sion for the repatriation of profits. Also significant were the measures, detailed in an earlier chapter, to promote indigenization of the economy, to enhance the expansion of agricultural exports and import substitution industrialization and to provide the basic infrastructure to support both. In pursuit of these goals, the government created or reorganized a num-ber of parastatal institutions in all sectors of the economy. In its desire to promote economic growth, moreover, the government never lost sight of the need to bring about a more equitable distribution of income. In fact, economic development was officially seen as essential for any effective assault on poverty, ignorance and disease, identified by Kenya's founding fathers as the nation's primary enemies.[3]

The initial economic planning pronouncements of the *nyayo* era made clear that there would be little break with past policies. Both the 1979-83 Development Plan and the 1979 Kenya African National Union (KANU) election manifesto emphasized this continuity.[4] Nevertheless, the documents did provide for some change in emphasis in development planning. Both allocated the highest priority to rural areas and emphasized the need for industry to turn from import substitution to production for export. Party and government leaders also recognized that, given Kenya's high rate of population growth, greater emphasis had to be given to the generation of new employment opportunities.[5]

Yet both political leaders and economic planners entered the *nyayo* era facing significant economic constraints. Largely the result of external factors and forces, notably the steep oil price rises of 1973-75 and the collapse of the East African Community, Kenya's rate of GDP growth had dropped to 4.7 per cent for the period 1972-77. While impressive in comparison with many neighbours, this growth rate was a far cry from the 6.5 per cent average for the period 1964-72.[6] The boom in coffee prices that benefited the Kenya economy in 1977 and 1978 provided only a temporary stimulus. By the end of 1979, the economy had entered a period of severe downswing, which would persist through 1982. This would mark a strong contrast with the 'golden days' of the 1960s and early 1970s.

Both external and internal factors combined to bring about this recession. The main external factor was the world recession that followed the oil price increase. Stagnation in world trade and the adoption of restrictive policies by the industrialized North had had a very negative impact on Kenya's extroverted economy for much of the 1970s.[7] Kenya experienced an accelerated deterioration in her terms of trade as prices for her main export crops fell, consumer prices rose and the GDP growth rate (at constant 1982 prices) fell from 8.2 per cent in 1977 to 3.9 per cent in 1980.[8] The government responded to this situation by new policy initiatives, summarized in Sessional Paper No. 4 of 1980. The government scaled down its projected rate of growth and development objectives. It introduced import constraints, initiated measures to promote exports, expanded external borrowing and attempted to cut back on government expenditure.[9] It initiated a number of measures that would be characteristic of a SAP aimed at industry.

A significant internal factor was the 1979-80 drought. This was an important element in producing a decline in agricultural production, particularly maize. This helped to cause the first food shortage in independent Kenya. During 1980 Kenya had to import substantial amounts of maize, wheat and milk. However, drought alone was not the cause of Kenya's food problems in 1979–80. The nation's large population growth, a shortage of unexploited, arable land and the high rate of urbanization played a role.[10] Government marketing policies were also responsible. Lack of storage capacity led the parastatal concerned to reduce the price and quantities purchased in 1978; government credit to large-scale farmers was also cut. Thus farmers, predictably, reduced the area planted with maize in the following year. In 1979, moreover, exports of maize left the nation without sufficient strategic reserve.[11]

The government soon realized the economic and social implications of the food shortage, and it sought to develop measures to deal with the situation so as to achieve 'a position of broad self-sufficiency in the main foodstuffs in order to enable the nation to be fed without using scarce foreign exchange'.[12] Above all, Kenya aimed at self-sufficiency in maize. Measures to achieve these ends were laid down in the 1981 sessional paper on national food policy. Most significant were the improvement of the marketing and processing mechanisms, an increase in storage capacity, improved credit for farmers, ensuring that adequate inputs were made available to farmers and, perhaps most important of all, providing adequate price incentives for the production of foodstuffs. Kenya, like many African nations, had followed, for the previous decade or more, a policy of keeping grain prices artificially low, which favoured the urban consumer at the expense of the rural producer. In the sessional paper, the government recognized the need to provide more attractive producer prices for basic foodstuffs.[13] From 1981 onward, moreover, the achievement of food self-sufficiency assumed a very high priority among Kenya's economic goals.

Another factor that adversely affected the economy was the 1982 coup attempt. It had a negative impact, particularly on the investment climate and on tourism. Nevertheless, the rapid restoration of order helped to promote a relatively quick recovery from any adverse effects of the coup attempt.

Nevertheless, Kenya's economy, beset by a prolonged international recession and local drought, continued to be characterized by crisis in 1981 and 1982. Rates of GDP growth were lower even than those revised in the 1980 sessional paper. The state was facing 'a serious financial crisis', which manifested itself in severe balance-of-payments difficulties and budgetary shortfalls that necessitated increased indebtedness. Imports grew more rapidly than exports between 1979 and 1981, while debt service charges were three times higher in 1981 than in 1979.[14]

The severity of the financial crisis led the government to take immediate action, through SAP, to try to check the situation. These were summarized in Sessional Paper No. 4 of 1982. Focusing particularly on the next two years, the government sought to renew growth while mitigating the budgetary and trade problems. In industry, future growth would have to be more export orientated. Thus the new strategies included tariff revision and the gradual elimination of protective tariffs that did not promote industrial efficiency, remission of price controls so that domestically produced products would compete with imports, devaluation of the shilling so as to make imports more expensive and stimulate exports, and a new system of import licensing.[15] In agriculture, future growth was seen as depending on more intensive use of existing farms and acreages through improved yields. Above all, this meant significant changes in institutional arrangements and incentives, especially better prices, as outlined in the previous year's food policy paper. Indeed, Sessional Paper No. 4 of 1982 emphasized the importance of agriculture: 'The rapid growth of agricultural production is the nation's highest development priority.'[16]

As a result of the initiatives undertaken by government and improved rainfall, food output increased in 1981 and 1982, and this had a stimulative effect on the Kenya economy. Although prices for coffee and tea generally fell during the same period, the Kenya economy obtained relief from recessionary influences in 1983. Oil prices dropped and export prices for coffee and tea increased. Kenya's inflation rate lowered, but the nation's debt-servicing burden remained very high, forcing the government to adopt a tight monetary policy so as to preserve foreign exchange.[17]

Thus the Kenya economy ended 1983 on a somewhat mixed note. There was reason for optimism, but significant difficulties continued to beset the economy. By 1983, external debt service took approximately 22% of foreign exchange earnings.[18] The situation was exacerbated by the deteriorating terms of trade that marked the *nyayo* era. In 1981, for example, an average unit of Kenya's exports could buy only 66 per cent of the imports it could buy in 1972.[19]

While external factors thus had significant negative impacts on the economy, the government faced domestic difficulties as well. Of primary importance in this regard was the huge rise in government expenditure and the resulting budget deficits. Government expenditure as a percentage of GDP increased from 24.7 per cent in 1976/77 to 35.5 per cent in 1980/81. This 'intolerable' rapid growth in expenditure was the result of population growth, the need for food imports necessitated by the drought, a rise in defence spending and increases in public-sector employment following the 1979 agreement linking government, the private sector and trade unions in an effort to provide more jobs. The government identified two other trends that aggravated, during the 1970s, the expanding expenditure picture. The state had attempted 'to provide more and better services to the people while reducing the share of the costs falling on the beneficiaries', and government expenditure on parastatals engaged in commercial enterprises had grown 'disproportionately'.[20] Far too high a proportion of government investment in parastatals was unproductive. The issues of the scale of government expenditure in support of parastatals and the cost of services to the population, such as education and health care, would remain pressing, and indeed controversial, throughout the 1980s. However, containing and reducing expenditure in these areas, first identified as important in the 1984–88 development plan, would prove difficult to accomplish.

Since the nation's external debt-service burden was approaching the limit set by government, a difficult choice had to be made. It was no longer feasible to borrow from external sources. The 1984–88 development plan summarized the situation succinctly. Kenya's choice was 'to accept a much lower rate of growth than is needed for development or to make every conceivable effort to mobilize the nation's resources in a major domestic development effort. The Government has chosen the second course of action.'[21]

Thus the major theme of the 1984–88 development plan was 'mobilizing domestic resources for equitable development'. Dismissing two means of reducing the nation's dependence on external sources of finance, raising taxes and increasing domestic borrowing, as 'not promising in present circumstances', the plan sought other means to accomplish the goal of mobilizing domestic resources. Among the most significant were the reduction of government investment in 'not-essential activities' and the divestiture of such investment in others, together with an improvement in government efficiency. The plan also proposed measures to promote private domestic savings, external trade and private foreign investment. It sought to provide means of promoting the use of underutilized productive capacity so as to expand output without substantial new investments in land, plant or equipment.[22] Also significant was the proposal to initiate 'cost sharing with beneficiaries' as it was 'both necessary and equitable to expect those who are fortunate enough to benefit from Government services and infrastructure to bear a larger share of their costs so that similar services can be further extended to others'.[23] Kenyans would be asked to meet a larger share of the cost of such services.

Moreover, the 1984–88 plan was the first to reflect the district focus for rural development that had been adopted by government as from 1 July 1983. Since the rural areas were the source of most food and export commodities and where some 80 per cent of the population lived, it was argued that it was there that the most effective mobilization of development resources could be accomplished. Thus responsibility for planning and implementing rural development was shifted from Nairobi to the districts. The objective was to 'broaden the base of rural development and encourage local initiative in order to improve problem identification, resource mobilization and project implementation'.[24] Throughout the rest of the decade, development efforts in Kenya would operate within a district focus.

Promoting equitable development involved, as in earlier development plans, efforts to alleviate poverty, enhancing a rural–urban balance and providing for a better balance of development among various regions of the country. Emphasis was also placed on measures to provide for basic needs, such as food, nutrition, health care, education and housing, for as large a cross-section of the population as possible.[25] This thrust fit in well with the prevailing emphasis on a 'basic needs' approach then popular with the World Bank and several industrialized donor nations.

Despite the economic difficulties noted earlier, the 1984–88 development plan was prepared with substantial optimism that Kenya could move forward to address them and continue with a high rate of economic growth. This optimism was soon altered by the disastrous 1984 drought. Kenya's agriculture was severely affected. Maize and wheat production fell by 35 and 45 per cent respectively, and dairy production was also reduced. As a whole, the Kenya GDP grew by a mere 0.8 per cent in 1984.[26] The devastating drought caused severe food shortages, and the government was forced to import more than one million tonnes of grain to avert a potential famine.

These and other measures undertaken by the government combined with rising prices for some of Kenya's exports (notably tea) to enable Kenya to surmount the crisis created by the drought. Indeed, the Kenya economy recovered rapidly in 1985 and 1986. Aided by a boom in coffee prices and a decline in oil prices, the GDP grew at 4.8 per cent in the former year and 5.5 per cent in the latter. The budget deficit and inflation were reduced, and self-sufficiency in maize was attained. Thus quick government action, a favourable international market for coffee and tea and continued growth in tourism combined to promote recovery and demonstrate the underlying strength of the Kenya economy in comparison with other East African neighbours.

Nevertheless, surmounting the problems created by the drought left the Kenya economy with relatively severe problems. The continued high level of population growth threatened to overwhelm the economy's capacity to expand. Kenya's terms of trade continued to deteriorate, and the nation was unable to significantly reduce its dependence on external borrowing. Neither was the state able to significantly reduce government expenditure on those activities not directly related to economic development. In early 1985, for example, 60 per cent of ministries' recurrent expenditure went to pay salaries.[27] These factors combined with external pressure to bring the government to alter economic policy so as to further a structural adjustment process.

SAP had become, by the 1980s, an article of faith with the World Bank and the International Monetary Fund (IMF) as far as Third World economies were concerned. Such policies were given strong backing by the Reagan administration in the United States. The SAP advocated by these international donors normally included exchange rate manipulation so as to spur exports by devaluing local currencies, a reduction of tariffs so as to facilitate imports, the elimination of artificial price controls in a market-based price structure for agricultural products, encouragement of domestic savings, a reduction of government expenditure on social services and employment, and privatization or the reduction of the number and role of parastatals in the economy.[28]

For Kenya, the new thrust was made part of the economic policy with the publication of *Sessional Paper No. 1 of 1986 Economic Management for Renewal Growth*. Focusing on the period from 1986 until the end of the century, the paper attempted to provide a framework for 'a new phase of development and the provision of basic needs'. The foundation of the new phase was to be 'renewed, rapid economic growth', specifically an average GDP growth rate of 5.6 per cent. This rapid growth would have to be generated by expanded job creation, a reduction of the rate of population increase, a dynamic informal sector that created jobs at low cost, and restructured industry that would move from import substitution to the creation of new export markets. It was particularly important to bring about increased productivity in agriculture so as to feed the nation, provide export revenues and raise rural incomes. The paper noted especially the need to promote widespread rural non-farm activity.[29]

Specifically, the government advocated a strategy that included:

> a flexible exchange rate policy that maintains over time sufficient rewards for exporting of all commodities and for efficient substitution for imports; farm prices that enable small and large farmers to earn adequate incomes to cover increases in the costs of inputs and the cost of living, thus moving towards greater food security and an improved rural–urban balance; import tariff and licensing policies that reduce the costs of imported inputs and gradually achieve more moderate levels of protection, thus inducing industry to improve its efficiency and ability to compete in world markets; wage guidelines that contribute to reduced inflation and encourage employment creation . . . prices that reflect real scarcities and thus influence users to conserve on those commodities, such as petroleum and wood fuels, that are most scarce and therefore most costly to the economy.[30]

These would remain key elements of Kenya's economic policy through the 1980s and into the next decade. The 1989–93 development plan would incorporate the structural adjustment process.[31] Economic and development planning during the first *nyayo* decade would thus be characterized by continuity with the preceding era. Nevertheless, the difficulties that plagued the economy in the wake of the world recession and oil price rises pushed Kenya towards SAP. These had come, by the middle of the 1980s, to occupy a major place in Kenya's economic policy.

Agriculture

As agriculture continued to be the most important sector of the Kenya economy, it would be the focus of SAP during the first *nyayo* decade. The major impact of SAP in agriculture may be seen in the frequency with which the government raised producer prices in attempts to spur increased production. This was particularly the case with food crops such as maize, wheat and sugar-cane. Despite considerable criticism of the performance of parastatals dealing with the agricultural sector, the state, turning a deaf ear to calls for privatization and competition from advocates of SAP, did little to alter the monopoly role these played in the marketing of produce and provision of inputs.

Agriculture was the nation's major source of food, foreign exchange, raw materials for domestic industry and employment. As noted above, the development plans and sessional papers of the period emphasized these facts, and the droughts of 1979–80 and 1984 served to give highest priority to the achievement of national self-sufficiency in food and the maintenance of adequate levels of strategic reserves. By 1989, the latter was defined as sufficient capacity to 'carry the country for at least six months in the worst of times'.[32]

An indication of agricultural performance for the decade can be obtained from Tables 6.1 and 6.2. In reviewing the data provided in the tables, it must be borne in mind that marketed production figures do not tell the whole story so far as the role of agriculture in Kenya's economy is concerned. A substantial proportion of food crops, for example maize, is consumed within rural households or sold in local markets rather than through the official marketing mechanism.[33] Both the 1978–79 Rural Survey and the 1986–87 Agricultural Production Survey, moreover, suggest that permanent cash crops, such as coffee and tea, account for only about 13 per cent of the total planted acreage on Kenya's small farms.[34]

As might be expected, the tables suggest a mixed, or uneven, performance by the agricultural sector of the economy. For none of the major crops listed, other than perhaps sugar-cane, was the decade one of continuous expansion or decline. The mixed fortunes of most crops were the result of environmental, economic (both local and international) and what may be termed bureaucratic factors. Among the first of these, the droughts stand out. The fall in marketed production of maize, wheat and milk in 1980 and 1984 illustrated this. The impact of international economic forces can be seen in the rise in the value of tea sales (higher world prices) in 1984 and the dramatic decline in the value of sales of pyrethrum extract in 1983 and 1984 (reduced international demand and prices). Bureaucratic factors also had an impact on agriculture. As in the preceding decades, government involvement in agriculture, through marketing boards, agricultural extension services and parastatals dealing

Table 6.1 Sales to Official Marketing Boards, 1979–88

Crop	Unit	1979	1980	1981	1982	1983	1984	1985	1986	1987	1988
Maize	000 tons	241.9	217.9	472.9	571.3	636.0	560.6	582.9	669.5	657.9	485.3
Wheat	000 tons	201.0	215.7	214.4	234.7	242.3	135.4	193.5	224.7	148.3	220.3
Coffee	000 tons	75.1	91.3	90.7	88.4	95.3	118.5	96.6	114.9	104.9	124.6
Tea	000 tons	99.3	89.9	90.9	95.6	119.3	116.2	147.1	143.3	155.8	164.0
Sugar-cane	mn tons	3.1	4.0	3.8	3.1	3.2	3.6	3.5	3.6	3.7	3.8
Pyrethrum extract	tons	114	162	241	258	87	34	50	74	93	102
Milk	mn litres	241	187	223	260	275	190	231	316	347	359

Sources: *Economic Survey 1984* and *Economic Survey 1989.*

Table 6.2 Value of Recorded Marketed Production at Current Prices, 1979–88 (K£ million)

Crop	1979	1980	1981	1982	1983	1984	1985	1986	1987	1988
Maize	9.36	10.39	23.64	30.78	48.95	49.05	54.56	66.50	68.09	54.18
Wheat	14.89	17.67	17.87	22.02	26.92	17.84	26.26	32.88	24.88	35.12
Coffee	105.68	118.86	102.47	122.87	166.25	227.67	181.89	288.32	192.16	278.11
Tea	67.34	71.52	80.59	93.19	130.31	301.12	247.60	242.33	194.76	203.72
Sugar-cane	23.30	29.52	30.88	29.40	34.34	40.99	46.75	52.79	55.46	68.77
Pyrethrum extract	5.7	9.74	13.39	14.78	5.03	1.94	2.92	4.48	5.64	6.63
Milk	17.47	15.01	22.80	28.51	32.80	25.78	36.26	56.51	62.08	60.67

Sources: *Economic Survey 1982, Economic Survey 1986* and *Economic Survey 1989.*

with specific crops, to take but a few examples, remained extensive. Such factors as government pricing policies, provision of inputs, processing and storage, and payment of growers by parastatals served to both encourage and discourage marketed production during the decade. It is clear, for example, that the decline in pyrethrum sales in the 1983–84 period was the result not just of an unfavourable international market, but also the failure of the Pyrethrum Board to release payments to growers.[35]

Despite problems such as these, the government had some success in meeting its highest agricultural priority during the 1980s, food self-sufficiency. Self-sufficiency in maize and milk had been attained by 1988. Marketed maize production in 1986 and 1987 was particularly important in enabling the government to establish the targeted level of reserves for food security. Production in 1988 roughly matched demand.[36] Marketed milk production, on the other hand, rose steadily from 1985 through to the end of 1988. This was the result of improved weather, a 42 per cent increase in producer prices between 1984 and 1988, and improved transportation and processing services offered by the Kenya Cooperative Creameries (KCC). As part of the structural adjustment process, moreover, the government had by 1988 ended the KCC's monopoly on sales of milk and dairy products. It faced competition from producer co-operatives in Bungoma and Meru.[37]

While domestic self-sufficiency was reached in maize and milk, such was not the case with wheat and sugar. Consumption of wheat flour outpaced domestic production throughout the decade. Partly, this was the result of a trend in Kenya agriculture since independence. Wheat was predominantly a large-farm crop and, with the breakup of many large, mixed farms for settlement schemes, land planted with wheat had declined by some 20 per cent by 1985. The government responded to the need to spur production after 1984 by offering higher producer prices, greater assistance with inputs, planting and harvesting, and improved marketing measures. The increased production and sale of 1988 represented considerable success, in reducing wheat imports by some 65 per cent. Nevertheless, self-sufficiency in wheat was still far from being reached.

The same was true for sugar in 1988. Unlike wheat, however, sugarcane production had attained domestic self-sufficiency by 1979. Kenya exported sugar between 1981 and 1984. From 1985, however, Kenya was forced to import at least 40,000 tonnes of sugar per year. This was largely the result of domestic consumption outstripping production. Between 1984 and 1989, for example, sugar consumption rose by 41 per cent while production of cane grew by only 11 per cent. Government measures to promote production and hold back consumption had limited success. Producer prices were significantly raised after 1984, but problems with acceptance and processing of cane and payments to growers served to hold down output. The closure of the Miwani and Ramisi sugarmills serves as an example of the latter deterrent to expansion of sugar output.[38] Shortages of sugar in the shops, a phenomenon of the late 1980s, was often attributed to smuggling of Kenya refined sugar to neighbouring countries.

Despite the achievement of food self-sufficiency, difficulties with food production remained. During the period from 1975 to 1986, calorie consumption per person went down. From a sufficient daily supply in the former year, it had fallen to almost 80 per cent of the standard rating by the latter.[39]

As in the preceding years, coffee and tea were Kenya's most important export crops. In 1982, for example, coffee and tea sales provided 60 per cent of total marketed production. In 1986, the figure was 68 per cent.[40] These suffered less from the ravages of drought than food crops, but, in terms of value returned to the grower and foreign exchange earnings, coffee and tea demonstrated great dependency on external market forces. Both experienced mini-booms: coffee in 1986 and tea in 1984. However, world market forces produced drastically lower prices in both cases within the next year. Table 6.3 demonstrates the fluctuation of coffee and tea prices in the 1980s. Coffee and tea were produced on both estates and small farms. Expansion in acreage planted during the *nyayo* era came more from the latter. By 1988, 66 per cent of Kenya's coffee was produced on small farms while approximately 45 per cent of tea came from that source. By the end of that year, coffee and tea were Kenya's second and third most important earners of foreign exchange. In neither case, however, does expanding acreage provide the main reason for the expansion in production shown in Table 6.1. Rather, rising yields were the major factors in increased output. According to official government figures, the average yield per hectare for smallholder tea increased by 59 per cent between 1983 and 1988.[41]

Table 6.3 Average Gross Coffee and Tea Prices to Growers, 1980–88 (KSh per 100 kg)

Year	Coffee	Tea
1980	2,635	1,591
1981	2,258	1,774
1982	2,780	1,940
1983	3,488	2,184
1984	3,844	5,184
1985	3,972	3,366
1986	5,020	3,382
1987	3,662	2,500
1988	4,465	2,037

Sources: *Economic Survey 1984* and *Economic Survey 1989*.

An important new undertaking of the *nyayo* era was the creation of *Nyayo* Tea Zones as a means of expanding tea cultivation on small farms. Established at the initiative of President Moi, the demarcation of *Nyayo* Tea Zones was followed by planting, improved communication and the construction of factories. A parastatal, the *Nyayo* Tea Zone Corporation, was set up to foster production in the newly planted areas.

Of all Kenya's major cash crops, on the other hand, pyrethrum experienced the greatest difficulty in sustaining export earnings. Declining international demand coupled with the 1984 drought and marketing problems brought pyrethrum extract exports to its nadir in 1984. The government expended considerable efforts to stimulate increased production after 1985 through increased producer prices and speedier payment of growers. These enjoyed some success as prices on the world market rose as a result of the reduction in the use of synthetic substitutes, but by the end of the 1980s Kenya production still fell short of meeting her world market quota.

In contrast, Kenya's most successful agricultural export during the *nyayo* era was horticultural crops. Among the latter were fresh fruits and vegetables and fresh-cut flowers. Table 6.4 illustrates the dramatic increases in export earnings from horticultural exports.

The structure of Kenya agriculture changed little during the first *nyayo* decade. Kenya continued to be characterized by large- and small-farm sectors. Less than 10 per cent of all Kenya's agricultural holdings were farms of more than 100 hectares, and all those classified as large-farm units (normally over 20 hectares) represented less than 3 per cent of all agrarian landowners. Thus Kenya remained a nation dominated by small-farm peasant producers. Available data point to little change in this pattern during the 1980s. The 1986–87 Agricultural Production Survey suggests that some 66 per cent of all agricultural holdings were less than 4 acres in size.[42]

Though relatively small in terms of numbers of units, the large-farm sector continued to play a significant role in agricultural production. A substantial proportion of such export crops as tea, coffee and sisal came from estates. These large units offer the advantage of higher yields for

Table 6.4   Value of Horticultural Exports (K£ million)

1979	9.7	1984	54.2
1980	11.4	1985	53.0
1981	12.6	1986	66.1
1982	13.6	1987	77.1
1983	17.5	1988	94.8

Sources: *Economic Survey 1984* and *Economic Survey 1989*.

such crops than on small farms. This was not the only reason for the continued importance and influence of the large-farm sector. Many such units were owned by members of the political and bureaucratic élite (including those known as 'telephone farmers').[43]

The small-farm sector in Kenya, on the other hand, remained highly stratified, as the process of differentiation, clearly visible by the end of the 1970s, continued to have an impact in the rural areas. The upper strata, whether called a middle peasantry or rural petty bourgeoisie, continued to prosper through sale of substantial portions of their production (both export and food crops) and participation in off-farm employment. At the same time, a portion of rural households was virtually landless and dependent on wage labour for its survival. Almost 50 per cent of small-farm households owned less than 2 hectares of land. These households, termed 'agricultural proletaroids' by Berg-Schlosser and Siegler, were forced to supplement agricultural production with off-farm income, often from the informal or *jua-kali* sector, in order to meet the needs of subsistence and reproduction.[44]

For small farms, therefore, the process of straddling remained characteristic of the majority of rural households. The vast majority did not take the 'exit option' and retreat to subsistence production; they remained 'captured' by the market economy. Certainly a critical factor in this situation was the responsiveness of such peasant households to market forces and price incentives and their success in influencing government policies.[45] So far as agriculture was concerned, it was in the latter area that SAP had the greatest impact.

Industry

Development in industry during the first *nyayo* decade was largely characterized by continuity rather than by change and by a heavy emphasis on SAP. The SAP in industry, as in other sectors of the economy, was aimed at insulating the industrial sector against the vicissitudes of the international economic situation and solving what was internally wrong with import-substitution industrialization (ISI). They were also undertaken to meet the conditionality of donors, such as the World Bank and the IMF.[46] They were further meant to provide incentives for private investors, mainly the multinationals. SAP never envisioned transformation of industry. They responded to the crisis in industry and to conditions imposed by donors, not by innovative initiatives but by guided continuity. Class interests, both external and internal, were involved in this and the state took them into account, taking sides rather than acting impartially.[47]

Industry experienced very hard times during the first *nyayo* decade. The droughts of 1979 and 1980 devastated agriculture, whose products fed Kenya's agro-based industries. Subsequent food imports diminished government spending in industry. The increase in oil prices, particularly between 1979 and 1983, substantially increased the cost of industrial production. Apart from the shrinking world market for Kenya's exports, recessions in the economies of industrialized countries, particularly between 1979 and 1983, substantially increased the cost of industrial production. Furthermore, the collapse of the East African Community in 1977, and the closure of the border, at one time with Tanzania, at other times with Uganda, barred Kenya's industrial products from next-door markets.

Added to these problems were those that were internal to ISI. ISI as a strategy was initiated by the colonial state, particularly after the Second World War. It was adapted and employed more vigorously by the Kenyatta regime, for rapid industrial growth, which it certainly brought about between 1964 and 1974. Thereafter, a crisis phase set in that drastically reduced and even stagnated the tempo of industrialization. Partly responsible for this was the rapid increase in oil prices in 1973 and afterwards. More fundamentally, ISI imposed limitations on further industrial growth and development by its very nature. The following have been identified in recent studies of ISI as problems inherent to and resultant from the strategy: underutilization of industrial capacity, little development of industrial skills, redundant investment, inability to produce intermediate goods, limited labour absorption, heavy dependence on imports of expensive inputs, protection and resultant exorbitant prices for ISI products, and poor terms of trade between ISI and domestic agriculture.[48]

It is therefore not surprising that industrial production sharply declined during the first years of the initial *nyayo* decade, never to improve appreciably throughout the period. Industrial output declined from 15.9 per cent in 1977 to 12.6 per cent in 1978 and from 7.1 per cent in 1979 to 4.6 per cent in 1980. Its share in the GDP similarly declined from 16 per cent in 1977 to 12.7 per cent in 1978.[49]

Although developments in Kenya's industry during the *nyayo* decade were influenced by the internal and international economic situations and by the structural weaknesses of ISI, the government's response to the situation was equally, if not more, decisive in shaping the structure of industry and determining its fortunes. During its first year, the *nyayo* regime adopted most of the policy objectives and orientation of the Kenyatta era.[50] Thus the objectives and strategies of industrial production which were formulated in the 1974–78 Development Plan were continued. These included production for domestic demand and for export at competitive prices, provision of employment, industrial diversification and sustained growth.[51] These were to be realized through commitment to a mixed economy and reliance on, and protection of, foreign and domestic private investment.[52] These remained the basic objectives and strategies of industrialization throughout the period as they were incorporated in subsequent development plans.

The 1979–83 Development Plan drew attention to the limitations of ISI and emphasized the need for alternative forms of industrialization. This, it was believed, would increase production for domestic and foreign markets, reduce the country's dependence on expensive foreign imports through a number of protection devices, create more jobs and increase efficiency in industrial production through fuller utilization of plant capacity, better use of local resources and application of better management policies.[53] All these were very difficult to realize, given the financial and other constraints of the time. It was this realization that prompted the government to formulate the *Sessional Paper No. 4 of 1980 on Economic Prospects and Policies*.

Sessional Paper No. 4 of 1980 noted that ISI investment in input industries was severely hindered by the small size of Kenya's market and high cost of production. It also pointed out that domestic industries were unnecessarily protected by the government, leading to their inefficiency. Government involvement in industry, it added, also contributed to poor performance in the sector. The sessional paper then proceeded to recommend the following structural adjustment measures: export promotion through the establishment of the export guarantee scheme; removal of qualitative restrictions on exports; reduction of industrial protection through import liberalization; and reduction of direct government involvement in industry through privatization and price decontrols.[54]

These measures, though necessary, were considered too drastic to be implemented immediately. The sessional paper was careful, for instance, to point out that 'rationalization of industrial protection' would be undertaken over several years and in a way that 'minimizes disruption and dislocation of existing firms'.[55] What necessitated this cautionary statement was the fact that the government did not want to alienate powerful foreign and local interests, which were deeply entrenched in Kenya's industry. As a consequence, SAP in industry were pursued half-heartedly and were frequently frustrated by administrative lethargy, intrigue and graft. These were manifested in the slow, uncoordinated and discriminatory aspects of SAP, such as the way in which the Export Compensation Scheme (ECS) and import licensing were administered.

Whether the process of industrialization would have experienced any rapid growth had the recommendations of the 1980 Sessional Paper been immediately implemented is difficult to tell. The fact, however, was that the recommendations never amounted to any drastic changes in Kenya's industry, and, even if attempts were made to implement them, it is doubtful whether they would have surmounted the economic problems that faced Kenya at the time. Increases in oil prices, a decline in domestic demand, stagnation in exports, recession in the world economy and acute balance-of-payments problems all reached a peak in 1982, making the year the worst one during the first *nyayo* decade. At 2.2 per cent, industrial output declined to an all-time low. The number of people employed in industry increased only slightly, from 141,300 in 1980 to 146,780 in 1982. This situation prompted the publication of *Sessional Paper No. 4 of 1982 on Development Prospects and Policies.*

Sessional Paper No. 4 appraised the local and international economic situation and found it, indeed, quite hostile to industrialization. But it also pointed out that the woes that faced the industrial sector included excessive government protection and participation.[56] The sessional paper recommended modification of protection to inefficient industries, positive incentives for exports and encouragement of the production of intermediate goods.[57] Again these strategies were not easy to implement. By 1984, two years after the publication of the sessional paper, industry had made very little advance. Industrial output grew at 4.3 per cent while its share in GDP was 3.4 per cent, barely higher than what it was in 1980. But the 1982 Sessional Paper was significant for two reasons: it revealed the extent to which the 1979–83 Development Plan had been overtaken by events as far as industrial development was concerned; it also set the tone for the industrialization strategy which informed the 1984–88 Development Plan.

The latter plan had as its thrust and strategy the consolidation of the existing industrial base through optimum utilization of installed capacity, mobilization of domestic and foreign measures for investment, increased indigenization of the industrial sector through the provision of training and advisory assistance to prospective and existing indigenous entrepreneurs, and, finally, the generation of employment through the establishment of labour-intensive industries.[58] Further, the Development Plan projected the following industrial growth targets: 5.4, 6.5, 7.0 and 7.5 per cent in 1985, 1986, 1987 and 1988 respectively. These percentages were very low compared with the previous decades.

Despite the fact that the economic strains Kenya experienced in the years before 1984 had slightly eased, industry made very little progress down to 1988. The volume of industrial output grew by 4.5 and 5.8 per cent in 1985 and 1986 respectively. Industry's contribution to GDP increased from 11.2 per cent in 1985 to 11.3 per cent the following year. Amounting to 164,800 in 1986, the number of people employed in industry experienced very little increase over previous years. There was increased need to invigorate industrial growth and development.

This was the essence of *Sessional Paper No. 1 of 1986 on Economic Management for Renewed Growth.* 'Up to the year 2000,' it declared, 'industry must be restructured to become more productive and attain rapid growth.'[59] The sessional paper emphasized increased privatization as a means of invigorating industrial growth.

Between the inception of the latter sessional paper and 1988, the condition of industry remained basically the same. The increase in volume of output was provisionally estimated at 5.7 per cent in 1987. Industry contributed 13.2 per cent to GDP in 1987. The number of people employed in industry only increased slightly, to 169,800 in 1987 and 170,300 in 1988. By 1988, only slight diversification had been achieved. This manifested itself in the establishment of new industries, such as plastic pressing and pharmaceuticals, steel rolling and galvanizing, oil-seed extraction and vehicle assembly. Rural industrialization was more politicized for populist purposes within the context of a district focus for rural development than was actually realized.

Indigenization or Kenyanization did not fare well either, enabling multinationals to dominate Kenya's industry. Most of the firms set up by indigenous entrepreneurs either failed to sustain operations or simply failed to start them. The Nile Investments, the Chui Soap Factory and Unisack simply ceased to operate soon after they were set up. Mathupaper International and J.K. Industries were placed under receivership. Even government projects, such as the Kenya Furfural Company, Ken Ren Chemicals and Fertilizers and the Kenya Fibre Corporation, also folded. The Kenya Meat Commission, a perennially ailing parastatal, remained a victim of bureaucratic mismanagement and corruption.

On the other hand, the continued establishment and proliferation of the informal industrial sector, *jua-kali*, in most of Kenya's urban areas must be seen not only as reflective of SAP but more clearly as people's response to the difficulty or impossibility of the small man to invest in the formal industrial sector. It also demonstrated the failure of the industrial sector to absorb the increasing number of unemployed. Easy entry and exit, low capital requirements, dependence on local resources and recycled waste, and employment of simple and easily adaptable technology were among the factors that aided the growth of *jua-kali*. The response of the state to this sector was marked by ambivalence. On the one hand, the *nyayo* government expressed a desire to assist, and to that end took action politically and financially. The government even wanted to incorporate the sector into the main stream of formal industrialization. On the other hand, the state, from time to time, ordered the demolition of *jua-kali* sheds, a course of action that became increasingly draconian after 1988.

Thus, by the end of the first *nyayo* decade, Kenya's industrial base was never substantially developed. This, together with the limited and unstable nature of Kenya's agricultural production, had a negative impact on the country's external trade.

External Trade

During the first *nyayo* decade Kenya's dependence on external trade continued to be high, as it had been since independence. The combined value of exports and imports to GDP in 1980 and 1984 was 68.6 per cent and 54.5 per cent respectively.[60] Kenya's external trade was characterized by one major feature: export earnings continually lagged behind import bills, resulting in growing deficits in the balance of trade. Responsible for this were the breakup in 1977 of the East African Community, where the country's export potential lay; depressed prices for Kenya's primary commodities; over-reliance on coffee and tea, whose prices often fluctuated; slumps in agricultural production due to drought conditions; and the import-substitution orientation of Kenya's industry.[61] The import bills continued to rise as the government continued to import oil and manufactured goods for industrial and agricultural development. The increasing demands of the public sector for a variety of imports and the tastes of a rapidly growing consumerist social class, the bourgeoisie, also needed to be met. Kenya was scarcely importing as much as was actually needed, even though imports alone constituted over half the value of external trade to GDP. But, as became obvious to the government, large deficits in external trade had a depressing effect on money supply and incomes, while shortages of essential imports affected industrial output and economic efficiency.[62]

The condition of external trade obviously posed multiple dilemmas, including the need to raise exports and imports while at the same time reducing the country's dependence on foreign trade, and the problem of keeping both exports and imports apace with the development needs of the country while at the same time ensuring that this did not result in high trade deficits and an adverse balance of payments. The latter, rather than the former, dilemma became a major concern of the *nyayo* regime.

The state continued, more vigorously, policies already formulated to promote exports during the Kenyatta era. As spelt out in the 1979–83 Development Plan, the strategy for increasing exports included the following: the growth of export-orientated agricultural and industrial production; diversification of exports through the development of new industrial exports and horticulture; government assistance to exporters through arrangements such as the Export Credit Guarantee Scheme (ECGS), and through increased roles for parastatals such as the Kenya National Trading Corporation (KNTC) and the Kenya External Trade Authority (KETA) in this regard.[63] ECS and ECGS were additional aspects of the scheme for export subsidies that were inaugurated by the Kenyatta regime in 1974 to encourage the exportation of local manufactures. Export subsidies were never a success before 1978. They were beset with bureaucratic delays, and they also constituted a heavy burden for the government. Besides, they were not very popular with most local manufacturers, who preferred to sell their products behind the highly protective tariff walls of the domestic market.[64] These problems continued during the Moi era, raising doubts as to whether export subsidies ought to be continued.

In June 1982, the ECS was scrapped, only to be restored by President Moi in September of the same year, perhaps as a result of pressure from the Kenya Association of Manufacturers. Announcing the restoration of ECS, President Moi said, in part:

> [The new ECS] will be based on a system whereby the more you export over the previous performance the more you benefit. There will be export compensation for all export earnings which qualified under the previous scheme at 10%. But any increase over the previous year will attract 25%; new business using new capital will only get 25% of export earnings on entry into the export market.[65]

This sudden reversal of policy shows that, despite the ineffectiveness of export subsidies, the government had almost no other option than to simply try to make subsidies more attractive to manufacturers. In fact, the number of such export incentives to manufacturers was increased by the 1984–88 Development Plan. The additional ones included manufacture under bond, which was designed to simplify imports for manufactures intended for export; the Export Credit Scheme, which required commercial banks to give higher priority to the financial requirements of exporters; the Insurance Guarantee Scheme; and a system of preferential allocation of foreign exchange for new materials intended for the manufacture of exports.[66]

The export situation between 1978 and 1988 improved, as shown in Table 6.5. Exports began to increase markedly from 1980 onwards. However, the increase was slower than that of imports. In 1980, exports covered only 55 per cent of imports, and half the total export earnings went towards financing imports of petroleum. In 1981, export earnings constituted only one-quarter of all income sources, and imports were still greater. In 1983, the increase in export earnings was largely attributed to improvements in world prices. Those improvements in the export situation were still considered inadequate, and 1984 was declared Kenya's Export Year, a year of intensive campaign aimed at publicizing Kenya's exports. The year also saw the reopening of the border with Tanzania. Whether the rise in Kenya's export earnings was the result of the export promotion, of an increase in production or of improvements in world prices for Kenya's products is not very easy to determine. It is safe to suggest that a combination of all these factors was at play. What is more clearly shown in Table 6.5 is the fact that primary products dominated exports throughout the period, and that the growth of exports on a year-to-year basis was low. The 1986 Sessional Paper on *Economic Management for Renewed Growth* therefore called for export growth of at least 5 per cent a year. It also urged diversification of exports and targeted concentration on Kenya's three largest exports, coffee, tea and petroleum products (re-export to other parts of eastern Africa), plus tourism, as the main means of export expansion.[67] Nevertheless, the

Table 6.5 Total Exports by Broad Category, 1978–88

	1978	1979	1980	1981	1982	1983	1984	1985	1986	1987	1988
K£ million											
Food and beverages	217.7	211.3	212.5	234.3	278.5	358.6	467.1	492.7	646.8	451.8	546.4
Industrial supplies	65.9	79.1	89.7	92.8	95.0	117.6	113.2	128.1	147.7	147.2	194.8
Fuel and lubricants	69.0	77.2	162.5	163.7	149.3	123.9	142.2	126.5	106.8	101.2	118.3
Machinery/capital equipment		1.5	2.5	2.0	1.8	2.6	2.1	2.6	4.1	4.1	5.6
Transport equipment	0.9	0.9	1.6	2.1	1.3	1.2	1.2	1.6	3.2	4.1	5.3
Consumer goods not elsewhere specified	14.6	15.2	18.4	18.7	19.9	25.0	28.4	33.8	49.9	44.7	47.5
Goods not elsewhere specified	0.2	0.3	0.2	0.1	0.1	0.5	0.2	0.3	0.2	0.2	0.2
Total	370.0	385.5	487.6	513.9	545.7	630.0	754.8	785.1	958.0	753.4	917.7
Percentage shares											
Food and beverages	58.8	54.8	43.6	45.6	51.0	56.9	61.9	62.8	67.5	60.0	59.5
Industrial supplies	17.8	20.5	18.4	18.1	17.4	18.7	15.0	16.3	15.3	19.5	21.2
Fuel and lubricants	18.6	20.0	33.3	31.9	27.4	19.7	18.8	16.1	11.2	13.4	12.9
Machinery and other capital equipment		0.4	0.5	0.4	0.3	0.4	0.3	0.3	0.5	0.6	0.6
Transport equipment	0.3	0.2	0.3	0.4	0.2	0.2	0.1	0.2	0.3	0.6	0.6
Consumer goods not elsewhere specified	4.1	4.0	3.8	3.6	3.6	4.1	3.8	4.3	5.2	5.9	5.2
Goods not elsewhere specified	0.1	0.1	–	–	–	0.1	–	–	–	–	–

Sources: *Economic Survey 1983* and *Economic Survey 1989.*

trend in Kenya's exports between 1986 and 1988 was no different from that of the previous years.

With regard to the import sector, the *nyayo* regime continued with the restrictive measures of the Kenyatta era and then gradually began to implement the policy of import liberalization. Import restriction consisted of import duties and a variety of credit restrictions on imports. Introduced in 1979, the Import Pre-Payment Scheme, for instance, required importers to place a deposit of 100 per cent for their imports with the Central Bank of Kenya. It was designed to make importers more selective and cautious with the use of foreign exchange and to make consumers purchase locally produced goods.[68] Another import restriction measure was the Letter of No Objection. These restrictions were resented, on the other hand, by manufacturers, traders, the IMF, other international donors and, of course, those consumers who recognized the negative impact these measures had on imports and their prices.

However, it was mainly as a result of pressure from the IMF, the World Bank and other donors that the *nyayo* regime gradually began to implement import liberalization as one of the SAP, along with devaluation of the Kenya shilling, reduction of government expenditure, strengthening the private sector and removal of price controls. In 1980, the sessional paper on *Economic Prospects and Policies* recommended the relaxation of the advance import deposit scheme, discontinuance of the Letter of No Objection practice and a shift from quantitative import restriction to tariff protection.[69] In 1981, the government made the exchange rate more flexible to encourage imports. But this effort was almost neutralized by two devaluations of the shilling.

Import liberalization, like the schemes designed to promote exports, was not easy to implement. Import licensing, apart from being beset by problems of corruption, was also delayed by administrative inefficiency. This prompted the President to issue a directive in September 1982 aimed at hastening the issuance of import licensing. He directed that

> those importing essential items for productive purposes will be assured of priority status on import licensing. On the allocation of import licences and foreign exchange, there must be control and we have a mechanism for doing this. However, to assure a more rapid and just allocation, I am requiring an immediate review of administrative machinery in order to bring about a fair application of the rules. This will be monitored by the various committees who will ensure that there is no undue delay and that importers are promptly informed of the position of their applications.[70]

Apart from such problems in the administration of import licensing, the government continued to be quite cautious with liberalization. The 1982 Sessional Paper *Development Prospects and Policies* still reiterated the need to pursue other measures to improve the economy. It noted: 'We must rather seek remedies through the expansion of exports, the reduction of non-essential imports, and special external finance to recover residual deficits until export earnings improve.'[71] But the shortage of these 'non-essential imports' reduced efficiency and output in the industrial, agricultural and public sectors of the economy.

Despite cautious import liberalization, the value of imports only declined sharply in 1979, by 6.3 per cent, when import restrictions were still in full force. As Table 6.6 indicates, 1980 saw a sharp rise in imports, partly due to the importation of large quantities of maize flour that year. Another major rise occurred in 1984, following the lifting in June of restrictions on the importation of 306 items, including petroleum products and fertilizers. A further adjustment of the exchange rate of the Kenya shilling was also responsible. As all this led to a dramatic rise in trade deficits, the 1986 Sessional Paper on *Economic Management for Renewed Growth* recommended a curb on imports. It particularly targeted extended import substitution (e.g. growth in agriculture and the *jua-kali* sector, which used relatively few imports, a shift towards labour-intensive methods), emphasizing the need to support 'efficient' import substitution while abandoning 'the highly protected generally *inefficient* substitution of the past'.[72] But, as Table 6.7 shows, the balance of trade continued to register increased deficits, attaining unprecedented heights in 1987 and 1988, as the terms of Kenya's external trade continued to worsen.

Thus by 1988, the Kenya government had not succeeded in reducing the country's dependence on foreign trade. Exports still lagged far behind imports. Deficits in the balance of payments rose to astronomical heights, and this adversely affected the country's balance of payments. They also certainly cast serious doubt on the wisdom of a country at the stage of Kenya's development trying to develop its economy through external trade.[73]

Balance of Payments and Government Finance

The first *nyayo* decade witnessed a continuation of the balance-of-payments, budgetary and financial problems that had characterized the preceding period of independent Kenya's history. Most noteworthy in this regard were, as noted above, a negative balance of payments, budget deficits, a rising level of external debt and increased debt-service charges. Kenya's position differed little in this regard from that of the economies of other African countries. Dependent on exports of raw materials and external sources of borrowing to promote development, these extroverted economies had experienced an increasingly adverse balance of payments, an increased need for external borrowing and a slowing of economic growth.

The main change in this situation that marked the initial *nyayo* decade

Table 6.6 Total Imports by Broad Economic Category

	1978	1979	1980	1981	1982	1983	1984	1985	1986	1987	1988
K£ million											
Food and beverages	38.5	32.9	41.3	44.3	52.8	83.2	127.6	109.0	116.2	98.1	101.0
Industrial supplies	179.8	179.7	261.6	240.4	224.9	253.0	289.1	353.3	408.0	469.0	641.6
Fuel and lubricants	117.8	147.3	322.4	343.7	332.6	338.2	332.4	376.2	238.6	282.4	245.9
Machinery and other capital goods	141.1	125.1	154.6	165.3	159.1	143.1	184.9	180.2	254.5	319.7	414.3
Transport equipment	126.6	94.9	121.2	88.15	85.6	66.0	113.5	122.2	259.6	190.7	267.2
Consumer goods not elsewhere specified	55.3	39.6	57.7	47.7	43.9	41.5	47.4	54.0	59.8	70.6	93.9
Goods not elsewhere specified	2.01	0.7	0.3	2.9	1.3	0.4	2.3	1.2	1.3	0.4	1.3
Total	661.1	620.2	959.0	932.4	900.3	925.4	1,097.2	1,196.0	1,337.8	1,430.8	1,765.0
Percentage shares											
Food and beverages	5.8	5.3	4.3	4.7	5.9	9.0	11.6	9.1	8.7	6.9	5.7
Industrial supplies	27.2	29.0	27.3	25.8	25.0	27.3	26.4	29.5	30.5	32.8	36.4
Fuel and lubricants	17.8	23.7	33.6	36.9	36.9	36.6	30.3	31.5	17.8	19.7	13.9
Machinery and other capital goods	21.3	20.2	16.1	17.7	17.7	15.5	16.9	15.1	19.0	22.4	23.5
Transport equipment	19.2	15.3	12.7	9.5	9.5	7.1	10.3	10.2	19.4	13.3	15.1
Consumer goods not elsewhere specified	8.4	6.4	6.0	5.1	4.9	4.5	4.3	4.5	4.5	4.9	5.3
Goods not elsewhere specified	0.3	0.1	–	0.3	0.1	–	0.2	0.1	0.1	–	0.1

Sources: *Economic Survey 1983* and *Economic Survey 1989*.

Table 6.7   Kenya's Overall Balance of Trade, 1978–88 (K£ million)

1978	1979	1980	1981	1982	1984	1985	1986	1987	1988
−265.4	−207.4	−443	−394	−375.7	−320.3	−384.6	−351	−641	−813

Sources: *Economic Survey 1982* and *Economic Survey 1989*.

Table 6.8   Kenya's Overall Balance of Payments, 1978–88 (K£ million)

1978	1980	1982	1984	1985	1986	1987	1988
−77.6	−72.2	−108.1	−32.3	−94.2	73.0	−75.9	−68.0

Sources: *Development Plan 1989* and *Economic Survey 1989*.

was a gigantic rise in the magnitude of the problem. Sessional Paper No. 4 of 1980 recognized the crucial impact of the shortage of foreign exchange resulting from 'an adverse movement in our international terms of trade and the imbalance between Government receipts and expenditure'.[74] These were rightly seen as serious constraints on economic growth and development. Table 6.8 shows the balance-of-payments situation for 1978–88, and it clearly indicates the dependent nature of the economy in this regard. Only in 1986, when a fall in oil prices coincided with a rise in coffee prices, did Kenya's balance of payments show a surplus.

The adverse balance-of-payments situation and its negative impact on the economy as a whole forced the government to give attention to SAP as a means of dealing with the situation. In general, these were directed towards expanding exports, reducing non-essential imports and, in the short term, arranging 'special external finance to cover residual deficits until export earnings improve'.[75] Thus the government arranged loans from the IMF and the World Bank. In fact, by 1987 the government had made use of IMF credits worth US$381 million.[76] In its efforts to spur exports and hold down imports, the government relied on export incentives, tariff hikes on imports, currency devaluation (two in 1981) and restrictions on imports of motor vehicles and on foreign travel.[77]

Despite government actions taken in 1981 and 1982, however, the constraints on development caused by an adverse balance of payments continued to cause official concern. Commodity exports paid for only 57 per cent of commodity imports in the first half of the 1980s. The SAP were not without some beneficial impact in so far as the balance of payments was concerned, but the sharp rise in oil prices and a drop in coffee and tea prices in 1987 demonstrated the difficulties that confronted them.

Nevertheless, one sector that made a positive contribution to the invisible component of the balance-of-payments position throughout the first *nyayo* decade was tourism. Amounting to K£62 million in 1979, tourist receipts grew to K£197 in 1985, and by 1988 these reached K£349 million, making tourism Kenya's leading earner of foreign exchange. The expanding earnings from tourism reflected the continuing appeal of Kenya to visitors from the northern hemisphere, but it was also a result of the fall in value of the shilling that marked the 1980s.[78] While the expansion in tourist receipts far exceeded the 5 per cent annual rate targeted in the 1986 Sessional Paper for export growth throughout the decade, the number of tourists visiting Kenya is dependent on factors beyond the control of the nation's economic planners. High rates of inflation in the industrialized North and a high rise in oil prices, for example, could curtail future expansion of tourist earnings.

On the budgetary front, moreover, the government, though faced with a world economic recession, strove to maintain an expanding level of expenditure on development projects and social services. The result was widened budget deficits, with a consequent need to expand government borrowing. Between 1978 and 1987, total government debt rose by 470 per cent![79] Debt-service charges rose at an even higher rate (665 per cent). Increased development expenditure in a climate of sluggish economic growth and more costly imports pushed the budget deficit from 5 per cent of GDP in 1979 to 9.5 per cent in 1981.[80] By 1987, service charges on external public and publicly guaranteed debt represented 37 per cent of the total value of all exports.[81] Within Kenya during the 1980s, the share of expenditure on economic services declined, while that on government salaries and social services, particularly education, expanded. The resulting adverse balance of payments and budgetary crisis was the target, as noted in the initial section of the chapter, of several of the SAP implemented during the same period.

The government recognized several causes for the expanding budget deficits and external borrowing. Among the most important was the international economic situation. As noted above, the costs of Kenya's imports rose dramatically and far faster than those of exports. External borrowing to finance the balance-of-payments deficit served to increase indebtedness. In addition, slower economic growth, especially during the droughts of 1979–80 and 1984, led to expanding budget deficits. At the same time, public spending increased, for a number of reasons. Increases in spending to support social services was one. A growing school-age population, the implementation of the 8-4-4 system of education after 1985 and the dramatic increases in university enrolment all pushed such spending upward. Government labour costs also accelerated, as the state expanded its role as the major employer of wage labour. Central government expanded employment by 7.4 per cent per year between 1974 and 1985. The result, as noted earlier, was that by 1985 60 per cent of ministries' recurrent expenditure went to pay salaries.[82]

Defence spending also expanded during the 1980s. Another reason for rising government expenditure was the multiplication of state parastatals and 'of a myriad of frequently complex development projects in every district and sphere of activity'.[83] Yet another factor was the fact that most ministries spent more than the original budget estimates presented to Parliament.[84]

Sessional Paper No. 4 of 1982 gave considerable attention to structural adjustment measures meant to redress the budget deficits. These included measures to control inflation and, as described above, to redress the nation's adverse trade position and balance-of-payments problems. The state also endorsed proposals to stimulate greater domestic savings as a means of enhancing the funds available for local borrowing. Extremely important were policies that would directly reduce the budget deficit by slowing the growth of expenditure. This, rather than a substantial expansion of revenue, was the focus of government strategy.

This was an 'austere' policy, but the Treasury saw no alternative in the dire economic circumstances of 1981–82. The government had to contain growth in expenditure while 'at the same time continuing to supply the essential services of Government in the quantities required'.[85] The approach was to improve government efficiency, on the one hand, and to slow expenditure growth in the development budget. Because of a concern to maintain essential services that depended on recurrent expenditure, that category of expenditure would be allowed to grow.

The austerity measures of 1981–82 did result in a fall in government spending. An improved international economic picture and Kenya's rapid recovery from the 1984 drought also played a part in the improved budgetary situation. By mid-1985, the budget deficit had been reduced to 4.3 per cent of GDP.[86]

Despite this advance, adverse budgetary pressures continued to hamper government finances and the economy as a whole. The government continued to place emphasis on SAP directed towards the budget deficit in Sessional Paper No. 1 of 1986. This meant putting 'a tight limit on ministry expenditures', cutting government employment, reducing parastatal activities and decreasing direct government involvement in managing development projects. Voicing the structural adjustment philosophy so favoured by Western capitalist nations, the World Bank and the IMF, the sessional paper maintained that 'fiscal stringency requires that the private sector, whether small-scale or large, rural or urban, must account for a larger share of investment, economic growth and employment creation in the coming years'.[87]

In addition, new budgetary initiatives would have to be undertaken. Government fiscal policy would have to dampen inflationary tendencies, restrain expenditure, reduce its claims on private capital markets, control the growth of public debt and give consideration to raising the level of taxation.[88] The 1986 Sessional Paper identified two major changes in the allocation of budget resources for the years ahead. The government would begin spending proportionately more on 'immediately productive services' that would promote agricultural and industrial expansion and proportionately less on education, health and other basic needs.[89] However, no precise means of accomplishing the latter were set out at that time.

The second major change was to come through a process of 'budget rationalization'. By this process, the state sought to reverse the emphasis on recurrent, as opposed to development, expenditure put forward in the 1982 Sessional Paper. Now projects with 'potentially high productivity' would be pushed to completion, while those with 'low potential benefits would be postponed or cancelled to free up funds for projects with higher rates of return'. New development projects would be funded only if they were 'productive investments with a very high priority'.[90]

The immediate impact of these structural adjustment initiatives announced in 1986 was hardly earth-shaking. Between 1986 and 1988, Kenya's budget deficit grew. Increased government expenditure was the major factor. The start of the 8-4-4 system, multiple university intakes and the construction of additional storage capacity for grain were all factors. By 1988, education ate up 38 per cent of Kenya's recurrent budget. A unique, but nevertheless very expensive, factor in the rising deficit was the loss incurred in hosting the 1987 All-Africa Games.[91] The escalating expenditure played a part in the continued rise in Kenya's external debt, which by 1987 made up a huge 76 per cent of total public debt.[92]

The ongoing budget problems did not lessen the government's commitment to the structural adjustment process. By the end of 1988, such measures to reduce the budget deficit were still strongly advocated. Among the most significant, and controversial, was the concept of 'cost-sharing' in the fields of health, education, water supply, agriculture and transportation. The 1988 report of the Presidential Working Party on Education and Manpower Training advocated increased cost-sharing in secondary schools, training colleges and the universities.[93] Cost-sharing was advocated for the health services so as to keep the share of the recurrent budget directed towards health below 9 per cent while allowing for an enhancement of service. While Kenyans would not feel significantly the effect of cost-sharing measures until 1989, the state had come down strongly in favour of such policies by the end of the first *nyayo* decade.

Money and Banking

The economic difficulties Kenya encountered during the first *nyayo* decade also manifested themselves in the areas of money supply, inflation and banking. As in other sectors of the economy, the impact of the philosophy and practice of structural adjustment was felt here as well. Yet, in banking in particular, SAP were not altogether successful; by the end of the decade, the government, far from loosening its control, was forced to exercise greater direction over banking.

As was the case with other Third World economies, Kenya experienced strong inflationary pressures during the 1980s. Kenya averaged double-digit inflation for the first *nyayo* decade. Inflation peaked in 1981 and 1982. The average rate of inflation for the former year was 20 per cent, while in the latter it was slightly over 22 per cent. Inflationary pressures emanated from such external factors as the steep rise in oil prices that marked this period, and the impact of the currency devaluations of 1981 and 1982, which effectively raised the price of imported goods. Among the most significant internal causes of inflation were the widening government budget deficit and sharp rises in food prices, necessitated by the need to spur domestic production.[94]

The government responded with monetary policies directed towards reducing the inflation rate. The Ministry of Finance sought to restrain its spending and domestic borrowing, and it used credit-control measures to encourage domestic savings and reduce the liquidity of financial institutions.[95] These measures enjoyed some success, as Kenya's rate of inflation dropped, on the whole, during the period 1983–86. Probably more important than the monetary measures, however, was a fall in world oil prices, a much more favourable international economic environment and a rise in the domestic production of foodstuffs. Kenya's inflation rate reached a low point for the decade at 5.7 per cent in 1986.[96]

This situation was followed by the renewed push of inflatory pressures in 1987–88. A rise in the price of imports played an important part in this, as did the expansion of the domestic money supply. A major factor was the 'mini-coffee boom' of 1986.[97] The impact of structural adjustment measures also contributed, in, for example, the price rises that followed decontrol of prices on food and beverages.[98] Given the dependent nature of Kenya's economy and the continued pressure to implement SAP, moreover, it seemed unlikely that Kenya could avoid double-digit inflation rates after 1988.

The impact of Kenya's dependent position in a generally inhospitable world economy and of SAP may also be seen in the declining value of Kenya's currency against those of the major industrial powers. Table 6.9 graphically illustrates this trend with reference to the US dollar. Obviously, the weak balance-of-payments position of the period made for a weaker Kenya shilling. In addition, devaluation so as to spur exports and reduce imports forms a central feature of structural adjustment orthodoxy. It was also advocated as a means of making Kenya more attractive to tourists from Europe and North America. Kenya undertook two major devaluations in 1981, with further significant devaluations in

Table 6.9 Exchange Rate as of 31 December, KSh to US$

1979	7.32	1984	15.71
1980	7.57	1985	16.28
1981	10.29	1986	16.04
1982	12.75	1987	16.51
1983	13.76	1988	18.59

Sources: *Economic Survey 1983* and *Economic Survey 1989*.

Table 6.10 NBFI Deposits, 1980–87 (K£ million)

1980	243	1984	608
1981	285	1985	702
1982	360	1986	806
1983	434	1987	884

Sources: *Economic Survey 1984* and *Economic Survey 1989*.

1982 and 1984. Overall, the value of the shilling against the dollar fell by 159 per cent between 1979 and 1988.

In the banking sector, on the other hand, the most striking feature of the first *nyayo* decade was the rise in number and significance of non-bank financial institutions (NBFI). Such institutions included building societies, hire-purchase companies, trade financiers and discount houses. As Table 6.10 shows, the expansion of NBFI was particularly rapid for the period 1980–87. During that time, the number of NBFI grew from 16 to 54.

The dramatic growth of NBFI in the 1980s in terms of numbers, mobilization of deposits and increased lending resulted from a combination of factors. The NBFI offered more attractive interest rates to depositors and borrowers than did the commercial banks. In contrast to the latter, NBFI required far less stringent conditions (e.g. substantial collateral) for the granting of loans. Also NBFI made loans for housing, building and construction more willingly than the commercial banks.[99] The mushrooming numbers of NBFI owed much to the fact that, thanks to the prevailing high returns on investments, these represented a very attractive business venture for entrepreneurs. They were particularly seen as 'a vehicle for indigenous Kenyans' entry into the banking sector'.[100] Another important factor was the relative lack of government regulation and control governing NBFI in Kenya.

The rapid rise of NBFI received a jolt in the banking crisis of 1985–86. A number of NBFI faced serious liquidity problems. Faced with demands for withdrawal of funds from depositors, a number were forced to close their doors. The first of the non-banks to go into receivership, in December 1984, was Rural Urban Credit Ltd. Starting in July 1986, further NBFI went under. These included Continental Bank, Continental Credit and Finance, Union Bank of Kenya, Capital Finance Company and Pioneer Building Society.[101]

The main reason for the banking crisis was poor management, combined with the lack of government control noted above. In far too many cases, the directors of NBFI failed to maintain a safe ratio between deposits and liabilities, and a number were undercapitalized. They were also guilty of poor lending policies (e.g. unsecured loans, loans to family members of directors) and excessive concentration of risk in certain areas. In addition to runs on several NBFI, there was a shift of deposits to the more established commercial banks.

Meanwhile, the government was forced to take rapid action to guarantee that depositors could recoup at least some of their money and to ensure that it could exercise far greater control over NBFI. Following the closure of Rural Urban, the Banking Act of 1968 was amended 'to instill discipline in the financial sector and to insure orderly growth'.[102] With further problems in 1986, the Central Bank of Kenya used the expanded powers to appoint special managers for ailing NBFI. Also a depositors' protection fund was set up, and special courts were established to deal with individuals and institutions implicated in wrongdoing by the crisis.[103] In subsequent years, the Ministry of Finance and the Central Bank of Kenya took further steps to bring banking under greater state control.

Moreover, the banking crisis of 1985–86 suggests a need for wariness in the implementation of SAP. The proliferation of NBFI represented the kind of growth of private ownership much favoured by advocates of structural adjustment. They provided opportunities for the accumulation of capital, and competition among NBFI and between the latter and commercial banks promised to benefit depositors and borrowers.[104] Yet, without adequate safeguards, 'market forces' and unbridled competition produced the uncontrolled growth of NBFI that eventually proved very costly to the national economy. As late as the end of 1990, the government was still involved in expensive activities (including a World Bank loan) aimed at sorting out the mess generated by the 1985–86 banking crisis.

Conclusion

Despite such negative impacts as those noted above, SAP had come to occupy a significant place in Kenya's economic policy by the end of 1988. Indeed, subsequent years would witness little modification in this situation. That SAP would exercise such an influence on the economy can hardly be viewed as surprising. Rather, the economics of structural adjustment were the logical outgrowth of the Western-orientated, capitalist structures and the patterns that made the European Economic Community the nation's dominant trading partner during the first *nyayo* decade, as well as in the preceding period of independent Kenya's history. Moreover, the severe economic problems that manifested themselves during the *nyayo* era forced government planners towards SAP. It also reflected the continued dependent nature of Kenya's economy; dependent on Western European, American and Japanese markets, development assistance and development models, Kenya would adopt SAP with less resistance than, for example, Tanzania or Zambia.

Yet perhaps the most significant characteristic of Kenya's economy during the initial *nyayo* decade was the fact that it was able to confront the economic crises of the period far more effectively than most African states. The continued growth of tourist receipts and the resiliency demonstrated by Kenya's small-farm sector, which had responded so remarkably to the opportunities of the Kenyatta era, in rebounding from the droughts and the negative international market conditions provide graphic examples of the underlying strengths. These, far more than SAP, allowed Kenya to survive the economic difficulties of the period without large-scale economic collapse and the resultant political turmoil that it would have produced.

Notes

1. Dirk Berg-Schlosser and Rainer Siegler, *Political Stability and Development: A Comparative Analysis of Kenya, Tanzania, and Uganda* (Boulder, Lynne Rienner, 1990), p. 59, and World Bank, *World Development Report 1989* (Washington, World Bank, 1989), p. 164.
2. World Bank, *World Development Report 1989*, p. 166.
3. Republic of Kenya, *Sessional Paper No. 1 of 1965: African Socialism and Its Application to Planning in Kenya* (Nairobi, Government Printer, 1965), pp. 30–31.
4. Republic of Kenya, *Development Plan 1979 to 1983* (Nairobi, Government Printer, 1979); KANU, *KANU Election Manifesto 1979* (Nairobi, KANU, 1979), p. 13.
5. Republic of Kenya, *Development Plan 1979 to 1983*, pp. 1–16; KANU, *KANU Manifesto*, pp. 11–22.
6. Republic of Kenya, *Development Plan 1979 to 1983*, p. 3.
7. Tiyambe Zeleza, 'The Global Dimensions of Africa's Crisis: Debts, Structural Adjustment, and Workers', *Transafrican Journal of History*, 18 (1989), pp. 3–7.
8. Republic of Kenya, *Development Plan 1989 to 1993* (Nairobi, Government Printer, 1989), p. 8.
9. Republic of Kenya, *Development Plan 1984 to 1988* (Nairobi, Government Printer, 1984), p. 41.
10. Republic of Kenya, *Sessional Paper No. 4 of 1981 on National Food Policy* (Nairobi, Government Printer, 1981), p. 1.
11. Ibid., p. 6.
12. Ibid., p. 2.

13. Ibid., p. 16.
14. Republic of Kenya, *Sessional Paper No. 4 of 1982 on Development Prospects and Policies* (Nairobi, Government Printer, 1982), pp. 5–7.
15. Ibid., pp. 10–14.
16. Ibid., p. 15.
17. Republic of Kenya, *Development Plan 1989 to 1993*, p. 8.
18. The Treasury saw 25 per cent as the upper limit; thus Kenya's capacity to borrow had been 'nearly exhausted'. Republic of Kenya, *Development Plan 1984 to 1988*, p. 40.
19. Ibid.
20. Ibid., p. 43.
21. Ibid.
22. Ibid., pp. 45–53.
23. Ibid., p. 47.
24. Republic of Kenya, *District Focus for Rural Development* (Nairobi, Government Printer, 1984), p. 1.
25. Republic of Kenya, *Development Plan 1984 to 1988*, pp. 57–58.
26. Republic of Kenya, *Development Plan 1989 to 1993*, p. 9.
27. Compared with only 47 per cent in 1979/80. Republic of Kenya, *Sessional Paper No. 1 of 1986: Economic Management for Renewed Growth* (Nairobi, Government Printer, 1986), p. 19.
28. Zeleza, 'Global Dimensions', p. 31.
29. Republic of Kenya, *Economic Management for Renewed Growth*, p. 1.
30. Ibid., p. 25.
31. Republic of Kenya, *Development Plan 1989 to 1993*, pp. 33–35.
32. Ibid., p. 104.
33. Official estimates were that 30 per cent of smallholder maize production went to the National Cereals and Produce Board while 10 per cent of such production went to local traders. Republic of Kenya, *Economic Survey 1989* (Nairobi, Central Bureau of Statistics, 1989), p. 97.
34. Republic of Kenya, *Statistical Abstract 1982* (Nairobi, Government Printer, 1982), pp. 123–124; *Economic Survey 1989*, 31.
35. Republic of Kenya, *Economic Survey 1984* (Nairobi, Central Bureau of Statistics, 1984), p. 56.
36. Republic of Kenya, *Economic Survey 1989*, p. 97.
37. Ibid., p. 102.
38. Ibid., p. 100.
39. Berg-Schlosser and Siegler, *Political Stability*, p. 60. See also World Bank, *World Development Report 1989*, p. 218.
40. Republic of Kenya, *Economic Survey 1987* (Nairobi, Central Bureau of Statistics, 1987), p. 105.
41. Republic of Kenya, *Economic Survey 1989*, p. 100.
42. Ibid., p. 28.
43. Berg-Schlosser and Siegler, *Political Stability*, pp. 33–34.
44. Ibid., pp. 37–38.
45. Ibid., p. 47. Smallholder coffee-growers, represented through the Kenya Planters Co-operative Union, provide an excellent example. In 1986–87, they blocked government attempts to reduce the share of coffee revenue paid to growers.
46. For details see W.E. Hecox, 'Structural Adjustment, Donor Conditionality and Industrialization in Kenya', in Peter Coughlin and Gerrishon K. Ikiara (eds), *Industrialization in Kenya: In Search of a Strategy* (Nairobi, Heinemann, 1988), p. 190.
47. For a further perspective on Kenya's industrialization see Colin Leys, 'Accumulation, Class Formation and Dependency: Kenya', in Martin Fransman (ed.), *Industry and Accumulation in Africa* (London, Heinemann, 1982), pp. 170–192.
48. Such studies include Fred Nixon, 'Import-Substituting Industrialization', in

Fransman (ed.), *Industry*, pp. 38–57; P. Anyang'Nyong'o, 'The Possibilities and Historical Limitations of Import-Substitution Industrialization in Kenya', in Coughlin and Ikiara (eds), *Industrialization*, p. 6.

49. These figures and subsequent ones on industry were compiled from the various issues of the Kenya government's *Economic Survey* between 1978 and 1988.
50. For a comprehensive analysis of the Kenyatta era see Arthur Hazlewood, *The Economy of Kenya: The Kenyatta Era* (Nairobi, London, Oxford University Press, 1979) and Tony Killick (ed.), *Papers on the Kenya Economy: Performance, Problems and Policies* (Nairobi, Heinemann, 1981).
51. Republic of Kenya, *Development Plan 1979 to 1983*, pp. 331–332.
52. Ibid.
53. Ibid., p. 327.
54. Republic of Kenya, *Sessional Paper No. 4 of 1980 on Economic Prospects and Policies* (Nairobi, Government Printer, 1980), pp. 22–23.
55. Ibid., p. 21.
56. Republic of Kenya, *Development Prospects and Policies*, p. 11.
57. Ibid., p. 12.
58. Republic of Kenya, *Development Plan 1984 to 1988*, p. 196.
59. Republic of Kenya, *Economic Management for Renewed Growth*, p. 92.
60. G.K. Ikiara, 'The Economy', in *Kenya: An Official Handbook* (Nairobi, Government Printer, 1988), p. 71.
61. These are identified as problems in the Economic Surveys between 1978 and 1988.
62. This was pointed out most emphatically in Republic of Kenya, *Economic Survey 1982* (Nairobi, Central Bureau of Statistics, 1982), p. 30.
63. Republic of Kenya, *Development Plan 1979 to 1983*, pp. 385–386.
64. Patrick Low, 'Export Subsidies and Trade Policy: The Experience of Kenya', *World Development*, 10 (1982), pp. 293–304; Delphin G. Rwegasira, 'Balance-of-payments Adjustment in Low-income Developing Countries: The Experiences of Kenya and Tanzania in the 1970s', *World Development*, 15 (1987), pp. 1321–1336.
65. *Weekly Review*, 24 September 1982.
66. Republic of Kenya, *Development Plan 1984 to 1988*, p. 212.
67. Republic of Kenya, *Economic Management for Renewed Growth*, pp. 20–21.
68. *Africa*, 100 (December 1979), pp. 89–91.
69. Republic of Kenya, *Economic Prospects and Policies*, p. 9.
70. *Weekly Review*, 24 September 1982.
71. Republic of Kenya, *Development Prospects and Policies*, p. 27.
72. Republic of Kenya, *Economic Management for Renewed Growth*, pp. 21–23.
73. For detailed discussion on the role of trade in developing countries, see Bela Balassa, 'Exports, Policy Choices, and Economic Growth in Developing Countries After the 1973 Oil Shock', *Journal of Development Economics*, 18 (1985), pp. 23–36; William G. Tyler, 'Growth and Export Expansion in Developing Countries: Some Empirical Evidence', *Journal of Development Economics*, 9 (1981), pp. 121–130; Irma Adelman, 'Beyond Export-led Growth', *World Development*, 12 (1984), pp. 937–950; Mieko Nishimizu and Sherman Robinson, 'Trade Policies and Productivity in Semi-industrialized Countries', *Journal of Development Economics*, 16 (1984), pp. 177–206; David Wheeler, 'Sources of Stagnation in Sub-Saharan Africa', *World Development*, 12 (1984), pp. 1–24; Stephen R. Lewis, 'Africa's Trade and the World Economy', in Robert J. Berg and Jennifer Seymour Whitaker (eds), *Strategies for African Development* (Berkeley, University of California Press, 1986), pp. 476–504.
74. Republic of Kenya, *Economic Prospects and Policies*, pp. 2–3.
75. Republic of Kenya, *Development Prospects and Policies*, p. 27.
76. World Bank, *World Development Report 1989*, p. 204. Prior to 1970, Kenya had not drawn on the IMF for such credits.
77. Republic of Kenya, *Development Prospects and Policies*, p. 29.

78. Republic of Kenya, *Economic Survey 1989*, p. 137.
79. Republic of Kenya, *Development Plan 1989 to 1993*, p. 15. Inflation partly accounts for the huge rise but, even taking that into consideration, the rate of increase was massive.
80. Ibid., p. 13.
81. Ibid., p. 16.
82. Republic of Kenya, *Economic Management for Renewed Growth*, p. 19. This included virtually guaranteeing every university graduate a job.
83. Ibid.
84. Republic of Kenya, *Economic Survey 1984*, p. 72.
85. Republic of Kenya, *Development Prospects and Policies*, p. 32.
86. Republic of Kenya, *Development Plan 1989 to 1993*, p. 13.
87. Republic of Kenya, *Economic Management for Renewed Growth*, p. 19.
88. Ibid., p. 26.
89. Ibid., p. 30.
90. Ibid., p. 31.
91. Republic of Kenya, *Development Plan 1989 to 1993*, p. 15.
92. Ibid., p. 16. External debt services had by the end of 1988 emerged for economic planners 'as one of the most critical issues that must be addressed if the growth of the economy is to be stimulated and sustained'.
93. Ibid., p. 61.
94. Republic of Kenya, *Economic Survey 1983* (Nairobi, Central Bureau of Statistics, 1983), p. 59.
95. Republic of Kenya, *Economic Survey 1984*, p. 59.
96. Republic of Kenya, *Development Plan 1989 to 1993*, p. 17.
97. Ibid., p. 11. Money supply rose by about 32.5 per cent.
98. Republic of Kenya, *Economic Survey 1989*, pp. 48–49.
99. Republic of Kenya, *Economic Survey 1982* (Nairobi, Central Bureau of Statistics, 1982), p. 62.
100. Republic of Kenya, *Development Plan 1989 to 1993*, p. 12.
101. *Weekly Review*, 11 July 1986, 8 August 1986 and 5 September 1986.
102. Republic of Kenya, *Development Plan 1989 to 1993*, p. 13.
103. *Weekly Review*, 15 August 1986.
104. Republic of Kenya, *Economic Management for Renewed Growth*, p. 37.

Seven

The Politics
of Populism

B.A. OGOT

The Making of a President – the Succession Story

The question of the succession to Kenyatta had been raised in different forums by different categories of Kenyans since 1964. Some Kenyan political leaders had even tried, on several occasions, to persuade Kenyatta to name an heir or to create the post of prime minister. Fortunately for Kenya, Kenyatta resisted all such temptations, preferring instead to adhere to the provisions of the constitution. Since independence, the country had produced several political leaders who could be considered as potential contenders for succession: Oginga Odinga, Tom Mboya and Ronald Ngala. None of these three was, however, fated to succeed. Odinga went into the political wilderness in 1966 when he resigned from the Kenya African National Union (KANU) to form his own party, the Kenya People's Union (KPU). Mboya was assassinated on 5 July 1969, and four years later, Ronald Ngala, former President of the Kenya African Democratic Union (KADU) died from an accident. This left Daniel Toroitich arap Moi, who had become vice-president in January 1967 in succession to Joseph Murumbi, who had resigned, Mbiyu Koinange, Njoroge Mungai and Mwai Kibaki as possible contenders for the presidency.

While attending the Commonwealth Conference in London in early 1969, Tom Mboya, in an interview with a Nigerian journalist, Sam Uba, had offered what he called 'an intelligent guess' about the succession issue in Kenya. According to his diagnosis, Kenyatta's preference for the job was Daniel Toroitich arap Moi, but he suspected that Kenyatta would do nothing about the intra-party struggle for the succession and would not name his successor. Mboya said,

I don't think the President will make any dramatic gestures. He may leave things to continue as they are so that power will slip quietly into the hands of Moi, who is bound to become Acting President should anything happen to the President. The hope will be that in the interim period of three months, as allowed in the Constitution before the election of a new President, Moi would establish his authority in the party or other contenders, out of respect for the former President, would withdraw and give Moi their support in the interest of national unity.

Mboya added that 'personally I am for Moi and will do everything constitutional to back him up . . . I believe that he will make an excellent President . . . In the last year or so, I have discovered excellent qualities of leadership in him.'[1]

In general, that is what happened on 22 August 1978 when Kenyatta died. Moi succeeded him in accordance with the constitution and, later in October, with the overwhelming support of the people of Kenya. But, prior to the succession, power had not been allowed to slip quietly into the hands of Moi as Mboya had predicted and the latter was not there to support the former. Moi faced considerable opposition from powerful economic, ethnic and political alliances and factions, who felt threatened by the prospect of having a president who might not protect their economic or ethnic interests.

The opposition took different forms. First, there was the Change-the-Constitution group, which was launched in Nakuru on 26 September 1976, led by Kihika Kimani, the Nakuru North Member of Parliament (MP), Dr Njoroge Mungai and the leaders of the Gikuyu, Embu and Meru Association (GEMA). The background to this movement was simple: Kenyatta's health was failing by the mid-1970s and hence the succession question could no longer be postponed. Chapter II Part I of the Kenya Constitution provides that on the event of the president's death, resignation, or incapacitation, the vice-president would act as president for a maximum period of ninety days, during which a national election to elect a new president would be held. Those who were opposed to Moi's candidature for succession wanted to amend the constitution to prevent such a possibility.

Had the movement succeeded in its objective, it would not have been the first time the Kenya Constitution had been changed to prevent a succession. The Independence Constitution had provided that, if the president dies, the vice-president would automatically succeed him for the rest of the term, similar to the American provision. But, in 1964, in order to exclude Oginga Odinga from any automatic succession, a new succession formula was introduced according to which, if the president died in office, the National Assembly would elect a successor for the balance of his term. Again, between July 1967 and June 1968, there occurred very acrimonious change-the-constitution debates which were aimed at excluding Tom Mboya from succession, Oginga Odinga having left

KANU in 1966. Mboya's political opponents were afraid of the tremendous influence he wielded over Parliament, which he could use to assure his election as president. Hence, the tenth amendment to the Constitution was passed on 25 June 1968, according to which the vice-president would succeed, but only for three months and with reduced powers.[2] The attempt to change the constitution to shut Moi out failed this time, mainly because of President Kenyatta's opposition to the way in which external and partisan pressure was being put on Parliament and on him to amend the constitution, partly because of the vocal opposition of ninety-eight MPs, who now began to refer to themselves as the Constitutionalists, and partly to an extremely legalistic posture adopted by the then Attorney-General, Charles Njonjo, who constantly reminded the politicians that, under the constitution, it was an offence punishable by death to speculate on the life and person of the country's president.[3]

Next, the anti-Moi forces turned to the party, KANU. The party plays a crucial role in the choice of president, for it is as president of the party that one becomes president of the country. Early in 1977, it was announced that KANU national elections would be held on 3 April 1977. It soon became clear that there were two factions within KANU, popularly known as KANU 'A', which supported the candidacy of Njoroge Mungai for the post of vice-president of the party, and KANU 'B', whose candidate was Moi. The line-up was similar to that for the change-the-constitution debate. Moi was aware that the party had been used to eliminate the challenge of a former vice-president, Oginga Odinga, in 1966 at the infamous Limuru Conference, during which eight provincial vice-presidents were created to replace the one national vice-president of the party. But, when it became evident that the battle for the party was likely to be won by the Moi group, party elections were again called off, on 1 April 1977, until after Kenyatta's death.[4]

As it gradually became apparent that Moi was likely to succeed Kenyatta, his political foes became desperate. An armed gang of would-be assassins (the *ngorokos*) based in Nakuru was organized to prevent such an eventuality. As part of the Stock Theft Unit which had been organized within the Kenya Police Force to fight cattle-rustlers in Northern Kenya, James Ephantus Mungai, Assistant Commissioner of Police in the Rift Valley Province, created the Rift Valley Operational Team. Consisting of 250 *ngorokos*, the team was trained in parachuting, and it acquired sophisticated weapons and vehicles and operated as an independent group of thugs who were supposed to eliminate certain leaders, including Moi, Kibaki and Charles Njonjo, on Kenyatta's death.

On 22 August 1978, Kenyatta died in Mombasa. The question: 'After Kenyatta what?', which had been asked by various commentators for over a decade, had now to be answered. In 1975, Colin Leys, a former professor of Political Science at the University of Nairobi, for example, had speculated that when Kenyatta died, 'the balance of forces within the ruling alliance, which reflected Kenyatta's special position in the country, would be upset and, in the ensuing struggle for power, class forces which had been repressed would quite likely be released'.[5] In short, Colin Leys was predicting a protracted power struggle in Kenya following Kenyatta's death.

On that fateful day, everything seemed to have worked well for the leaders who were on the *ngoroko* assassination list. Moi reached Nairobi from his Kabarak home before the *ngoroko* could set up their road-blocks, Kibaki was safely in Mombasa and Njonjo, who had been in London, arrived that morning in Nairobi. At 3.00 p.m. that afternoon, Moi was sworn in at State House as Acting President. Those behind the *ngoroko* had again failed in their last bid to prevent Moi from becoming Kenya's second president.

Although Moi was now Acting President, the constitution required that a presidential election be held within the next ninety days. Could the anti-Moi factions produce a presidential candidate? The death of Kenyatta had obviously caught the opposition politicians napping, and the idea of marshalling support for an opposition candidate for the presidency was beginning to appear remote. For the moment, at least until the general elections scheduled for 1979, it was now evident that only Moi could hold the country together during this transitional period.

An important characteristic of this period of transition was the meticulous manner in which Moi followed constitutional procedures. For instance, since the constitution required that a presidential candidate must be the leader of his political party, the ruling party, KANU, convened a delegates' conference for the first time since 1966 to elect a national party executive and to elect a new leader for the party. Mombasa Central MP Shariff Nassir announced on 1 September that Mombasa KANU branch had met that day and decided to nominate Moi as the sole candidate for the party presidency as well as the national presidency. Soon every other KANU branch followed Nassir's lead. Even politicians who had earlier been thought to have been interested in the presidency jumped on the bandwagon.

On 4 October 1978, the national executive party elections were held, and Moi was elected unopposed as President of KANU. One significant aspect of these party elections was that, besides the post of president, almost all the remaining party posts were hotly contested, including that of the vice-president. Considering the number of times national party elections had been postponed for over a decade, and bearing in mind the serious political issues that were at stake, the elections were remarkably democratic, transparent and peaceful. In a sense this was a reflection of Moi's confidence and the political maturity of Kenyans.

On 14 October 1978, Daniel Toroitich arap Moi, an astute politician who had grown with the country's political system, was formally installed as the second President of the Republic of Kenya. A new era had started.

But how was Moi able to have such a peaceful and smooth succession, given that, by 1978, the Kikuyu élite dominated the political, administrative and economic life of the country? Two factors favoured his ascendancy. One was that many of his would-be political enemies underestimated him. They believed he was not ambitious and they therefore referred to him as a 'passing cloud'. Secondly, despite their strong presence in all important fields, the Kikuyu were fragmented into various camps that were hostile to one another. Moi effectively exploited these deep-seated divisions among the Kikuyu. He decided to side with one group, the Charles Njonjo/G.G. Kariuki/Mwai Kibaki group, to which he gave a blank cheque to deal with all the other Kikuyu rival groups. In the new administration, Njonjo and G.G. Kariuki, especially, teamed up with Moi to form a mighty triumvirate of power never before witnessed in the history of Kenya. These two were to be axed in 1983 during the 'traitor' affair, leaving only Kibaki, whose influence steadily declined until 1988, when he was replaced as vice-president by Jasphat Karanja, following that year's general elections.

Theoretical Perspectives on Populism

President Moi has often been referred to as a populist and the policies of his government as populist policies of the right. The meaning of populism as a concept is unclear and seems to change from one historical context to another. The various organized populist movements in history have taken both left-wing and right-wing forms, and, invariably, they are the precursors of authoritarianism or dictatorship.

But, in general, there is agreement that populism in its ideal form has two main aspects: the supremacy of the will of the people and the desirability of a 'direct' relationship between people and leadership. In the words of Peter Worsley, who has written extensively on populism in the Third World, 'Populism is better regarded as an emphasis, a dimension of political culture in general, not simply as a particular kind of overall ideological system or type of organization.'[6] It is in this sense that we shall be using the term 'populism' in the context of Kenya history and not as a movement or an ideological system.

As the name suggests, 'populism' must refer to the people, both in terms of their relationship with leadership and also with regard to popular participation in policy formation in general. From this definition, it follows that a populist leader must have a political rapport with his followers, especially with the ordinary people. He must also be able to formulate policies which meet popular needs and which engender a sense of close identification.

The Ideology of the Moi Regime: Nyayoism

The period following Moi's accession to power was full of anxieties and apprehensions on the one hand and high hopes on the other hand. There were those groups and individuals who had enriched themselves at the expense of the public through links with the state and who feared economic reprisals. Some communities, such as the Luo of western Kenya, were hoping, under Moi's leadership, for a return to the main stream of political life in Kenya. But a more general apprehension was felt by a large section of the public about the tremendous increase in smuggling and corruption, activities known as *magendo*, which had become a marked feature of Kenya's public life. At a three-day 'The Kenya We Want' conference, organized in January 1978 at the Kenya Institute of Administration in Nairobi and attended by ministers, assistant ministers, Members of Parliament, Permanent Secretaries and Provincial Commissioners, corruption had been referred to as a festering sore that appeared to have taken root in modern Kenya. The leaders accepted that many high-ranking government officials and the police were involved waist-high in corrupt practices.

This was the Second Leaders Conference with the theme 'The Kenya We Want'. The same theme had been the subject of a mammoth leaders conference (the First Leaders Conference) soon after independence. The opening address of the January 1978 Conference was given by Daniel arap Moi, then vice-president. The other key speakers were Mwai Kibaki, then Minister for Finance, and Robert Ouko, then Minister for Community Affairs.

The conference had thus diagnosed corruption in public life as the biggest problem facing Kenya. In a very real sense, the report of the conference represents an excellent summary of the state of the nation at the end of the Kenyatta era.

President Moi, on acceding to power, was therefore faced with combined public and political apprehension and with the task of defusing opposition. The challenge before his government also raised fundamental questions about how a one-party government that rules over a fragmented and clientelist society can apply corrective policies to redistribute power and resources away from those who have previously most enjoyed them (and who know how to defend them) and towards those least favoured by the previous regime, with the consent of the majority. Many Kenyans, therefore, expected Moi to break in a significant manner with the old era in order to demonstrate that his was a different and uncorrupt regime.

Instead, President Moi responded with the philosophy of nyayoism. *Nyayo* is a Kiswahili word meaning 'footsteps'. He announced that he would follow in Kenyatta's footsteps. In other words, he told Kenyans not to expect a revolution, for he was determined to continue with Kenyatta's policies. There would definitely be social, economic and political reforms, but he assured Kenyans that these would be carried out without any discontinuity. *Nyayo* thus became a national motto, symbolizing continuity, love, peace and stability. The succession was thus portrayed as a continuation of Kenyatta's legacy and this defused opposition, especially from the groups that expected economic reprisals. Continuity was also exhibited by the fact that Moi retained Kenyatta's cabinet for a year, neither dropping a minister nor bringing into the cabinet a new face. He preferred to wait for the 1979 general elections to make more comprehensive changes in government.

Moi defused opposition further by practising a policy of reconciliation and forgiveness instead of pitching open battles with his adversaries. He justifies such a policy by quoting a Kalenjin proverb: 'Do not carry your anger in your heart, but in your lungs.' The lungs expand while the heart does not.[7] On the fifteenth anniversary of the country's independence (*Jamhuri* Day, 1978) and by coincidence the thirtieth anniversary of the Universal Declaration of Human Rights day, Moi launched a new era of tolerance in Kenya by releasing all political detainees. He showed his fellow Kenyans that a new chapter was opening in Kenya's political life, a chapter of political tolerance and reconciliation. In his *Jamhuri* speech, he called for a spirit of tolerance among politicians and leaders in Kenya. He also suggested that there would be room for constructive dissent so long as such dissent was offered in the context of a united stable Kenya. Twenty-six detainees were released, including Ngugi wa Thiong'o, George Anyona, Joseph Martin Shikuku, John Marie Seroney, Michael Koigi wa Wamwere and Wasonga Sijeyo – the longest-serving detainee and former MP for Gem, who was detained in 1969. This was a popular proclamation which sent the University of Nairobi students to the streets chanting pro-Moi songs.

Moi also forgave the change-the-constitution group, dismissing the whole episode as having been in accordance with the nature of politics. Furthermore, he told the Kenya public to forget the *ngoroko* affair. James Mungai, the former head of the '*ngoroko* squad', who had fled the country in November 1978 to Switzerland, was allowed to return to the country and the government decided not to prosecute him. In essence, the succession issue had now been satisfactorily settled and there was therefore no need to reopen old wounds.

As Moi consolidated his power and the strength and confidence of the new regime grew, nyayoism expanded to acquire ideological functions. It gradually became a blanket ideology under which the various ideologies, such as constitutional democracy, African socialism, Christian and Islamic morality, nationalism, patriotism, developmentalism, anti-tribalism and other positive ideas were subsumed. This, however, meant that any person who acted contrary to *nyayo* philosophy was also acting against the *nyayo* government. In short, being anti-*nyayo* soon meant being anti-government and anti-party, because nyayoism was already depicting a new social order and restructuring political categories. This marked a further entrenchment of the political monolithism which had been introduced under Kenyatta.

In a series of shrewd moves, President Moi had succeeded within a year in neutralizing his opponents. He also made himself accessible to the Kenya public. He set about touring the whole country, meeting the ordinary Kenyans and condemning corruption and inefficiency. His populism soon revealed itself in his concern for the common man, which gradually emerged as a central point of his rule. At times, he spoke in the language of the ordinary people, especially when castigating bureaucracy for inefficiency or the politicians for their tribalism or corruption.

The 8 November 1979 national parliamentary elections, coming so soon after the succession issue, provided a golden opportunity for any opposition groups to try their political strength against Moi's government. But, as it turned out, the elections, which were peaceful and hotly contested, gave Moi a sweeping mandate. Seven of Kenyatta's ministers (including Mbiyu Koinange) and fifteen assistant ministers lost their seats. Moi now formed a new and enlarged cabinet, a *nyayo* cabinet, from a broad popular base, bringing in new blood to serve the nation. In his desire to promote national unity and reconciliation, Moi included in his government persons who had tried to block his own succession, much to the consternation of a section of the foreign press. He also appointed a former vice-president and former leader of the defunct KPU party, Jaramogi Oginga Odinga, Chairman of the Cotton Lint and Seed Marketing Board, in order, as President Moi explained, 'to give Mr. Odinga a chance to prove that what people have been saying about him was untrue'.[8] In May 1980, Moi directed the press to stop referring to people as ex-KPUs. This marked the completion of his reconciliation with the Luo.

But the national ideology (nyayoism) in its expanded version was soon to come under heavy attack by voices of dissent, most of whom preached what the government regarded as foreign ideologies. The dissenting voices were largely based in Kenya's institutions of higher learning or in some of the professional organizations, such as the Law Society of Kenya. President Moi had to address the problem of 'foreign ideologies' or dissent constantly between 1979 and 1988. For example, on 14 December 1979, President Moi, speaking as Chancellor of the University of Nairobi, warned that there was no room for foreign ideologies in Kenya and called upon all Kenyans to concentrate on practical problems facing the nation. He stressed that Kenya nationalism was the source of the country's strength, saying that no imported ideology would solve the local problems. He continued: 'All our experience since independence shows that there is no substitute for hard work, community discipline, practical management of national affairs, and *harambee* spirit linking goverment and the people together in all our endeavours.' He pointed out that what was happening in some other countries, including those previously committed to scientific socialism, indicated the success of 'the immense sense of pragmatism instead of blind commitment to ideologies which invariably disguise more than they illuminate'. He then concluded his address by appealing to the professors and lecturers to get more involved in nation-building: 'I sometimes feel that professors and lecturers could be of greater use to our society if their initiatives, springing from knowledge, could be made more constructively apparent, and if their occasional intolerance could be transformed into something more helpful.' He stressed that the university should be looked upon as a fertile forum for dialogue, bridging gaps which might frustrate co-operation between academic and practical experience.[9]

Although President Moi was holding up an olive branch to the university in this address, the university did not reciprocate. Very soon, confrontational politics reappeared at the university. In February and May 1980, there were student riots at the University of Nairobi. Later, in July of the same year, President Moi revealed that a neighbouring country was hatching a plot to use the University of Nairobi to cause political unrest and even assassinations in Kenya.[10] During the next two years, 1981–82, dissidence or, more accurately, opposition to Moi's government at the University of Nairobi became more vocal and more violent. But this is to anticipate.

Outside the university, the general elections of 1979 had not produced the kind of national consensus that the country's espousal of nyayoism had suggested. Squabbles and factionalism became rampant in the first half of 1980. In July 1980, President Moi convened the Third Leaders Conference since independence (but the first since Moi took over from Kenyatta) at the Kenya Institute of Administration in Nairobi. These conferences were used by the government to produce a national consensus on any burning issue. It was attended by over 300 Kenyan leaders, including ministers, assistant ministers and senior civil servants. President Moi gave a keynote address, which was on the need for national unity. It was a tough speech in which Moi made it clear that he was the president and that in the exercise of his powers no other minister was involved. He emphasized that no leader was indispensable and each leader must be personally and directly accountable to the people and cannot therefore hide weaknesses in a generalized collective leadership.

It was at this conference that the leaders called for a national code of ethics to be drawn up by a body appointed by the President. But the conference is chiefly remembered for its assault on ethnic organizations. Among the resolutions passed was the one calling for the dissolution of all ethnic organizations for the sake of national unity. GEMA, the Luo Union (East Africa), the New Akamba Union (NAU), the Abaluhya Association, the Kelenjin Association and the Miji-Kenda Association were targets. While ostensibly welfare organizations, these groups had become highly politicized.

GEMA was founded in 1971 as a cultural and social welfare organization, but was viewed by most Kenyans as a political organization because both its national chairman, Dr Gikonyo Kiano, and its national vice-chairman, Jeremiah Nyaga, were politicians. In 1973, in order to allay the fears of non-GEMA Kenyans, all the politicians were removed from positions of leadership in the organization, and were replaced by people who had no apparent political ambition at the time. These included Njenga Karume, a prominent businessman, as national chairman, Duncan Ndegwa, then Governor of the Central Bank, as vice-chairman and Kihika Kimani, a farmer and businessman, as national organizing secretary.

In October 1973, the new leaders launched the 50 million shillings GEMA Holdings Ltd. And, in the following year, GEMA entered national politics in a big way. Njenga Karume was nominated to Parliament after the 1974 elections, and Kihika Kimani was elected MP for Nakuru North. By 1976, GEMA was a political power unto itself, almost rivalling KANU under Kenyatta. It was GEMA – euphemistically known as the 'Network' – that spearheaded an attack on Kenyatta government critics, following the murder of the former MP for Nyandarua North, Josiah Mwangi Kariuki. It was also the GEMA leaders who spearheaded the change-the-constitution campaign to prevent Moi from succeeding Kenyatta.

In 1975, Martin Shikuku and Jean Seroney were detained by Kenyatta for warning Parliament of attempts by GEMA MPs to kill the august House the way they had killed KANU. By July 1980, GEMA Holdings Ltd assets were estimated as between 70 and 90 million shillings. Hence the role of powerful organizations such as GEMA in the context of national unity had to be considered very carefully.

The Luo Union (East Africa) was another welfare organization that was deeply involved in politics. Founded in the mid-1940s to promote the welfare of the Luo people, the Union had since independence increasingly become involved in politics, especially through Oginga Odinga. And, although in Luoland the people were divided, since 1966 when Odinga left KANU to start an opposition party, into pro- and anti-Odinga camps within the Luo Union, the organization had the potential for becoming an organized political force. Indeed, before 1978, the Odinga faction of the Union had made strenuous efforts to revive the Kikuyu–Luo alliance of the early 1960s by trying to forge links with GEMA.

Then there was NAU, which was founded in 1960 to promote the social welfare of the Akamba people. In 1974, the chairman of NAU, Mulu Mutisya, was nominated as MP. Also, all parliamentarians from Ukambani, except Paul Ngei, who wanted NAU banned, were members of NAU and were to a certain extent beholden to its leader, Mulu Mutisya.

The three remaining, ethnic organizations – the Abaluhya Association, the Kalenjin Association and the Miji-Kenda Association – were less political than the three organizations we have already discussed.

The important question facing participants of the Third Leaders Conference was whether ethnic loyalty and solidarity could be reconciled with national loyalty and unity. The leaders took a bold decision to dissolve all ethnic organizations so as to promote national unity. The fact that the leaders could take such a drastic step after only two days of deliberation showed the extent to which Moi had consolidated his position. Consequently, a major source of potentially well-organized opposition to him in the future was eliminated. With this accomplishment and with the mass support which he had, Moi's political control appeared tight-sealed and was destined to become even more so when KANU was revitalized, as we shall discuss below.

The stability of the Moi regime was, however, increasingly threatened by the growing opposition, stigmatized as 'dissidence', from the intellectuals, based largely at the University of Nairobi, and from political activists, such as Oginga Odinga, Masinde Muliro, George Anyona, Martin Shikuku and Koigi wa Wamwere. These two major streams of dissidence were to merge in 1991 to constitute the pro-democracy movement. The problem was that Kenya lacked mechanisms which could permit open criticism. And, as is evident from history, whenever public opinion is denied expression through the proper channels, it finds its way by the sewers. This is what seems to have happened. Throughout the 1980s, various groups opposed the one-party rule, using different strategies. This included academics from the University of Nairobi and Kenyatta University; an attempted coup by junior Air Force officers; and underground movements, such as *Mwakenya*, *Umoja*, Kenya Patriotic Front, Kenya Revolutionary Movement and the December Twelve Movement.

Dissent was an important historical phenomenon in Kenya, especially from 1966 and more especially from 1982. Its contribution to the transformation of Kenya from a single-party to a multiparty society therefore deserves serious attention. What were the satisfactions, successes, defeats and frustrations of dissidents? As has already been pointed out, there were two main groups of dissidents: the intellectuals at the University of Nairobi and the political activists.

Dissidence at the University of Nairobi started even before it became an autonomous institution in 1970. In January 1969, the Kenya government intervened for the first time in order to prevent a public lecture by Oginga Odinga, who was then the leader of KPU, an opposition political party. This was the beginning of academic intolerance and censorship at the university. The students boycotted lectures in protest and the university was closed for a brief period.

In 1970, Nairobi became an independent university. Direct government interference intensified. For example, in 1972 the editors of the student newspaper, *University Platform*, were arrested for criticizing government policy. The students rioted, the university was closed and *Platform* was subsequently banned. In February 1975, students boycotted classes and demonstrated in the streets following the assassination of J.M. Kariuki, an outspoken and popular MP. They demanded a full and objective inquiry. The government reacted violently, beating up students and closing the university. This episode marked a turning-point in the relations between the government and the university community. Thereafter, a climate of distrust and confrontation emerged, with the state regularly using force to curtail academic freedom.

In January 1978, Ngugi wa Thiong'o, the country's leading novelist and Chairman of the Department of Literature of the University of Nairobi, was arrested and detained after establishing a community-based theatre group at Kamuriithu village in Limuru, where they performed a play he co-authored with Ngugi wa Mirii, called *Ngahaahika Ndeeda* ('I will marry when I want'), which attacked the government's policy towards the 'wretched of the earth'. The open theatre was closed, permission to perform the play revoked and Ngugi's appointment with the university was revoked on the grounds of 'non-performance of contract'. He thus became the first Kenyan intellectual to be detained because of his works.

The waning years of Kenyatta's rule witnessed a decline in the tolerance of academic freedom. The government exerted control over public lectures given on campus by outside speakers by insisting that such speakers had to obtain a permit from the vice-chancellor, a crude way of trying to insulate the university against what were regarded as subversive ideas. But the fire of dissent was already kindled in the academic circles at the University of Nairobi. A whole generation of dissident scholars, such as Katam Mkangi, Mukaru Ng'ang'a, Peter Anyang' Nyong'o, Micere Mugo, Atieno Odhiambo, Shadrack Gutto, Willy Mutunga and Gibson Kamau Kuria had emerged. They delivered fiery public lectures in Taifa Hall or at seminars and symposia critical of the Kenyatta regime. The campus was ablaze with Marxist revolutionary ideas, from which the students were not free.

This was the volatile situation which Moi inherited on succeeding Kenyatta in August 1978. He released all political prisoners and thereby elicited demonstrations by the University of Nairobi students in support of the decision. But any hopes of a cordial relationship between the university community and the government were quickly dashed as confrontation continued.

In September 1979, the students criticized the government's decision to ban Oginga Odinga and three other former opposition figures from contesting the general elections. The university was closed and the students' leaders expelled. The Nairobi University Students' Organization

(NUSO), which had emerged as a strong proponent of the autonomy of the university, was proscribed. In the following year, the Academic Staff Union was banned and in May the same year riots broke out at the university in protest against the barring of outside speakers. As a result of the riots, the passports of twelve lecturers regarded as critical of the government were seized. Among the lecturers affected were Micere Mugo, Ooko Ombaka, Michael Chege, Mukaru Ng'ang'a, Okoth Ogendo, Atieno Odhiambo, Peter Anyang' Nyong'o and Shadrack Gutto.

By June 1982, the political temperature in Kenya had risen to a high degree. Addressing a massive KANU rally at Nakuru Afraha Stadium, President Moi revealed a plot by university lecturers to arm school and university students to cause chaos in the country. Their action was intended to coincide with a call by some politicians for the establishment of a second political party to rival KANU. He singled out six university lecturers who he said were teaching nothing but 'politics of subversion through textbooks majoring in violence'. The President vowed to root out plotters and agitators from within the Kenyan nation.[11] Later that month, several staff members of the university were arrested and accused by the government of teaching subversive literature aimed at creating disorder in the country. They were Al-Amin Mazrui, a lecturer in linguistics and a playwright (the author of *Kilio cha Haki*); Edward Oyugi, a lecturer in educational psychology; George Mkangi, a sociologist; Kamoji Wachira, a biologist; Willy Mutunga, a lecturer in law; and Mukaru Ng'ang'a, a historian. They were all detained without trial for varying periods of time. It should also be added that earlier in the month, on 3 June 1982, Maina wa Kinyatti, a lecturer in history at Kenyatta University College, had been arrested and charged with possession of a seditious publication and being a member of the underground movement, *Mwakenya*. He was convicted and sentenced to six years in prison. A number of lecturers fled the country or left their posts at the university in order to avoid imprisonment or detention.

On 1 August 1982, junior members of the Kenya Air Force attempted a *coup d'état*. Although the attempt failed, this event affected the intellectual integrity and autonomy of the university in several ways. First, many of the students who took to the streets of Nairobi to celebrate were arrested and charged with offences ranging from rioting to sedition. One of those students was Tito Adungosi, the chairman of the Students' Organization of Nairobi University (SONU), a body which had been established in 1982 as a central body representing students. Adungosi, who was SONU's first chairman, was on 24 September 1982 sentenced to ten years' imprisonment for sedition. He later died in prison, on 27 December 1988, under suspicious circumstances. Sixty-seven other students were held from August 1982 to February 1983, when they were granted presidential clemency, except for six students who were tried, convicted and sentenced to prison terms of five or six years.

Secondly, the Vice-Chancellor began to operate more and more as a political appointee and less as an academic. And, through him, the government was able to stifle any open political activity or criticism. No faculty member dared to speak out in public and the students adopted a low profile.

Thirdly, the coup attempt resulted in the longest closure of the university, from August 1982 to October 1983, a period of fourteen months. The result was a backlog of students waiting to be admitted, which could only be handled by introducing the 'double intake' in 1987, with all the dire consequences for the quality of university education.

During the *Mwakenya* crackdown of 1986–1988, several students and staff of the university were jailed or detained. In November 1987, SONU was invited to participate in an international students conference in Cuba. The government refused to issue a passport to the SONU chairman, Wafula Buke. The students reacted violently. SONU was banned and Buke jailed for five years.

Dissidence at the university had thus been brought under control, and it did not resurface until 1990, when the crusade for multiparty democracy started in earnest. Is it any wonder, therefore, that, during the 1991 heated debate on democracy, 140 academics from the University of Nairobi argued for the status quo and accused the pro-democracy activists of being agents of foreign powers? It should, however, be noted that many of the radical academics who had been compelled to leave the university emerged as leading opposition figures from 1990.

The 'Traitor Affair'

Hardly had Kenyans recovered from the shock of the coup attempt than the country was faced with a new and more complicated challenge. This was the 'traitor affair'. At a public rally in Kisii in May 1983, President Moi revealed that a powerful politician in his Cabinet was plotting to overthrow his government, with the assistance of some foreign governments. The traitor was soon identified as Charles Mugane Njonjo, who was then Minister for Constitutional Affairs and MP for Kikuyu constituency.

Charles Njonjo was at that time the most feared minister in Kenya. He had over a long period, as Kenya's Attorney-General, established an elaborate machinery involving the police, senior civil servants and the judiciary, which provided him with a formidable power base. As the Miller Commission Report was later to reveal, Njonjo had worked out a two-pronged strategy for ousting President Moi from power: he tried to get a majority among MPs to pass a vote of no confidence in the President, and he tried to influence KANU sub-branches and branches to support him for the party presidency.[12]

With the traitor identified, the party and the government swung into action. Disloyal elements within the party were identified and subsequently expelled. In all, fourteen associates of Njonjo were purged from the party, in addition to Njonjo himself. Njonjo's elaborate machinery in government was dismantled; and a Judicial Commission of Inquiry, consisting of three judges – Justice C.H.E. Miller (Chairman), Justice Chunilal E. Madan, Queen's Counsel (QC) and Justice Mrs Effie Owuor – was appointed in July 1983 to inquire into allegations made within and outside Parliament involving Njonjo. President Moi also decided to call a snap election in 1983. Most of the Njonjo associates, including G.G. Kariuki, former Minister of State in the President's Office, and Joseph Kamotho, former Minister for Higher Education, were removed through election. The notable survivor was Stanley Oloitiptip, formerly Minister for Culture and Social Services, who was not reappointed to the Cabinet. He later died following a short illness.

The findings of the Commissioners who had been appointed to inquire into the conduct of Charles Njonjo were made public on *Jamhuri* Day, 12 December 1984, by President Moi himself. The Commissioners found that all allegations against Njonjo, except the crucial one of treason, had been proved. In the same speech, the President announced his pardon of Njonjo, giving Njonjo's age and past service to the government as among the reasons for the clemency. To many Kenyans the magnanimity of the President towards someone who had clearly been bent on undermining his powers was incomprehensible. Silence, therefore, greeted President Moi's announcement of his forgiveness of Njonjo. The least punishment they expected to be meted out to Njonjo was detention. Even the University of Nairobi students took to the streets of Nairobi to demonstrate against the President's pardon.

The destruction of Charles Njonjo's power base and his subsequent removal from the centre stage of Kenya politics left President Moi unchallenged. Henceforth, the President turned his attention more towards the control of basic institutions, such as the party, the university, the public service, the judiciary and Parliament and less towards individual political rivals. Consequently, the period following the attempted coup up to 1988 was to be characterized by the further concentration of power in the executive, the over-bureaucratization of life and the increasing marginalization of civil society.

The One-Party State and the Revitalization of KANU

Although KANU had played a crucial role first in the struggle for independence from 1960 to 1963 and subsequently in consolidating and safeguarding that independence, it is also a fact that the party went through a period of internal confusion and dormancy following the banning of Oginga Odinga's KPU party in 1969. Kenya had become a *de facto* one-party state. And, from 1970 onwards, there were several highly publicized campaigns by the leaders to revitalize KANU to make it more relevant to the majority of Kenyans. But little came of these campaigns. Also, although the party constitution stipulated that party elections should be held every two years, the last national elections were held in 1966 at Limuru. Indeed, none were to be held until after Kenyatta's death in 1978. Throughout this period of about twelve years, there were constant demands for party elections and on several occasions dates were announced for these elections.

In April 1970, for example, KANU President Jomo Kenyatta set up a 'KANU Reorganization Committee', whose task was to 'reorganize, reactivate and revitalize' the party in order to meet the demands of changing times and the rising expectations of the members. Daniel arap Moi, then vice-president of the country, was appointed chairman of the Committee. They submitted their report on 19 August 1971, although it was not published until 1974. The report concentrated more on the structure of the party than on making it more effective in national life. The proposed amendments to the party constitution included the introduction of a new post of national chairman; the scrapping of the provincial vice-president, leaving only one national vice-president, as had been the case before 1966; and the requirements for clearance of former KPU members wishing to contest civic and parliamentary elections on a KANU ticket. Between 1974 and 1978, the party remained largely dormant, only coming alive during elections, to carry out the exercise of clearing (or barring) candidates, or during times of political crisis, such as occurred following the assassination of J.M. Kariuki, MP, in March 1975, to seek ways of containing dissent.

Between 1969 and 1982, Kenya had remained under *de facto* one-party rule. In May 1982, George Anyona was detained without trial and Oginga Odinga was put under house arrest when they tried to register an opposition party, the Kenya African Socialist Alliance. A constitutional amendment was then rushed through Parliament making KANU the only political party. Kenya had thus become a *de jure* one-party state.

But there were those Kenyans who were apprehensive. They wondered whether, within the one-party system, there would still be room for differences of opinions on important matters of public interest and whether the freedom entrenched in Chapter Five of the Constitution of Kenya would continue to guide the party.

The biggest challenge facing KANU now was whether matters of national importance would be aired publicly now that the party had become the sole guardian of the public good. Would the party allow debate at all levels of the party on a controversial issue before a decision was taken? There was also the question of 'party clearance'. Could this be used to restrict debate on national issues? Moreover, there was a provision in the constitution of KANU concerning ex-KPU members. Did it have any meaning in the new situation?

An even bigger challenge was that, although KANU was a popular party in the sense that its leaders were popularly elected, it was not yet a mass party. Indeed, up to 1984, it had only about one million members. How was it to be transformed into a mass party?

Finally, although ethnic associations and alliances had been abolished in 1980, KANU continued to be divided not on an ideological basis, as was the case between 1960 and 1970, but on the basis of factions. Generally speaking, the existence of political factions indicates a system where relationships and events are determined by groups thinking mainly of personal advantage. Factions also entail the existence of patrons and clients. The main function of a patron in such a system is to promote his own standing and reputation by promoting the interests of his clients. But the existence of factions must be seen in the wider context of the power struggle. Patronage is part of the political battle, and such a patron tries to exert and maintain as much influence with the central authority, in this case the President, as possible. At the national level, KANU had two influential patrons – Charles Njonjo and Mwai Kibaki – and there were several patrons at the district and provincial levels. This made KANU a factious party which could not provide the kind of coherent policy decisions that were necessary, especially in a one-party state.

The national trauma of the 1 August attempted coup forced the country to examine all organs of state, including the role of KANU. It is in this context that we should consider the major policy statement that President Moi issued on *Jamhuri* Day in 1982. The statement answers the critics of the one-party state and it enunciates the principles underlying the policies of KANU so clearly and so succinctly that it can be claimed with justice that the rejuvenation of KANU and its transformation into a mass, disciplined and coherent party started with this clearly enunciated policy statement. He said:

> There had to be a party giving people everywhere a sense of belonging and an arena of unity. The party was also to serve as an institution which the government and the people had in common – so that philosophies, policies and aspirations all sprang from the grass-roots of society. It was further visualized that the party, as a political instrument, must be appropriately involved in sustaining the countrywide momentum of nationalistic forces and feelings . . . Kanu is required – through all its elected leaders and appointed officials – to educate the people about the policies and challenges to safeguard constitutional rights and uphold the rule of law, to establish standards of conduct and impose any necessary discipline in the cause of national integrity . . . I also want to stress that if Kanu is to fulfil its critical mission intelligently and effectively, there are at least three important prerequisites. First, it must be and remain a countrywide popular movement, serving as a political outlet, but succeeding as well in being a source of answers and attractions covering

much broader spectrum of human need. Next the party must be and remain at all levels and all times, a democratic institution, so that its members are able to feel convinced that their individual votes and their opinions do count in reaching decisions. Thirdly, the party must be ready, and make itself competent, to look both ways, offering guidance to the Government on a wide range of issues while also being a forum of enlightenment for all the people.[13]

The President explained that he was outlining these objectives and possibilities partly in order to assure Kenyans that revitalization of the party was being taken very seriously. He announced that the enrolment of members throughout the Republic would start on 14 December 1982 and that the recruitment exercise would be followed by party elections from sub-location to national levels. President Moi stressed that, at every stage of this process of election, 'democratic principles must and will be upheld in a manner which everyone can witness'.

This speech embodied Moi's vision of a revitalized KANU as a popular mass party and also his concept of a one-party state which is strong and united, and yet democratic. To his critics, however, the speech represented an amateurish rationalization of political monolithism by the powers that be.

The *Jamhuri* speech gave KANU the mandate and challenge to mobilize the country to meet the requirements of national development. Was the party ready for this formidable task? The party was still poorly organized, especially at the grass-roots level. Hence, its role, as we have already pointed out, had been limited largely to that of an electoral party. Secondly, the party had found it difficult to develop a consensus or hold party conferences and regular elections in accordance with its own constitution. These two weaknesses had to be overcome if KANU was to be transformed into a popular mass party.

But, before KANU revitalization could get far, the country, as we have already discussed, was faced with the 'traitor affair'. KANU organized public rallies throughout the country to denounce the 'traitor'. Disloyal elements within the party were purged. A snap general election was called, and hence the task of revitalizing the party had to be postponed until after the general election.

President Moi, who emerged from the general election even stronger than before, now turned his attention to strengthening the ruling party. Throughout 1984 and during the first half of 1985, President Moi spearheaded the KANU recruitment drive all over the Republic. Over five million people were recruited as party members, thus turning KANU into a mass party.

On *Madaraka* Day (1 June 1985), President Moi announced that KANU grass-roots elections would be held throughout the country between 22 and 25 June. These were going to be the first grass-roots elections since 1976. But, in that year, there were no agreed rules according to which the grass-roots elections were to be conducted. Party branches were told to hold elections any time before 31 December. Officials of the party therefore held elections at times convenient to them, a procedure which led to many irregularities. Moreover, there was no agreed procedure for appeal by losers who felt aggrieved. But, for the 1985 party elections, the first problem had been solved since President Moi had fixed four days during which grass-roots elections had to be held.

The grass-roots elections were followed by branch and national elections from 24 June to 1 July 1985. Only three of the previous nine officials of the national executive were returned: President Daniel arap Moi, Vice-President Mwai Kibaki and Justus ole Tipis as national treasurer. All the remaining six officials were new faces, with David Okiki Amayo as national chairman and Burudi Nabwera as secretary-general. In electing members of the national executive, the principle of fair geographical distribution, which was initiated by Moi in 1978, was maintained.

In his address to the delegates who had gathered at the Kenyatta International Conference Centre in Nairobi to elect members of the party national executive, President Moi warned that KANU was entering a new era and major reforms were needed within the party to transform it into an effective and efficient organization which could meet the aspirations of all Kenyans. He suggested that the party should establish a disciplinary committee to deal with party members, particularly councillors, MPs, assistant ministers and ministers, who might contradict the party consensus.

Following the successful elections, the party now turned its attention to the reform agenda. Several provincial conferences were held to discuss a wide variety of topics, such as the party structure, constitution and finances and the role of KANU in the district focus for rural development strategy.

The provincial seminars culminated in the KANU national seminar, which was held from 2 to 4 December 1985 at the Kenya Institute of Administration in Nairobi. It was attended by over 300 delegates, consisting of six elected members of each branch and the branch and national executive committees. The national seminar addressed itself to several major problems and made a number of far-reaching recommendations aimed at strengthening and streamlining the party.

In his opening speech, President Moi stressed the need for party members and officials to be self-disciplined in order to give a good example to other Kenyans. His address also dealt with several other national issues such as tribalism, corruption, unemployment and environmental degradation.

The proposed reforms covered discipline within the party, national development, relations between public officers and party finances. The seminar recommended that party elections should be held every five years, as is the case with parliamentary elections. In order to strengthen the administrative structure of the party, the seminar recommended that the post of secretary-general of the party should be a full-time and paid post at the level of cabinet minister.

The seminar also agreed that a disciplinary committee of the party, consisting of one representative from each province and four appointees of the president, should be formed to deal with party discipline.

On investment, the seminar reiterated the fact that the Kenyatta International Conference Centre is a KANU building, which should generate substantial funds for the party. Other KANU investments at the time included the Kenya Times Ltd newspapers (the *Kenya Times*, the *Sunday Times* and *Kenya Leo*) and the Press Trust Printing Company. These two companies had been acquired by the party in April 1983. Despite the fact that the companies had by then lost 27 million shillings, the seminar recommended that the party should continue to own and support its papers and press.

There were, however, other major constitutional issues which the seminar did not discuss. For example, the seminar did not deal with how disputes arising out of party elections should be resolved. The seminar also failed to tackle the sensitive issue of the clearance of candidates for both party and general elections.

Most of the recommendations made at the national seminar were subsequently adopted and implemented by KANU. One of the major changes was the establishment of the disciplinary committee. This was viewed as one of the positive changes in the party constitution. Now aggrieved politicians had the opportunity to defend themselves, unlike in the past when a group of party officials would decide the destiny of others without listening to their side of the story. The disciplinary committee was empowered to deal with all disciplinary matters in the party. It had the power 'to hear and determine cases recommended by the branch executive committees and others which may be referred to it by the President of KANU, the National Executive Committee, the National Governing Council or an appeal from an aggrieved member'.

The disciplinary committee rapidly developed into the party court of justice, where both the accusers and the accused were heard in the open before the committee passed its judgement. The committee became an even more powerful instrument when KANU introduced a new rule under which those recommended for suspension or expulsion by the disciplinary committee lost all party and public offices they held. Nor were suspended members allowed to address any public meetings.

Very soon KANU's new strength raised the question of whether it was the party or Parliament that was supreme. The issue became critical when the party's disciplinary committee summoned the then Minister for Labour, Peter Okondo, to appear before it and show cause why disciplinary action could not be taken against him for attacking the committee chairman, David Okiki Amayo, in Parliament. In the opinion of some MPs, especially in the opinion of the then MP for Butere, Martin Shikuku, the action taken against Okondo amounted to violation of the Powers and Privileges Act, which gives MPs immunity for anything they say in Parliament. In an interview with the *Weekly Review*, the then national chairman of KANU, who was also chairman of the disciplinary committee, David Okiki Amayo, explained the relationship between the party and Parliament by saying that political supremacy rests with the party while legislative supremacy lies with Parliament.[14]

Another reform which proved controversial was the queuing system of voting in preliminary elections as part of election procedures. KANU had announced, in April 1987, that there would be preliminary elections in which voters would be required to line up behind candidates. The method of voting by queuing was one of the major political reforms introduced during the first decade of the *nyayo* era. Queue-voting had already been used during the 1985 KANU grass-roots elections, even before it was formally endorsed as party policy. In 1986, KANU revised its constitution and formally incorporated queue-voting as party policy. In the February–March 1988 general elections, voting by queuing was used as a nomination procedure, followed by secret-ballot polls. This idea of nominating candidates for elections had replaced the old informal and often biased process of clearance, which was carried out by a few power-brokers (usually the secretary-general, the treasurer and the organizing secretary) at the party headquarters. The new nomination procedure now gave the party's rank and file a final say in who should be cleared for party and general elections.

There was, however, one aspect of the new nomination procedure which caused the most controversy, namely the 70 per cent rule, according to which those who obtained 70 per cent and above votes cast at the queue-voting nomination were declared elected unopposed.

The queuing debate, which had started in 1986, reached its climax in 1988, when it developed into a great national political debate. The critics of the queuing system, who included the representatives of the various church groups and the Law Society of Kenya, argued that the system was divisive in the sense that several categories of Kenya citizens, including the clergy, the armed forces and some cadres in the civil service, could not participate in the lining-up nomination exercise, for fear of being publicly identified with a particular aspirant. The critics also argued that the 70 per cent rule meant that the non-KANU member who is a registered voter could not exercise his or her right under Section 32 of the Constitution to vote in his or her constituency for an MP.

The party consensus, however, favoured the queuing system of nomination. It had proved itself during the party nomination process: it was conducted in the open and hence it was difficult to rig. The party also argued that identifying with candidates publicly during queue-voting nomination was not any more divisive than openly supporting a candidate during election campaigns.

But the debate on the queuing system of nomination continued unabated until the system was finally abolished in 1991 (see Chapter Nine).

In 1987, the party decided to affiliate the *Maendeleo ya wanawake* organization, which was founded in 1952, to KANU. This is a nationwide women's organization, whose affiliation to KANU was meant to add strength to the party in the rural areas, where the majority of the membership of *Maendeleo ya wanawake* is based. The modalities of this affiliation were not worked out clearly. For example, it was not clear whether KANU-*Maendeleo ya Wanawake* would remain an autonomous body. Nor was it clear how the women's wing of KANU, the Women's League, would coexist with KANU-*Maendeleo ya Wanawake*. Some women leaders condemned the move as a clever machination aimed at side-tracking the political demands of Kenyan women.

By the end of the first *nyayo* decade, KANU had thus become the supreme political body in the country. As President Moi said in his *Message to the Nation* on the twenty-fifth anniversary of Kenya's independence on 12 December 1988.

> We have made strenuous efforts to strengthen the party. Particularly during the last decade. But we did not strengthen the party to give it dictatorial powers. Kanu is the protector of the public against selfish and divisive interests of a few individuals in our society. It is the unifying force by which our people can fully participate in the democratic process which is one of the most cherished goals of our freedom struggle.[15]

But this very success which transformed KANU into a strong mass party engendered widespread fears and opposition, which resulted in a determined campaign for multipartyism from 1989.

The Dynamics of National Politics

The death of President Kenyatta in August 1978 marked the end of an era in Kenya, during which the country's independence was consolidated. The Kenya of 1978 was vastly different in its social character from the Kenya of 1963. Settler influence on social life had all but disappeared. The Africanization of the former 'White Highlands' and the settlers' city under the sun, Nairobi, was unmistakable. And, despite the persistent pull of horizontal ties of ethnicity, fuelled by struggles over allocation of resources, a Kenyan nation had emerged by 1978.

But, despite this remarkable achievement of the Kenyatta regime, significant portions of the Kenyan population still remained on the fringes of society. They felt deprived of a place of dignity in the national life by barriers of class, ethnicity, gender or even geography. On the other hand, many Kenyans who were already enjoying the fruits of independence were reluctant or even opposed to sharing their fortunes with the disadvantaged groups. Questions were asked as to whether Kenya could any longer be regarded as one large community, one large family, when a significant number of its members felt alienated.

On becoming president in 1978, Daniel Toroitich arap Moi insisted right from the beginning that Kenya could only be built on the concept of a greater Kenyan community, which had been advocated in the early 1960s. In his view, the idea of a national community entailed a rigorous call to unity, discipline, public-spiritedness and compassion directed towards the nation as a whole.[16]

In practical terms, President Moi's government, during the first *nyayo* decade, designed and implemented social, economic and political programmes aimed at incorporating those who were rapidly becoming alienated from the main stream of national development. For a long time, for example, the North Eastern Province of Kenya was referred to simply as '*Shifta* area' and many of the inhabitants of the region did not feel they were part of Kenya. But, through a series of deliberate political, economic and social programmes, the province regarded itself as an integral part of Kenya by 1988. Also, most of the disadvantaged groups, such as the *jua-kali* workers, women and the disabled, were being integrated into the national socio-economic system.

One of the causes of the feeling of alienation which was beginning to develop among some sections of Kenyans was the distance which had gradually developed between 'the government' (which in this context meant the bureaucracy) and the people. The latter felt that important decisions affecting their lives intimately were being made by a bureaucracy which they neither participated in nor controlled. History has shown that, if you put public affairs entirely in the hands of a powerful, distant, central government, citizens soon lose interest in public matters. Public-spiritedness or civic virtue is possible only when the government is close to the people. In such circumstances, the citizens feel themselves to be part of a genuine community, in which members feel concerned about the welfare of one another, where gross inequalities in wealth can be avoided and where no one individual or group is permitted to exert undue influence on the policies of the state.

During the period under discussion, various measures were taken by the government aimed at reducing the gap between the government and the people. The most important action was the introduction of a participatory democracy through the District Focus for Rural Development strategy in July 1983. The strategy is based on the principle of government ministries and administrative districts having complementary responsibilities. The districts are responsible for the operational aspects of rural development while the ministries retain responsibility for broad policy as well as for planning and implementation of multi-district and national projects.[17]

But the viability of the larger Kenyan community demands a commonly shared and vigorously inculcated ethical code. The 1980 Leaders Conference had recommended the establishment of a national code of conduct. In October 1982, President Moi appointed a fourteen-member Working Party, chaired by B.M. Gacaga, a lawyer and businessman, and including religious leaders, lawyers, trade union and women leaders and politicians, to formulate a national code of conduct. The conduct of some of the leaders in carrying out their public responsibilities, the deterioration of public and private institutions, tribalism, mismanagement and misappropriation of public funds and property, quarrels among leaders – all these had reached alarming proportions in the country. When announcing the appointment of this Working Party, President Moi had stated that Kenya's national objectives were to achieve political equality; freedom from want, disease and exploitation; equal opportunities; and high and growing per capita incomes, equitably distributed. He continued: 'Regrettably, some persons in authority, others in responsible positions, and even out of greed and selfishness, exploited the general public through misappropriations, corrupt practices, blackmail and bribery. Such people are blatantly undermining our objectives.'[18]

The Working Party completed its work in October 1983, but the report was never published, and no action was taken to implement its recommendations. Meanwhile, the problem of greed, selfishness and corruption continued to undermine the national objectives so clearly spelt out by President Moi in 1982.

One issue which dominated public debates during the first *nyayo* decade was human rights and the rule of law. Church leaders, the Law Society of Kenya and various critics, local and foreign, participated actively in this debate. They repeatedly argued that respect for human rights guarantees peace, development, freedom and justice; that human rights are indivisible and interdependent; and that there is no hierarchy in human rights; they form a whole in which no rights are more dominant than others.

But any meaningful discussion on human rights must not be abstract and theoretical: it must be concerned with real human beings in specific historical and cultural conditions. Although it is true, as the international lawyers contend, that the human rights of nationals can no longer be considered to fall within the exclusive national jurisdiction, since human rights are the concern of all human beings, the fact still remains that the primary responsibility for the protection of human rights rests with the state and with the nationals of that state. Hence, human rights in Kenya must first and foremost be the concern of Kenyans.

The bitter debate on human rights during the *nyayo* era started in earnest with the promulgation of the law turning Kenya into a *de jure* one-party state in 1982. It set the stage for a confrontation between the advocates of one-party rule, on one side, and the opponents, who regarded such a move as the beginning of authoritarianism. The critics contended that the kind of national unity that was then needed for social and economic development was different from the almost spontaneous unity that the anticolonial struggle called forth from the people. The unity which was now needed for national reconstruction called for a new kind of politics, based on open discussion, consultation and consensus, which the single party, by its very nature, could not stimulate.

Additional constitutional amendments and political changes that were introduced in the 1980s helped to drive more groups and individuals into the opposition. In 1986, for example, the KANU delegates conference ratified the queue-voting system, despite strong opposition from church and legal fraternities as well as other individuals. In the same year, in November, an Amendment Bill, which sought to abolish the post of chief secretary within the civil service and to remove the security of tenure of the offices of the Attorney-General and the Controller and Auditor-General, was issued. The amendments drew fierce criticisms from the Christian churches and the Law Society of Kenya, as well as from other human rights advocates. But, when the Constitutional (Amendment) Bill 1986 was taken to Parliament, it was passed with relative ease, with Charles Rubia, then MP for Starehe, being one of the few parliamentarians who opposed it.

Two years later, in 1988, another constitutional amendment was issued. Called the Constitutional (Amendment) Bill 1988, it sought to remove the security of tenure of office for High Court and Court of Appeal judges, as well as for members of the Public Service Commission. It also aimed at empowering the police to detain capital offence suspects for fourteen days instead of for twenty-four hours, as had previously been the case. There was a widespread outcry.

Three Nairobi lawyers, Kiraitu Murungi, Paul K. Muite and Gibson Kamau Kuria, issued a joint statement arguing that the proposed amendment negated the objectives of the Kenya society and constitutional principles which were agreed upon at the Lancaster House Constitutional Conference of 1962, which regarded an impartial and independent judiciary as being of fundamental importance. They further contended that the provision of giving policemen in Kenya the power to arrest and detain any person without trial for at least fourteen days 'offends the basic requirement of the rule of law that no one should be made to suffer in his body or goods except for a distinct breach of the law established by the Courts'. On the security of tenure for the Public Service Commission officers, the three lawyers argued that the electoral process, which means changes in political leadership, 'ought not to be allowed to disrupt the smooth running of the civil service through changes based on political consideration' and that 'the Kenya society was and still is made up of various racial, religious and ethnic groupings which would require an impartial arbiter of their conflicting interests in the civil service'. They concluded by warning that whoever drafted the Bill 'is paving the way for the very evils which the Lancaster Conference sought to guard against'.[19]

Before the Bill was moved in Parliament, the then Minister of Health, Mwai Kibaki, moved a procedural motion requesting that the requirement for its notice of publication be reduced from the usual fourteen days to five days. The then Attorney-General Justice Guy Muli introduced it at 3.00 p.m. and by 6.00 p.m. it had gone through its third reading without even token opposition! Here was a Bill which touched on some of the most fundamental tenets of the country's constitution, involving the independence of the judiciary and the public service from political control and the basic rights of individuals in the custody of the police being rushed through in three hours without any debate! Parliament was rapidly forfeiting its right to be the supreme legislative body in the land. Seconding the motion on the Bill, the then vice-president and leader of government business in the House, Jasphat Karanja, ridiculed the criticisms voiced by the lawyers and a number of clergymen, saying that the clergymen had become the 'laughing stock of the nation' while the lawyers 'exhume doctrines that have been eroded by time'.[20]

No wonder Hilary Ng'weno, Editor-in-Chief of the *Weekly Review*, was moved to write in his 'Letter from the Editor':

> This is not the first time that a law has sailed through parliament in a matter of hours. In 1986, similar speed accompanied the passing of a major constitutional amendment. It is a trend which needs to be reversed, especially where matters affecting major components of the country's constitution are concerned. Admittedly, all constitutions get amended in light of changing circumstances, but a constitution is presumed to be the codification of a contract between the people who make up a nation. It is important that in both its formulation and any subsequent amendment, maximum support of the public be sought and secured. In Kenya, this is provided for by the procedure that normally requires that bills be published several days before they are brought to parliament for deliberation, which deliberation usually allows sufficient time for various views to be considered by law-makers. When the procedure is telescoped, as was the case this week, and when M.Ps. unanimously support a bill without giving themselves enough time to say why they support it, . . . there is much cause for concern.[21]

In the same issue, the review pointed out that:

> Whatever the government's reasons and objects in proposing the constitutional amendments and rushing them through parliament, the amendments raise some disturbing questions about the government's and parliament's perception of the sanctity of the constitution and the guarantees pertaining to freedom and independence of the judiciary as well as the rights of freedoms of the individual enshrined in it. Even more disturbing in the long-term, are

questions likely to arise regarding the role of the country's parliament, both as supreme guardian of the constitution and as an estate of government separate and independent from the executive. Kenyans will have to examine these issues more closely after the dust and mistrust raised by the manner in which the whole affair has been handled has settled.[22]

Unfortunately, the dust and mistrust never settled. Instead, more dust and mistrust, which had been generated by the 1988 party and general elections, which were characterized by an unprecedented wave of rigging and other malpractices, spread to the whole country. The image of the government, the party and Parliament was marred, the trust in those institutions eroded and their legitimacy challenged. A strong civil society with a public voice was beginning to develop outside the state. Was the state willing and prepared to listen to that voice?

Notes

1. Charles Otieno, *Viva - 20 Years of Uhuru*, Special Issue of *Viva* (Nairobi, 1984) pp. 5 and 71.
2. Y.P. Ghai and J.P.W.B. McAuslan, *Public Law and Political Change in Kenya* (Nairobi, Oxford University Press, 1970), pp. 228-231; David Goldsworth, *Tom Mboya - The Man Kenya Wanted to Forget* (Nairobi, Heinemann, 1982), pp. 269-271.
3. Joseph Karimi and Philip Ochieng', *The Kenyatta Succession* (Nairobi, Transafrica, 1980), pp. 8-51.
4. Ibid., pp. 88-106.
5. Colin Leys, *Underdevelopment in Kenya* (London, Heinemann, 1975 & James Currey 1987), p. 274.
6. Peter Worsley, Chapter 10, 'The Concept of Populism', in Chita Ionescu and Ernest Gellner (eds), *Populism - Its Meanings and National Characteristics* (London, Weidenfeld & Nicolson, 1970), p. 245.
7. *Daily Nation*, Nairobi, 14 October 1978.
8. *Standard*, Nairobi, 1 December 1979.
9. *Standard*, Nairobi, 15 December 1979.
10. *Standard*, Nairobi, 5 July 1980.
11. *Daily Nation*, Nairobi, 7 June 1982.
12. *Miller Commission Report on Njonjo Inquiry* (Nairobi, Government Printer, December 1984).
13. *Message to the Nation* (Nairobi, Government Printer, 12 December 1982).
14. *Weekly Review*, Nairobi, 8 May 1987.
15. *Message to the Nation* (Nairobi, Government Printer, 12 December 1988), pp. 12-13.
16. For a general introduction to President Moi's philosophy, see Daniel T. arap Moi, *Kenya African Nationalism - Nyayo Philosophy and Principles* (London, Macmillan, 1986).
17. *District Focus for Rural Development*, Office of the President (Nairobi, Government Printer, 1983).
18. *Standard*, Nairobi, 6 October 1982.
19. *Weekly Review*, Nairobi, 5 August 1988, pp. 5-6.
20. Ibid., p. 4.
21. Ibid., p. 1.
22. Ibid., p. 6.

Eight

The Construction
of a National Culture

B.A. OGOT

Culture and Development: A Shifting Focus

The histories of most societies indicate that, in working out developmental priorities, the sequence is usually from the economic and technological priority to social concerns and finally to cultural problems. The predominant emphasis on output goals, such as capital formation and the raising of gross national product (GNP), soon leads to problems of social justice: equity and human rights. In other words, the reckless pursuit of wealth, unaccompanied by broader social objectives, aggravates social tensions and generates disharmonies and conflicts which are bound to have unsettling effects on the social order. Often, during these first two stages of development, the cultural objectives of development are either left undefined or stated in very general and vague terms. It is usually when the forces of destabilization are unleashed that societies are forced to show more concern for culture. This normally means making an attempt to find an alternative approach to development, and a realization that the concept of development itself is value-loaded. In short, it is during this third stage that societies realize that the development paradigm is not an economic matter but a cultural one.

With the attainment of political independence, Kenya, like other African countries, was preoccupied with the question of modernizing and developing the new nation. Development as a process and an objective was interpreted to mean modernization, defined largely in economic terms. Culture was not accorded a central place, either as a goal or as an instrumentality. It was still believed that traditional values and institutions were incompatible with modernity. Economic growth and development were of such paramount importance that tradition and social institutions that stood in the way of the attainment of these objectives had to give way.

In the minds of many Kenyan leaders, modernization was also equated with Westernization. In the 1960s and early 1970s, Western countries were referred to in development literature as 'modern', 'industrial', 'affluent' or 'developed' and the countries of Asia, Latin America and Africa as 'underdeveloped' (later 'developing'). Development came to be seen as a process of change towards those types of social, economic and political systems to be found in Western societies. Western societies were once in that original state, the traditional stage, and they had transformed themselves into modern societies by passing through various development phases before reaching their final developed stage. From this it was inferred that African countries, including Kenya, would inevitably go through the same process and stages of development. They could not modernize unless they altered or abandoned their traditional institutions, beliefs and values to suit the demands of development.[1]

A detailed discussion of this theory of modernization as applied to Kenya is found in Edward W. Soja's book, *The Geography of Modernization in Kenya – A Spatial Analysis of Social, Economic, and Political Change*. According to Soja, the colonial impact had produced 'transitional societies', or those societies 'in transit' between traditional and modern ways of life. Nation-building and changes accompanying modernization are crystallized around the drive to build cohesive, national communities within the state area. In 'transitional societies' such as Kenya, therefore, the process of social mobilization must promote the weakening of traditional forms of organization and behaviour and provide 'alternative avenues for alternative means of regrouping and restructuring of traditional society within a modern framework'.[2] Abandoning traditional institutions was thus considered by the modernizers as a precondition for development. Instead, these so-called 'transitional' societies were to adopt economic, political, social and psychological processes characteristic of Western societies.

The modernization writers, however, did not realize that institutional transfer, that is, the wholesale and indiscriminate adoption of the Western institutional framework, was infinitely more complex and difficult than technological transfer. How was Africa in general, and Kenya in particular, to go about changing traditional institutions and the associated value system? The possibility that the so-called traditional societies could modernize themselves without necessarily having to discard their institutions, beliefs and values was never seriously discussed until the latter part of the 1970s and the early 1980s, when it became evident that the one-dimensional economic man created by the economists was finding himself in a spiritual void and alienated from his physical and social· environments. Culture contributes to an individual's or nation's sense of identity by providing bases of social integration and offering guidelines to action during periods of uncertainty. So, during the first decade of the *nyayo* era which we are considering in this chapter, we find that there was a general realization in society that culture has to move to the centre stage to influence the process of economic growth and the distribution of its benefits. Attempts were therefore made to reconceptualize 'modernization' and 'development' and to emphasize development policies, strategies and programmes which took into account the cultural dimension and objectives of any process of economic and social change.

Development of the Social Sector

In a paper written in January 1980, Dr Ben Kipkorir, then Director of the Institute of African Studies at the University of Nairobi, concluded that the socio-cultural sector of the Kenyan nation was still under-developed. He bemoaned the fact that, although the founding father of the Kenyan nation, Jomo Kenyatta, was an eminent anthropologist, who had risen to political prominence by championing the cause of Kikuyu traditions, Kenya, under his leadership, was increasingly shaped by Western cultural values. The country lacked a dynamic cultural policy; it had no ministry of culture; it had a National Theatre that was national in name only, but Western in every other way; it had a Cultural Centre that was in reality a centre of European culture; and it had a National Museum which was supposed to be the chief repository of national culture but which was preoccupied with biological and palaeontological research. Kenya had not even ratified the Organization of African Unity (OAU) Cultural Chapter for Africa, adopted at Port Louis, Mauritius, in July 1976. The cultural future of Kenya, according to Kipkorir, looked bleak.[3]

But perhaps Kipkorir had overpainted the bleakness of Kenya's cultural scene. Much had been attempted and achieved towards the development of the social sector by the government, some institutions and individuals. To begin with, political leaders and social thinkers were agreed that, in the words of the OAU Cultural Charter for Africa, colonization had introduced cultural domination, which 'led to the depersonalization of part of the African peoples, falsified their history, systematically disparaged and combated African values, and tried to replace progressively and officially, their languages by that of the colonizer'. They further agreed that there was a need to develop the social environment through cultural revival and innovation.

There was, however, disagreement as to what constituted development in the socio-cultural field. The purists were only interested in the culture of the past, in remaining true to their cultural heritage, in authenticity. Such people put more emphasis on the preservation of cultural traits, beliefs and practices. Others were interested in the arts or aspects of traditional knowledge and practices which they believed had contemporary relevance. For instance, the Kenya government attempted, in Sessional Paper No. 10 of 1965 entitled *African Socialism and Its Application to Planning in Kenya*, to convey the spirit of the extended family to the state and the nation through the principle of mutual social responsibility. It looked at the concept of mutual social responsibility as an extension of the African family spirit. A few social thinkers argued that a more dynamic and creative view of culture must be adopted, which would lend support to living creativity by paying special attention to artists and writers. They thus saw socio-cultural development in terms of creative innovations which related more to the needs and aspirations of contemporary societies. New art had to be created to be displayed in art galleries or exhibition halls; new music had to be composed to be performed in concert halls on the stage to a passive audience; and new plays had to be written to be performed in national theatres. This was because the social settings for the new creative works were also different. Instead of kinship groups or ethnic festivals and rituals, we now had educational institutions, churches, political parties, sport organizations, trade unions and similar organizations. The creators of the new works often used traditional art forms, mythology and symbolism, but they did this in a creative manner that reflected contemporary experience.

Despite the different approaches adopted towards the problems of socio-cultural development, there was a general consensus that priority should be accorded to those social programmes which promoted the growth of national consciousness instead of ethnic loyalties. The heated debates on Kenya's cultural policy which were conducted in the 1960s and 1970s were agreed at least on four broad objectives. First, the African heritage had to be made meaningful to the present generation. Secondly, contemporary society and its arts and culture had to be interpreted in the context of the achievements of the African past. Thirdly, there was general agreement that Kenya could not, and should not, isolate itself from the scientific and technological developments that were taking place in the world, in order to preserve and develop her cultural heritage. Finally, the leaders and thinkers were united on the point that African cultural heritage must be a vehicle for promoting national unity.[4]

In order to achieve the above objectives, some thinkers advocated a synthesis of the dualities that they believed constituted the realities of contemporary Africa: the dualities of traditional and contemporary, ethnic and national, indigenous and foreign. One of the most serious attempts to formulate a cultural synthesis was carried out by Kwame Nkrumah, whose concept of 'African personality' was generally received sympathetically all over the continent. These ideas later received a more elaborate treatment in his theory of consciencism. According to Nkrumah, traditional African culture and Western and Islamic traditions coexist in Africa in a state of tension and conflict. Traditional

African culture is characterized by a humanist and socialist ethos, Western culture is motivated by acquisitive capitalist values and Christian ideas of man as sinful and Islam has its own rules on how to organize a society and on what is a good life. Nkrumah argued that a new harmony needs to be forged between these elements from the three roots. A new ideology to replace the African traditional ideology was required. The philosophy behind this social and ideological revolution is what he called consciencism. It would enable African society to synthesize traditional, Islamic and Western cultures into an amalgam animated by humanist values.[5]

Other cultural syntheses were also suggested. Kenneth Kaunda tried to combine the humanist values of traditional culture with Christian ideas of man to produce the philosophy of humanism.[6] In the famous Sessional Paper No. 10 of 1965 on *African Socialism and Its Application to Planning in Kenya*, the Kenya government attempted a synthesis between the socialist ethos of traditional culture and the acquisitive capitalist values of the West. The result was capitalism dressed in socialist clothing. More recently, Professor Ali Mazrui of Kenya, in his famous television series and book entitled *The Africans*, has argued, like Kwame Nkrumah, about Africa's triple heritage. But, whereas Nkrumah looks forward to a new and complete synthesis of the triple heritage, Mazrui foresees a reconquest of Africa's cultural space by traditional and Islamic culture.[7]

But how were all these theories and models to be implemented on the ground in Kenya? First, it was realized by both the Kenya government and the University of Nairobi that a research and documentation centre was needed to provide information on socio-cultural institutions, mythology, rituals, oral literature, history, music, dance, visual arts, material culture and aesthetic values of the different nationalities of Kenya. Such a research centre was also to test some of the assumptions about social and cultural development needs and strategies.

Besides the research and documentation needs of the country, there was the question of the cultural image of the university, which had to be changed from that of a colonial institution promoting Western values to that of a national institution with an African personality. Such a transformation called for an organized research institute in African studies.

There was, however, considerable debate as to whether it was really necessary to have an Institute of African Studies in an African university. The opponents of the idea argued vigorously that all departments of an African university are, in effect, departments of African studies. Special research institutes dealing with African studies should only be established in non-African universities.

In 1965, the Institute for Development Studies was established at the University of Nairobi, with two main divisions: the Social Sciences Division and the Cultural Division, each with a director. The writer was privileged to be appointed the first Director of the Cultural Division. It was this Cultural Division of the Institute that developed into the Institute for African Studies in August 1970, when Nairobi University College became an independent national university.

The Cultural Division was given formal responsibilities for promoting and conducting original research in the fields of African archaeology, history, social anthropology, musicology, linguistics, oral literature, traditional arts, crafts and belief systems. Multipurpose in conception and interdisciplinary in organization, it was intended that the Cultural Division (and later the Institute of African Studies) should make a major contribution to the need to Africanize the content of cultural instruction within the university and throughout the Kenya nation, both by the production of teaching materials and by the rapid dissemination of research results through university lectures, public displays and publications.

The Institute soon attracted some of the most original and creative minds in the East African cultural field: Okot p'Bitek, Owuor Anyumba, Taban lo Liyong, William R. Ochieng', Elkana Ongesa, Washington Omondi, H.S.K. Mwaniki, George W. Mathu, Janet M. Bujra, Achola Pala, G.M. Manani, Francis X. Nnaggenda and P.N. Kavyu. Many foreign scholars were also attracted to the Institute.

The Institute was able to develop resources in subject areas not catered for in the structure of the university. It also helped the university to develop as a centre for the creative arts. Finally, the Institute served as a link between the university and institutions and ministries responsible for national development in the social and cultural fields.

On the government side, the Ministry of Culture and Social Services was created in 1981. This was a clear demonstration that culture was no longer on the periphery of government planning. The Ministry was charged with responsibility for initiating cultural activities and co-ordinating cultural programmes in the country. It was to 'rehabilitate, develop and integrate indigenous cultures to national life'.

But the task of organizing cultural programmes was not left to the Ministry of Culture and Social Services alone. In 1981, the District Socio-Cultural Profiles Project was formulated jointly by the Institute of African Studies of the University of Nairobi under the directorship of Dr Ben Kipkorir and the Ministry of Economic Planning and Development. It was generally realized that, in framing and implementing development programmes, knowledge of local social and cultural practices enables the nation to avoid costly errors. The Institute's material culture project also made great strides in the period from 1977 to 1982. The collection, preservation and documentation of the material culture of all the peoples of Kenya had been a basic concern of the Institute since its inception in 1965. The systematic collection was started by Jean Brown, an expatriate Research Fellow of the Institute. She was succeeded by Sultan Samjee in 1976. He started research into the methodology of systematic collection, documentation and conservation. The aim was to document material culture items in order to understand their relevance to society. The studies were meant to give insight into traditional technology and how this could be further developed and integrated in national development.

In the same year, 1981, the then Ministry of Higher Education took a significant step towards integrating African culture in education. It introduced oral literature in the secondary school syllabus and made it compulsory. Kenya was now taking steps to liberate herself from cultural imperialism.

But even this literary innovation was hotly debated. In the 1960s and early 1970s, the historians had succeeded in establishing the authenticity of oral traditions as historical sources. But the historians were careful not to treat oral traditions separately as a distinct genre or branch of history: they were used merely as sources in conjunction with other sources, such as archaeology, linguistics, anthropology and written sources to reconstruct the precolonial history of Africa.

But the students of literature decided to create orature, or spoken literature, as opposed to written literature. A major debate then ensued, especially when oral literature was introduced in schools, colleges and universities as a subject. Those opposed to the inclusion of oral literature in school, college and university syllabuses argued that oral literature encouraged tribalism, especially among the youth, and that it promoted the study of belief systems and cultural practices, such as ritual sacrifices, that were obsolete and irrelevant to the present and future needs of Kenya. Thirdly, they argued that oral literature was based on race and asked what oral literature Kenyans of Asian or European origin would study. Finally, the opponents warned that there was a real danger of romanticizing oral literature by assuming that all African writers must make use of oral traditions in order to produce good books. They quoted, with approval, Wole Soyinka's warning that the African writer needs an urgent release from the fascination of the past. They urged that each work should be judged on its own merit, for there were excellent African works of literature, such as A.K. Armah's *Why Are We So Blest?*, that do not make reference to African traditional life. Are we to condemn such works?

But the champions of oral literature, led by Ngugi wa Thiong'o, Owuor Anyumba, Taban lo Liyong and Okot p'Bitek – all of the University of Nairobi – contended that oral traditions, which include folk-tales, legends, myths, beliefs, songs, poems, tongue-twisters, puns, proverbs and rituals, offer a dynamic source of content and form in the search for authentic African literature. And they emphasized that oral literature must be viewed as part of a living and vigorous tradition, not a dead past. The African youth must therefore be exposed to this reservoir of African culture, especially as the traditional 'fire-place schools' are non-existent or obsolete. The proponents of oral literature had won the debate by the end of the first *nyayo* decade.

A problem closely related to the issue of oral literature was that of national languages and development. It is reckoned by linguists that there are about 1,250 African languages, a quarter of all the languages in the world. But, at the Berlin Conference in 1884, the European capitalist powers carved out Africa with a multiplicity of peoples, cultures and languages into different linguistic zones. African countries came to be defined and to define themselves in terms of the languages of Europe: Anglophone, Francophone and Lusophone African countries. The political frontiers drawn up at the Berlin Conference and adopted by the OAU were thus not only political and economic but also cultural.

Since the attainment of political independence, most African countries have continued to define themselves in terms of the languages of imperialist imposition. The language of the former colonizer has tended to remain the main vehicle for educational activities and English, French, Spanish and Portuguese dominate the school syllabuses. There are also African lingua francas, such as Kiswahili, Hausa and Lingala, used between speakers of different languages. Then there are the other national languages, the mother tongues. Hence, most Africans speak at least three languages. But the choice of language and the use to which language is put is central to a people's definition of themselves in relation to their natural and social environment.

English has been recognized as the official language in Kenya. All official documents are published in English. It is also the medium of instruction from standard four in primary school to university. Kiswahili is the national language. This is appropriate since Kenya is the undisputed homeland of Kiswahili. It played a very significant role in communication between the different nationalities of Kenya during the struggle for independence. Hence, Kiswahili is also the political language of Kenya. In the rural focus for development strategy, Kiswahili is playing a fundamental role as an instrument of administration and mass mobilization.

During the first *nyayo* decade the teaching of Kiswahili in schools, colleges and universities was vigorously promoted. In 1983, for example, 100,000 O-level candidates sat for the Kiswahili language examination. In 1985, 500,000 students were examined in Kiswahili at standard eight level, following the introduction of the 8–4–4 system of education in the country. Kiswahili is also an examination subject in teacher training colleges and a degree subject at national universities.

But Kiswahili must also be developed as a vehicle for promoting Kenyan culture. The Kenyans and the government have an obligation to promote the language as an important cultural heritage, and this was already being attempted during the period under discussion.

But what is the future of the other national languages? Are they doomed to a slow death?

In April 1986, President Moi raised the question of the use of mother tongues in formal education. He said that the mother tongues should be used as the medium of instruction in the lower classes of primary school. He emphasized that there were many children who could not read, write or speak in their mother tongues. In many Kenyan families, he pointed out, children only spoke English. This was an unhealthy situation which he said should be corrected.

The issue of language in education had long been a controversial one in Kenya. But the statement of President Moi is supported by results of research in child development, which has shown that children learn best in their mother tongues, especially at the early stages. The mother tongue is the most potent to awaken the dawning imagination through songs, stories, nursery rhymes, folk-tales and proverbs; it touches the heart as well as the brain. Moreover, the language is part of the child's cultural heritage. Much of the African culture is embedded in the oral traditions, music and dance, which are all expressed in mother tongues. Hence, the mother tongue should be an important medium of instruction and a useful tool of social and cultural development.

Another factor which has been established through educational research in Africa is that the use of foreign languages such as English and French has contributed to high failure rates in public education. Because of poor mastery of these languages, African students find it difficult to understand concepts in many subjects.

Despite these well-established advantages the teaching of mother tongues and their use in instruction has been played down in Kenya since independence. The decline of the mother tongues had actually started much earlier, in the late 1950s, when the colonial educators became alarmed at the poor performance of Africans and Asians in the English language in public examinations. They attributed such poor results to the fact that Africans and Asians were taught their mother tongues in standards one to four, in line with the Beecher Report of 1949, which had recommended such a policy. The African leaders had opposed the policy because they believed it was part of the overall strategy of giving the Africans inferior education. They demanded that English be the medium of instruction right from standard one.

This idea was given official support in the Ominde Report of 1964, which endorsed the use of English as the medium of instruction from standard one. The report stated dogmatically, 'We see no case of assigning the vernaculars a role to which they are ill-adapted, namely the role of being the educational medium in the critical early years of schooling.' The report therefore relegated the mother tongues to what it called 'domestic verbal communication'.

The new language policy created more problems than it solved.

Children learned English by rote and their writing skills deteriorated. They could neither read nor write in their mother tongues; and teachers discovered that it was difficult to teach other subjects in lower primary without using mother tongues.

The Gachathi Report of 1976 reversed the Ominde Report. It recommended that the medium of instruction from standard one to three should be the language predominant in the school's catchment area. In the urban areas, where children came from different ethnic groups, the report recommended Kiswahili as the medium of instruction. In all schools, the report recommended that Kiswahili should be taught as a subject from standard one and English should be used as the medium of instruction from standard four. The 8-4-4 syllabus for primary schools emphasized the teaching of mother tongues and their use in instruction in lower primary.

But even this policy was faced with many problems. Many children had not mastered the mother tongues; and there was a general lack of teaching materials in all Kenyan languages, especially primers. Moreover, there was a lack of qualified teachers since the younger teachers were the product of the Ominde Report period, when mother tongues were ignored in schools.

But are we to limit the use of indigenous languages to the classroom? African peoples are today faced with an encroaching, universal and alienating modernism, and they are finding it absolutely necessary to go back to the use of their mother tongues, full of life and reason, as a guarantee of their identity.

The language debate in Kenya became more general and widespread in 1977, when Ngugi wa Thiong'o publicly announced that he would henceforth write in Gikuyu after seventeen years of involvement in Afro-English literature. He had come round to the conclusion that African literature can only be written in African languages, that is, the languages of the African peasantry and working class.

What generated much heat was not the question of writing in African languages. This was nothing new, although Ngugi sometimes tried to create an orthodoxy out of the language problem. Gakaara wa Wanjau had written novelettes, songs and poems in Gikuyu in the early 1950s; the students at Maseno High School had produced *Thuond Luo* (Luo Heroes) in the 1940s; and Shadrack Malo had written short stories and folk-tales in Dholuo. In 1966, Christian Konjra Alloo, a Tanzania Luo, wrote *Otieno Achach*, a full-length novel, in Dholuo and, in 1983, Okoth Okombo published *Masira Kindaki*, a novella. In Uganda Sir Apolo Kagwa and M.B. Nsimbi had written stories in Luganda. Then came that great African humanist, Okot p'Bitek, whose novel in Acholi, *Lak Tar* ('White Teeth'), was published in 1953. In 1965, he wrote *Wer pa Lawino*, the Acholi version of his famous *Song of Lawino*, published in 1966. The former was not published until 1969. At a time when English was supposed to reign supreme in East Africa, Okot p'Bitek wrote in the language of his people and without any apology. Kiswahili literature goes back to the eighteenth century, when a verse literature flourished around Lamu. In the early part of the nineteenth century the focus shifted to Mombasa, where nationalist poets like Muyaka bin Haji were writing their *mashairi*. So Ngugi was not doing anything new.

What created much controversy was that Ngugi had become prescriptive. He declared that only those works written in African languages qualified to be called African. Since 1977, Ngugi has written in Gikuyu (with Ngugi wa Mirii) a play, *Ngaahika Ndeenda* (I Will Marry When I Want), a novel, *Caitaani Mutharabaini* (Devil on the Cross), a musical drama, *Maitu Njugira* (Mother Sing For Me), another novel, *Matigari ma Njinuungi*, and three children's books. His case for the total production of African literature in African languages has been vigorously stated in his book *Decolonizing the Mind: The Politics of Language in African Literature*, which is dedicated 'to all those who over the years have maintained the dignity of the literature, culture, philosophy, and other treasures carried by African languages'. But Ngugi ignores the fact that, as an established writer, whatever he has written in Gikuyu has immediately been translated into English for wider distribution. A new author, writing for a small ethnic community, faces formidable problems, which should not be glossed over.

The other Kenyan writer who has taken up the challenge of producing serious works of literature in indigenous languages is Grace Ogot. She has published a novel *Miaha* (The Strange Bride), a novelette, *Ber Wat* (The Beauty of a Relative) and a folk-tale, *Aloo Kod Apul-Apul*. Her most ambitious work to date is the novel in Dholuo, *Simbi Nyaima*, published in 1983. It is a historical novel which deals with the settlement of modern South Nyanza in western Kenya in the eighteenth century and the formation of the different social groups in the area. Topics such as the role of women in decision-making processes, in trade and in the evolution of the new ethno-linguistic identities; the inter-generational conflicts; the use and abuse of political power, especially in a plural society; and the problems of corruption and immorality, particularly among the wealthy and the powerful, are dealt with in this novel.

It is true, as we have argued, that the African languages were neglected during the immediate post-independence period, and more recently by the enthusiasm of the Kenyan youth for English, which they see as the way into the modern world. But Kenya is a land of many nationalities, many cultures and many languages. These cultures should not be preserved as museum pieces for the curious tourist or a foreign scholar with a taste for the exotic. They should be developed as living cultures so as to enrich the national culture. The development of regional cultures must involve the development of regional languages and literatures. In this way, Kenya will end up with multilingual literatures of all her peoples, and this will constitute the national literature. Kenyan literature must be seen not simply as literature in English but as literature which has been created by authors of many Kenyan nationalities writing in their own languages – Kiswahili, Kikamba, Gikuyu, Luhya, Kalenjin, Kimaasai, Dholuo, etc. – as well as in English. Kenyan literature will thus be a collective name for dozens of literatures. Instead of dividing the people, this will actually enrich the spiritual lives of the citizens of Kenya, and bring closer unity based on understanding and appreciation of one another's values.

But, for such a policy to succeed, the different literatures must aim at stressing both the universals and the peculiarities and must maintain creative relations with one another. In that way each regional literature will make its own contribution to the cultural treasure-house of Kenyan literature. The artistic taste of readers should be developed by literary critics so that they can enjoy reading works from different regions. This also means organizing the work of literary translation systematically. The Kenyan readers will then be given the opportunity to acquaint themselves with the best works of all literature, local and foreign, and this will enhance their spiritual development.

Since independence, very little had been done to promote Kenya's heritage of arts and crafts. The designs which decorated objects like gourds, wooden vessels, shields, leather garments and personal ornaments; the beautiful beadwork; wood sculpture; the carving of dolls, human and bird heads and grave posts; pottery and basketry – all these constituted a rich artistic heritage which awaited development. True, art and design courses were offered at the University of Nairobi, and later at Kenyatta University. But these courses were merely perpetuating the élitist idea of 'art for the few'. In order to disseminate artistic activities as widely as possible, creative activities involving all sections of society and at all levels should have been organized.[8]

Consequently, many talented Kenyan artists were condemned to oblivion for lack of opportunities to show off their talent. Most of them could not afford the expenses of staging an exhibition in the expensive commercial art galleries of Nairobi and other urban centres. Those who were lucky enough to get appointments to exhibit found assistance at foreign cultural centres, notably the French Cultural Centre, the Goethe Institute, the American Cultural Centre and the British Council. But these are foreign centres which are primarily concerned with promoting the cultures of their respective countries and which, therefore, cannot be relied upon to organize national artistic activities. After all, art is a product of society, born out of the experience of the artist in a particular environment. Any meaningful art must reflect the dynamic and contradictions of the society of the artist. It must have form, content and history. A national organization or institution is therefore needed to develop indigenous artistic talent.

It was in this context that an art exhibition organized in Nairobi by the Ministry of Culture and Social Services in December 1981 was greatly welcomed. The exhibition, entitled *Utamaduni wa Sanaa* and including about four hundred items of paintings, sculptures and material culture selected from all over Kenya, was organized to coincide with the *Jamhuri* (Republic) week, because the artists felt they have a role to play in making independence meaningful.

This was the first exhibition of Kenyan art and material culture which gave the local artists a forum to express themselves and a Kenyan audience a chance to view, appreciate and share Kenyan works of art based on the ideas that bind them together as a nation. Some of the artists whose works were exhibited showed anger at the way the Kenya society was developing, while other artists of hope saw a chance of the society being reborn. It was a proud beginning, which raised great expectations but which unfortunately has never been repeated. It should have been followed by the establishment of a national art gallery and shops where works of art and crafts could be sold in urban areas. Local artists have therefore continued to rely on foreign cultural centres in Kenya for assistance and encouragement.

Another area of artistic creativity is music, which is easily the most powerful cultural medium in any society. This is especially so in countries like Kenya, where the other forms of communication and cultural expression, such as the written word, are not yet fully developed.

The history of many developing countries where colonial domination was a factor shows that the colonized people were always able to express themselves through song and dance in complete defiance of their oppressors. In Kenya, for example, the people resisted cultural domination with as much vigour as they resisted economic exploitation. African songs, dances and musical instruments, such as *wandindi*, *shiriri*, *Chemonge*, *chivuti*, *bung'o*, *nyatiti*, *orutu*, *obokano*, *litungu*, *limba*, *marimba* and drums, were not driven out of existence by the colonial system. Revolutionary songs, such as *mutherego*, spread like bushfire throughout Kikuyuland in the 1930s. Even in the urban areas, the *ngoma* performances, consisting of song and dance provided the main entertainment and commentary on current affairs for Africans. During the weekends, Kinyamkela dance was performed at Nubian Kibera and Swahili Pumwani in Nairobi. Kisokoto dances entertained Kaloleni residents and Manyatta slum-dwellers of Kisumu. The most famous venues for these *ngoma* performances were at Pangani in Nairobi, Mnazi Moja in Mombasa and Bondeni in Nakuru. These were weekend showpieces, which attracted whole towns. It was a mass movement on a country-wide basis, against which the colonial 'civilizing mission' failed.

Then there was the *twarab* music, which is a fascinating mixture of different languages, traditions, musical sounds and Kiswahili poetry. The music has had a major cultural and political impact on the East African

region, especially Kenya, Somalia and Tanzania. The most representative of this music has been included in a collection of *twarab* songs by
a Dutch researcher, Dr J. Knappert, called *A Choice of Flowers*.

This local heritage of a rich repertoire of songs has had, all along, a
relevance to Kenya's environment and traditional values. With independence, there was the need to produce the kind of music and dance
that would be in tune with post-independence realities. The country has
traditional forms of music belonging to over thirty-six indigenous
Kenyan nationalities, in addition to Indian and European-orientated
forms. The teaching of foreign-orientated forms had been concentrated
at the East African Conservatoire of Music in Nairobi and in educational
institutions. As a private venture, the Conservatoire had to charge high
fees to the private students, which, in effect, cut off those willing and able
to study music but who lacked the finances to pay for tuition. But there
was no centre for the teaching of African music and dance.

All these music forms met once a year during the Kenya Music
Festival. The festival started in 1927 as a private organization which
catered solely for the Europeans living in Kenya. It was sponsored by
the British Council and its primary aim was to promote European music.
In the late 1930s and early 1940s, other musical festivals, organized by
Africans, emerged in different parts of the country. These festivals were
autonomous. Among such festivals were the Nairobi Music Festival in
Eastlands, the Nyanza Music Festival (later Western Kenya Music
Festival), the Coast Music Festival and the Music Festival in Eldoret.
In 1969 these different festivals merged into the Kenya Music Festival,
which became a government undertaking and which saw phenomenal
growth and improvement in the late 1970s. It incorporates all classes and
traditions of music – Western, oriental and African. The festival involves primary and secondary schools, training colleges and, more recently,
universities, churches and other non-institutional groups.

The festival has for many years served as an important talent-tapping
forum. It is meant to encourage the study and creation of music. But,
unfortunately, not much has been done to help the many talented
children, the budding vocalists and composers, who possess talent but
lack guidance or knowledge to develop their musical careers. The question that was increasingly crying for an answer was: How was the country
to nurture these creative talents?

A department of music was inaugurated at Kenyatta University in
Nairobi in 1970. Initially it offered a certificate course, which was later
replaced by a Diploma in Education course. In 1977 the Diploma course
was discontinued and instead a Bachelor of Education degree course in
music was introduced. But, since this course was intended largely for
producing graduate music teachers for secondary schools, what was to
happen to the many other talented young people who might not meet
the minimum entrance requirements into a university or who merely

wished to develop their music talent without any intention of becoming teachers?

It was in response to such a demand that, in early 1982, the government toyed with the idea of starting a school for music, drama and dance, whose graduates were to teach and train dancing groups in the rural areas. The school was to enable Kenya to harmonize her various cultures in order to enable each cultural group to understand and appreciate the cultural values of other groups. This was to bring about the mutual understanding essential for the nation's development.

But this idea came to naught. There were those culture experts who contended that this was a backward-looking idea. They argued that it was high time the country looked at music as an industry and the musicians as people drawing from the past but moving forward, capable of performing to audiences far beyond their ethnic or national boundaries and being accepted as not just Kenyan musicians, but also good musicians.

It was while the debate about the necessity for such a school was still raging that President Daniel T. arap Moi decided to appoint a high-powered Presidential National Music Commission, in November 1982, 'to prepare detailed plans and recommendations on the preservation and development of music and dance in the Republic'. The Commission was to be chaired by Professor Washington Omondi and was to consist of five other top musicologists in the country – Peter Kibukosya, Gerishom Manani, Boniface Mganga, George Kakoma and Senoga Zake – as members. This was the first time that a head of state in Kenya had taken a deep and personal interest in solving the problems hindering the development of music in the country.

The Commission spent five months in the field and about a year in analysis and writing. More than 10,000 people submitted their views either orally or in writing to the Commission. The most widespread demands from all sections and geographical areas of Kenya were three:
1 The need for an institution where musicians of various kinds could learn and pursue their trade. In other words, the people were demanding a national institute of music and dance with country-wide outlets.
2 The need to incorporate the teaching of traditional music at all school levels, just as oral literature and drama were beginning to be part of the curriculum.
3 The need for a national organization representing all the people involved in music development.

The Commission presented a 214-page report on the music situation in the country to the President in January 1984. On the same occasion, the President made the Commission permanent and appointed it to implement the recommendations of its report. The report included, among other things, how best to improve and develop the nature and character of the performance of the traditional and non-traditional music and dance. The Commission produced 367 recommendations on research, dissemination and development of music and dance; music education; music and dance performance; music in the media; musicians; and the training of music personnel.

The government had thus come to realize the importance of music for entertainment and in uniting people and mobilizing them for national development. It decided to have music taught in all schools and at teacher training colleges.

But the Presidential Permanent Music Commission seems to have got off to a slow start. And, by November 1987, when the President moved the Commission from the Ministry of Culture and Social Services to the Office of the President, its activities had almost come to a standstill. At the beginning of 1988, the Commission announced its programme of establishing an archives centre of Kenyan music and dance. It also planned to transcribe various Kenyan national songs into a song book to be used in schools.

But, of the three major demands presented to the Commission by the public, only one had been implemented by the end of 1988, namely the introduction of traditional music in schools and colleges. The other two demands, especially the establishment of a national institute of music and dance, which was regarded as critical, were yet to be implemented. There was, however, the International Music Academy, which was to be built at Kisumu with some assistance from the United Nations Educational, Scientific and Cultural Organization (Unesco). The construction started in 1988 and, on completion, it would train music personnel, conduct research, document African music and offer music recording facilities.

An area that has been ignored completely is that of popular music. Like other areas of development, popular music must change with time. But, because of the tendency to look down upon popular music, little or no assistance has been provided to pop music groups, despite the fact that it is the music with the widest following, especially among the youth. Generally speaking, there is a lack of musical instruments in the Kenya market for those who wish to play or they are too expensive; and the musicians are generally out of work. Consequently, the Kenya market is flooded with music from America, Europe, Latin America and the Carribean and even from other African countries, especially Zaïre, Cameroon and South Africa. This music is available twenty-four hours a day, everywhere. There is the stereo in the home, in the car; there are music videos; and there are Walkmans. This foreign musical diet must be assimilated into the local cultural milieu, into a local popular musical tradition.

Another major aspect of our theme relates to culture and literature in society. It has a historiography which reflects an encounter between contemporary history and the socio-economic and political realities. The cultural nationalism of the 1950s and the 1960s finds expression in optimistic literature. The writer is part of the nation-building effort, a teacher with a direct influence. The late 1960s and the 1970s in Africa witnessed a general disillusionment with independence, developmentalism and modernism. The people had sought and found the political kingdom, but not much had been added to them. There was therefore a renewed struggle against neocolonialism and cultural decolonization was interpreted to mean the search for a new socio-cultural order. Most of the writers invoked socialist ideology in their fight against imperialism and many of them claimed to speak for the 'people' against the national élite or the dependent bourgeoisie, who were regarded as the local enemy.

By the 1980s, it was becoming evident that the new African societies demanded much deeper and more comprehensive analyses than the doctrinaire socialist rhetoric that was being offered. The writers had to make the society aware of itself by having social visions and by being builders of the future rather than destroyers. They had now to explain Africa to fellow Africans and not to foreigners. The discussion on culture and literature in Kenyan society has therefore to be conducted against this historiographical backdrop.

The post-independence literature of Kenya has generally concentrated on interpreting the experience of colonialism and independence. The novelists, the short-story writers, the playwrights and the poets have tried to provide some meaning to the changes that have taken place in society and in individual lives.

They have discovered that colonization has alienated the African from his culture, from his roots. They have also noticed that alienation has continued during the post-independence period, as a result of a strong presence of cultural neocolonialism. Africans themselves now exploit and dehumanize each other, sacrificing their cultural identity. The writers are unanimous that, in order to remake the Kenya society, it is essential to re-evaluate what has been done to the African societies in the past and what we are doing to one another today.

The conflicts between indigenous and foreign cultures, between past and present, run through almost all of the literature of Kenya. But the conflicts are never simple or clear-cut. The characters in these literary works are men and women whose lives have undergone so many changes that they can no longer choose between two ways of life. The line between what is indigenous and what belongs to the present is indivisible. Hence most of the characters do not want to, or cannot, choose. Many are also unable to forge a synthesis. Those who suffer most in Ngugi wa Thiong'o's novels, for example, are those characters who attempt to reconcile the opposing forces by selecting from the past and the present or from the local and the foreign, those things which are most useful or relevant. Waiyaki in *The River Between* is a case in point. He fails to convince both sides on the need for reconciliation and he is therefore sacrificed. Ngotho in *Weep Not Child* is also such a person, who is sacrificed because he is unable to reconcile his traditional beliefs with the violence of the rebels. Thus the sensationalized image of the educated African as 'a child of two worlds' is a gross over-simplification of the socio-cultural reality.

From the works of other Kenyan writers, such as Leonard Kibera (*Voices on Dark*, 1971; *Potent Ash*, 1968), L. Okola (*Drum Beat*, 1967), Jared Angira (*Juices*, 1970; *Soft Corals*, 1973; *Silent Voices*, 1972), Charles Mangua (*Son of Woman*, 1971; *A Tail in the Mouth*, 1973), Meja Mwangi (*Carcase for the Hounds*, 1974; *Going Down River Road*, 1976; *Kill Me Quick*, 1973; *Taste of Death*, 1975), Rebecca Njau (*Ripples in the Pool*, 1975), Grace Ogot (*Land Without Thunder*, 1968), G.K. Murua (*Never Forgive Father*, 1972) and Francis Imbuga (*Betrayal in the City*, 1977), we glean a picture of a new Kenyan society that is fragmented into three main discordant elements. First, there is the wealthy and insecure élite; secondly, there is a poor and frustrated urban working class; and, finally, there is a mass of people who fit nowhere – the peasantry, the unemployed urban migrants living off their relatives or by their wits, criminals, beggars and prostitutes. Thus the experience of independence has often been painful and hollow for many Kenyans, in both the rural and the urban sectors.

What is the cure for this fragmentation? Many of Kenya's writers adopt a moralistic approach to this question. Some writers have chosen to remain uncommitted about the situation. They are convinced, however, that part of the answer lies in each individual attempting to synthesize the contrary influences in his or her own life. Some of the writers have adopted a negative stance by refusing to see any meaning in independence and have blamed both individual frustration and alienation as well as social fragmentation on the policies adopted by the ruling élite. They therefore place their hope in a revolution. Still others see great hope in the future. For such writers, the optimists, the conflicts between the past and the present and between the indigenous and the foreign can be resolved, if the Africans can reaffirm the traditional humanistic ideals, such as pride, respect, self-confidence, dignity, industriousness and communal spirit. They believe that the problems of individual frustration and social fragmentation have been caused by the neglect and devaluation of the old African values. One need not be powerful or wealthy to be considered a valuable and respectable person. These writers are thus condemning the imported value system, which tends to stress the importance of wealth and power at the expense of all other norms.

The problem of culture and literature in Kenyan society is perhaps best illustrated in the works of Ngugi wa Thiong'o. He regards writing as 'an attempt to understand myself and my situation in society and in history'.[9] As an Afro-English writer, he portrays himself as a cultural exile. Hence, writing to him is a quest for identity. This quest is pursued in his trilogy, *The River Between, Weep Not Child* and *A Grain of Wheat*, which together represent a history of colonialism in Kenya. They start with the alienation of land and end with the alienation of the social and individual psyche of the colonized. He considers colonialism as a major cause of alienation, of universal exile, because it destroys the cohesion of society.

In his fourth novel, *Petals of Blood*, which covers the first twelve years of Kenya's independence, Ngugi raises the important question as to what should be done about alienation, which continues to afflict the post-independence period. In an independent Kenya, what is the answer to alienation? Ngugi does not provide a satisfactory answer to this question, except to predict a resurrection of the old colonialism, which he says will bring the same disasters.

He raises another basic question, however: 'how best to build a true communal home for all Africans'.[10] To do this, Ngugi suggests that the exile must first of all return home. The African and the Caribbean exiles are in search of themselves and their place in the world, which should end 'in a kind of homecoming'.[11] Once they are back, they should be actively involved in the construction of a new home.

But the writer's position, according to Ngugi, must be a dual one, simultaneously swimming in the main stream of his country's history and standing on the bank watching. He writes:

> And the novelist, at his best, must feel himself heir to a continuous tradition. He must feel himself, as I think Tolstoy did in *War and Peace* or Sholokov in *And Quiet Flows the Don*, swimming, struggling, defining himself, in the mainstream of his people's historical drama. At the same time he must be able to stand aside and merely contemplate the currents. He must do both: Simultaneously swim, struggle and also watch, on the shore.[12]

But, in the 1970s and 1980s, Ngugi increasingly became the swimmer and not the bystander. Whereas *Homecoming*, his first collection of essays, contains some of his articles and lectures covering the 1960s and distilling his ideas on culture and literature in society, his second collection of essays, *Writers in Politics*[13] serves a similar purpose for the 1970s. But it is evident from the latter book that Ngugi's thoughts had evolved in the interim period. In *Writers in Politics*, he now reveals himself as an uncompromising champion of cultural independence who has now taken the plunge. He has identified his alienation, his exile, and has decided to fight it. Marxist ideology runs through each of the thirteen essays. They all repeat the same abstract generalization: since capitalist or neo-capitalist society is divided between a ruling minority idle class and a dominant majority working class, true literature is produced for and by the majority. He therefore calls for the production of a peasant and working-class literature in Kenya. Ngugi does not test this doctrinaire view of society and literature against the socio-cultural realities in Kenya through detailed analyses. As a petty-bourgeois intellectual, Ngugi merely states rather dogmatically what he regards as his class role in society as well as his ideological assumptions about the Kenya society. He is thus still in search of himself and his place in the world. Culturally, he is still in socialist exile. And, since he believes in a cyclic concept of history, we must await his second homecoming to participate in the construction of 'a true communal home for all Africans'.

The ideas of Okot p'Bitek could serve as a conclusion to this discussion on culture and literature in society. Though a Ugandan, Okot p'Bitek contributed immensely towards the development of African culture in Kenya. In fact, he spent most of his working life in Kenya and not in his homeland. He worked in the Extra-Mural Department of the University of Nairobi at Kisumu in the 1960s. In the 1970s he moved to Nairobi, first in the Department of Sociology, then in the Institute of African Studies and finally in the Department of Literature, where he merged sociology and literature. At the national level, P'Bitek was in demand everywhere, addressing large public gatherings. He soon gained eminence through his writings, teaching and public lectures as a cultural critic of modern African society.

Okot p'Bitek, who died on 20 July 1982 at the age of 51 at his Kampala home, was loyal to his African roots, and his scholarship was geared towards integrating African philosophy into modern development challenges.[14] He was concerned, like all the Kenyan writers we have considered, with how to create a new African society from the shambles left behind by the years of slavery and colonialism. He did not believe in irrelevant traditionalism. He instead called for change within the framework of African philosophy, as opposed to Ngugi, who is calling for change within the Marxist context. An intellectual to him is one who understands, interprets and promotes the thoughts and beliefs of his people. The African intellectuals must therefore be those who attempt to incorporate African ideas or philosophies into African social institutions. Those who are going to implement development policies must be deeply versed in African philosophy and culture and not experts who are well versed in foreign philosophies and cultures but who are thoroughly ignorant about the homeland.

But for Okot p'Bitek philosophy and culture are one and the same thing. He believes that 'Culture is philosophy as lived and celebrated in a society.'[15] The dichotomy between philosophy and culture is false and, in any case, is part of the Western tradition, which is irrelevant in Africa.

The view of culture as something separate and distinguishable from the *way of life of a people*, something that can be put in books and museums and art galleries, something which can be taught in schools and Universities for examination purposes, or enjoyed during leisure time in theatres and cinema halls – the western tradition that regards culture as something that can be bought and sold, where the artist is some very special fellow who is paid with money for his works – is entirely alien to African thought.[16]

He therefore urges that what is going on under the label 'culture' in the towns and cities, in schools and universities and in the Ministry of Culture should be based on a relevant social philosophy, otherwise they will not contribute anything to moral life. In short, culture should not be 'a thing added like sauce to otherwise unpalatable stale fish'.[17]

Ethnicity, Culture and National Integration

Since the Second World War, movements rooted in ethnicity have assumed a global dimension and enhanced ferocity. New assertions of distinctiveness and claims to cultural autonomy manifest themselves not only in Asia, Africa, the Middle East and Latin America, but also in countries like the United Kingdom, the United States of America, Spain, Belgium, France and Yugoslavia, which are normally considered to be stable with well-established political institutions. These movements have a strong cultural component. Cultural symbols drawn from tradition are manipulated for political mobilization. And, since ethnicity cuts across class-based interests and identities, the goals adopted by ethnic groups often override the growth and development of objectives of the wider society of which, politically speaking, they are a part. In the process, a new mystique gets invested into the notion of culture and begins to provide powerful motivation for new trends. Such trends often result in the politicization of culture, which has its own inherent dangers. It can lead to the erosion of cultural values, conflict or even violence.

But ethnicity and cultural differences are not bad in themselves, nor can they be obliterated. All nations in the world today possess a vast assortment of different peoples, customs, languages, traditions and life styles. This means that every nation is multiethnic and multilingual in its make-up and hence multiculturalism is destined to be one of the distinctive features of the world of the future. This diversity is needed to enrich and inspire contemporary life as well as to protect it from the dulling and deadening effects of modern technology.

The new Kenya, which is multilingual and multiethnic, will have to cultivate new attitudes and new ways of living together if recognition of the equal dignity of all cultures is to become an everyday reality.

Since independence, one of the basic objectives of Kenyan leaders has been to build a national political community as a basis for maintaining state power. The question that has sometimes been asked is about the nature of this political community. Is it to be an all-embracing political community or is it to be selective or even exclusive? There are those who contend that the national political community must include all Kenyan nationalities and all classes: peasants, the petty bourgeoisie, the élite, former loyalists and forest fighters. This was the thesis put forward by Jomo Kenyatta, who refused to classify Kenyans on the basis of past history. He argued that history should be used to unite Kenyans and not to divide them. He therefore preached the doctrine of 'we all fought for independence' and suggested that the divisions of the past be buried in order to build a new nation, a new Kenya.

Those who condemn the Kenyatta thesis would like to reopen old wounds and to use history to divide Kenyans into the sheep and the goats. Maina wa Kinyatti and Ngugi wa Thiong'o, for example, believe that the only true Kenyan nation must be a proletarian one. Those who wish to develop a multicultural and multiethnic Kenyan nation are condemned as petty bourgeoisie, who want to promote a false consciousness, and therefore they do not belong to the new national political community, the new Babylon that is to be created by the Kenyan Marxists.[18]

It should, however, be emphasized that what is really at stake is the question of national identity. What kind of civil society Kenya should have is ultimately dependent on the question of national identity, which is basically a cultural question. In Kenya, as in most African countries, people do not live in a nation state. They live in a state with a nation still to be built, but with many nationalities, with multiple identities. But the goal of the construction of a national culture, that is, the objective of the self-examination which we have sketched in this chapter, must be to transform Kenya into a modern nation state embodying our political and cultural identity. In the words of John Lonsdale, an eminent historian who has contributed immensely to the study of Kenya history, 'If we have to construct a new national political culture, new national political communities, we have to broaden our historical experience to embrace the multicultural and multi-ethnic Kenyan State.'[19]

Notes

1. See Tom Mboya, 'The Impact of Modern Institutions on the East African', *The Challenge of Nationhood* (London, André Deutsch, 1970), pp. 168–181.
2. Edward W. Soja, *The Geography of Modernization in Kenya – A Spatial Analysis of Social, Economic and Political Change* (Syracuse University Press, Syracuse, 1968), pp. 1–2.
3. B.E. Kipkorir, 'Towards a Cultural Policy for Kenya: Some Views'. Institute of African Studies Seminar Paper No. 131, 29 January 1980.
4. For a fuller discussion, see Kivuto Ndeti, *Cultural Policy in Kenya* (Paris, Unesco Press, 1975).
5. Kwame Nkrumah, *Consciencism* (London, Heinemann, 1964).
6. Kenneth Kaunda, *A Humanist in Africa* (London, Longmans, 1966).
7. Ali A. Mazrui, *The Africans – A Triple Heritage* (London, BBC Publications, 1986).

8. See Jean Brown, 'East Africa's Heritage of Arts and Crafts', in *East Africa's Cultural Heritage*, Contemporary African Monographs Series No. 4 (Nairobi, East African Institute of Social and Cultural Affairs, 1966).
9. Ngugi wa Thiong'o, *Secret Lives* (London, Heinemann Educational Books, 1975), preface.
10. Ngugi wa Thiong'o, *Homecoming* (London, Heinemann Educational Books, 1972), p. xix.
11. Ibid., p. 94.
12. Ibid., p. 39.
13. (London, Heinemann Educational Books, 1981).
14. See the following works: Okot p'Bitek, *African Religions in Western Scholarship* (Nairobi, East African Literature Bureau, 1971); Okot p'Bitek, *Religion of the Central Luo* (Nairobi, East African Literature Bureau, 1971); Okot p'Bitek, *Africa's Cultural Revolution* (Nairobi, Macmillan Books for Africa, 1973); Okot p'Bitek, *Song of Lawino* (Nairobi, East African Publishing House, 1966); Okot p'Bitek, *Artist, the Ruler* (Nairobi, Heinemann Kenya Ltd., 1986).
15. *Artist, the Ruler*, p. 13.
16. *Artist, the Ruler*, p. 14.
17. Quoted by Herbert Read in, *To Hell with Culture and Other Essays* (New York, Schocken Books, Third Printing, 1976), p. 106.
18. See Ngugi's *Barrel of a Pen*, (Trenton, N.J., Africa World Press, 1983).
19. John Lonsdale, 'Mau Mau Through the Looking Glass', *Index on Censorship*, London, February 1986, Vol. 11, No. 2, p. 22.

Part Four

Epilogue
1989–93

Nine

Transition from Single-Party to Multiparty Political System 1989–93

B.A. OGOT

Multipartyism in Kenya has had a chequered history. Beginning with a multiparty system from 1960, the country was transformed into a single-party state with the merger of the Kenya African Democratic Union (KADU) and Kenya African National Union (KANU) parties soon after becoming a republic in 1964. Two years later the one-party system was challenged by Oginga Odinga, the father of political pluralism in Kenya, who left KANU to form an opposition party, the Kenya People's Union (KPU). With the banning of KPU by Kenyatta's government in 1969, Kenya reverted to the one-party system, a position that held strong until 1982, when Odinga, together with George Anyona, again sought to establish another opposition party, the Kenya African Socialist Alliance (KASA). This move did not materialize, for in June of the same year Parliament amended the constitution, inserting Section 2A, making Kenya a *de jure* one-party state. Thus what had been fluid was now frozen. And between 1982 and 1988 a strong opposition to political and intellectual monolithism gradually developed, spearheaded by the dissidents (see Chapter Seven). With their emphasis on 'human rights' and 'liberties', they challenged the dominant political discourse of self-aggrandizement and power. They questioned the tacit assumption of the majority of political bystanders that all resistance was so dangerous that it was impossible.

But the right political climate had to be created in Kenya before dissidence could make an impact. Up to 1989, openly defiant and even seditious appeals had failed because the national and international conditions were not ripe for change. In fact, struggle for the 'second liberation' in Kenya had started with independence. Several leaders, led by Oginga Odinga, began to realize that the country had attained a false freedom and hence it was 'not yet *uhuru*'.

But, from 1989, the world conjuncture had changed, thus favouring the struggle of the people against authoritarian states in Europe, Latin

America, Asia and Africa. The reforms of Gorbachev inspired transformations which led to the fall of the Berlin Wall in 1989 and which swept through Eastern Europe and the former USSR. The dramatic collapse of the one-party communist regimes gave a fresh impetus in 1990 to the pro-democracy movements in Africa. In 1991, several African states moved towards multipartyism: Benin, Cape Verde, Sao Tome and Principe, Burkino Faso, the Central African Republic, Guinea-Bissau, Madagascar, Mauritania, Rwanda and, above all, Zambia, where the twenty-seven-year old reign of Kenneth Kaunda was ended by his defeat at the polls by Fredrick Chiluba. In May of the same year, the Ethiopian leader Mengistu Haile Mariam was forced to flee his country. All these events were followed with keen interest in Kenya.

The pro-democracy movement in the country was spearheaded by veteran politicians, such as Oginga Odinga, Masinde Muliro, George Anyona and Martin Shikuku, prominent clergymen, such as Dr Henry Okullu, Bishop of Maseno South, and the Presbyterian cleric the Revd Timothy Njoya, lawyers and academics. The movement was greatly encouraged by policy statements from Western nations and the World Bank that in future financial assistance would be linked to respect for human rights, transparency, accountability and democratization. New magazines, journals and newspapers, such as the *Nairobi Law Monthly*, *Finance* and *Society*, and well-established newspapers, such as the *Daily Nation* and the *Standard*, provided the crucial media support without which most of the opposition views could not have been known to Kenyans and the world. But whatever the opposition said had to be acceptable to a Western audience of patrons, benefactors and well-wishers: 'civil libertarians', publishers, editors, journalists, academics, churchmen, functionaries of non-governmental organizations, Members of Parliament (MPs), diplomats, spies and other busybodies. These were the people who could give them fame and protection. Prizes and honorary degrees were awarded liberally to the so-called human rights activist. (It is, however, noteworthy that the great champions of the second liberation, such as Oginga Odinga, George Anyona, Masinde Muliro and Martin Shikuku, were never recognized by these international organizations.) They had to support the neo-liberal policies of the Western governments in order to earn recognition.

But the West has inherited its ideas of civil society from Locke, Burke, Hegel and Tocqueville. Burke, Hegel and Tocqueville, in particular, had addressed the problem of cohesion, order and civic virtue in a free, democratic society. What contribution did the Kenya dissidents make to this? Was there any innovative side to dissident thought? What were their ideas about civil society, human rights and democracy? From their writings and statements, published in papers, journals and magazines, it is evident that they simply swallowed the whole Western political tradition, with human rights forming the main principle behind their concept of civil society. But many of these dissidents had, only a few years back, been Marxists, who were critical of such universalist Enlightenment notions. It is therefore most likely that human rights rhetoric was forced upon them as a price for winning Western support.

Years of reckoning for the KANU government were 1990 and 1991. Dr Timothy Njoya proclaimed on New Year's Day 1990, that it was high time Kenya adopted a multiparty system, arguing that what had happened in Eastern Europe would inevitably occur in Kenya. He was supported by several lawyers and by George Anyona, who expressed their views in the *Nairobi Law Monthly*, edited by Gitobu Imanyara. A few months after Dr Njoya's sermon, another clergyman, Dr Henry Okullu, produced a programme for radical change, which was soon adopted by the advocates of pluralism as their agenda for the next two years. He demanded the scrapping of Section 2A of the constitution, which had made Kenya a single-party state, the dissolution of the sixth parliament, which he regarded as illegitimate, the limitation of presidential tenure to two terms of five years each, and the convening of a national convention to chart out Kenya's political future.

Okullu's call provoked a violent reaction from KANU leaders, who reiterated the orthodox position that multipartyism would generate ethnic tensions and threaten political stability. The introduction of the system should therefore wait until Kenyan society was more 'cohesive'.

It was at this time that two former cabinet ministers, Kenneth Matiba and Charles Rubia, both from Muranga in Central Province, both expellees from the KANU party and both extremely wealthy, raised loud voices against the single-party system. They received the support of thousands of Kenyans, who were similarly frustrated and dissatisfied with the way politics were being managed. Furthermore, they enlisted the support of Oginga Odinga, the doyen of multipartyism.

To the government, the 'cat was out of the bag', as President Moi declared. From June 1990, the KANU government carried out a major offensive against pro-democracy activists, denouncing them as 'traitors', 'agents of foreign powers', 'tribalists' and 'anarchists', who were out to fan ethnic violence in the country. Matiba and Rubia asked for a licence to hold a public rally at Kamkunji in Nairobi on 7 July 1990 to prove to the government that the Kenyans were yearning for political pluralism. But, to their dismay, their request was rejected and the two, together with Raila Odinga, were arrested and detained. But, on the date that the aborted meeting was to be held, thousands of people streamed into the venue! Police had to use force to disperse them and there were riots in Nairobi and its environs.

It was now evident that pluralism had enormous support in Kenya, contrary to KANU propaganda. More and more people began to speak openly and defiantly against the regime. The demand for reforms had reached a crescendo and the government had either to prepare for a major confrontation, possibly a violent one, or introduce controlled change. It is a great credit to the Moi government that it opted for a peaceful transformation.

The KANU Review Committee and After

On 21 June 1990, the KANU Review Committee had been appointed, under the chairmanship of Professor George Saitoti, the vice-president of the party, to look into three areas: the KANU nomination rules, the KANU election rules and the KANU code of discipline. But, in fact, the Review Committee had been appointed in response to growing demands for political changes. Nothing dramatized the extent of the public disaffection with the political system and yearning for sweeping reforms than their reaction to the composition of the Review Committee and its narrow mandate. Consequently, the President enlarged the committee from ten to nineteen, adding mostly non-party members. The chairman of the committee was also compelled to widen the scope of the mandate so as to hear and entertain views on all national issues. Those who appeared before the Review Committee demanded the abolition of the queue-voting system; dissolution of Parliament as it was no longer representative of the wishes of the majority; the removal of Section 2A of the constitution to allow multipartyism; limitation of presidential tenure; restoration of the security of tenure of the Attorney-General, judges, Controller and Auditor-General, and Public Service Commissioners; immediate abolition of detention without trial; immediate release of all political detainees; and strict observance of human rights. In its wisdom, KANU had decided to listen to the grievances and views of the public. Was it willing to accept the demand for major reforms that had been expressed so loudly and clearly?

President Moi called a special KANU Delegates Conference on 4 December 1990 to discuss the 170-page Saitoti Report. The Delegates Conference adopted, with only a few minor amendments, the report. They abolished the queue-voting system, the 70 per cent rule and expulsion as a method of discipline. Much of the credit for this achievement should go to President Moi, who was acutely aware of the need for change. He particularly reminded the delegates of the need to heal the wounds that queue-voting had opened in the body politic. Reminding the delegates to be open and frank, the President said:

> Whatever you say should be said from true conviction. A number of Kenyans who made their presentations to the KANU Review Committee expressed the views they held on various issues because Kenya strongly believes in the principle of free expression. They expect you, as their representatives to be equally free in expressing views to defend their interests. The decisions or resolutions you arrive at today have the potential to build or destroy this nation.[1]

For the first time, KANU was facing the issue of reform squarely. The party thus acted wisely in listening to and acknowledging voices that had been demanding change. Some of these voices were for moderate reforms and improvement of the current structures, and others for a radical overhaul of the existing system and an immediate transition to a multi-party system of democracy. Very few advocated unconstitutional methods of achieving change, and these had no influence in the country. Hence, the period 1989–92 was more a period of constitutional reform than of revolution. Even KANU at this special Delegates Conference rejected the position of the hawks – the extreme rightists – within the party, who were so rabidly opposed to any change. The conference rejected extremist positions, whether of the opposition or KANU members, and came out squarely for managed change. It also promised more change by not closing the door. Indeed, President Moi had already set the trend before the Special Delegates Conference by instructing the Attorney-General, Justice Muli, to introduce a Bill restoring the security of tenure for the judges, the Attorney-General and other public officers. It was this determination of the party and the government to take the issue of political reform firmly in hand and to guide events in a meaningful direction that saved Kenya from violent change.

The country's critics, from both within and outside Kenya, took advantage of these reforms to clamour for even more change. For Oginga Odinga, it was the introduction of a multiparty state that would prove the genuineness of the President's reform programme. The church leaders, the lawyers and the academics demanded the dissolution of Parliament and the release of all political detainees.

On 13 February 1991, Oginga Odinga called a press conference at the Press Centre at Chester House. He announced to the local and foreign press that he had called them to witness the launching of a new political party, the National Democratic Party (NDP). He reminded them that, in his New Year message to the people of Kenya, he had said that the year 1991 would be the year for the repeal of Section 2A of the Kenya Constitution so as to establish multiparty democracy in Kenya. Then he issued a statement entitled 'Our Stand', in which he stated:

> There is no doubt in the minds of most Kenyans that we need fundamental changes in this country. We need to establish a government which is truly acceptable, legitimate and responsive to the people's needs.
>
> We need to establish a government led by men and women of integrity; people committed to national development and not the looting of the national economy.
>
> There is also no doubt that Kenyans want these changes to come *peacefully*. *They want change by constitutional means and not by a military coup d'état or guerrilla warfare.*[2]

On the same day Odinga released the NDP's Manifesto, whose preamble read:

> A crisis has engulfed Africa. It is a crisis of governance. Everywhere established governments are being challenged from below to listen to the voices of the people. Everywhere they are being challenged to deliver the fruits of independence and to ensure development. Where military dictatorships have held sway for decades, the masses have risen up to overthrow them, and to demand representative government. Where one-party authoritarian regimes have survived on bankrupt ideologies, the multi-party democracy has demanded democracy. The one-party regime has been thoroughly discredited, and only rearguard politicians with no new ideas to offer, and only their ill-gotten wealth to protect, can continue to defend the one-party system of misgovernment.[3]

In these stirring words, almost reminiscent of Karl Marx's *Communist Manifesto*, did Oginga Odinga issue his clarion call to the Kenya democrats. But the party was stillborn. An attempt by Odinga to register it was refused by the Registrar of Societies and an appeal against the refusal was summarily dismissed by the High Court as unconstitutional in July. Nevertheless, radical lawyers and clergymen continued to plead Odinga's case. Magazines such as the *Nairobi Law Monthly* and *Finance* carried interviews with him and details about his proposed party. Odinga was thus acting as the symbol of opposition in Kenya. He himself, however, had undergone a transformation, discarding his old socialist message and seeking legitimacy by playing to modern international and local audiences that subscribed to liberal democracy.

In August 1991, Oginga Odinga was involved in the launching of yet another political movement. He teamed up with five other veteran politicians – Masinde Muliro, Martin Shikuku, George Nthenge, Philip Gachoka and Ahmed Bamahriz – to form the Forum for the Restoration of Democracy (FORD), a pressure group whose stated objective was to fight for the restoration of democracy and human rights in Kenya. The founders of the Forum stated that they were brought together by a shared vision of 'multi-party democracy as the most effective mechanism for the establishment of good governance, public accountability, the rule of law and social justice'. Citing 'their duty to this country' and 'their obligation to bequeath to the future generation a stable, democratic and prosperous nation', the members of FORD demanded the immediate convocation of a constitutional convention that would provide multiparty democracy; an independent electoral commission; the entrenched protection of fundamental rights; abolition of all forms of detention without trial; and the limitation of the presidential tenure to two terms of five years each. They demanded that no parliamentary and presidential elections should be held until the constitution was drafted and agreed upon.[4]

The Forum was supported by an assortment of people with different agendas, but who were united in their determination to get rid of the Moi government and KANU. On 16 November 1991, the leaders of FORD attempted, unsuccessfully, to organize a pro-democracy rally in Nairobi in defiance of a government ban. Later that month the Donors

Consultative Group was scheduled to meet in Paris to consider Kenya's request for financial assistance for the following year. Throughout 1990 and 1991 Kenya had been given a bad press in practically all the major newspapers in the West. She was accused of suppressing the pro-democracy movement, violation of human rights and rampant corruption. The Consultative Group deferred consideration of Kenya's request for financial assistance for the next six months pending the introduction of political and economic reforms. This was the first time such an action had been taken by the international community against Kenya. Could the country afford to ignore these economic red lights?

A week later, on 3 December 1991, some 3,600 KANU delegates, meeting at Kasarani Sports Centre in Nairobi, adopted the recommendation by the KANU Governing Council to ask Parliament to repeal Section 2A of the country's constitution. This was another historic conference. The situation was, to a large extent, reminiscent of the December 1990 conference, when President Moi nudged the party's hardliners into accepting the changes proposed by the KANU Review Committee headed by George Saitoti. This time the delegates were informed that they were to make a choice between retaining KANU as the sole party or permitting the formation of more parties. The hardliners used the same old argument that the country would be torn apart by ethnic animosities if pluralism were introduced. In the words of Kalonzo Musyoka, organizing secretary of the party and one of the hardliners: 'The choice is between KANU and violence. It is upon you to decide.'[5] Again it was President Moi who saved the situation, by indicating that there was a third choice – allow multipartyism. He said the time had come to 'choose between the good eggs and the bad eggs by putting them in the water'.[6]

Subsequently, on 10 December 1991, Parliament passed the constitutional amendment repealing Section 2A, thereby effectively ending KANU's legal monopoly of political power.

The Concept of Transition

Simply defined, political transition means a passage from one type of political system to another. Often, it refers to the passage from an essentially authoritarian regime to a basically democratic one, which ends with the introduction of the new democratic regime. In the case of Spain, for example, 'the transition' meant the process by which a discredited authoritarian regime was legally and peacefully replaced by a pluralist democracy after General Franco's death in November 1975. The transition saw the emergence of consensus politics, which culminated in the elaboration of the democratic constitution of 1978, hammered out in committee meetings between socialists, communists and former Francoist notables. Consensus politics ended in 1982 with the socialist political victory. This is in contrast with the 'transitions' attempted in the former Soviet bloc, where the process involves democratic transition as well as the creation of market economies. In Latin America, transition deals with democratic transition and consolidation processes, especially those that result from the collapse of authoritarian military regimes.

But transitions do not solve the problems of democratization and transformation of society: they are processes which only restore a particular type of political system. The resolution of other social problems comes with the consolidation of democracy, which implies the completion of transition by furthering overall democratization. Democratic consolidation must also imply redefining the development model, since the neo-liberal model which many champions of democracy embrace is likely to promote a new type of dependence, a new type of neo-colonialism. Secondly, consolidation should also mean the establishment of a new model of relations between the state and civil society, particularly by strengthening the latter. Thirdly, democratic consolidation implies the establishment of a strong system of political parties which are independent of the state and social movements and which represent the real divisions of society. This is what would permit the establishment of majority governments and loyal oppositions. Fourthly, underlying this transition or political redemocratization is the need for a new political culture which can define the direction of collective action and the ways to harmoniously living together.

In the case of Kenya, the first phase of the democratic transition was marked by the reintroduction of multipartyism in December 1991 and by the formation of new political parties, such as FORD, which transformed itself from a pressure group into a political party, with Odinga as its interim president, and the Democratic Party of Kenya, led by Mwai Kibaki, which was launched on Christmas Day in 1991. This, in itself, was a remarkable achievement for the pro-democracy movement, which had fought for the establishment of a new constitutional order that would dismantle monolithic systems and lay the foundation for building democracy in Kenya. But, in order to introduce the new constitutional order, the opposition parties demanded certain changes to be made first before they could enter the arena of electoral politics as part of the democratic process. These demands included the immediate convocation of a National Constitutional Conference; the dissolution of Parliament; the resignation of President Moi and his government; the establishment of an interim Government of National Unity; and the holding of free and fair civic and parliamentary elections within twelve months, on the basis of a multiparty democracy. These demands, however, were not met, and no new constitutional order was created. Instead, the parties rushed to an election within the framework of a constitution that preserved, in large measure, the structure and powers of the one-party regime. In this context, it may be asked what role these multiparty elections played in the democratization process.

Also, how democratic were these popular movements? Suffering at the hands of the establishment does not in itself guarantee that a popular movement is democratic in nature. The political platforms of the opposition may have responded to genuine social needs and demands, but were they not premised on an equally élitist and undemocratic basis? It is in this connection that the *Nairobi Law Monthly* warned, in January 1992, that the repeal of Section 2A of the Kenya Constitution did not guarantee democratic governance. The significance of the repeal was that it increased the options open to the citizens in their choice of who governs. It continued in a commentary:

> The formal openness of a system is no guarantee of substantive openness. To create a system that is substantially open demands patience, diligence, discipline, commitment and at times, heroic sacrifice. Each citizen must repeal the Section 2A in his heart . . . In a word, the formal democratization of public power needs to go hand in hand with the democratization of private power. Dictators in the household do not make democrats when they enter public office . . . Democracy concerns itself not with the annihilation of opponents but the peaceful resolution of conflicts. It rejoices not at the supplantation of an enemy but at the triumph of an ideal. It does not resent argument, it resents those that make argument impossible . . . Unfortunately, concepts are easier to love and be enamoured of than people. Concepts – democracy, rule of law, justice, freedom – are manageable. A person may be moved to tears by contemplation of the injustices afflicted on an indeterminate and abstract mass of people but the same person may stare abstractedly and with ruthless detachment as a parent clubs a child to death. Loving concepts and ideals and fighting for them carries no reciprocal responsibility. Concepts do not demand love. They do not give back love. Our love is strong, pure and selfless only if we love something or someone that cannot love back. It is here that democracy becomes difficult. It is easy to be a pro-democracy activist, it is difficult to be a democrat. It is easy to campaign for justice, it is difficult to be just. It is easy to preach chastity, it is difficult to be chaste. It is easy to moralize and exhort people to love, it is difficult to love.[7]

In short, were the opposition leaders mere pro-democracy activists or were they genuine democrats?

The repeal of Section 2A had raised the hopes of many who felt suppressed under the single-party system. And the party on which many Kenyans hinged their hopes for 'the second liberation' was FORD, because it had grass-roots support in most parts of the country. But, by August 1992, the party was on the verge of a major split. This put to question the sincerity, seriousness and commitment of the party officials in their fight to restore democracy. It should, however, be emphasized that, given the diverse backgrounds and objectives of the factions that constituted the original FORD, the rupture was bound to come sooner or later. After all, political parties bring together like-minded individuals in pursuit of defined political objectives. Members have to agree on methods as well as aims and, when agreement over such basic issues cannot be reached, then it is time for the party to break and disaffected members to look for alternative avenues for their political activity. In the case of the FORD party, initially the common bond was their joint hatred for the KANU leadership, which soon proved inadequate to hold them together.

Things began to take an unexpected turn when the party's interim secretary-general, Martin Shikuku, disagreed with the interim chairman, Oginga Odinga, on the method to be used during the party elections. Initially, FORD was unanimous that all officials would be elected directly by the *wananchi*. Later, a faction led by Odinga and including the 'young Turks' – a group of young political activists, James Orengo, Paul Muite, Gitobu Imanyara, Raila Odinga, Mukhisa Kituyi and Anyang' Nyong'o – contended that direct elections would be too expensive and the party had no funds. They argued that the national officials should be elected by a caucus of delegates, the KANU style.

The group championing direct elections was led by Shikuku. They argued that electing leaders through delegates was tantamount to denying Kenyans their right in a democratic system. The delegates would be manipulated and bribed by the rich, leading to unpopular but wealthy leaders being elected to high office. When Kenneth Matiba, a former Cabinet Minister and an ex-detainee, returned to Kenya after undergoing treatment in Britain for a stroke he suffered while in detention, he joined the Shikuku faction of the party.

As party elections drew near and various presidential candidates – Odinga, Matiba, Shikuku and Masinde Muliro – declared their candidacy, cracks along ethnic lines began to show, as it appeared that ethnic loyalties would determine the eventual winner. The disagreement about the date on which party elections should be held led to the formation of two splinter groups – one of Odinga and his 'young Turks' and the other of Matiba and four of the founder members of the party – Philip Gachoka, Shikuku, George Nthenge and Ahmed Bamahriz. Muliro later joined the Odinga faction.

With the formation of the two factions, which were soon to develop into two separate parties – FORD-Asili and FORD-Kenya – it became increasingly evident to many Kenyans that the party leaders were not interested in the 'second liberation' but in the right for the occupation of State House. Matiba, for example, made it clear that he had always dreamt of leading Kenya, and this was his chance to realize his dream of being a president of Kenya. He would therefore not compromise, negotiate or reconcile. 'Let the people decide,' he thundered. Odinga answered that Matiba was just an ordinary member of the party and a sick one at that. He therefore declared his intention to fight on in a bid to grab the presidency. He argued that he had not benefited by leaving the presidency to Jomo Kenyatta. 'This time, I won't leave it to anybody else,' he swore.[8] The final show-down was now around the corner.

Within FORD, there were already ethnic divisions, particularly between the Kikuyu and the Luo. Ethnic claims to leadership had become much more important than Kenya's struggle for greater democratization. Raila Odinga, for example, said 'no' to another Kikuyu president. George Nyanja, an architect and a supporter of Matiba, reacted by exhorting the Kikuyu and Kenyans in general to reject a Luo president. He denounced FORD's interim chairman, Oginga Odinga, calling him a 'traitor' and 'an uncircumcised person' (a *kihii*). He swore that the Kikuyu would never agree to be led by a Luo.[9]

After the final split, which saw the Matiba faction staying out of the polls, the FORD founding congress was held at the Nairobi City Stadium, on 4 September 1992, and Odinga was unanimously elected president of the party, with Paul Muite as first vice-president, Kijana Wamalwa as second vice-president and Gitobu Imanyara as secretary-general. The elections were, however, marred by boycotts and allegations of massive rigging, selections and violence. The polls also led to the defections of former leading activists, such as Mborio Mashengu wa Mwachofi, Peter Kibisu, Dr Katama Mkangi, who was the editor of *Mbiyu wa Magambo*, and Emmanuel Karisa Maitha. The MP for Molo, Njenga Mungai, was moved to lament that: 'We keenly watched the way the Agip House faction of FORD held its recent elections and I have personally concluded that all those office bearers were hand-picked in the same way Kanu has been selecting leaders.'[10]

By the end of September 1992, FORD was losing the confidence of the public. The euphoria that had accompanied its foundation at the beginning of the year was rapidly disappearing. Its internal power struggle had led to a split, which had now resulted in two political parties. Personal ambition and ethnic chauvinism had taken the front seat, as nationalism and patriotism had faded into the rear.

Moreover, since 1960 political parties in Kenya have been, in reality, coalitions of ethnic-based factions. Hence, the party elections have been more fiercely fought and are viewed as being more important than the national elections. This is because victory in party elections ensures the leader and his supporters of a dominant position in the country; and, in case of victory in the national elections, a bigger share of the national cake is guaranteed to his ethnic group. It is widely believed by Kenyans that the ethnic group from which the president of the country comes is likely to benefit more by being given more access to employment and other financial resources. This would explain why there was so much campaigning for the presidency in Kenya to rotate among the different groups so that each might have an opportunity to loot. The political and economic goals are thus viewed not in terms of individual welfare and happiness but in terms of collective ethnic security and welfare. Each ethnic group tries to ally itself with a presidential candidate who is likely to promote its interests and any member of the group who prefers to support a different presidential candidate is regarded as a traitor by the group. Basic human rights are thus sacrificed at the altar of ethnic solidarity.

As the country approached the date for the general elections, there was much apprehension and fear among the different ethnic groups. In an effort to assuage such fears, attempts were made to partition Kenya into protected political zones whose borders coincided with the ethnic boundaries. In many areas, groups preferred to look at their future in terms of a new federal constitution, which would institutionalize the political zones. It soon became apparent that the concept of a 'second liberation' had different meanings among different ethnic groups: to the leaders of the original FORD party, for example, it meant freeing Kenya from the shackles of authoritarianism and neo-colonialism, whereas to the federalists (*majimboists*) it meant freeing the smaller ethnic groups from the hegemony of, and the exploitation by, the majority groups. The two perceptions of the concept were contradictory, and the resulting political situation provided an ideal recipe for ethnic animosity and conflict.

It was, therefore, not surprising that the ethnic clashes, which first broke out in October 1991 at Meteitei farm in Tindaret Division, Nandi District, soon spread to Western, Nyanza and Rift Valley provinces. The underlying causes of these clashes have yet to be explained. Instead of factual information, what has been coming out are claims and counterclaims by politicians, clergymen and individuals seeking to make political capital out of the plight of the clash victims. Even the Kennedy Kiliku Parliamentary Select Committee, which was appointed by Parliament on 13 May 1992 to 'probe the root cause of fighting and make recommendations with a view to averting such incidents in the future', failed to produce any objective evidence. The 238-page report consists largely of data on the number of deaths; property destroyed; minutes of meetings; and lists of alleged witnesses, which are not made use of in the report. Much of the evidence is superficial and full of hearsay and unsubstantiated allegations. In the end, the committee admits that it did not do a good job and so recommends further investigations to find out the truth.

It is also important to note that key members of the committee, including the chairman, were opponents of KANU, and most of them were soon to end up in the opposition. The report was clearly part of the campaign to discredit the Kalenjin community in particular and KANU and its president in general. Its findings were presented to Parliament in September 1992, debated and rejected by a majority of Members of Parliament as a shoddy piece of work. In the view of KANU parliamentarians, the report was clearly part of the disinformation campaign to cover up the terror that the opposition unleashed on Kenyans in the form of clashes which were intended to force KANU out of government. Be that as it may, the fact remains that the ethnic clashes continued even after the elections, and hence more scholarly research is needed to account for their genesis and continued existence.

By December 1992, when the Chairman of the Electoral Commission,

Justice Zachariah Chesoni, announced 29 December as the date of the first fully-fledged multiparty general election since 1963, the Kikuyu leaders had opted to huddle together in the Democratic and FORD-Asili parties, to face the rest of Kenya in the battle for political hegemony. For example, there was a mass exodus of the Kikuyu MPs from Kiambu District from KANU to the Democratic Party (DP) the party that soon emerged as the party of the Gikuyu, Embu and Meru Association (GEMA) élite. At least that was the allegation. This alleged GEMA–DP link evoked memories of the enormous political clout GEMA once wielded, during the latter years of Kenyatta's rule, when it appeared to be more powerful than KANU. It aroused suspicions of designs by the Kikuyu community to manipulate multiparty politics to get back in power. Other Kikuyu people, especially the peasants, the wage-earners, the *jua-kali* artisans, the unemployed and underemployed in the rural and urban areas were violently pro-Matiba. In fact, Matibaism developed into a kind of cult, which inspired political fanaticism.

The original FORD was, in many ways, a resurgence of the earlier Kikuyu–Luo alliance of 1960–66. Odinga believed that since he had supported Kenyatta in the earlier alliance the Kikuyu leaders would be willing to support his bid for the presidency this time. But he was mistaken. He soon discovered that most of the Kikuyu leaders who had rallied around him during the formation of FORD were now ready to fight him to the bitter end, either within the party or by hiving off to form their own parties. Hence, by election time, FORD-Kenya was viewed by many Kenyans as basically belonging to another large ethnic group – the Luo. It is true that there were strong Kikuyu and Luhya elements, represented by Paul Muite and Wamalwa Kijana and his Bukusu group respectively, but there were fears that Muite was fronting for Charles Njonjo and that the Bukusu elements were really the remnants of the followers of the Masinde Muliro supporters from Bungoma and Trans-Nzoia Districts, who remained in FORD but who might find it difficult to win a sizeable Luhya support. Thus the Kikuyu–Luo alliance was failing before the general elections.

The voting patterns were to be influenced enormously by presidential candidates. Those ethnic groups with presidential candidates tended to vote for their candidate. This was particularly so in the case of the Kikuyu, the Luo and the Kalenjin; the Kikuyu voted for Matiba and Kibaki, the Luo for Odinga and the Kalenjin for Moi. There were virtually no competitive elections in those areas. Opponents were intimidated and threatened with violence. This undemocratic practice is clearly a form of rigging, but it follows naturally from the ethnic approach to democracy, according to which it is the ethnic group that can exercise its democratic rights to choose its candidate but not the individual within the group. Various desperate attempts were made by the opposition to merge or form coalitions of the various opposition parties before the election, similar to what occurred in Zambia. In particular, much pressure was put on the opposition leaders by the clergy and the American Ambassador in Nairobi, Smith Hempstone, the 'Messiah' of the Kenya opposition, to form a united front against KANU and Moi – all to no avail. Such attempts failed because of the ethnic factor and because of the personal ambitions of presidential candidates.

On 29 December 1992, the long-awaited civic, parliamentary and presidential elections were held. Eight political parties participated, including KANU, FORD-Kenya, FORD-Asili, DP, Kenya Social Congress, Kenya National Democratic Alliance and Party of Independent Candidates of Kenya. Moi emerged winner of the presidential elections and KANU won a majority of parliamentary seats. Many of the opposition MPs went to Parliament not because of their own popularity with the electorate but as a result of the euphoria following the introduction of many parties, a euphoria that swept the country because of dissaffection with KANU. The Commonwealth elections observer team concluded in their report that, though the general election was marred by numerous flaws and irregularities, it reflected the will of the Kenyan people, who are committed to meaningful democracy, and that the election itself was a major step towards the desired democracy. The international observers concurred that, despite a few flaws, the election was none the less representative of the popular will of the people of Kenya.

Smith Hempstone, who was in Kenya from 1989 to February 1993, had witnessed the formation, growth and development of the opposition movement, which culminated in a legal opposition in Parliament. Asked to assess the process on his day of departure from Kenya, he replied that he was disappointed by the way the opposition got fragmented, particularly closer to the general election.

> The opposition leaders failed particularly at the level of personal ambitions for the Presidency. If they had been united, backing one candidate, one of them would be in State House today . . . This was a terribly high price the country had to pay for the lack of consensus and concessions among the opposition leaders.[11]

This assessment confirms how partisan Hempstone was, for why should it be a national tragedy because KANU won? He, however, felt that all was not lost. He grudgingly conceded that some progress had been made.

> Despite the obstacles encountered along the way, Kenya has made significant progress. Today there is a legitimate opposition in Parliament, there is greater freedom of the press and association, but I can only hope that the opposition will have learnt through their mistakes. But Kenya is heading in the right direction.[12]

This, coming from a person who had spent three years harassing and attacking the Kenya government, was at least something.

The Concept of an Alternative Government

It was not so much the lack of opposition as that of an 'alternative government' in many African countries that caused certain tendencies inimical to the nurturing of sound political relations to be reproduced and entrenched in African societies. South Africa and Zaïre, for example, had opposition political parties but no 'alternative government'. For it to work, the system of 'alternative government' must be enshrined in a country's constitution, in which rules governing political behaviour, to which all must subscribe, are outlined. Multipartyism can only work if due recognition is given to the primacy of a country's constitution.

In the democratic system, the vanquished in a general election are expected to accept defeat and transform themselves into critical judges of the victor. The vanquished henceforth become the opposition – loyal opposition – and assume a particular political etiquette which defines them as genuine custodians of democracy. It is only in doing so that a sound democratic culture can be nurtured. With elections over, agitational and confrontational politics must be discarded by both the winners and the losers. In its place should be established a positive political contribution to debate in Parliament and recourse to law outside Parliament should be encouraged.

In Kenya, following the 29 December 1992 general elections, FORD-Asili and, to a lesser extent, the DP continued with confrontational politics and agitational 'Moi must go' tactics. The former initially even refused to accept the results of the elections, claiming that they had been rigged. In the case of FORD-Kenya, a major division later developed among the leaders, resulting, by September 1993, in a major split, with Paul Muite, MP for Kikuyu and the party's first vice-chairman, charging that FORD-Kenya had 'been incorporated into President Moi's political apparatus and had become opaque, corrupt and authoritarian in its management'.[13] He was vehemently opposed to what he called 'incorporation' precisely because, he said, his aim was to remove President Moi from power. He argued that Moi must not be given any rest and FORD-Kenya must therefore organize strikes, civil disobedience and any other action that would force an election in under five years. For Muite, democracy is not a style of life which empowers the citizens: rather, it is a way of acquiring power by non-military means. As James Orengo, FORD-Kenya spokesman for legal affairs and MP for Ugenya, commented, 'People desired the second liberation, but their desires have been hijacked by those who wanted to lead. In great revolutions, the real leaders of the struggle have never been beneficiaries. One must distinguish between activism in a struggle and leadership in governance.'[14]

The leader of opposition in Parliament, Oginga Odinga, persuasively defended his policy of co-operation with the government. His reasons were succinctly summarized by Kwendo Opanga, a feature-writer with the *Sunday Nation*, as follows:

(i) Once the Opposition parties agreed to take their places in parliament they had, in fact, agreed to cooperate with KANU precisely because this entailed sitting on the same Parliamentary Committees and the District Development Committees.

(ii) As a member of the colonial legislature, he and other African elected members used the institution that was dominated by the white people to force change. There is no reason why over 80 opposition M.Ps. cannot do the same in parliament.

(iii) Democracy can only work if contestants can sit, talk and use the institutions in place for the common good, for the opposite of this is perpetual war.

(iv) An Executive President like Moi wields immense power, constitutional and personal, and if he is pushed against the wall, he could unleash his might in retaliation and the consequences would be disastrous.

(v) It is not worth fighting to the extent that people die in their thousands as had been the case in Angola when J. Savimbi rejected the results of a general election.[15]

Odinga thus transformed himself into the leader of a loyal opposition in Kenya, by eschewing belligerent political behaviour and by encouraging his party to act as the political watch-dog for the masses. Increasingly, FORD-Kenya is being seen as an alternative government.

But democracy also demands tolerance. Diverse ideologies, ideas and views have to be accommodated both within the individual parties and between the parties so as to forge consensus on basic issues of national concern. Without such a consensus, it is difficult for a state to develop a minimum base-line which is beyond party or factional differences. On such a minimum, all political parties or individuals, whatever their ideologies or outlook, must have a broad consensus. Kenya is still far from developing such a consensus, mainly because of the political intolerance which exists in all parties.

Ethnicity, Nationalism and Democracy

The main consequence of the Soviet communists' collapse was expected to be the ever-widening spread of peace, democracy and the market economy. Instead, there has been an unprecedented level of ethnic strife in ex-Yugoslavia, the former Soviet Union and other ex-communist countries. Moreover, the phenomenon of ethnic fragmentation is not confined to former communist countries. Everywhere in the world, ethnic separatism, religious fanaticism and xenophobia appear to be on the rise. In Western Europe, for example, there has been a marked increase in violence against foreigners and immigrants, particularly in Germany, France, Italy and Britain. In short, what we seem to be witnessing is a retribalization of humanity. Individuals, in different places and for different reasons, are abandoning their former allegiances to established ideologies and nation states to seek a new identity in smaller, particularist groupings, based on ethnicity, religion or other characteristics.

In Kenya, the repeal of Section 2A of the constitution had encouraged many Kenyans, especially the well-educated, articulate and wealthy petty bourgeoisie, who had not been represented in the *ancien régime*, to jump on the bandwagon of 'second liberation'. Many of them defined liberation to mean the removal of Moi and KANU from power. They saw multipartyism as a chance to gain power and to have access to wealth. The opposition, and specifically the 'young Turks' in FORD-Kenya, were soon embroiled in conflicts that had nothing to do with differences over political philosophy or ideals, but which marked political competition, accentuated by ethnic suspicions and fears. Instead of being liberators, as they had claimed to be, many of these leaders betrayed the trust that had been reposed in them by the masses.

In FORD-Kenya, for example, there was a second major split in September 1993, which was reminiscent of the original split that rocked the once-mighty FORD in mid-1992. At that time, the split was brought about by disagreement over Section 13 of the original FORD constitution, which had factions led by Shikuku and Odinga part ways in a most acrimonious manner. The Shikuku group, as we have discussed above, insisted that the party's national elections be held through a direct vote system, as was provided by Section 13 of the constitution. The Odinga faction, the future FORD-Kenya, insisted that the system would be time-wasting and costly.

But, in September 1993, ethnicity was the fundamental issue. Paul Muite, for instance, charged that FORD-Kenya's second vice-chairman, Michael Wamalwa Kijana, and the party's deputy director of Elections, Raila Odinga, had subjected him to what he called 'ethnic discrimination in reverse'. In his view, 'both Wamalwa and Raila are short-sighted in believing they can take FORD-Kenya to State House through Luos and Bukusu'.[16] He was supported in this by Gitobu Imanyara, the dismissed secretary-general of the party, and two other key officials, Kiraitu Murungi and Farah Maalim who, like Muite, quit their positions in protest.

Raila, on the other hand, had claimed that Muite and Imanyara were part of the conspiracy to bring down the main opposition parties in Kenya and that the two were being manipulated by influential people who wanted to form their own opposition party. These few individuals were using ethnicity to advance their interests. He accused Muite of having been instrumental in establishing a group of leaders from different opposition parties, known as the Thika Caucus, whose intention was to work out a scheme through which leaders of existing political parties could be dislodged. The group was also supposed to work out new approaches of destabilizing the government because, as Muite confessed, the parties as they were then constituted could not effectively check the excesses of the ruling party.[17] Thus the protagonists in FORD-Kenya – Muite, Imanyara, Raila Odinga and Wamalwa Kijana – were all convinced that ethnicity was responsible for tensions in the party.

But the Thika Caucus was also supposed to examine the possibility of reviving GEMA. On 2 October 1993, Paul Muite and Gitobu Imanyara, 'the desperate and fallen heroes of multipartyism', as Michael Wamalwa Kijana had branded them,[18] declared their determination to revive GEMA. They asserted that a lot of groundwork had been done to revive it and other ethnic organizations in different parts of Kenya, with the aim of forming a national party. But why would the Kikuyu want to withdraw from existing political parties in order to form what would, in effect, be a coalition of ethnic organizations? The answer seems to be that it is a question of political arithmetic. The Kikuyu, who are the largest ethnic group in the country, make up, together with their Embu and Meru cousins, about 43 per cent of the electorate. GEMA unity, they believed, would pave the way for one of their own to ascend to power in 1997. In the words of Njenga Mungai, MP for Molo, FORD-Asili–GEMA unity will open doors for 'political negotiation'. He explained: 'We are not calling for GEMA unity merely to allow a member of our community to become president of the country. We think that a united GEMA can be a major force if it throws its weight behind a candidate, even if the candidate is from outside the community.'[19] Another vociferous exponent of GEMA revival is Ngengi Muigai, a former MP, a DP member and a prominent member of the Kenyatta family. He categorically stated that 'We shall see to it at all cost that GEMA unity is back.'[20] Thus the new move to revive GEMA, which was first revealed by Paul Muite at a political rally in Murang'a in May 1993, is more explicit in its political implications, unlike the earlier one in the 1970s, which was disguised as a cultural and economic organization. Contrary to the claim by Mwai Kibaki, chairman of the Democratic Party of Kenya, that the revival of GEMA would 'reinforce democracy',[21] the aim is to revive the defunct organization as a means of putting the Kikuyu back into leadership.

But other commentators have pointed out that it is not simply a question of ethnicity and politics: there is a major class element involved in the GEMA revival. Mukaru Ng'ang'a, for instance, who is chairman of the Kenya Democratic Alliance (KENDA), a former history lecturer at the University of Nairobi and a Kikuyu himself, has strongly opposed the revival of GEMA. In a letter published by *Society*,[22] he contended that the 'call for the revival of tribal association is an indication that democracy is in danger and this move should be condemned by all progressive forces in the country'. He was surprised that educated people like Paul Muite and Gitobu Imanyara, who were in the forefront of the struggle for the restoration of political pluralism, should be unable to read the political realities in Kenya today. He wrote:

> GEMA was a club of wealthy Kikuyus and was created to exploit the poor Kikuyu masses. It was responsible for the support Moi got from the poor Kikuyu masses to enable him to take power. GEMA having been oppressive to the common Kikuyu was looking for a saviour, and they embraced Moi. GEMA is KANU's political wing.

According to him, GEMA, KANU and DP are one and the same thing, one animal with different heads. He sees the upsurge of the ethno-cultural nationalism in GEMA as not being genuine, and ascribes it to the machinations of disgruntled members of the Kenyatta 'Family' who include: Mama Ngina Kenyatta, Ngengi Muigai, Njenga Karume, Isaiah Mathenge, Andrew Gumba and George Muhoho. Mukaru Ng'ang'a therefore concludes that the call for the revival of GEMA by this clique is a kind of political revenge on Kenneth Matiba, who had marginalized them among the Agikuyu people.

His fear is for the ordinary Kikuyu dispersed all over Kenya, who are likely to be penalized by their host communities. He laments the fact that, though these GEMA activists are very wealthy, they are not spending their money in fostering a national democratic culture. Instead they are promoting ethnic separation; and, in his view, GEMA can only cause more disunity within Kikuyu-based political parties.

A former sociology lecturer at the University of Nairobi, Professor Katama Mkangi, comes to a similar conclusion that the revival of GEMA would be a retrogressive step. He writes, with characteristic candour:

> The Kikuyu or the GEMA group is its own worst enemy. For instance, before last year's general election, the group refused to accept the fact that they needed Jaramogi Oginga Odinga in order to win the elections. If the Matibas and the Kibakis really read the situation, they would have realized that the only way to remove Moi was by rallying behind Odinga, but they were so blinded by their own ethnically-based ambitions that they never saw this! So when they failed to remove Moi they came with GEMA. Unfortunately, this fits squarely in Moi's scheme of things. By trying to revive GEMA, the Kikuyu will simply alienate themselves more and more from other communities . . . If the original GEMA was really interested in the advancement of the Kikuyu Community, we would not be having so many poor Kikuyu. Right now, Kikuyu are still some of the most oppressed Kenyans. GEMA was an elitist organization which Kenyatta used to legitimize his power. It was not an organization with the interest of the ordinary Kikuyu in mind, and even if it were revived, there is no doubt that it will still remain an elitist political organization.[23]

The attempt to revive GEMA was bound to frighten other ethnic groups. The smaller ethnic groups, who had interpreted KANU's victory in the December 1992 election as their victory over the larger communities, are reacting to the new GEMA threat by closing their ranks. Even the larger communities, such as the Luo and Luhya, are frantically re-examining their relations with the GEMA peoples. The current desperate search for a future leader among the Luo to succeed Odinga, for instance, is a clear manifestation of the fears and uncertainties about the future which have encompassed the whole country. The Luo are, in fact, scared of possible fragmentation after Odinga's demise, and are therefore seeking ways and means to consolidate the apparent ethnic unity within FORD-Kenya. In a sense, this phenomenon is similar to the concerns the Kikuyu élite are expressing in their effort to revive GEMA.

It is also a fact that the fear of Kikuyuism has revived the clamour for *majimboism* or federalism. But, unlike the *majimboism* of 1963–64, which was brought about by the fear of the smaller ethnic groups of being dominated by the Kikuyu and the Luo, the present demand is coming from all groups, large and small. It started in 1991 in a series of political rallies organized in the Rift Valley by KANU leaders to counter the calls for a multiparty system. The *majimbo* debate generated so much controversy that President Moi was forced to call a halt to the rallies.

By October 1993, however, the *majimbo* campaign, which was originally a KANU effort, was beginning to attract support from other parties, especially from the Luo members of FORD-Kenya. Achieng' Oneko, Ochola Ogur, Otieno Mak'Onyango, Tom Obondo, Clarkson Otieno Koran and Professor Joseph Ouma Muga have all supported federalism on the basis of 'equitable development', contrary to FORD-Kenya's official party line, which favours a unitary system of government. As a sign of the openness of the debate, two KANU stalwarts and Cabinet Ministers from Nyanza – Dr Zachary Onyonka and Dalmas Otieno – have strongly spoken out against *majimboism*. From the GEMA peoples, two scholars have come out strongly in favour of federalism. Kiraitu Murungi, the FORD-Kenya MP for Imenti South, and a lawyer, has advocated *majimboism* as the one system that would take care of the ethnic dimensions of Kenyan politics. Michael Chege, a political scientist and a former lecturer in political science at the University of Nairobi, working with the Ford Foundation in Harare, Zimbabwe, recently advocated that African countries and thinkers should revisit the question of ethnicity so as to try to reconcile it with nationalism in a novel constitutional framework, preferably a federal structure. Writing in *Foreign Affairs*, he said:

> Africa must learn to live with its fissiparous subnationalism and ethnic diversity. 'Tribalism', indeed, is an issue that calls for further reflection among African political reformers seeking to recast the social bases of their govern-

ments. Governments in sub-Saharan Africa have long repressed ethnic interests, centralizing power and economic resources purportedly to promote a new 'integrated' national consciousness. Their critics now demand proportional ethnic representation and an end to nepotism as the high road to the same elusive national unity. But the political and constitutional institutions congruent with ethnic pluralism are not found in strong centralized states. Rather they are found in the opposite. African states may now have to try a formula for stability and equity that disaggregates centralized power, allows freedom of association, including ethnic organization, and in particular promotes federalism.

Federalism may ironically strengthen national political loyalty. By diffusing autocratic power and providing cultural autonomy and control over local resources, it may satisfy varied and sometimes highly idiosyncratic provincial demands. Strengthening the parts could then provide solidarity for the whole. African leaders and many of their external advisers have argued that, outside Nigeria, African states are too small for federal arrangements. But it is the complexity of the social organization, not the size of the population, that mandates decentralized power. Switzerland, for instance, is both smaller and more federalist in constitutional character than the United States.[24]

But is federalism the formula for stability and equity in Kenya? Is it congruent with ethnic pluralism? Will it produce a democratic culture that will enable the citizens – whatever their origins, colour of their skins, the land or language of their ancestors – to join together in support of certain ideals and principles which make it possible for them to live together? A truly democratic culture should deny no specific identity, be it ethnic, religious, linguistic or cultural, any more than it should develop at the expense of national identity, collective solidarity and the shared hopes of all. It should promote integration by reconciling the double imperative essential to citizenship – of unity and freedom, of membership in the community and individual liberty. Will federalism permit the free exchange of ideas, which is the corner-stone of democratic culture, in so far as the freedom of information and expression alone can ensure the transparency that is indispensable to the exercise of choice and responsibility? And, finally, will federation permit the free movement of people? In short, the important question Kenyans should be asking themselves is not whether they should have a unitary or federal structure, but what kind of unitary government or what kind of federal structure. Are the *majimboists* demanding the devolution of powers to clearly defined regions or are they proposing the creation of homogeneous 'Bantustans'?

Conclusion

In a situation where democracy does not address the community's demands and does not generate new bases for social integration and collective identity, the influence of populist or fundamentalist movements in the country develops or heightens, leading to new authoritarian regimes. Kenya is at the crossroads now. It must re-create a shared normative order for the day-to-day renewal of trust in the promises of democracy if the populist–authoritarian cycle is to be broken. This entails the forging of new institutions and the restructuring of the socio-economic system. And the fundamental question which must be raised is whether Kenya is any less neo-colonial economically, culturally and intellectually as a result of the reintroduction of the multiparty system. The economy is being managed according to the dictates of the World Bank and the International Monetary Fund (IMF). But for political stability to be sustained, free market policies alone are inadequate: a frontal attack on poverty is essential. Hence, there is a desperate need for more social policies aimed at fighting poverty.

Also, there is a need for mass participation in the political process. At the moment, the 'national conflict', embodied in the rivalries for the executive power among the élite in the various political parties, takes priority over 'social conflict', concerned with the interests of most of the inhabitants of the country. It is a democracy of the élite, for the élite and by the élite. This yawning chasm between the élite and the masses must be bridged.

Culturally and intellectually, the élite of all parties continue to compete for the favours of the West, whose leaders and thinkers act as the reference group, the originators of concepts, models and paradigms and the final Court of Appeal. A new 'civilizing mission' by the West has been launched in Africa.

Notes

1. *Weekly Review*, 8 December 1990, pp. 6–7.
2. *Nairobi Law Monthly*, 30 (February 1991), 28.
3. Ibid., p. 30.
4. *Nairobi Law Monthly*, 35 (August 1991), 16.
5. *Weekly Review*, 6 December 1991, p. 7.
6. Ibid., p. 9.
7. *Nairobi Law Monthly*, 40 (January 1992), pp. 17–18.
8. *Weekend Mail*, 18 February 1993, p. 24.
9. *Kenya Times*, 28 August 1992, pp. 1–2.
10. *Society*, 28 September 1992, p. 14.
11. *Sunday Nation*, 28 February 1993, p. 10.
12. Ibid., p. 11.
13. *Sunday Nation*, Nairobi, 26 September 1993, p. 10.
14. Ibid., p. 11.
15. Kwendo Opanga, *Sunday Nation*, 26 September 1993, pp. 10–11.
16. *Weekly Review*, 17 September 1993.
17. *Weekly Review*, 20 August 1993, p. 3.
18. *Standard*, 4 October 1993, p. 2.
19. *Weekly Review*, Nairobi, 13 August 1993, p. 5.

20. Ibid., p. 6.
21. *Sunday Nation*, 10 October 1993.
22. *Society*, 18 October 1993.
23. *Society*, 35 (8 November 1993), p. 19.
24. Michael Chege, 'Remembering Africa', *Foreign Affairs*, 1 (1992), 151.

Index

Inguka, George, 99
Institute for Development
    Studies, 218-19
Institute of African Studies, 142, 219, 233
Insurance Guarantee Scheme, 171
International Labour Organization,
    89-90, 131
International Monetary Fund, 157, 165,
    173, 176, 178, 260
International Music Academy, 229
Islam, 112, 217-18

Jamaica, 38
Jeremiah, Jimmy, 57-8
Josiah, Samuel Onyango, 31
jua-kali, 165, 169, 174
judiciary, 70, 72-3, 211-12

Kadima, J.G.W., 55
Kaggia, Bildad, 35, 68, 94-6, 98, 101
Kagwa, Sir Apolo, 223
Kairi, Rebecca Njeri, 37
Kakoma, George, 228
Kalenjin Association, 195, 197
Kalenjin peoples, 31, 65, 67, 250-1
Kalenjin Political Alliance, 65
Kamotho, Joseph, 201
Kanyana, J.F., 68
Kanyua, J.F.G., 41
Karanja, Jasphat, 191, 212
Karari, Reuben, 41
Karia, Govindji Karsandas, 30
Kariuki, G.G., 67, 191, 201
Kariuki, J.M., 103-4, 196, 198, 202
Karume, Njenga, 104, 196, 257
Kasyoka, J.M., 56, 58
Kaunda, Kenneth, 218, 240
Kavyu, P.N., 219
Kebaso, John, 31, 55
Kennedy Kiliku Parliamentary Select
    Committee, 250
Kenya African Democratic Union, 51,
    65-6, 68-77, 92, 94, 107, 187, 239
Kenya African National Congress, 52
Kenya African National Union, 31, 51,
    53, 68-73, 77, 96, 98-101, 103, 106,
    153; Delegates' Conference (1990),
    242-3; Disciplinary Committee,
    206-7; founding of, 65-6; Kenyatta
    Elections (1963), 75, 137; Lancaster
    House Conferences, 70-3, 75-6;
    land question, 88, 92, 94-5; and

nomination of Moi, 190; philosophy
    of government, 83-5; and
    post-Kenyatta succession, 187-213;
    Reorganization Committee, 202;
    Review Committee, 242-3, 245;
    and transition to multi-party
    system, 239-60
Kenya African People's Party, 65
Kenya African Rifles, 31, 41
Kenya African Socialist Alliance, 202, 239
Kenya African Study Union, 31
Kenya African Union, xii, 28, 30-1,
    33-6, 41, 52, 55-7, 100
Kenya Air Force, 197, 199
Kenya Association of
    Manufacturers, 171
Kenya Coalition, 62, 72-3
Kenya Co-operative Creameries, 162
Kenya Court of Appeal, 108
Kenya Cultural Centre, 141, 216
Kenya Democratic Alliance, 256
Kenya Education Commission, 126-9,
    137, 222-3
Kenya External Trade Authority, 170
Kenya Federation of Labour, 49, 64
Kenya Independence Movement, 61, 65
Kenya Industrial Estates, 86
Kenya Institute of Administration, 192,
    195, 205
Kenya Land Commission, 29
Kenya Literature Bureau, 140
Kenya Meat Commission, 169
Kenya National Council of Arts and
    Culture, 143
Kenya National Democratic
    Alliance, 252
Kenya National Party, 61, 65
Kenya National Trading Corporation,
    86-7, 170
Kenya Patriotic Front, 197
Kenya People's Union, 18, 98-103, 187,
    194, 197, 202-3, 239
Kenya Revolutionary Movement, 197
Kenya Social Congress, 252
Kenya Tea Development Authority, 87
'Kenya We Want' Conventions, 73,
    192
Kenyatta, Jomo, 2, 18, 43, 60, 84-5,
    88, 114-15, 126, 132, 140-1, 196,
    198, 216, 235, 251; and colonialism,
    30, 33-4, 39-40, 63, 65-6, 68-70,
    73, 89; Constitutional Amendments,
    107-8; death, 122, 189, 202, 208;
    elected president, 55, 75-6, 248;

Index